The Vikings
and
Their Enemies

The Vikings and Their Enemies

Warfare in Northern Europe, 750–1100

Philip Line

Skyhorse Publishing

Skyhorse Publishing books may be purchased in bulk at special discounts for
sales promotion, corporate gifts, fund-raising, or educational purposes. Special
editions can also be created to specifications. For details, contact the Special
Sales Department, Skyhorse Publishing, 307 West 36th Street, 11th Floor,
New York, NY 10018 or info@skyhorsepublishing.com.

Skyhorse® and Skyhorse Publishing® are registered trademarks of Skyhorse
Publishing, Inc.®, a Delaware corporation.

Visit our website at www.skyhorsepublishing.com.

10 9 8 7 6 5 4 3 2

Library of Congress Cataloging-in-Publication Data is available on file.
Cover design by Jon Wilkinson

Print ISBN: 978-1-5107-5836-0
Ebook ISBN: 978-1-63220-872-9

Printed in the United States of America

Contents

List of Plates

Acknowledgments

First of all, I would like to thank my wife, Mervi Mattila, who not only insisted on helping with the laborious task of indexing, but had to endure a considerable amount of complaint (most of it about my own inability to live up to the demands I place on myself) during the process of writing this book. Her brother, Jari Mattila, has also earned my gratitude by turning my draft maps into very good maps and making the photographs look as good as possible. Many thanks are also owed to several friends who research or have an interest in various aspects of the subject and gave me their comments after reading through parts of the manuscript: Aleksandr Koptev, Paul Elvidge, and Karolina Kouvola. I am also grateful to those who have agreed to supply me with the photographs used in this book: Peter Jan Bomhof of the Photodepartment in the Rijksmuseum van Oudheden, Leiden; Ingvild Tinglum of the Department of Documentation/Photo at the Museum of Cultural History, Oslo; Siv Falk of the Historiska Museet in Stockholm; Derek Craig of the Corpus of Anglo-Saxon Stone Sculpture; Dr. Neil Christie, one of the project directors of the Wallingford Burh to Borough Research Project; Terry Joyce; Gabrielle Roeder-Campbell; and Grzegorz Kulig (aka Thorkil) for the pictures of his excellent replica helmets of the period. Finally, I have to thank the people at Pen and Sword: Rupert Harding, the Commissioning Editor, not least for tolerating my shifting deadlines; Sarah Cook, who did such a meticulous job checking through the text in preparation for printing; and the typesetter Noel Sadler. This is their work, of course, but nowadays not all publishers take so much care.

Introduction

There have been many books on the Vikings, and a number on Viking warfare, and the reader is entitled to ask why there is a need for another. The purpose is not to give the chronology or history of Viking expeditions, which have been related in many other works, but to concentrate on some of the aspects of Viking-Age warfare that have either not been dealt with, or have been dealt with inadequately, in previous general books. This includes military organization and contemporary attitudes to war, both among the Vikings and among their enemies in northern Europe, which obviously affected the way wars were fought and even why they were fought. To the Christian lands that suffered from their raids, the Vikings represented a terrifying and alien phenomenon, as they were non-Christians whose activities caused a dramatic increase in the level of pillage, destruction, and slave-trading. Yet none of these practices was unfamiliar to any of Europe's inhabitants before the Viking Era. Similarly, although the Scandinavians presented their enemies with some new problems, in many ways their military methods were similar to those of their opponents.

Many previous books on Viking and Anglo-Saxon warfare have looked at the subject entirely from a modern perspective, as if Vikings and their contemporaries were modern soldiers in fancy dress, and have taken the accounts of medieval writers (and often their numbers) at face value, without taking much notice of who they were, why they were writing, or even how long after the events they describe they were writing. As a result, things that are very uncertain have all too often been presented as facts. We all *want* to know what really happened, and it is easy to fall into the trap of accepting the only account we have of a certain campaign or battle as the truth, but if there is reason to question it, this should be done.

Since the aim of this book is to look at Viking warfare in the context of warfare in northern Europe in general, the discussion covers the period 750–1100 and ranges over the British Isles, the Carolingian Empire and its successor kingdoms (including East Frankia, generally referred to as Germany after 917), and the areas north and east of the Balkans occupied by the Slavs. Although they are not fully covered here, there are also occasional excursions into Italy, Islamic Spain, the Byzantine Empire, and the steppes to the southeast of Russia (then inhabited largely by Turkic-speaking nomads).

England and Wales in the Viking Age

100 km
50 miles

Legend:
- Offa's Dyke
- ○ Burh
- ● Other site

Dumbarton
Edinburgh
Clyde
Tweed
STRATHCLYDE CUMBRIA
Lindisfarne
Bamburgh
Hexham
Tyne Corbridge
Galloway
Solway Firth
Carlisle
Durham
Isle of Man
Ripon
York Stamford Bridge
Ouse
Anglesey
Rhuddlan
Wirral Thelwall Manchester
Bromborough Runcorn
Eddisbury
Chester
Torksey Goltho
Lincoln
Gwynedd
Bakewell
Trent
Derby
Powys Shrewsbury Stafford Nottingham
Buttington Lichfield Repton
Chirbury Wednesfield Tamworth Leicester Stamford
Bridgnorth Severn Warwick Norwich
Ceredigion EAST
Worcester Avon Huntingdon Ely Thetford ANGLIA
St David's Deheubarth Northampton Tempsford
Dyfed Brycheiniog Hereford Towcester Cambridge Ipswich Sutton Hoo
Mynydd Carn? Buckingham Bedford
Gloucester St Albans Colchester
Morgannwg Lea Hertford Essex Witham
Cirencester Thames Oxford Maldon
Cricklade Wallingford London Benfleet
Sherston Malmesbury Sashes Southwark Isle of Sheppey
Chippenham Ashdown Rochester Graveney Isle of Thanet
Bath Chisbury Reading Canterbury Sandwich
Axbridge Avon Southampton Dover
Glastonbury Warminster Grateley Eashing Agglethorpe
Watchet South Wilton Winchester Eorpeburnan Hythe
Pilton Cadbury Salisbury Lewes Rye Lympne
Lyng Shaftesbury Southampton Burpham Hastings
Crediton Athelney Sherborne Porchester
Devon Langport Bridport Badbury Chichester
Exeter Twinham Isle of Wight
Tamar Wareham
Cornwall Lydford
Halwell

Francia, Germany, west Poland, Bohemia, north Italy

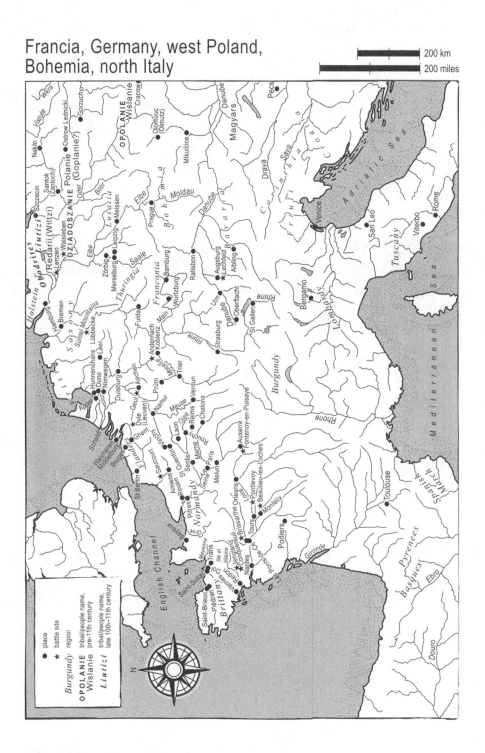

Ireland in the Viking Age

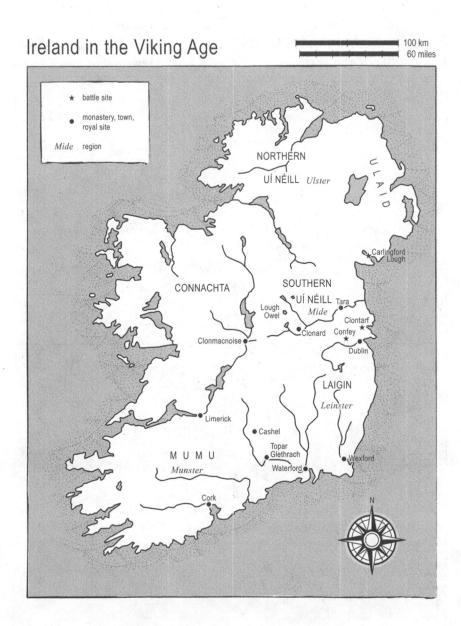

100 km
60 miles

★ battle site
● monastery, town, royal site
Mide region

NORTHERN
UÍ NÉILL *Ulster*

U L A I D

Carlingford Lough ★

CONNACHTA

SOUTHERN
UÍ NÉILL
Mide

Lough Owel ●
Tara ★
Clonard ●
Confey ★
Clontarf ★
Dublin ●

Clonmacnoise ●

LAIGIN
Leinster

Limerick ●

Cashel ●

M U M U
Munster

Topar Glethrach ●
Waterford ●
Wexford ★

Cork ●

N

Russia, east Poland & Baltic

500 km
300 miles

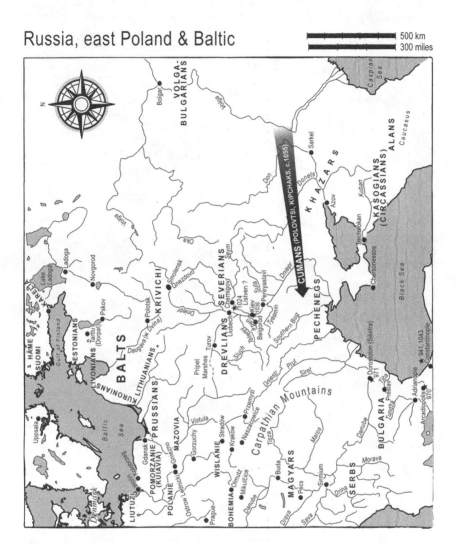

Scandinavia

200 km
150 miles

- ● ○   town, fortified site   ★   battle site   <u>Rani</u>   tribe
- *Jutland*   region, island   **LIUTIZI**   name of tribe/people   ‖   dyke

Scotland in the Viking Age

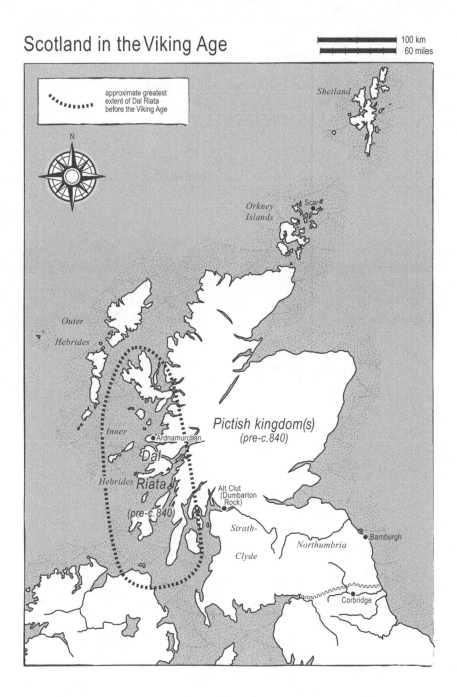

100 km
60 miles

approximate greatest
extent of Dal Riata
before the Viking Age

N

Shetland

Orkney
Islands

Scar

Outer

Hebrides

Inner

Ardnamurchan

Dal

Pictish kingdom(s)
(pre-c.840)

Hebrides

Riata

Alt Clut
(Dumbarton
Rock)

(pre-c.840)

Strath-

Northumbria

Bamburgh

Clyde

Corbridge

Chapter 1

Viking-Age Warfare and History

Court poets, monastic scribes, and saga writers

The Battle of Maldon, 11 August 991

In the late summer of 991 an English ealdorman, Byrhtnoth, addressed his assembled troops in the town of Maldon. With him were his own personal following or household of relatively experienced warriors and a levy from the local shires, assembled to confront a Viking force that had come in ninety ships and was encamped on an island offshore not far from the town. The ealdorman incited his troops, and they incited one another. Following this, the army traveled to the shore at a point where a causeway connected it with the island, the horses were driven away, except for Byrhtnoth's, and the army formed a battle line along the bank of the nearby River Pant. Byrhtnoth then rode up and down the battle line to ensure that all was in order, telling the troops how to form up, hold position, and grasp their shields, after which he dismounted and joined his most loyal companions. Many of those among his host feared the worst, one of them releasing his hawk, his most valued and personal possession, to fly off to the woods.

The first contact with the enemy occurred when the tide was still high, covering the causeway. A spokesman for the Vikings asked for a payment of tribute, in return for peace—there was no need for them to kill each other. He received a disdainful and ironic response from Byrhtnoth—gold rings cannot be gained so easily, and their tribute will be spearpoints. Besides, when they have traveled such a long way, it would be shameful for the Vikings to leave without a fight. Æthelred's land was not prepared to pay. An exchange of arrows across the channel ensued. This did not mark the end of the conversation between the two sides, however. As they could make no headway while a force led by Byrhtnoth's nephew Wulfstan blocked the causeway, the Vikings requested that they be allowed to cross it, in order to fight on more even terms. Byrhtnoth conceded, and as the tide ebbed the Vikings crossed the causeway to attack the main English army. Arrows flew, spears were thrown and thrust at their opponents, swords wielded, and shields were used to ward off the thrusts and blows of the enemy and to dislodge enemy weapons. Wulfstan fell in the first onslaught, and eventually Byrhtnoth too was wounded by a spear. He dispatched this attacker, but another spear struck him. This time a young man, Wulfstan's son, pulled the spear from his lord's body and hurled it back at the Dane who threw it, killing him. Finally Byrhtnoth's arm was disabled by a sword-blow, but before he died he commended himself to God and exhorted his men to continue the fight. Alongside him fell two of his household, but at this crucial point in the battle another of his own retinue, Godric son of Offa, failed to remember his obligation to his overlord, stole his horse, and fled the battlefield, by this act encouraging others to do the same. But many among those closest to Byrhtnoth remembered their duty: they had only two choices, to avenge their lord or to die with him. Their feeling was expressed most eloquently by one of their number, Ælfwine, who spoke of his own great lineage and emphasized that he wished to avoid the worst thing of all, to be mocked for abandoning the host after his lord had been cut down. Offa and Leofsunu echoed his sentiments. Incited by the speeches of their fellow-warriors, Byrhtnoth's "hearth-companions" hurled themselves at their enemies and died fighting, taking many of the enemy with them.

This is how the old English poem now known as *The Battle of Maldon* describes the battle that took place on 11 August 991. It illustrates many of the problems facing the historian of Viking Age warfare. Even to someone who knows little of heroic poetry and its conventions, there are improbable elements in the description. One of Byrhtnoth's followers carries his hawk to battle on his wrist and then releases it shortly beforehand. Byrhtnoth is able to kill his attacker just after receiving his third severe wound, and, even more unlikely, an inexperienced youth is able to pull a spear from his body and throw it back where it came from with deadly accuracy. Byrhtnoth also commends himself to God at some length and with great eloquence, despite his crippling injuries. After his death two of his followers make long appeals to their fellows to continue the fight, supposedly during the heat of battle. Throughout the poem, we are presented with the thoughts of the English warriors taking part, imputed or imagined by the poet, who could not have known such details.

To anyone familiar with the traditions of Anglo-Saxon poetry and heroic culture, or even heroic poetry in general, other standard motifs become obvious. Almost from the beginning of the surviving section of the poem, there are indications that Byrhtnoth and his warriors are about to sacrifice themselves. The sending of the hawk to the woods indicates that its owner does not expect to go hawking again, while Eadric's declaration of his intent to use his weapons "as long as he can" and the dismissal of the horses are signals that there will be no flight should things become difficult. The exchange between the Viking demanding tribute and the ealdorman, while not impossible in itself, follows literary convention in that the expressions used by the "deceitful" Viking were recognizably "Viking" to the audience of the tenth and eleventh centuries, while Byrhtnoth's response is conventionally dismissive. The element of betrayal is also familiar in numerous poetic portrayals of heroic defeats, not only those of the Anglo-Saxons. Here it is the theft of Byrhtnoth's horse by Godric, one of his trusted followers, who, the poet tells us, has been given many a horse by his lord in the past, and his subsequent flight that causes the bulk of the English army to flee, in the belief that it is Byrhtnoth who is abandoning them. Godric's treachery is contrasted with the loyalty of Byrhtnoth to his king and his land, and the loyalty to their lord of those who die around him. They are heroes in the sense that they fulfill their duty to the last, having been placed in a situation not of their own making and confronted with the stark choice of facing death or ignominy. In fact, this poem is an exception in suggesting that the duty of a lord's retinue was to die with him if he was killed: other Anglo-Saxon literary works about war and warriors, such as *Beowulf*, suggest that their primary duty was to avenge his death.[1]

To the historian, other improbabilities become apparent. No other source indicates that tribute was demanded or promised while rival armies faced each other prepared for battle. Here this demonstrates that Byrhtnoth would rather face death than endure such shame. The tribute is talked of as a payment in "gold rings," when we know that they were paid in coin. The poem centers on Byrhtnoth and a band of close companions. The ealdorman is the "giver of rings" and other valuable gifts and in return they have vowed to be loyal to him, an exchange that has occurred during feasts in his hall. Already by the ninth century this was a long-established image: the chieftain and his *comitatus* (personal war-band or warrior household), sworn to protect him to the last. The poem is written in an "old style" and uses old imagery: we cannot be certain, therefore, that it reflects the reality of military obligation and organization in 991. After an initial reference to the "battle-hedge" (line of battle), the description suggests individual duels rather than concerted movements by masses of men which would probably have occurred, at least until the battle line was broken. The poet also describes at length the finery that Byrhtnoth wears, such as his decorated robe and gold armbands. Whilst it is indeed probable that his sword hilt was gilt, his saddle fit for a lord and his clothes better than those of his followers, no mention is made of armor or helmet, whereas the Vikings are said to have had them. It is quite possible that more Vikings had armor than their opponents, especially if their army was larger, but it is improbable that a man who could afford such fine clothes would not protect himself and his immediate retinue. It seems that the poet is more interested in emphasising Byrhtnoth's nobility than describing what he actually wore in battle.

The Battle of Maldon is a rare late example of a genre now known as "heroic poetry," for the purposes of this book considered poetry from Germanic-speaking northern Europe. The principal structurally unifying factor in this type of poetry is alliteration. One of the chief difficulties with all written sources, of course, not just poetry, is establishing the date at which the version we possess was written, whether it is closely based on an earlier version, and what its sources were. In many cases only copies or fragments of the original texts survive. In the case of *The Battle of Maldon* the beginning and the end are missing. When we note that it is one of the best sources we have for a battle of the Viking era, since it is nearly contemporary, the reader can imagine what the historian endeavoring to uncover the reality of warfare is up against. As will be seen, the poem does include information related to actual events, but it is not easy to distinguish this from the imaginative episodes and embellishments.

The accounts of only two heroic poems (if we exclude the skaldic verse discussed below) seem to bear a close relationship to what actually happened, one being *Maldon*, the other the *Ludwigslied*, which concerns the

Battle of Saucourt between the Vikings and Franks in 881.[2] However, the heroic ethos that is demonstrated in these epics, not only in these two but in others that were recited during the period 800–1100, such as *Beowulf*, presumably reflects attitudes of the period. This ethos is detectable in other literature of the era and also later material such as the Icelandic Kings' Sagas. It may present an ideal of the noble warrior, but ideals affect practice. The few examples of "heroic poetry" that purport to describe actual warfare at least include details of fighting and events during battle, which theoretically, if correctly analyzed, can tell us a considerable amount about the actual experience of war, or how people idealized it, or how they hoped it would be.

Heroic poetry is only one type of written source available to us for the Viking period. The vast majority of written material was produced by scribes trained in the Church, or, in Ireland, one of the bardic schools, which taught how to make literary compositions on law, history, poetry, or medicine in Irish. Among the manuscripts we possess are charters, letters, and other documents related to specific events, but those that give an overall view are chronicles or histories, or annals. The last differ in that they are lists of events considered important to the scribe or patron, which are dated but not necessarily related to one another, nor written in such a way as to give a continuous narrative. The vellum, paper, or parchment on which the text of any of these is written may be dateable, but that does not tell us the origin of the text or how it has been copied or altered. The recording and copying of annals and chronicles was a laborious task and one of the duties of a monk, but it was not simply done as proof of forbearance, as it was believed that the keeping of records of events would lead to a better understanding of the works of God and His purpose.

What was considered of most importance to people of the Christianized regions of the Viking Age does not often correspond to what is considered most important to the majority of us nowadays, and this is very noticeable in records of warfare. Moreover, almost all such works were produced with an audience in mind. Religious houses favored those who had been generous to them and similarly showed those who (in their eyes) had persecuted them in a poor light. In addition, many of those trained to write in ecclesiastical establishments were employed in the service of royal or ecclesiastical administrations, as were the Irish bards, and many of the most important sources available to us were produced as a form of propaganda for rulers, often one or other of the protagonists in internal struggles for power, or the ultimate victor. For instance, the version of the *Anglo-Saxon Chronicle* produced under Archbishop Wulfstan's direction after King Æthelred II's death was clearly adjusted to show his favored candidate for the English throne, Edmund, in a favorable light by comparison with his father. If we travel to the other end of the Viking world, our chief written source for the early history of Rus, the Russian *Primary Chronicle*, was also altered to favor Prince Yaroslav Vladimirovich ("the Wise") after his victory in his struggle with his brothers for control of Kiev. Fortunately, the reliability of many of the existing texts can often be tested against other evidence, as a vast amount of analysis has been done on their content, style, and palaeography. Increasing evidence from archaeology, aided by good dating methods, numismatics and climatology, and an improving understanding of economic and social conditions has also contributed significantly, although this is more true in the west and north of Europe than in the east.

Most of the sources will be introduced where relevant, but the most important of them are listed below. For the Viking invasions of England, the best known of the contemporary or near-contemporary annals is the *Anglo-Saxon Chronicle*, which has a complicated history and exists in several versions. A valuable supplementary source to this is the *Chronicle of John of Worcester*, which was written some hundred years after the events it describes, but uses the ASC and other earlier sources that have since disappeared. From the mid-eleventh century we also possess the *Encomium of Queen Emma*, which drew on the evidence of witnesses to the Danish Conquest earlier in the century.

There is also a vast range of manuscripts from Viking-Age Francia, although Viking attacks were not of such central importance to most of the Frankish scribes as they were to the Anglo-Saxons. The *Royal Frankish Annals (Annales regni Francorum)* have a strong Carolingian bias. After the division of Francia into west and east kingdoms in 829 these annals were continued in the west as the *Annals of St. Bertin* up to 882 and in the east as the *Annals of Fulda* up to 887, or 901 if an addition is included. Like the ASC, the manuscript tradition of these royal annals is rather complicated. Among their sources, however, were a number of minor annals, sometimes more contemporary. Other sources such as chronicles of abbeys and bishoprics provide a less pro-Carolingian view. The most important sources for

Viking attacks are the *Xanten Annals* and the *Annals of St. Vaast d'Arras*, to which can be added the verse description of the Norse siege of Paris in 885-6 by the monk Abbo and the invaluable chronicle of Regino of Prüm. There are fewer sources for the tenth century, but the *Annals* of Flodoard of Reims and the *Historiae* of Richer of Saint-Rémi which takes up where Flodoard left off are both valuable, while Rodolfus (Ralph) Glaber's *Histories* take us into the eleventh century. For East Francia, generally referred to as Germany after the end of the Carolingian line in 919, our most important sources for the period 900–1050 are the works of Widukind of Corvey and Thietmar of Merseburg, although Liudprand of Cremona, who was mainly concerned with Italy, also has useful information.

Along with the rest of the British Isles, Ireland suffered severely from the Viking attacks. The surviving Irish annals (or, as they are usually less appropriately named, chronicles) have very similar wording up to the year 911, which has led to the hypothesis of an earlier *Chronicle of Ireland*, or *World Chronicle* (as it includes many events beyond Ireland taken from earlier foreign sources). The consensus appears to be that the chronicle's second annalist was working in the Irish midlands in the period 741–911, probably in Brega (or *Breagh*) and possibly in the monastery at Clonard, although some scholars believe it may have moved to Armagh by the end of the period. After 911 the successor chronicles were produced in two main areas, one in Armagh, later integrated into the *Annals of Ulster*, and the other in Clonmacnoise. The latter included the *Annals of Clonmacnoise* (in Irish); the fragmentary *Annals of Tigernach*, the abbreviated version of these; the *Chronicum Scotorum*; and the *Annals of the Four Masters*. After 800 a large number of entries in the Irish chronicles concern Viking raids. In addition to Irish material, these sources are useful for England and Scotland, the chronology of English events sometimes making more sense than that of the *ASC*. However, the extant ones all date from the fourteenth century and (mostly) later.

For events further east, written sources are rare. Many of the lands visited by the Vikings were at a similar level of development to Scandinavia. The Slavs, Letts, and Estonians of the Baltic coast left no records, and almost the sole record from Russia is the *Primary Chronicle*. The extant version of this dates to 1347 and the amount of rewriting makes the task of finding out what was actually recorded in versions from the era before 1100 very difficult. A considerable amount of work has been done on it, but much of this is controversial. In many ways the same problems apply to the Scandinavian records of events in the east, which were written much later. What can be gleaned from these sources can be supplemented by information from more contemporary German and Byzantine chronicles, which sometimes refer to events outside their own main spheres of interest, on which Viking activities occasionally impinged directly. These include Thietmar's *Chronicon*, the records of missions to Scandinavia such as Adam of Bremen's *Deeds of Bishops of the Hamburg Church* (Gesta Hammaburgensis Ecclesiae Pontificum) and Rimbert's *Life of Ansgar* (*Vita Anskarii*), the *Chronographia* of Michael Psellos, John Skylitzes's *Synopsis Historiarum*, and the *History* of Leo the Deacon. The lack of good sources for eastern Europe, together with our westocentric view of European history, accounts for the relative lack of interest in Viking activity in the present region of Russia, although it is arguable that the lasting effect of their presence there was greater. Unfortunately, the western bias must remain in this work, as the limited sources give little information on the conduct of warfare in that region, but they will be considered as far as possible.

What of the Vikings themselves, the Scandinavians whose depredations between 800 and 1100 have defined the parameters of this work? Almost all the contemporary written sources we have were produced by their enemies in the lands they raided or settled. Thus we have a view of the Vikings that is almost universally hostile to them, particularly before their conversion to Christianity. The Christianization of Scandinavia was a slow process, ultimately brought about through the contact resulting from their voyages and pressure on Denmark from Germany. First to be converted were those who settled in the regions they had initially raided, and subsequently, towards the end of the tenth century, the kingdoms of Denmark and Norway, and finally Sweden, through which Christianity made steady headway from Götaland to Svealand, the region north of Lake Mälar being converted only at the end of the eleventh century.

A written culture like that of Latin Europe did not begin to develop in Scandinavia until the twelfth century. Just how little accurate information was preserved in Denmark is shown by the *History of the Danes* (*Gesta Danorum*) written by Saxo Grammaticus at the end of that century. His account of the era before the early twelfth century is highly suspect and colored by Christian belief, and he had no access to English sources such as the *ASC*. However, as a source of tradition and mythology it has its uses.

His contemporary Sven Aggesen also wrote a short history, as well as the *Lex Castrensis* (perhaps in the early 1180s), purporting to be law for soldiers in the king's service dating from Cnut's time, which has been used by both Danish and English historians as evidence for late Viking or English military organization. In fact, it is a learned text in Latin in the European juridical tradition of Sven's own era, "a political work written in a pseudo-historical form," and it tells us little of Cnut's time.[3]

Runestones are our only source of contemporary written evidence from Scandinavia. They first appeared in Denmark, whence the fashion for raising them traveled to Norway and Västergötland by the end of the tenth century and eastern Sweden in the early eleventh. There they continued to be raised for a century, whereas the practice largely died out further west during the mid-eleventh century. A few famous inscriptions provide limited information about those who went to war, where they went, and whether they made a profit and whether they survived or not. Sometimes people are designated by a particular title, such as "steersman" or "thegn," evidence which is useful when illuminated by other sources. However, the primary purposes of runestones were commemoration of the dead and their living relatives who raised the stones, and as declarations of religious and political affiliation.[4] They are more useful as sources for social organization than for warfare.

Another genre of source material from Viking Age Scandinavia that has come down to us is skaldic poetry, but whether it may be considered contemporary is a matter of opinion. In modern usage "skaldic verse" refers to poetry composed between the ninth century and the end of the Middle Ages in an alliterative style and a variety of meters. It belongs to the same Germanic tradition as Old English and Old High German or Old Saxon heroic verse. Skaldic verse is one way in which the pagan Vikings kept an oral record of their exploits, although tales must have been passed down in other forms as well. The skaldic verse is "historical" in the sense that it refers to definite historical events, at least in theory, in a specific historical context.[5] Although the Old Norse word for it may have meant "libel in verse" originally (an alternative view is that it meant simply "poetry"), the majority of what has come down to us was composed by court skalds in honor of kings or jarls. Most celebrate battles or other notable deeds, although a few are funeral poems, and they praise the subject for his generosity and boldness. However, skaldic verse has several characteristics that make it very difficult to follow even for those who understand Old Icelandic: the word order is infinitely variable and clauses can be split and intermixed, vocabulary is varied by the use of name alternatives (*heiti*) in place of common words and riddle-like kennings, themselves often split between lines and clauses, in place of common words or short phrases. These are also used in Old English poetry, but not to the same extent.

Many of the kennings include allusions to mythological figures and the same ones can sometimes be used as substitutes for more than one other word: for instance some of the battle kennings can mean "warriors." Like the heroic poetry of Anglo-Saxon England, the end result is more likely to give a picture of how noble warriors wished to be seen or possibly hoped to be, rather than a realistic portrayal of battle. Skaldic verse contains numerous images of the grim side of battle, such as weapons running with blood, blood-stained clothes and warriors, blood-soaked decks of ships, crushed bones and carrion birds that feed on the corpses of the slain; but these are "stock phrases" employed by the poet to describe virtually every battle. Only rarely is pain mentioned, whether physical or emotional.

Since skaldic verse usually tells of the patron's battles or other noteworthy exploits, it is contemporary in character, although verse that dealt with past events began to appear in the twelfth century, much of which is of extremely doubtful historical value. Because it was not written down until the twelfth century or later, the whole corpus of skaldic verse is suspect. Many modern scholars nevertheless maintain that much of it preserved its form and content largely unchanged from an earlier era, having been transmitted by mouth by memory to successive generations of skalds.[6] It has been shown that formulaic poetry, particularly when used for ritual purposes, can be transmitted orally over many generations and preserve many of its original themes, sometimes even when these cannot be fully understood by the later reciters or singers.[7] However, it is impossible for successive transmissions to occur without some change in wording or content, even if only accidental, while re-interpretation of passages that do not make sense to the generation of the new poet is entirely possible.

As far as the practice of warfare is concerned (its religious or ritual aspects are another matter), there is little in the skaldic verse of the Viking era that would not have made sense to Scandinavians seven generations later. In the thirteenth century Snorri Sturluson himself cited the antiquity of skaldic poetry as one of his reasons for using it as a source and quoting it in his history of the Norwegian kings, now known as *Heimskringla*, and it is to him that we owe much of our knowledge of skaldic verse and the practice of its composition.[8] All the skaldic verse that has come down to us exists in fragments of varying length that were used by twelfth- to fourteenth-century saga writers in their works. This has created problems in itself, as the quotations, mostly quite short, have been taken out of context in such a way that they could be used to support or emphasize something different from what they originally concerned. Moreover, since the compilers or writers of the sagas of Norwegian and Danish kings were often themselves accomplished skalds, they were also capable of skilfully altering skaldic poems or even creating spurious skaldic poems or fragments to back up their tales if they wanted.

As noted above, the prose sagas that we possess were written from the late twelfth century onwards, which makes any uncorroborated material suspect as history. Many modern Scandinavian works on the Vikings, and particularly Viking warfare, have tended to take them at face value, on the unwritten principle that "this is all we have, so we have to believe them."[9] These sagas may be regarded as works of historical tradition, rather than historiography in the modern sense. They appear to have used a variety of sources, including the earlier works of their former enemies, particularly the English. Earlier sagas were used, as well as genealogical lists. A great part of their source material, however, is clearly derived from oral tradition, either directly or via earlier works. Of this the skaldic poetry (if genuinely from the period it told of) is the most likely to have been passed on unaltered, as it had a form and structure that aided memorization and was held in a respect that made it less likely to be adulterated. Tales passed down to kinsmen and friends are likely to have been embellished or adjusted, or simply remembered wrongly.

Of the kings' sagas, the most coherent and convincing "history" appears to be *Heimskringla*, but this does not necessarily mean that it is reliable. Snorri clearly used his own intuition, and employed dramatic reconstruction in a way that a modern historian would never do. In a sense *Heimskringla* resembles those historical novels of our time that are closely based on what the novelist knows of history. In some ways Snorri's skill in compiling his history makes it more difficult to identify seams in the text. Moreover, *Heimskringla*, like the other Icelandic saga-histories, includes numerous incidents that we would consider little more than interesting anecdotes, many of them highly improbable. Among them are many supernatural events or unlikely tales, such as Harald Hardrada's use of incendiary birds to capture a city in Italy. These may be derived from folk tales and tradition, but an important source of information for the saga/chronicle writers may have been their own imaginations. The "history" they wrote was intended to be entertaining, and if there was a gap in the known sequence of events it needed to be filled. In the Icelandic sagas there are many episodes that appear to reflect the political reality or reproduce events of the authors' own day rather than what might have occurred in the Viking Era.

Battle of Niså, 1062

In the sixteenth year of Harald Hardrada's rule over Norway, during his long war with King Sweyn Estridsen of Denmark, he took his fleet south, where he found the Danish fleet waiting at the mouth of the River Niså. Harald had 180 ships, but Sweyn had twice as many, commanded by six jarls. In each line of battle many of the ships of the center were fastened together with ropes, with the king's ship in the center. The ship of Harald's marshal, Ulf, took up a position next to the king's, and they led their fleet forward towards the enemy. Other ships on the flanks acted individually, among them a contingent led by Jarl Håkon, who had previously served King Sweyn, after which he acted as a freebooter before volunteering to fight with Harald. The two fleets came together in the evening twilight. A long and bloody battle ensued, involving savage hand-to-hand combat alternating or accompanied with showers of stones and arrows, Harald himself using his bow to good effect.

Håkon's ships cleared many of the Danish ships operating independently on one flank, so that those remaining retreated from the battle. However, the ships on Harald's other flank were not faring so well, although fine ships commanded by the chieftains of the Trondheim district. On hearing of this, Håkon rowed to the other flank, where he proceeded to turn the tide in the Norwegians' favor. The battle continued all night, but eventually Harald captured King Sweyn's ship. This led to a general flight of the Danish ships that could escape, but many of them were fastened together or grappled by Harald's ships, and their crews had no choice but to jump overboard if they could not reach an unattached ship. No one knew whether Sweyn was alive or dead, but, having fought bravely, he managed to escape the slaughter at the end of the battle and find another ship, which skirted the shore to avoid the confusion. Taking a false name, he enlisted the help of Jarl Håkon to escape. King Harald was hindered from pursuing as he would have liked by the mass of ships ahead of him, some abandoned and others attached to the Norwegian ships. Nevertheless, he captured more than seventy Danish ships and the Jarl of Halland, Finn Árnason, who had abandoned his service earlier.

This account is based on those of the Icelandic–Norwegian saga writers of the late twelfth and thirteenth centuries. They are remarkably consistent, but they probably drew on the same sources. Among these were a number of skaldic verses, which are said to have been composed by Stein Herdísarson, who was on Ulf's ship; Thjóðólf Árnason, who was Harald's court skald; and Stuf (one stanza). They in turn probably provided the basis for one or more prose accounts that may themselves have been followed by the sagas we still have. Some of these verses are quoted in the saga accounts, and they give us the location of the battle, information on fleet sizes and losses, the basic fleet formations, the showers of stones and arrows during the battle, and the capture of Finn Árnason. The other details, such as the roping together of Harald's center ships, Jarl Håkon's part in the battle, the presence of the Trondheim chieftains on one flank, and Sweyn's escape are all given in the main text of the sagas.

There are all sorts of problems with these accounts. Much of the detail, such as the flying stones and arrows, was made up of stock phrases used for battles, although it is also likely that these things did occur during every battle. Why was the battle fought at night? Did it really last all night, or is this just rhetoric? Why is so much prominence given to Jarl Håkon? He is supposed to have cleared both flanks of "loose" Danish ships, yet these (alleged) successes played no part in the ultimate victory, and thereafter Håkon is said to have operated on the fringes of the battle. Finally, how was Harald able to win, if the fleets were really engaged all night, when he was outnumbered two-to-one?

We do have another account of this battle, that of Saxo, written from the Danish perspective. According to him, it was the Danes who were heavily outnumbered. He states that Sweyn decided to fasten the Danish ships together with grapples so that they could remedy their weakness by uniting into one indissoluble unit which might bear all before it. Among the Danish ships was one commanded by Skialm the White, one of whose oarsmen, Aslak, armed with an oak tiller, clubbed and drowned an entire Norwegian ship's crew. However, after this initial clash, the Norwegians received reinforcements led by "a jarl" and the whole Scanian contingent deserted the Danish fleet as night fell. The linked "fighting platform," it seems, was not so indissoluble, as the Scanians managed to remove the grapples silently before escaping into the night. Sweyn nevertheless decided to fight on, and battle was rejoined. Despite heroic resistance, victory went to numbers, and Skialm himself was wounded and captured after his ship was beset on all sides by enemy craft.

Saxo's account includes a number of incidents that defy credulity. How could a whole regional contingent escape the fleet unnoticed, even at night? It is more likely, if this defection occurred, that the rest of the fleet had no way of stopping it while the enemy fleet was still facing them. The tale of Aslak is plainly ludicrous, but it is also written in clear imitation of an anecdote by the Roman author Valerius Maximus, with the Dane substituted for Julius Caesar's centurion Caesius Scaeva.[10] Saxo writes that Aslak's actions would exceed belief, had Absalon not told the tale to him in his own words. Archbishop Absalon of Lund was Saxo's patron and also Skialm's grandson, which gives us the reason for Skialm's prominence in Saxo's account; it is derived from family (oral) tradition. It is probable that the origin of the Jarl Håkon episode in the Icelandic–Norwegian accounts was also a family or local tradition. Was he the jarl who reinforced Harald's fleet? Saxo does mention him later, claiming that he served Sweyn after the battle rather than before, as the sagas state.

We can dismiss some elements of his tale out of hand, but Saxo does give a reason why the decisive phase of the battle may have occurred at night, as reported by the sagas: if there was an initial clash which ended at sunset, and Harald was aware of the desertion of the Scanians, or simply decided to attack with his reinforcements when least expected, he may have made this decision. Saxo gives no indication of a date for the battle and no detail of fleet sizes, and seems to have had very little knowledge of the battle other than Hvide family tradition. The Danes' inferiority in numbers, as reported by him, gives a reason for their defeat, which also makes their fight appear a heroic effort against the odds—overwhelming odds, once the Scanians have fled. Sweyn's decision to continue the fight in these circumstances seems suicidal, although there have been many strange decisions in the history of warfare. In the late Viking Age the Danes should have been able to call upon more resources than their opponents, although not all available contingents need have been present at the Niså. The saga accounts do give fleet sizes, but the numbers are multiples of ten, or twelve if the duodecimal system is used, and the Danish fleet is exactly twice the size of Harald's, which makes the numbers highly suspect.[11] Even the skalds who were possibly present at the battle may not have known how many ships were engaged, or may have falsified the numbers for effect. Even if Sweyn did have more ships at the start of the battle (but probably not twice as many), Saxo's reported desertion of some of his side and the reinforcement of the Norwegian fleet may have reversed the odds. Here, however, we are entering the realms of speculation.

We can only guess at the reaction of the audience to a recital of heroic poetry or skaldic verse. One possibility is that some who had experienced battle viewed it with a certain cynicism or distaste, much as some modern war veterans have viewed *Rambo* or other "heroic" films. However, unlike these modern productions, the same people who were celebrated, or perhaps exhorted to behave as the heroes of the Viking Age poems, were those most likely to be their audience, and often the patrons of the poets. No doubt it was possible for the warrior nobility to divorce the content from reality and admire the skill of the poet. The poetry may even have represented a way of suppressing the fear of close combat or the very real horror of it. We can only guess at how seriously the audience took references to the enemy as wolves and the like. Often they were simply impersonal—the foe that the heroes of the epics were able to measure themselves against. As an example, no Viking is named in *The Battle of Maldon*. There is no indication that the poetry was primarily intended to function as a sort of hate propaganda, nor is there an obvious moral viewpoint on the enemy or his behavior, as there is in some of the chronicles written by churchmen; on the other hand, the lack of description of enemies as named people and occasional references to them as beasts dehumanizes them.

It has been argued that Germanic heroic poetry is "political," in the sense that it is an appeal to duty and sacrifice for the good of one's overlord or community, as appears to be the case with *The Battle of Maldon*.[12] Its heroes are not primarily glory-seekers, but men prepared to sacrifice themselves in the fulfilment of their duty, to their lord, to their kingdom or nation, or to God, and it is this achievement that is glorified. Some contemporaries may have looked askance at this as a form of propaganda, but we should not assume that people of Viking-Age Europe were as cynical as we are today. Although the Church expressed doubts about warfare in some contexts, particularly between fellow Christians, there was no "anti-war" movement such as that of recent times, particularly after the mass slaughter of two world wars. The "Peace of God" (*Pax Dei*) movement that sprang up in parts of Francia after 989 was an objection not to war as such but to general endemic disorder, a clergy-led appeal to warlord nobles to allow local communities to function without the constant destruction caused by their feuding. The world of men was imperfect, and it was believed that there could be no absolute peace until the Day of Judgement.

Heroic verse is the only surviving written material from the Viking Era that gives anything like a detailed account of combat. The clerics who wrote most of our source material were generally not interested in the detail of what men did in combat or battlefield tactics. By contrast, Greek historians of the classical era, whose experience of battle cannot have been dissimilar, did write about tactics. Their tradition was continued to some extent in the Roman Empire and then in the Byzantine Empire. A little more information on such matters is provided from sources as the Viking Era progresses, and the Scandinavian historical sagas provide considerably more, but they are much more likely to be reliable when they tell of the twelfth and thirteenth centuries, the period closer to their composition. Nevertheless, given the greater interest of Byzantine and later western sources in the conduct of warfare, the lack of comment in Viking-Age western Europe cannot be attributed solely to the influence of Christianity.

A key difference between the Scandinavian kings' sagas and the majority of medieval European chronicles is that they were composed by secular writers. Is it possible that the lack of interest in the detail of Viking warfare was a result of the sources being composed by ecclesiastical writers? Contrary to what some authors have stated in the past, churchmen who wrote in the Viking Era were not ignorant of warfare. Monks and clerics came from the same aristocratic background as warriors, a large proportion of them would have practiced fighting in their youth, and some had actually been warriors before taking the cloth. Nevertheless, from the time of the Church Fathers onwards, doubts had been expressed about the justification for warfare and the warrior's trade by clerical writers such as Augustine of Hippo. In the former territories of the Western Roman Empire a separation of Church and state developed and the tradition of questioning was much stronger there than it was in Byzantium.

Although hagiographers and biographers of kings indicated that their subjects wished to become monks or clergy, if only they could, there were certainly many for whom the monastic life held little appeal. We know that there existed a certain rivalry (or mutual suspicion or contempt) between those who fought and those who prayed in the High Middle Ages, and the same was probably true in the Viking Era, even if we have no direct written evidence of it. It is possible that clerics actually produced some of the "heroic verse" we possess, but others may have disliked the glorification of war and violent death, even if they thought it was sometimes necessary. Parts of the poem *Waltharius*, which was in Latin but drew on older Germanic tales, appear to parody the Germanic hero, notably when Guntharius appears as a rabid dog gnashing his teeth. There is little doubt that the writer was a churchman.[13]

More commonly, perhaps partly in response to epics of heroic war and partly inspired by it (even if unconsciously) monastic scribes wrote of their own heroes, men and women prepared to endure extreme hardship to spread the word of God, intended as examples for Christians to follow. Like the warrior, carrying out their duty sometimes required them to pay the ultimate price, in this case as martyrs for the faith, often enduring extreme torture and very violent deaths which the scribes did not shrink from describing. Their heroism lay in a resolute refusal to deny their faith, to "go down fighting," in this case metaphorically rather than literally. From Ireland, Anglo-Saxon England, and Francia there are many lives of missionaries and ecclesiastical leaders, and queens or kings who played a significant part in the conversion of their people to Christianity. Some became accepted as saints and subsequently had more "lives" written. These texts were not biographies as we understand the term: they were intended for the teaching of a largely illiterate population, to set them an example, and functioned as a handbook of rhetorical methods for priests and theologians to use when they taught about the truth of the word of God. Saints imitated the life of Christ, and the common folk were encouraged to imitate them in turn. For this reason there was a heavy emphasis on the saints' suffering and miracles, performed both before and after death. Rather like heroic poetry, although not founded on an oral tradition, saints' lives tended to follow a set pattern and included well-known motifs. Naturally, these tales also gave prestige to any ecclesiastical institution or royal house that had produced the saint, or possessed his or her relics. As evidence of actual events, however, they have to be used very carefully, and some are of no value whatever.

Nowhere is the lack of interest in the detail of battle more apparent than in the near-contemporary account of the Battle of Fontenoy, fought on 18 October 841, and related by Nithard, a grandson of Emperor Charlemagne, who fought in it.[14] It is a rare report by an eyewitness, yet his account of the actual fighting is extremely short and formulaic, notable more for its high-quality Latin than for anything it can tell us of warfare in the mid-ninth century. Nithard was not a cleric, but his account of the strife between the sons of Louis the Pious that broke up the empire created by Charlemagne was written in Latin and shows the same preoccupations. Like other medieval authors writing in Latin, his main concern was to demonstrate his knowledge of classical writings, the works of the Church Fathers, and of scripture. They tried to understand what happened and to explain it according to their world view. Scholarly learning provided the basis upon which an understanding of the workings of God in the world could be reached. In this context the detail of troop movements on the battlefield was less significant than signs sent by God, many of them what we would understand as "natural events."

The *Annals of Fulda* entry for the year 876 gives a very short and confusing description of the Battle of Andernach between Charles the Bald of West Francia and his nephew Louis "the Younger" of East Francia, followed by evidence that God fought against Charles and the following explanation: "This happened on October 8 against the new Sennacherib [Charles], so that he who in his self-confidence would not remember God may now, defeated and shamed, realize that victory in war lies not in the greatness of armies but that strength comes from heaven, and may also at last set some bounds to his greed and pride."

Like the Fulda annalist, Christians everywhere believed that God determined who was to be the victor in any military encounter. The rationale behind this was the same as that behind the judicial duel, the battle being a duel between armies rather than between individuals. Here the pro-Louis annalist interprets Charles's defeat as punishment for excessive greed, pride, and duplicity, which had included the swearing of false oaths, and makes allusions to the Bible. However, although God may have decided the outcome, this did not mean that there was no point in the protagonists making decisions and taking actions themselves. The second coming and the end of the world were inevitable, but man nevertheless had to do his utmost to bring about God's world on earth, and the same applied on a smaller scale. Therefore, as will be seen later in this work, commanders did make what we would call military decisions designed to bring about the result they wanted, but equally (or perhaps more) important in their preparations for war and battle were religious and ritual acts. They acted in such a way as to please God, in the hope that he would favor them. For this reason prayers were said before battle, masses were held, and sometimes even ordeals were undergone, while relics or other religious symbols accompanied the armies. But what those who recorded these events afterwards were most interested in were the signs of God's works. In this they were following the example set in the Old Testament, the source of inspiration for the kings of the emerging polities of Europe, in particular the Book of Kings, in which little is said of how battles were won or lost on the ground, but there is much about divine intervention and its influence on their outcome.

The Siege of Paris, 885–886

In 885–886, seven hundred ships carrying a huge Viking host of forty thousand warriors approached Paris. They came from Rouen, attracted by the wealth of the city, led by a chieftain named Sigfred. The Parisians retreated to the Île de la Cité and prepared to withstand a siege under the leadership of the Count of Paris, Eudes (Odo, later king), and Bishop Gozlin. They had the support of Odo's brother Robert, the ailing Hugh, abbot of Saint-Germain d'Auxerre, two more counts and a marquis. The city had stone walls of Roman origin, and was connected to the land by two bridges, one crossing the Seine to the north of the island, one to the south. On the north side, the *grand pont* (where the modern Pont au Change is) had stone foundations and was of greater width than its wooden counterpart, the *petit pont*. Both were protected along their length by palisades and had wooden towers on stone foundations at the ends, surrounded by ditches. They were low enough to prevent passage beyond them for the Viking longships, which seriously hindered the attackers as they could not cut off the city by controlling the river. The city also had powerful spiritual protection in the form of the relics of Saint Germain.[15] The saint intervened at several points to aid the defense, as shown by convenient changes in the wind and rocks in the river which blocked the enemy fire-ships.

The Danes arrived on 24 November and two days later launched an assault on the tower defending the end of the *grand pont*. During the nighttime lull in this assault another story was added to the tower. Covered by ballistas and slings (catapults?), the Vikings tried to dig away the foundations with iron spikes, but the defenders poured a mixture of oil, pitch, and wax over them. On the second day Bishop Gozlin joined the defenders, armed with bow and axe, and set up a cross on the parapet. Although the Vikings started a fire at the door, a change in the wind caused the smoke to blow into the faces of the attackers. They were driven back, the fire was put out, and the damage repaired. The Danes realized that the city would not be taken quickly and set up camp, ravaging the country around for supplies. However, they prepared another attack, constructing huge roofed battering rams with sixteen wheels each. Progress was slowed when the two builders were killed by a ballista bolt from the city, but the rams were ready by the end of January and shelters were made for the besiegers to operate close to the defenses. To prepare for the attack the defenders manned the bridge and deployed catapults on it. In order to reach the tower with their rams, the Vikings needed to fill in the ditch to provide a flat approach. The attack was made on 31 January. For two days the attackers attempted to secure an approach for their rams, but they suffered heavy casualties. A crowd of them were killed by an enormous stone thrown from a machine "commonly called a *mangana*," and at one point seven Vikings were skewered on one ballista bolt. On the third day the Danes sent ships filled with burning brush against the bridge, but rocks in the river prevented them reaching the bridge or causing any serious damage before they sank. The attackers then withdrew a distance, abandoning their rams. Finally the besiegers did take the tower of the smaller bridge, but only after the swollen river had caused the bridge to collapse, isolating it and its twelve defenders.

The siege finally ended in March, when a relief army approached and the Vikings agreed to withdraw on payment of sixty pounds of silver. They returned in the following summer, but the defenses had been strengthened and they soon left after another payment.

For this siege of Paris we have an eyewitness account, written in Latin verse by the monk Abbo. He seems to have written his account a decade after the siege, but the possible fading of his memory is not the most serious problem for the modern interpreter. As usual, no reference is made to military decision-making, as the real heart of the defense is St Germain, although Odo and Gozlin are given due credit for their bravery. Other than the leaders, we have no idea how many people there were in the defended city, or how many of them were warriors. Furthermore, the city itself is not clearly described. Abbo mentions only the Île de la Cité, which still had walls of Roman origin at this date, probably with towers. By the ninth century the city had already grown beyond the island, and there were suburbs beyond the bridges, particularly on the north side, although there is no evidence that these had any form of defenses at this date. Were they cleared so that the Vikings could not use them as cover or quarters? What happened to the population? They may have fled, either into the countryside or into the walled city, but we have no way of knowing.

Abbo clearly exaggerates for effect: quite apart from the enormous stone that kills a crowd of Vikings and the ballista bolt that skewers seven Vikings, the size of the enemy force must be grossly inflated. It would have been impossible for the Vikings to assemble well over thirty thousand men and seven hundred ships, even though the Vikings in Francia had received reinforcements from England shortly before the attack. Although Abbo says the Vikings devastated far and wide, they could not have maintained such a force near Paris for several months over the winter. In addition, there is no indication that the Parisians were running short of supplies, which suggests that there was no blockade, or at most an incomplete one. The attacks described are almost all on the *grand pont*, but the Vikings may also have attacked the other bridge tower, which is mentioned clearly only when it falls after the river demolishes the bridge. Abbo appears to have concentrated on, and embellished, those things that he saw or heard described in detail. Doubts have also been expressed about his descriptions of siege machines and stone throwers, which might have been borrowed from classical authors.[16] The difficulty in following Abbo's descriptions is shown by the various interpretations of the rams, some modern authors reporting them as siege towers, although these are unlikely to have had sixteen wheels (unless, of course, the number of wheels was a way of exaggerating the size of the towers). However, use of engines at this siege is mentioned in other sources of the period, so his account is not impossible in this respect.

Abbo's account is valuable to the modern historian, but shows clearly the preoccupations mentioned above: what was important was the way in which the will of God was manifested, rather than details of tactics, descriptions of technology or the accurate (as we would see it) recounting of events. Abbo hoped to make an impression, so literary style had a part to play—and, like the *Maldon* poet, he chose the medium of verse. In this case his own abbot was not very impressed with the poetry, an opinion echoed by many modern commentators.

Modern historians and Viking-Age warfare

Historians of the ancient and medieval worlds are familiar with the problem of a lack of written sources, but that has not stopped many of them, even some of those with an academic training, from selecting and combining pieces of information from different centuries or regions to construct a composite picture of "New Kingdom Egyptian administration" or "Dark Age society." Frequently recourse is made to analogy. These methods may be legitimate, provided that it is made clear that we are dealing in probabilities or possibilities and why an analogy should be valid. Unfortunately, in recent times academic historians who have specialized in the early Middle Ages have taken little interest in warfare. The bloodletting of the twentieth century has discredited any form of history seen to glorify war, and history that considers warfare as an art and concerns itself largely with strategy and tactics is seen by many as such. This criticism is not wholly unjustified, as war is not a game of chess and its victims are not wooden pieces, but the fact that much history of human conflict is badly written or only considers part of the question is not a good reason to exclude the subject from serious study. With some notable exceptions, mostly published within the last two decades, war history has remained the province of enthusiastic amateurs, ex-soldiers, re-enactors, and wargamers.

Unfortunately, the vast majority of those who have written about medieval (and ancient) warfare have ignored the social and religious context in which these wars were fought and the way in which contemporary world views influenced decision-making. Books on Viking warfare have often contained a lot of good information on armor and weaponry, but have been less successful in tackling the problems of strategy, tactics and attitudes to war. There has been a tendency to see the "rules of war" as timeless, in the sense that when ninth-century Vikings or Franks made decisions on how to act in war, they took the same things into consideration as soldiers do nowadays. Thus analogies can be drawn with wars from different eras without any qualification and actions reconstructed using the logic of a modern military thinker. Similarly, it is assumed that the behavior of people was basically the same. It is of course true that we remain the same species as our ancestors and as a result we have the same instinctive responses, many of which are common to other large animals, but our responses are moderated by cultural factors. As we know only too well from recent experience, deeply held beliefs can overcome fear and enable people to endure all sorts of deprivation. To make matters worse for the historian, what medieval writers meant by emotional terms such as love or anger (or the supposed equivalents in the original language) may differ from our understanding of them. In addition, the way in which armies were raised was determined by the structure of the society around them and the nature of the economy.[17]

Experiences from modern war may be valid; for instance, Ryan Lavelle has recently argued that Francis Peabody Magoun's experience as an ace pilot in the First World War was of great assistance to him in interpreting the *ASC* account of clashes between English and Viking ships around the southern English coast in 886, as he understood the importance of the experience of the crews in manoeuvring their craft and did not simply base what happened on analyses of tides, currents, and technology.[18] In more general terms, the importance of instilling a feeling of duty to comrades into men required to fight, so as to make the shame of running away greater than the fear of dying, is as valid now as it was in 991. The equivalent of this modern "regimental pride" then was the pride in belonging to the lord's household, and one purpose of heroic poems such as *Maldon* was perhaps to appeal to this. On the other hand, there are significant differences between the experiences of the warrior on the battlefield in different ages. If we exclude the mounted archer armies of central Eurasia, most battles from the era of the first city-states in the Near East to the seventeenth century were determined by the outcome of close combat. Increasingly from the end of the sixteenth century onwards, and certainly from the end of the seventeenth century, battles were determined by firepower and battlefield artillery came into its own. This ultimately brought about the second great change in battlefield combat, as the range and accuracy of firearms and artillery increased, along with the latter's destructive power. The use of hand-to-hand combat or massed short-range firearms to determine the issue required that men stood shoulder to shoulder in multiple ranks, which initially contributed to solidity but probably also to mass flight when such a formation was broken.

In recent times formations have become much more dispersed. Coordination of forces over a wide area has been increasingly facilitated by the advent of radio and electronic communication, which means that the commander is no longer dependent upon someone delivering messages by hand, whether on horseback or on foot, and no longer has to be near the front line. Even before this, population increase and social and economic change had led to a steady increase in the size of armies since the Middle Ages, with a significant leap in the French Revolutionary and Napoleonic Wars. It is worth remembering that the population of Europe as a whole was probably twenty-five to thirty million in 800 AD, perhaps rising to about fifty million in 1100.[19] In the Middle Ages large armies of many tens of thousands were unusual in Europe, but the balance of evidence suggests that they were raised by the Carolingian and Ottonian kingdoms, just as they were by ancient states such as Macedonia, Carthage, or Roman Republican Italy and the large tribal confederations of the Migration Period (400–550 AD) that moved en masse and deployed a large proportion of their able male population (and occasionally some females as well) as warriors.

Archaeology as evidence of warfare

Nowadays everyone with any interest in the past knows that we are very heavily dependent on archaeology when written sources are lacking. It also has a huge contribution to make when they do exist, especially when they are rare, which is the case for the Viking Era. On the face of it, archaeology provides "hard evidence," whereas the written word is inevitably tainted by the opinions and aims of the writers. However, archaeology provides selective evidence; only those things that have survived and have been discovered and analysed are available. Some things survive better than others, depending on the durability of the material, the environment in which it was lost or abandoned, and the context in which it was deposited—material from burials, for instance—is over-represented. Furthermore, those who possessed more, almost invariably the social elite, and especially those who chose to take more of it with them when they died, are much more visible than the majority of the population who lived alongside them. In many ways the problems of analysing written and archaeological material are comparable: the written material of the Viking Age and most of that of succeeding periods was produced by a small number of people, the vast majority from a select group of aristocracy who became Christian clerics. A text may survive in a version written down by one scribe, but the material in it is like an archaeological site in which all the settlement layers have been compressed into one—disentangling how many previous authors compiled the contents, when they did so and where they got their material from is extremely difficult, and sometimes impossible.

In addition, although it is true that the evidence detected by archaeology is "material" in a sense that written texts are not, artifacts or detectable alterations to the landscape tell us very little in themselves—they have to be interpreted, either in the light of written evidence, or the accumulated knowledge of ancient beliefs and psychology that is derived from it. Even if it is dateable, we need to know more of an archaeological find than what it is: the find of a single sword, for instance, may tell us how it was made and perhaps when, and the sword may show signs of contact damage, but we do not know who made it or how it was used without all the other equipment that its owner used, comparable finds from elsewhere, or written evidence about the use of similar weapons. Even if we did know everything about its owner (or owners) and his equipment, how could we know how far from the next man he stood in the battle line? Even the assumption that the owner was male cannot be certain. We make educated guesses or assumptions on the basis of everything else we have learned, but some of those made in the past have been very questionable. To take an example, Guy Halsall has suggested that late Roman and early "dark age" European armies fought in a looser formation than did armies from the eighth century onwards, as suggested by the lighter shield bosses, often designed for "catching" opponents' weapons, and the greater number of throwing weapons found in grave deposits.[20] This is possible, but can we make these judgements about shield bosses when the rest of the shield (i.e. what was usually the wooden part) is missing? Some interpretations of material remains in the landscape are highly dubious, and some have later been proved hopelessly wrong: for instance, at the end of the twentieth century it was shown that archaeologists who had earlier excavated and interpreted the site of Büraburg in Hesse, in the Frankish–Slav frontier zone of the eighth and ninth centuries, had mistaken natural erosion as deliberate movement of earth by humans and Neolithic remains as Carolingian.[21] A number of forts that were actually Frankish foundations were mistaken as Slavic and an assumption that stone fortifications of the tenth or eleventh centuries were of the eighth or ninth century had been made on the basis that Frankish methods must have been more sophisticated than those of the Slavs.

Unfortunately, finds of actual battlefield remains are extremely rare, although a few mass burials have been found, which testify to the horrific injuries inflicted in medieval warfare. The above examples represent two of the most obvious and common archaeological contributions to the knowledge of warfare: finds of offensive and defensive equipment of the individual warrior and defensible structures or features in the landscape. There are also many problems with the interpretation of the latter category, however: fortifications are not merely defensive in function, nor even simply military in function. Apparently military features may also have non-military functions. The non-military aspects of many of these received increasing emphasis in recent decades, so much so that military functions began to be underplayed. However, this highlights a central problem with interpretation of sites such as Offa's Dyke or the Danevirke, which may be frontier markers rather than defensible walls, the Viking ring-forts of Denmark, which may be garrison sites rather than defensible forts, or the round towers of Ireland, which may or may not have been wholly or partly defensive in function. Conversely, many other aspects of social life or human physical condition are relevant to the study of warfare, even if this is not immediately obvious. An example is the study of disease from human remains and hygiene (or the lack of it) from habitation sites, as it is no secret that deaths from disease outnumbered deaths in combat and constituted one of the greatest threats to any medieval army, forcing the abandonment of many campaigns. Climate and settlement patterns also have obvious relevance to warfare.

Even more controversial than the dating and examination of material remains and assessment of their use is "cognitive archaeology." Is it possible to determine how people thought, or what people believed, hundreds of years ago? This is difficult enough when we have both archaeology and written sources, as in the case of the Christianized parts of Europe in the Viking Era. Use of finds as evidence of the mentalities of past societies is also controversial, so that some archaeologists reject it altogether, arguing that we only have evidence of material culture from the prehistoric period. Although we are in a far better position when written material is also available in some quantity, that too is very problematical. Nevertheless, in this book an attempt will be made to address all these problems, at the risk of over-simplifying them because of space limitations.

Chapter 2

Equipment

Weapons

Our information about the equipment used by soldiers of the Viking Era derives almost entirely from archaeology and manuscript illustrations. The terminology used by contemporary chroniclers, annalists, and poets was usually vague. Some words used by Latin-language authors were no more exact than the kennings of skaldic verse, for instance, the use of the noun "iron" on its own to refer to any weapons with iron points or edges, including swords, axes, and spears, both for thrusting and throwing. Unfortunately from our point of view, the practice of burying people with their equipment ceased almost entirely during the eighth century in Christianized lands, although the Vikings, Slavs, Balts, and Finns continued it. Many of the weapons used by them were of Frankish manufacture.

A general view is that the spear was the primary weapon of most footsoldiers. This is partly based on numbers of finds and partly on their usefulness in the context of the phalanx-like formation. As an example, 85 percent of Anglo-Saxon graves containing weapons had spearheads in them. Nevertheless, none of the requirements specified for levy troops listed the spear as a minimum requirement. The spear was also, of course, an effective weapon for use on horseback, and frequently appears as such in illustrations. The lighter "javelin" variety was certainly used by Slav horsemen and by Breton horsemen in the eighth and ninth centuries. A problem with identifying light javelins is that their heads are not necessarily distinguishable from arrowheads. However, they were almost certainly used in Ireland, as Irish warriors carried more than one "spear" and they were characteristic weapons of the Irish up until the end of the sixteenth century, clearly not derived from external influences.

Spear shafts rarely survive, but the limited number of finds and references in heroic poetry and other sources indicate that a variety of woods were used, ash being perhaps the most common. There was a considerable variety of spearhead forms, but they can be divided into three basic types.

The most common were socketed and had a diamond-shaped cross-section and angular blades. Others, like most of the known Viking examples, were more leaf-shaped with a lentoid (lens-shaped) cross-section. Some of these were corrugated, which increased the strength of the blade without adding to the weight. The third type were more or less spikes with a square cross-sectioned midrib. Some had sword-like blades of up to 50 centimeters in length. In the early Viking Era many of these spearheads had two small iron "wings" at the socket end, the so-called "winged lance" (Ger. *Flügellanzen*), which seems to have appeared in eighth-century Francia and spread to England, Scandinavia, and the Slavic-speaking regions, and even to Hungary after the raiding period was over. The wings were possibly designed for parrying. Spears with these heads also appear in tenth-century illustrations of mounted soldiers, among other weapons. Spearheads were socketed and fitted to the shaft with rivets.

Spears are shown wielded both overarm with one hand and underarm (supported by the length of the forearm) grip in combat, in both cases enabling the soldier to strike at his opponent above the shield.[1] A few illustrations, such as the eighth-century Pictish Aberlemno Stone, also suggest that spears might have been wielded two-handed with the spear hung on a strap round the neck. This would provide less protection but enable greater force to be used in the strike. Leaf-shaped blades could also be used for cutting strokes.

It is very difficult to estimate the length of a spear from its head, but on the basis of all available evidence most specialists in this field estimate that Viking-Era spears were between 150 and 280 centimeters long.[2] There is no indication that spears were of a uniform length or that foot soldiers in any European armies attempted to create a solid and uniform line of spearpoints. Their primary purpose was probably for use in mêlée or throwing. Byzantine infantry did employ longer and heavier spears in the tenth century, as they were faced with heavily armed and armored Arab cavalry, essentially the same problem faced by western infantry from the twelfth century onwards and one of the main motivations for the use of long spears or pikes of more uniform length.[3] There is no evidence that Frankish cavalry used couched lances in the Viking Era, nor that their horses were armored.

In place of the spear, or in addition to it, many troops were armed with a sword. Especially during the eighth and ninth centuries, the relatively short and single-bladed *seax* must have been a common weapon among footsoldiers. Its blade varied from 50 to 80 centimeters in length, although there were shorter "knife" versions of 30 centimeters or less. However, the double-edged long sword, referred to as *spatha* on the continent, had become the weapon of choice for those who fought mounted or other elite troops. The design of this sword improved substantially during the Viking Era. Although its length remained fairly constant at 90–100 centimeters, the eighth-century (and earlier) weapon lacked a point: in other words, it was primarily a slashing weapon, perhaps designed largely with use by horsemen in mind. During the ninth century it was improved so that the blade tapered more from the hilt to a point. Not only did this make it a thrusting as well as a cutting weapon, but the center of gravity moved towards the hilt, making handling it in combat easier. It therefore replaced the *seax* as the sword of choice for foot soldiers. In Ireland the pre-Viking sword was a short form of the late Roman *spatha*, but this was quickly replaced among those who used swords, the aristocracy, by the Viking type after the Irish came into contact with it.

Manufacturing methods involved forging a blade from many small pieces, either from stacked thin sheets to form a laminated blade or from iron rods laid side by side and welded together. The problem faced was the variable quality of iron ore and furnaces that did not produce a high enough temperature to melt the iron into a homogenous billet. The best swords were made by twisting iron strips together and welding them into rods, which were welded side by side, a technique known as pattern-welding. The use of this time-consuming method declined during the Viking Era as the quality of iron improved and higher temperatures that removed more of the slag were achieved in the furnaces, with less than half of those found in England being made by pattern-welding by the mid-tenth century. Many of the long swords had a groove or fuller running down the center, which reduced the weight slightly. At the end of the sword blade was the hilt, which was round or oval in shape in the early Viking Era, but developed into a bar of metal at right angles to the blade in the tenth century, probably in late Viking swords. This crossguard became a standard feature of later swords, such as those used by the Normans, as it provided better protection for the wielder's hand. Below the guard was a narrow tang, over which the hilt of horn, wood, or bone was fitted with a pommel on the end. In the Viking Era the form of the pommel was usually the most distinctive feature of the sword, as it could be designed in variable ways without diminishing the effectiveness of the weapon. Many hilts were quite short, but a few *seax* hilts were long enough to suggest that they may have been used two-handed.

Swords were suspended either from a waist-belt or a shoulder-belt, so that they hung on the left-hand side and could be drawn across the body. Scabbards were normally made of wood covered with leather and with metal fittings. There is no doubt that the sword was the high-status weapon of the era. In both Scandinavian sources and English heroic poetry swords are often named, and some found with burials in Scandinavia, Finland, and Slavic regions had been ritually bent or "killed" to accompany their dead owners. Spearheads could be decorated with bronze or silver inlay, and some shafts found in Denmark were also decorated. However, decoration of swords, especially the pommels, was more common. Some blades had inscriptions on them, the best known being the "Ulfberht" blades (the name of the maker) of the tenth century, long thought to have been of Frankish manufacture.[4] Only 171 have been found: they were very high-status weapons, and are found throughout the areas the Vikings visited. However, while some were of incredibly high quality (high carbon content, so-called "crucible steel") and made of steel that originated in Iran and Afghanistan, others were much poorer and more brittle, imitations made from locally worked iron in Europe. Unfortunately, it was impossible to tell the difference until they were used in combat.[5]

Aside from knives, which were probably carried by most men for various uses, including combat if all other weapons were lost, the other main hand-arm was the axe. Many of those unearthed resemble modern axes used as tools, which is probably what these specimens were. They include a number found in female graves in Scandinavia. It is certain that the axe was a favored weapon of the Scandinavians, and from them it was adopted by various peoples, especially the Irish. Unlike the "tool-axe," which could serve as a weapon if need be, many Viking axes were clearly designed for combat. Some of them are light slender specimens with spurs on either side of the head, but the broad-bladed battle-axes, also with spurs, are the best known. They became more common in the late Viking Era. In the form with long shafts and wielded two-handed, these were adopted in England after Cnut became king, and remained in use among the king's housecarls and others until the Norman Conquest. Similar axes were still used in Europe after the Viking Era. Two rarer forms of axe head found in Scandinavia—those with very long spurs and a variety with a "helm" at the back—probably originated in the southern and eastern Baltic regions respectively.[6] The axe also appears to have been used by the Slavs and Balts.

Missile weapons

Bows were used by most peoples, but not, it seems, in Ireland until its introduction by the Vikings. They were employed *en masse* from horseback by the Khazars, Hungarians, Pechenegs, and other steppe peoples, and on foot by European armies in the eleventh century. Before this, there are only very rare mentions of them employed in this fashion by armies in northern and central Europe. With the exception of several depictions of bows in Frankish manuscripts, all the evidence suggests that central and northern European troops used so-called "flatbows" or "self-bows," basically a stave made of one type of wood, which could vary in length and pull according to the strength and ability of the user.[7] Few have survived, as wood perishes in most environments, but eighth-century Alemannic bows were found at Oberflacht and Viking bows at Hedeby, Nydam, and Thorsbjerg. The bows of both finds were comparable to the later longbow: for instance, the first one found at Hedeby was 192 centimeters long and made of yew.[8] Two Carolingian texts also recommend this as the material for wooden bows.[9] However, this does not necessarily mean they were drawn in the same way as they were in the fourteenth century, as far back as possible. Good yew bows were made with the back of the bow of sapwood and the belly (facing the archer) of heartwood, as the most suitable to be stretched and compressed when the bow was bent.

Arrowheads in Scandinavia had an iron tang, unlike most of those from continental Europe, which were socketed. The most common military type was lanceolate, usually with a square or triangular cross-section, like the so-called "bodkin." Leaf-shaped and barbed arrowheads are more likely to be for hunting, although they would have been highly effective against unarmored men and more difficult to extract. Narrower arrowheads were more aerodynamic and had better chain-mail penetration. Fletching improves accuracy, but adds weight and air resistance. Similarly, arrows begin to lose velocity as soon as they are fired, so a strike from one at point-blank range is more damaging than one at longer range, but conversely the chance of missing a target is higher, as the danger to the archer from the approaching enemy is greater and a minor error in aiming can cause the arrow to land short of the target or fly overhead. In general and in good conditions, accuracy might be possible at 50 to 60 meters, but accuracy was not so important when aiming at a mass target. Maximum effective range may have been anything from 100 to 150 meters, depending on the bow and other factors.

The arrow shafts from Nydam were between 74 and 94 centimeters long, turned to taper from the middle. Later medieval sources claim ash was the best wood, but poplar was also used, while some found at Chessel Down on the Isle of Wight (fifth/sixth century) were of hazelwood. Quivers were made of wood, such as the one found at Nydam, and probably of leather. All archers need to wear a leather bracer on the left wrist to protect it from the bowstring during release.

There is little evidence that the Anglo-Saxons used bows to any great extent. Nevertheless, in the *Maldon* poem both sides employ them. Finds have been rare in England, even in the pre-Christian period, possible arrowheads appearing in about 1 percent of graves. Some of these finds may be javelin heads. The appearance of only one English archer in the Bayeux Tapestry is hardly evidence on its own of limited use of the bow, but reinforces the impression given by other evidence. Use of the bow appears to have been more common on the continent. Some Carolingian capitularies mention bows as required equipment for noble cavalry. Although it has sometimes been assumed that they must have been carried by the nobles' retainers, there is no reason why the elite cavalry themselves should not have used them. Charlemagne and his sons in the eighth and ninth centuries, and William the Conqueror and his sons in the eleventh, are known to have been proficient archers. Although they and their predecessors in Francia may have used bows primarily for hunting, they may also have been used by heavily armed horsemen in skirmishes, possibly even in battle. The "Golden Psalter" of St. Gall shows one armored Frankish horseman firing a bow. Bows portrayed in manuscripts and the main panel of the Bayeux Tapestry are somewhat shorter than the finds of longbows, although those in the tapestry margins appear to have longer bows. In his *Strategikon* Emperor Maurice made the point that bows should be suited to the strength of each man and not above it, a principle that would have made sense for all archers, whether on foot or horseback.[10]

The bow used by the Hungarians, Pechenegs, and Byzantines was a very different weapon from the self-bow. The Huns had first made the short but powerful composite bow a feared weapon in central Europe and the stirrup had since given more stability to the rider. Those who made composite bows were highly skilled craftsmen. The bow was made from horn, wood, and sinew laminated together. The horn is glued to a wooden core on its belly, and the sinew is glued to the back of the core. When the bow is drawn, the sinew is stretched on the outside and the horn on the inside, which stores more energy for the length of the bow than an all-wood "self-bow." However, although it was superior weapon in ideal conditions, the composite bow took many years to make, perhaps as long as a decade. Also, not only did moisture adversely affect the glue used during manufacture, but it could even cause the bow to become unglued afterwards. This was obviously a problem in the maritime climate of central and western Europe, which was damper than the steppes of southeastern Europe and inner Asia, and presumably one reason why the Magyars made such efforts to protect them. They carried their bows in special cases of soft leather. As in the case of other bows, the effective range was considerably less than the maximum range, and certainly less than the ranges achieved by firing flight arrows in competitions. The same factors applied to the flight of arrows from composite bows as from self-bows. In his study of Islamic archery, W.F. Paterson assessed that constant accuracy with a composite bow was possible at 60 meters or less for a foot archer, and considerably less for a horse archer.[11]

Whether the composite bow was used in western and northern Europe is controversial. At Birka mounts normally associated with closed quivers of eastern type were found, along with arrow types used with eastern composite bows.[12] Birka was at the western end of the trading routes through Rus, so it is likely that this equipment came from there, and perhaps its owners too. In Carolingian manuscript illustrations some of the bows used by mounted troops also appear to be composite, but there is no way of knowing whether this is artistic licence or an accurate representation. Carolingian troops must have come across them in Italy and when campaigning against the Avars, but whether they or any of their successors used them, especially given the problems of more northerly and westerly climates, is another matter.

The crossbow was probably introduced into western Europe at the end of the ninth century, although it is portrayed as a hunting weapon on four Pictish stones from early medieval Scotland (sixth to ninth centuries).[13] The earliest record of its use is at the siege of Senlis in 947, in Richer's *Historia*.[14] Thereafter it makes occasional appearances in written records and pictures, such as Haimo's *Book of Ezekiel* (tenth century) and the gospel book of Otto

III dating to 998–1001, where it is used by both sides in a siege of Jerusalem, as usual represented as a contemporary event.[15] The *Carmen de Hastingae Proelio* ("Song of the Battle of Hastings") and William of Poitiers mention them as being used at Hastings, although they do not appear in the Bayeux Tapestry.[16] Until the twelfth century the prods of crossbows were self-bows, made out of one piece of wood. Although more powerful than ordinary bows, they were not as effective as the later crossbows. All in all, it is likely that use of crossbows was limited before the twelfth century.

Light spears or javelins were probably common to all armies, although rarely mentioned or clearly depicted. The smaller spearpoints found in archaeological excavations may belong to throwing weapons, while some "arrowheads" may in fact be javelin-heads. Slings may have been used in warfare, but there is no good evidence for this. In his edition of Vegetius's *Epitome*, Rabanus added material about use of slings, but this was derived from the Old Testament account of David and Goliath.[17] They are mentioned in sources, but not as used in warfare. Similarly, on the Bayeux Tapestry the only slinger, depicted in the margin, is hunting birds. However, they appear in an illustration representing a siege of Jerusalem in the above-mentioned gospel book of Otto III, which otherwise clearly portrays contemporary medieval weapons and equipment.[18] The staff sling was certainly used in some regions, at least in sieges. With this weapon, a sling attached to the end of a long straight stave used as a lever when throwing, it was possible to hurl the slingshot a greater distance and at a higher trajectory. Its maximum range may have been some 150 meters, with more accuracy achieved at 50 meters or less.[19] It appears in two eleventh-century (or possibly tenth-century) illustrations of sieges from Spain, and was certainly used further north in the High Middle Ages.[20] It is probably this sling that Adalbert of Magdeburg refers to as used at the siege of a fort on the island of Garda in 961.[21]

Protective equipment

The most common piece of protective equipment was the shield. There is no evidence that the Magyars carried shields, but the vast majority of men in other European armies were equipped with them. The importance of this piece of equipment is underlined by the requirements of law-codes that men should carry one as a basic item. Carolingian and Ottonian kings demanded that monasteries and fiscal units maintain shield makers for their household troops. The trade of shield maker must have been profitable, the more so in times of war. The *Annals of St. Bertin* records shield sellers as among the following of Charles the Bald's army before the Battle of Andernach. For them, a battle must have represented an exceptional opportunity, as many shields must have been broken or lost in a short space of time. For most of the period shields were round. European shields consisted of a wooden board with an iron boss in the center and a rim of metal or hardened leather. With its boss a round shield could be used offensively, although this was clearly not the shield's primary purpose. Michael Spiegel argues that the main purpose of the boss was to enable a formation described in the Byzantine emperor Maurice's *Strategikon* (seventh-century), in which the second rank rested their lower shield rims on the bosses of those of the front rank to create a two-tier shield barrier against missiles as they advanced, but this is highly improbable, even if it could be used for this. The alternative use that he dismisses is for parrying blows, but it is probable that this too was a secondary use, as the main purpose must have been to cover the hand grip.

Various woods were used for the board, despite the English poetic tradition of referring to them as made of lime. Behind the boss there was a hole in the center, spanned by a handgrip, usually of iron but sometimes of wood. Many shields may also have been fitted with a leather strap so that they could be slung on the back, which is presumably what Nithard referred to when he talked of using them to protect the backs of the cavalry in feigned flight (below). The front of the shield, and sometimes the back as well, was covered with leather. The pattern of curved lines shown radiating from the center in artistic representations may well be stitching, although alternating colors in similar patterns are shown in pictorial sources. [22] Evidence for the painting of shields is not plentiful, but traces of red paint have been identified on some Danish shields and those with the Gokstad ship burial were black and yellow, a similar pattern, in fact, to the shields on the Bayeux Tapestry. Shields in an illustration in the tenth-century Frankish "Golden Psalter" of St. Gall also have a spiral segmented pattern in green, red or both colors (at least in their present condition). There are also references to colored shields in *Beowulf* and skaldic verse. The diameter of shield boards varied considerably in size, from 35 to 100 centimeters. Those of the Vikings appear to have been large, between 70 and 95 centimeters in diameter. It is probable that this was common among soldiers who fought in a phalanx, but small shields must have been common in Ireland, given the number of small bosses found there.[23] There was also variation in the flatness of the board. Convex shields would be more likely to deflect a blow, but were probably a little more difficult to manufacture. Literary references to shield damage may in some cases be exaggerated, but there is no doubt that the board could be pierced by thrown or thrusted spears or split by repeated axe or sword blows. Whenever possible, the bearer of the shield probably endeavored to use the boss to parry.

In the late tenth century the "kite"-shaped shield appeared. In the Viking Era it was normally a reverse teardrop shape, which tapered to a distinct or rounded point at its foot. It was possibly a development of the round shield designed to guard one flank of a rider when in combat, perhaps inspired by Byzantine teardrop shields. It became popular with foot soldiers as well in the eleventh century, probably because it provided protection for the foreleg in mêlée. The kite shield was made of the same materials as the round shield and was either flat in section or curved round its longitudinal axis. At this date most kite shields had a boss, but this was probably decorative as the shield was not gripped by a central handle. Manuscripts show them as strapped in a variety of ways designed to distribute the weight along the arm.

It is much more difficult to assess how common armor was. Armor and helmets are frequently referred to in written sources, but much of this material is either "heroic" and/or poetic, or influenced by classical writings, and naturally concentrates on the elite warriors. There are also extant law-codes, but when they required men to be armored, as Carolingian legislation does, they were stating an ideal. It is probable that the most common piece of metallic armor was the helmet. Few examples of helmets have been found intact and these show considerable diversity, possibly because they were often specially commissioned items that belonged to the elite. The type known as the *spangenhelm*, which consisted of a bowl made from several parts joined by bands that reinforced it and covered the joints, still existed in the Viking period, but if we can judge by the limited number of finds, the design that was widespread in the fifth, sixth, and seventh centuries, on which the bands widened to join together above the band round the base of the helmet, seems to have become rarer, while the number of joined pieces no longer exceeded four. However, a spangenhelm very similar to sixth-century examples is portrayed in the Corbie Psalter from *c.* 800, indicating that it was still in use amongst the Franks in the Carolingian era. A ninth-century spangenhelm of that type, thought to be Frisian, was also found at Groningen, but this also had spikes on the bands, as did an earlier (supposedly) Merovingian helmet. The well-known tenth-century Viking helmet found at Gjermundbu in Norway, with spectacle-like rings protecting the eyes, was of similar design, although the back to front ridge makes the finished product resemble the ridge helmet.

Another common helmet type in northern Europe was the "ridge helmet," derived from late Roman designs. The bowl of the helmet was made of two pieces held together by a clasp that formed a ridge running from back to front. This type was still in use in the Viking Era. One example is the late eighth-century Coppergate helmet from York, but similar types are depicted on the slightly older Franks Casket. Carolingian Frankish manuscripts depict a differently shaped helmet, but apparently of similar construction. It is most clearly portrayed in the Golden Psalter: the cap tapers to a projecting neckguard and it has a rim which encircles the helmet, rising to a point to meet the ridge at the forehead.[24] In the Stuttgart Psalter the helmets are similar, but with a less pronounced taper. Since the design was not a copy of a classical form, in all probability these helmets were common in Carolingian armies.[25] Another two-piece helmet of the ninth or tenth century, but with a flat band riveted to the ridge and of more conical form, was found at Gnezdovo in the Ukraine. Many of the above types, although not the Carolingian helmets, had cheek-guards and some had aventails. The Coppergate helmet had both. The Anglo-Saxon examples mentioned above had nasal bars, but, if we can judge by illustrations, these seem to have gone out of fashion until the mid-tenth century, when they reappeared.

In the late ninth or tenth century helmets beaten from one piece of metal appeared. The examples we have all come from east-central Europe: the "Wenceslas helmet" from Prague, and another Czech helmet from Olmutz, and one from Ostró w Lednicki in Poland. A similar helmet was found at Nemia in Russia, although it belonged to the eleventh century. In one example from Orchowskie Lake, Poland, the nasal and bowl were beaten from one piece, but it is not certain whether this belonged to the eleventh or a later century. No examples of single-piece helmets are known from western Europe, but one appears on one folio of the (Frankish) Bern *Psychomachia*, which dates from the late ninth or early tenth century.

Several other helmets have been discovered in Russia and Ukraine, three of the so-called "Chernigov type," similar to a late tenth-century example found there. These have four pieces joined in similar fashion to the span-genhelm, with wide bands of metal riveted to the plates, but with a separate band round the rim and a plume holder or "spike" on the top. None of these had nasals, but a second helmet from Gnezdovo had one as part of the band round the rim. A tenth- or eleventh-century helmet from Pecs, Hungary, is of similar form but different construction, of plates directly riveted together, the raised and scalloped edges at the joins decorated with copper. It closely resembles the Gorzuchy helmet from Poland, although this is more conical in form, while another more conical helmet from Pecs is of similar construc-tion but with a vertical band riveted to the front, which extended below the rim to form a nasal. Any or all of these may have had aventails, similar to that found with the helmet from Kazazovo in the Kuban. This was ninth century and almost certainly Khazar. If some of the Magyar or Pecheneg nobles wore helmets, they were probably of this type or similar to the Pecs or early Russian examples. In general, Russian and east European helmets display a mixture of western or Viking and Asiatic styles.

The helmets depicted in several Carolingian manuscripts were prob-ably quite common, but it is difficult to tell how typical individual finds were. Especially those with decoration and inscriptions, like most of the Russian-Ukrainian examples above and the Coppergate helmet, must have been valuable items. In this era it seems that the helmet was the piece of armor most likely to display individuality for many nobles, just as the sword was among weapons. This may be an accident of the finds and pic-torial sources, but this aspect of helmet design appears to have diminished in the late tenth and eleventh centuries, at least in western and north-ern Europe. However, even in that period, as in the later Middle Ages, helmets may have been painted and the bands on nobles' helmets were probably of a metal color distinct from steel, such as brass. Many helmets throughout the period were probably simple caps. The helmets worn in the ninth- or tenth-century St. Gall *Book of Maccabees* look much simpler than others in Carolingian manuscripts, although this may simply be the artist's representation of them. Indeed, thick leather may have been used to make helmets, although none has survived from the period. Leather hardened by scalding would also have been a suitable material for the plates inside the iron-banded frame, and can also be riveted. The Anglo-Saxon "Benty Grange" helmet from Derbyshire, although from an earlier period (late sixth or early seventh century) had horn plates on either side.

It is also possible that basketwork helms covered in hide or leather were used but, again, if they were, none has survived from our period. There are also possible helmets of Phrygian form depicted in certain Anglo-Saxon manuscripts, such as one showing an early eleventh-century battle scene. They could be caps, but they appear quite stiff in what appears to be a fairly realistic depiction of combat.[26] On the other hand, as helmets their design would represent a drastic departure from contemporary styles, and, despite their special shape, they are depicted as worn by otherwise unarmored men.

The helmet that became increasingly common in the west and Scandinavia during the tenth century and apparently even more so in the eleventh was also of a similar construction to the spangenhelm, four plates joined by bands and with a rim, usually with a nasal, the type familiar from the Bayeux Tapestry, or a single piece metal cap reinforced by bands. An Ottonian illustration showing armored horsemen attacking unarmored horse archers appears to show one helmet with one of the "Carolingian" features, the rising rim at the forehead, but with vertical bands and another round the rim. Since the other helmets appear to be "standard" domed types, this may be an unintended difference. These helmets have a small ball at the top, whereas others in tenth-century illustrations appear to have a point, of similar shape to some Byzantine helmets. The influence of Byzantine styles on Ottonian art is undeniable, but there is no way of knowing whether the actual helmet style was independently developed or copied, or whether only the illustration style was copied. In general, helmets everywhere became less domed and more conical as the Viking Era progressed, usually taking the form depicted in the Bayeux Tapestry by the eleventh century.

Mail coifs were also worn from the ninth century onwards, to cover the top and back of the head, the cheeks, chin, neck, and perhaps part of the shoulders. Coifs are mentioned but have never been found, so we can only guess as to their original shape. By the beginning of the tenth century these had become quite common among professional warriors, and by the eleventh century the coif was often integrated with the hauberk, becoming a hood. The "ventail" section of mail on the chest that folds up over the neck and chin, and hooked into position over the lower face, is the best explanation for the squares represented on horseman's armor on the Bayeux Tapestry. Padded arming caps would be probably be worn under the coif, and may even have served for protection on their own.

Body armor was certainly used in the Viking Era, but it is very difficult to know how common it was. It was expensive, so it is unlikely that levy troops or the majority of Vikings could afford it, although individuals may have captured it on occasions.[27] It appears in numerous illustrations, but although a case can be made for many of these being reliable representations of contemporary equipment, they tend to give soldiers a uniform appearance. One illustration of the Golden Psalter shows a band of horsemen who have no body armor except for two: the draco-bearer and another who may be an officer. All other illustrations of horsemen portray them with body armor, while all have helmets. However, the one Golden Psalter illustration of soldiers on foot also shows them in armor, although they may represent elite troops on foot, as they look identical to the cavalry. The Utrecht Psalter shows almost all troops without armor or helmets, which also appears to be a convention of the artist(s). Body armor was usually referred to as *brunia* or *lorica* in Latin. Given that the former term, a Germanic loan, appears in law texts and the latter in narrative sources that consciously imitated classical works, it seems unlikely that these terms denote different types of armor.

Charlemagne's capitularies regularly made references to armor. Royal vassals with twelve or more mansi (see Chapter 3) were required to possess a brunia, and any man who owned such armor but failed to bring it on campaign would be deprived of both his armor and his benefice. Carolingian lists of equipment do not demand that common infantry or cavalry possess body armor, although churches and monasteries apparently owned stocks of armor from which to equip their household troops (*milites*). Various written sources suggest that some Bretons wore armor,[28] and that the Vikings acquired it from Franks despite the repeated attempts of Frankish rulers to prevent its sale to them.[29] From the late Anglo-Saxon period many wills survive in which *heriot* (from OE *heregeat*, "war-gear") bequeathed to the king was recorded. When a noble died, he was obliged to leave a specified set of military equipment to the king, which often included swords, shields, spears, helmets, and horses.

As in the case of helmets, some material worn as armor may not have survived. It is probable that both chain-mail and metal scale armor were used throughout the Viking Era. The Utrecht Psalter, the Milan diptych, and illuminated Bibles from Tours all portray soldiers wearing a classical cuirass and pteruges. These look suspiciously like imitations of classical armor, but the weapons and helmets appear to be contemporary, so certain troops may have been armored in this fashion, perhaps as a deliberate copy of Roman custom. The general assumption of historians and art historians is that the less suspect Carolingian illustrations portray scale armor. However, it is not clear that the illustrations of the St. Gall *Golden Psalter* and the Stuttgart Psalter do not attempt to portray mail, which the St. Gall *Book of Maccabees* certainly does. Rabanus Maur mentions mail twice, once in imitation of Isidore of Seville and once in his own words. Of the three sources just mentioned, the first two show scale or mail armor extended below the waist, while the third does not. Both types are also shown in Byzantine illustrations, and there seems no reason why both forms should not have been used by eighth-, ninth-, and tenth-century troops further west, given that many troops supplied their own armor. When troops belonged to noble or ecclesiastical households each household may have had batches of armor made, but there is no reason why there need have been consistency between batches. Other troops probably had their own armor made or acquired it through individual purchase or looting from battlefield casualties. By the eleventh century the knee-length hauberk appears to have been common, usually of chain-mail, if we can judge from illustrations.

In the eleventh century the hauberk that reached to the knees and split at front and back below the waist appears to have become more prevalent, at least in central and western Europe. As usual, this cannot be certain, as we have only a limited number of illustrations. As is well known, the Bayeux Tapestry appears to show a hauberk with chain-mail trousers. Virtually everyone accepts that this is a way of representing the hauberk described above. Such armor would have been impractical for riders. In the "tapestry" it appears that the whole suit was in one piece, so it would have to be split at the back and fastened by an assistant when put on. Nicholas Brooks suggested that this armor did in fact exist among English warriors, and that the English women who made the tapestry simply portrayed the armor of both Norman and English soldiers with armor they were familiar with. His argument was that English warriors always fought on foot, so they could have used this form of armor, but they may have fought mounted on occasions and even if they did not it is likely that they sometimes rode to battle in their armor.[30]

No armor for legs or hands or arms below the elbows was listed in capitularies, but we know that some warriors used them. They appear as *bagnbergas* ("leg guards") in the seventh-century *Lex Ribuaria* (Law of the Ripuarian Franks), which was still in use with additions in the Carolingian period and formed part of the Lex Saxonum of 803. They also appear in Count Eberhard of Friuli's will and Notker's unreliable collection of anecdotes about Charlemagne.[31] Since they have a high price in the law-code, Notker is probably right that they were made of iron. The Stuttgart Psalter depicts tight scale leggings, and greaves may be shown on an ivory tablet from Florence. A form of limb protection that appears to have been in use in the contemporary Byzantine army was splint armor, consisting of thin bands of metal or possibly wood linked by straps to make a tube round the lower leg or forearm. It was used by some troops in western and northern Europe in the sixth and seventh centuries, so it is possible that it was still in use in the early Viking Era. Both Eccard and Eberhard also mention gauntlets or arm-guards, although, with the possible exception of armguards on an ivory in Leipzig, none is depicted.[32] A capitulary of 803 forbade the sale of armguards, referred to as *bauga*. Given that leg and armguards are not mentioned in lists of required equipment, it is probable that they were rarely used and available only to the wealthiest, such as Eberhard.

Horses

From the time when horses were first domesticated they were valuable to humans, and their value became considerably higher once the two-wheeled light chariot was devised and they began to play a significant part in warfare. Selective breeding for whatever use they were intended must have started very early, but we now know that the warhorses of the early Middle Ages were not very big by modern standards. The horses of the late ninth-century Gellone Sacramentary, the St. Gall *Book of Maccabees* and the tenth-century depictions of cavalry listed above do not appear large, and those of the Bayeux Tapestry not much larger, but with a soldier mounted on them they were sufficiently big to dominate infantry. Size was not the only criterion, however. A warhorse had to be strong enough to carry an armed man at some pace, steady enough not to panic when faced with the noise of battle or a line of armed enemies, and brave enough to endure wounds. Whether the eighth century was really the period when large numbers of horsemen were first used in central and western Europe, as was once claimed by several historians such as Heinrich Brunner, is difficult to prove, but the number of benefices granted to warriors so that they had sufficient resources to equip themselves with a horse and other war gear certainly seems to have increased in the early Carolingian period.

Production of warhorses was a major industry in medieval Europe. The indigenous horse of northwestern Europe was useless for heavy cavalry. The warhorse of the Middle Ages derived from two sources, the "Bactrian" horses of Central Asia, which first enabled the Assyrians and their neighbors (and later the Chinese) to employ worthwhile cavalry, and North Africa, horses which may or may not have originated in Asia. The largest of the Bactrian horses from the Altai Mountain region were 15 hands high. Good quality horses of both large and small types were in Mediterranean Europe a century before the time of Philip II and Alexander of Macedon, and the Romans developed a sophisticated horse breeding industry. As R.H.C. Davis made clear in his book on the medieval warhorse, breeding requires great care, selection of the right foals, segregation of mares from all but select stallions, and so on. Periods when political and social disorder was sufficiently bad to make the proper management of herds and the operation of stud farms impossible can not only halt the improvement of a breed, but possibly lead to its contamination and disappearance.[33] This may be what occurred after the disintegration of the Western Roman Empire in the fifth century, although it is possible that the Merovingian Franks and the Visigoths in Spain inherited some good stock.

The vital ingredients to the breeding stock of western Europe were the so-called Arabian horse, which was not Arab in origin but was carefully bred and nurtured by the Arabs, and the North African "Barb." Although the largely Berber armies that overran the Visigothic kingdom in the early eighth century seem to have been composed mainly of infantry, the Islamic conquest introduced a small number of Arab horses and breeding methods to Spain. Alongside them came a large number of North African horses ("Barbs"), which were probably also of good quality, as those of the Libyans and Numidians used by the Greeks and Romans had been earlier. Possibly these were interbred with good Spanish horses surviving from Roman times. We first hear of a Spanish horse ("Iberus") outside Spain in the life of St. Corbinian, written in the 760s.[34] Some of these Spanish horses were acquired by the Carolingians.

It is known that Charlemagne had a strong interest in horse-breeding. The *Capitulare de Villis* from the end of the eighth century and the *Brevium Exempla* of *c.* 801 laid down regulations about the segregation of mares and care of the stallions on the royal estates ("vills").[35] Both sources indicate that the Franks were practising good breeding methods by that time, and had a small number of high-quality stallions for the purpose. As well as learning from their own experience, the Franks must have derived their practices from the Moors in Spain and Byzantines in Italy, and also from surviving Roman works like that of the first-century agronomist Columella and the fourth-century Palladius.[36] The royal estates were not specialized stud farms like those of today, but a large part of their resources was used for provisioning the army. Alongside arms and female slaves, stallions were specified as items that should not be sold outside the kingdom in the Capitulary of Mantua (781). Almost a hundred years later Charles the Bald threatened any who sold arms and horses to the Vikings with death in his Edict of Pitres (864). By the end of the ninth century it seems that Frankish horses had a high reputation; when Paul the Deacon wrote that the Lombards had earlier been envious of their herds of mares, he may have been thinking of the herds of his own time. Ermold the Black claimed that the Carolingian horses were so big that it was difficult to mount them. Although he was clearly exaggerating, from his early ninth-century perspective they must have seemed big.

As an example of what might happen to a stock of good warhorses, a disease wiped out a huge number of them during Charlemagne's campaign against the Avars in 791.[37] Fortunately the main breeding area was far away in northeastern France, but the replenishment of the stock was a major undertaking that must have lasted three years. Once they were old enough, the colts bred for the purpose went to the households where they were trained as warhorses, when some would prove unsuitable and be relegated to other tasks. This may have been one of the main reasons why the final reckoning in the Avar War was delayed for several years. From the evidence of this Carroll Gillmor estimated the effectiveness of Carolingian horse-breeding and the numbers of horses involved.

Horses from the steppes or eastern Europe were also used in East Francia, as capitularies mention that they imposed tolls on them at Rafelstetten on the Danube in 903–906. Although Henry I of Germany (918–936) built up a force of heavy cavalry to counter the Magyars, not much has been written about the horses or where they originated from. Davis suggests that he captured some from the Magyars, in which case they would have been quite small, but they may still have been acquired from Slav merchants through Bohemia or bred from earlier Frankish or imported horses. There were Carolingian estates that bred horses in Bavaria and Alsace, which became part of the Duchy of Swabia in 870, as well as in West Francia. As well as training and increasing the number of horsemen in the nine-year truce Henry agreed with the Magyars before 933, the Germans were breeding horses, as he is credited with the institution of studs. At the end of the eleventh century William of Apulia claimed that the Germans preferred to fight on foot as they were not such expert horsemen as the Normans, referring to the Battle of Civitate in 1053, when the Normans defeated a papal army.[38] Assuming that he was right, this does not tell us whether the men or horses were less well trained or the horses were less well bred. Certainly knighthood developed later in Germany than in France, but this may be a consequence of a variety of social factors as well as the lack of use of horses in battle. Moreover, the seven hundred Swabians recorded as present at Civitate need not have been typical of German armies.

We do not know where the opponents of Pope Leo IX at Civitate, the Normans, sourced their horses. The Normans of Italy also acquired Barb and Arab horses from southern Italy, and may have acquired them from Sicily even before their conquests there, either by purchase or captured from the Saracens. In addition, good Byzantine horses may have contributed to the breeding stock. Whatever their sources, the Normans must have the known the value of good horses and good breeding when they first went there as mercenaries in the early eleventh century. In West Francia–France many horse-breeding centers were inherited directly from the Carolingians, and a surprising number survived in Normandy, despite the Viking origin of its ruling dynasty. The success of the Norman dukes also attracted warriors from other parts of France to their service. Valuable horses appear in transactions involving both lay nobles and monasteries from the reign of Robert (1027–1035) onwards. Some horses were also acquired from Spain as gifts or trophies from the activities of Norman adventurers there.

If the Franks generally had the best warhorses of northwestern Europe, or at least most of them, it is quite clear that good quality horses were bred elsewhere, not least in Anglo-Saxon England. The possible use of horses in battle is dealt with in Chapter 5, but the question of whether they were regarded as war-gear is slightly different, as they would still have been so if English warriors had ridden to battle and dismounted to fight in the battle-line, possibly mounting again to pursue a beaten foe. Both sculptural evidence and decorated equestrian equipment found in earlier graves show that the horse was an important part of Anglo-Saxon culture and a symbol of status, one of the items that distinguished a warrior from a *ceorl*. Figures apparently fighting from horseback are shown in many Viking-Era sculptures and armed men on horseback appear in manuscript illustrations as well. As stated most clearly by Guy Halsall, the question of the use of horses in warfare in the post-Roman to Viking Era period has been heavily influenced by modern distinctions between cavalry and infantry that belong to the era of specialization that began in the sixteenth century, in which soldiers who fought both mounted and on foot were themselves specialized troops, known as dragoons.

Ann Hyland, herself a horse-breeder, argued that "the English would have been totally blinkered" had they ignored Frankish military practices. R.H.C. Davis before her and Sarah Keefer after her both pointed out that there is plenty of evidence for stud farms and good breeding practices in pre-Conquest England. Like Charles the Bald, Æthelstan forbade the selling of horses "across the sea" in his Grately Law-code, which also demanded the provision of mounted men "from every plough."[39] Cnut attempted to ensure the supply of (good quality) horses from his nobility by codifying legal heriots, and it is in his reign that we first hear of the "staller" as an officer of the court. This may have been in part an honorary title by this time, but it still indicates that in origin, as one who looked after the king's horses, the task had considerable importance and status—the staller was no stable hand, let alone a mucker-out. The English had good horses and they knew how to ride, as Harold and his retinue must have done when they accompanied William on his campaign in Brittany.

The sculptures of late Anglo-Saxon Northumbria also have implications for the Viking use of horses. From Scandinavia itself the evidence is mainly archaeological. There are a number of finds of horses in individual Iron Age and Viking Era Scandinavian graves, just as there are from pre-700 Anglo-Saxon England, and a quantity of horse trappings in the sacrificial deposit of Illerup Ådal (Denmark), thought to represent the equipment of an army defeated in *c*. 450. Horses were buried with the deceased in many graves from the Iron Age and Viking Era all over Scandinavia.[40] It has been suggested that they, like the boats of the boat burials, functioned as a means of transportation to the otherworld. Sometimes horses were buried together with boats and occasionally without, as in the early ninth-century Arninge grave at Täby, Sweden, which contained seven horses, although some of them were not the finest of specimens.[41] In pagan Scandinavia it seems that the horse had a cultic importance, perhaps a special role in sacrifice, as well as a material and economic importance. Undoubtedly it played a part in warfare, but whether it was used in battle, as Johan Engström suggested in a speculative article about the Vendel Period in Sweden, is another matter.[42] It is reasonable to assume that specific types of horses were ridden by men of stature, the same who were buried with them or with boats.

In Denmark, with the exception of Hedeby and some graves on Bornholm, all the graves that contained weapons and other items, including horses, are from the tenth century.[43] Horses are common, as are powerful bits and stirrups of Hungarian style that suggest use in warfare. It has been suggested that horsemen became more important in warfare as a result of Frankish and more especially German influence in the Ottonian period, although Henry the Fowler's invasion of Denmark and even his reforms in Germany occurred after the custom of "horseman burial" started in Denmark. Klaus Randsborg is right, however, to link their distribution with the Jelling province and the Trelleborg-style forts, at least insofar as they mark the emergence of the kingdom of Sweyn Forkbeard and Cnut.

Near the start of our period, the 804 entry in the *RFA* refers to King Godfred's Danish army as cavalry, although this may simply mean that many of the men had mounts.[44] Three hundred years later, in his account of a disastrous Danish campaign in Wagria (now eastern Holstein) in *c.* 1113, Saxo suggests that the "Danes had still not adopted the use of mounted troops outside their own land," which seems to imply that they used them in Denmark but not abroad.[45] Even then, he may not be referring to the use of mounts in battle. The reason for this is very likely that virtually all Danish campaigns abroad involved the transport of forces by sea and that they did not use horse transports. In the Wagrian campaign the army was supposed to be joined by a contingent with mounted troops led by the jarl of Schleswig, who was to march by land but failed to turn up. Having said all this, it is also clear that Saxo had very little knowledge of Denmark before 1100, so his statement is probably "received tradition."[46]

In Viking Era Sweden artifacts associated with horses were found in twenty-one cremation graves and twenty-four chamber-graves at Birka, and horses in twenty of the latter. Spurs and stirrups were found in nine of the horse graves and all the chamber graves contained weapons as well. By comparison, the horses of the Viking Age graves at Tuna, Vendel and Vals-gärde were of varied ages and stirrups and spurs appeared less frequently, indicating that the horses were not all ridden by warriors and the graves were not primarily warrior graves.[47] Possibly, as Olof Sundqvust suggests, the graves of Birka were those of the king's *hirð*. A further indication that the deceased belonged to a military organization is the uniform structure of the chamber graves. Suggestions that those buried at Birka were of for-eign (eastern) origin because of the eastern-style clothes and other items found there seem less plausible than that the men adopted eastern styles, as Svealand had strong connections with the eastern Baltic and Rus.[48]

The difficulty of relating horse burials to possible horse use in warfare in Viking Age Scandinavia applies equally to many other regions of Europe in the same period, where the horse clearly had a cultic function and was sacrificed with the dead in northeastern Rus, the region where Slavic, Scan-dinavian and Finnic-speaking groups met, and the whole of the area where Baltic languages were spoken (Prussia and present-day Latvia and Lithu-ania). Although horse burials are rarer in the other areas settled by Slav-ic-speaking tribes, the horse was at the center of many cultic practices, as at Arkona on Rü gen, Pomerania, a center of the Rani.[49] The evidence suggests that smallish horses were used in warfare in all these regions in the early Middle Ages, but the lack of written sources gives little clue to breeding methods or sources of the horse stock. In some ways the horse equipment resembled that of the steppe people, Avars, Khazars, and Magyars, and in some ways western European traditions. For instance, spurs, not used by the steppe cavalry, are found in burials, but only rarely.

It is not clear from ninth- and tenth-century illustrations whether the horses used by warriors of Latin Christendom were mares, geldings, or stal-lions, but the Bayeux Tapestry clearly shows the Norman cavalry mounted on stallions. By the time of Hastings, and probably considerably earlier, western European soldiers used only stallions in battle, and preferably else-where. In battle the warhorse was expected to rear and kick at opponents, in other words, to fight, and the perception was that stallions had a courage and bearing that geldings and mares did not. In a sense this was a reflec-tion of human society, and it was a prejudice that lasted for the rest of the Middle Ages.

Apart from the impact of importing and breeding warhorses, the other controversial aspect of mounted warfare is the impact of new riding equipment. Many stirrups have been found in the region occupied by the Avars, chiefly modern Hungary, and it was probably they who introduced them into central Europe and Byzantium in the late sixth or early seventh century. Maurice refers to the stirrup in his *Strategikon*, but not by a special name, which suggests that it was something new in his time.[50] However, many of the stirrups found in various parts of Europe are not of Avar type. There is no clear pattern as to how and when stirrups came into use in different parts of Europe. Some Carolingian manuscripts of the ninth century still appear to depict riders without them, yet they are found in Vendel grave III in Svealand, Sweden, dated to the eighth century and of a different style to the Avar ones. It has been argued that the stirrup made mounted shock combat possible, but to my mind this has been convincingly refuted.[51] It enabled the mounted warrior to stay in the saddle more easily and to stand in the stirrups to give downward blows to the side with greater force, but the development of the saddle with high back and front panels was more important for the use of the couched lance, a change in the method and culture of combat that did not occur for several centuries after the stirrup was introduced. Earlier western saddles sometimes had a high front pommel with decorated plaques, but otherwise those in illustrations appear to be low. Both saddles and harness were often highly decorated.

Riding horses were not the only animals to play an important role in war, as horses unsuitable to be ridden by warriors, alongside mules, donkeys, and oxen, played a vital role as pack or draught animals, providing support to armies in the field. The numbers required were enormous, a question dealt with in the next chapter.

Ships

It is no secret that Scandinavians were great seafarers in the Viking Era. Boats had always been of vital importance in Scandinavia. Waterways offered better communication routes than inland paths over mountains or through forest and marshland, and the vast majority of settlements had access to the sea via fjords, straits, and river and lake systems. There were cultural reasons for engaging in raiding and warfare, which probably took place at least as early as the Bronze Age. However, the vessels of that era were essentially war canoes, like the Hjortspring boat of Pre-Roman Iron Age Denmark, apparently buried as an offering after its crew were defeated. Such vessels were made from sewn planks, a method still used for construction long after this date. One example is the Tuna boat from Sweden, in which a woman was buried in the eighth century. Boats similar to this were still built in northern Russia up to the 1950s: they were rowed, but they were not suitable as troop carriers or warships. These vessels were designed primarily for use in coastal waters and inland waterways.

Viking ships were very different, built shell-first on the backbone of stem, keel, and stern. Planks were fastened with clench-nails hammered through their overlapping plank edges, a technique known as "lap-strake." During the construction the gaps between the overlaid planks were caulked with a suitable material such as loosely spun yarns of wool, making them watertight. The method probably came into use in the early centuries AD in northern Germany and Scandinavia, replacing sewn planks, and produced strong and flexible hulls. Frames of naturally curved timber and thwarts were inserted afterwards, lashed to cleats cut out of the planks. The thwarts also served as seats. At the same time as this building method developed oars replaced paddles as the means of propulsion. In early ships of this type the oars were mounted on rowlocks on the gunwales, which meant that the height of the ship was restricted by the rowing height. A side rudder mounted starboard aft was used for steering. Although the method of hull construction was the great leap forward, further improvements appear in the various ship finds of the Roman and pre-Viking eras. Lashing of frames was replaced by three-nailed fastenings in the Sutton Hoo and Gredstedbro (Denmark) finds, while the slightly later Avaldsnes ship from Norway has a solid plank above the curved frame with oarholes instead of rowlocks. Coins and pictures depict shields arrayed along the gunwales of the ships. It is likely that this was done only for display and perhaps for additional protection from missiles in battle, but certainly not on the open sea. Some form of rack must have held them in place, which was probably not very robust, and on some of the surviving ships shields would have obstructed the oarholes. It is difficult to envisage their use in battle in this case, as ships had to row into position because the masts were taken down to prevent the sail from falling on the deck.

The final leap was probably the introduction of the single square-rigged sail. This type of sail allowed sailing close to the wind. With the additional capability to row during adverse wind conditions, ships could run in to shore easily and escape easily. The earliest evidence for the use of sails in Scandinavia may be the Gotland picture stones of the eighth century. However, in

2010 a site where a 17-meter long and 3-meter wide ship had been covered (rather than buried) was unearthed at Salme on Saaremaa (Estonia), where a smaller 10-meter rowing vessel had been found two years earlier. Thirty-five men were buried in it, with high-status weapons, shields, four dogs, hunting birds, and assorted other items. The manufactured items were of Scandinavian type. The ship is dated to *c.* 750, the end of the Vendel Period (or the very beginning of the Viking Era). Its keel and keelson indicate that it was a sailing ship.[52] By *c.* 800 ships with sails are also found depicted on runestones, coins, and graffiti. Until the Salme discovery, the oldest certain find was the Norwegian Oseberg ship of *c.* 820. However, sails may have been used earlier, perhaps south of Scandinavia, as they must have been known from Roman ships, and they were certainly used in the Mediterranean. Like the hull, the sail was an expensive item, as it was made of homespun wool.

The raw materials for shipbuilding, wood, iron, and wool, were all produced in Scandinavia. Nevertheless, shipbuilding required a huge investment of time, while long voyages meant that men were not producing anything at home and had to be supplied by others for their journeys. Long-distance expeditions had to hold a good promise of profit to be worthwhile. Experimental archaeologists have estimated that forty thousand working hours may have been needed to produce all the components of a 30-meter longship, consuming the surplus production of one hundred persons for a year.[53] There has been a very long debate about why Scandinavians set out on long-distance voyages of trade and plunder. Undoubtedly there were many factors involved, such as increasing awareness of trading networks, perhaps brought about by the appearance of trading emporia such as Dorestad, and possibly pressures at home caused by the attempts of certain chieftains to extend their authority, but it was the technology of the Viking ship that enabled Scandinavians to make the voyages. Whether they began to use sails because they felt the need to travel further afield, or traveled further because they began to use sails is a chicken-and-egg question. We can be certain that the raiding culture existed long before the end of the eighth century, and we know that Scandinavians were active around the Baltic in the Vendel Period, and even earlier in Francia, as Gregory of Tours's account of the Clochilaich raid makes clear. Precisely how the Vikings navigated is still uncertain. A variety of aids has been suggested, but none is named in any sources.

The three best known Viking ships, found at Oseberg, Gokstad, and Tune, the last two from *c.* 900, all represent ships of the elite. Since they were used in funerals, we cannot know how typical they were, even of chieftains' ships. Whether the Oseberg ship would have been suitable as a long-distance sailing vessel or warship is debatable, as it is less robust than the other two. There are no thwarts for the rowers to sit on, although they may have used chests or benches. The bottom of the ship is also more v-shaped than the later vessels. The keelson that holds the mast above deck level spans only two frames and the fish at the base spans four beams. This had split and had been repaired at some stage, indicating that the ship had been used. The Gokstad ship is 23.2 meters long, 1.7 meters longer than Oseberg, has a similar beam (5.2 meters) and a higher gunwale (2 meters above the keel). It has thirty-two oars as opposed to thirty. The keelson spans four frames and the mast fish six. The Tune ship is smaller, 19 meters long and 4.2 meters wide, and of similar construction. A ship of similar date was buried at Ladby, and this has been reconstructed from the soil impression. It was not much shorter than the Gokstad ship at 21.5 meters, but had a narrower beam (2.9 meters), and a height amidships of only 1 meter. It was thus similar to the Nydam/Sutton Hoo rowing vessels. As such it was probably used in the Baltic and coastal waterways rather than to cross the North Sea.

From the tenth century we have many more examples of ships, not only those used in funerals. The Hedeby ship was a fine vessel, but was obviously reaching the end of its days when it was used as a fireship in an attack on Hedeby, some twenty-five years after it was constructed in c. 985. It was 30.9 meters long, 2.6 meters in beam, and 1.5 meters high amidships, with sixty oars. The wood came from the western Baltic and the dimensions, similar to those of the Ladby ship, suggest its use in those waters. By contrast, the ship known as Skuldelev 2 was over 29 meters long. Although it was eventually filled with stones and sunk as part of a barrier in Roskilde Fjord in northern Zealand, presumably restricting access to Roskilde itself, it was built in the Dublin area in 1042. It has a larger beam of 3.8 meters, reflecting its use in the Irish and North Seas. Skuldelev 5 was also a warship, built between 1030 and 1050, probably in the region where it ended up. It is interesting for several reasons, not least its lighter construction and the number of times it had been repaired before being sunk in c. 1080. It was 17.5 meters long and 2.5 meters in beam, and probably had twenty-six oars. This type of ship may well be representative of the majority of warships in the Viking Era.

In Roskilde itself a partially scrapped vessel, Roskilde 6, was probably 36 meters long with a beam of 3.5 meters and a height of some 1.7 meters. It had been joined together from three parts with two 2-meter-long scarfs. It has been dendrochronologically dated to the second quarter of the eleventh century. Is the method of construction evidence that eleventh-century shipwrights were struggling to make bigger and bigger ships? If so, it casts further doubt on the dubious claims made by saga writers that some Viking ships of this era were enormous: for instance, *Heimskringla* claims that Olaf Tryggvason's *Long Serpent*, built in Trondheim Fjord in 998, was 42 meters long and that Cnut had a ship of 120 oars. Rike Malmros suggests that these claims were made because the sagas were written in an era when ships had indeed become bigger. Particularly during the Baglar Wars (1195–1217), there was a "naval race" in Norway. As she says, the authors probably thought that the heroic kings of the Viking past ought to have had similar-sized ships to the kings of their own recent history.[54] In general, skaldic verse and the Icelandic sagas use the term *skeið* to refer to the ships we call "longships," a term that was used in the Middle Ages but rarely in skaldic verse. The sagas describe the *Long Serpent* as a dragon ship, where the qualities of the sea-going sailing ships are combined with the warship's need for oars and rowers.

Although there were variations in size and structure according to where the ship was intended for use, certain functions were common to all of them. Their primary purpose was as troop transports, although there was no strict ship specialization such as that of the modern era and they could be lashed together side by side to form fighting platforms. They were built to allow easy beach landings, their shallow draft allowed movement in waters less than 2 meters deep and the light weight of the smaller ones allowed them to be carried over portages from one waterway to another. Even the larger seagoing ships could be moved over short portages with rollers. Since the longship had a symmetrical bow and stern, it could be reversed easily. Average speed appears to have ranged from 5 to 10 knots, although theoretical speeds of up to 15 knots or even more may have been attained in ideal conditions.

The Scandinavians were not alone in building longships. Several ships built using the same construction methods have been found in the Slavic areas of the southern Baltic, for instance at Szczecin, Ralswiek (Mecklenburg), and Puck (at the western end of the Bay of Gdansk). Almost all are trading vessels, but one of the finds, Puck 2, is a very well-preserved longship, whose construction was dated by dendrochronology to the early tenth century. Its original length was 19–20 meters and its width 2.2 meters. Unlike the Viking ships, it was assembled with treenails (wooden pegs), not iron nails. In known examples of Slavic ships moss was used for caulking and a mast rib supports the heel of the mast rather than a keelson, but Puck 2 was an exception in having a "Scandinavian" keelson. No generalization can be made about the sizes of Slavic longships on the basis of this one find, but their range of activity was largely restricted to the Baltic and they had to be capable of operating in the shallow and marshy inlets of Pomerania and Mecklenburg. It is clear from Saxo's account of the twelfth-century wars between the Danes and Wends that some of the Danish ships were bigger than any of the Wendish ones, while a large Norwegian ship given as a gift to the Danish king Valdemar I proved useless in one of his attacks, as it grounded on the bed of a river.

Clinker-built boats of similar construction to the Viking longships have been found in various regions besides Scandinavia, Saaremaa, and the southern Baltic coast, such as the tenth-century boats used for burials at Port an Eilean Mhòir, Ardnamurchan, on the west coast of Scotland, and Scar in Orkney, both Viking burials, and the Lapuri find in Finland. None is a warship, but they indicate that longships were probably also built in these regions, just as Skuldelev 2 was built in Ireland.[55] Later in the Middle Ages the people of the West Highlands and Islands of Scotland had their own fleets of birlinns, smaller warships (troop-carriers) derived largely from the Norse tradition.[56] In passing, the *ASC* refers to Frisian ships, but little is known of them although they were probably similar to Scandinavian ones. The ships of the Bayeux Tapestry appear no different from Norse ones, but this is hardly surprising when Normandy was ruled by a dynasty of Norse origin. More controversy has surrounded the type of ship employed by the English as a response to Viking attacks.

It is well known that Alfred decided to build ships, although the number of them built in his reign was probably small. It is perhaps noteworthy that Æthelweard did not even refer to the new ships of 896 in his *Chronicon*, as the *ASC* does. Unfortunately no examples of warships from the Viking Era have been found in England. The *ASC* indicates that the ships built by Alfred were "built neither on the Frisian nor on the Danish pattern," and that they were almost twice as long as contemporary Viking longships.

Edwin and Joyce Gifford suggested that the pattern drew on southeastern English traditions of shipbuilding such as that of Sutton Hoo, which might also be represented in the smaller Graveney ship of the tenth century.[57] On the other hand, there is no certainty that Alfred's ships were not a short-term experiment, or that they were ever replicated after what appears to have been a mid tenth-century decline in the fleet. Given that Cnut and his sons employed Scandinavian crews (*lithsmen*) and ships in their fleet, the ships of the "English" fleet revived after the Danish period in the eleventh century were probably of Viking type, similar to those portrayed in the Bayeux Tapestry.

The Chronicon of the tenth-century ealdorman Æthelweard contains a number of terms for different ships.[58] His Latin is problematical, as his ability to construct sentences correctly was somewhat limited, although he attempted to use very elaborate vocabulary. Nevertheless, he had first-hand experience of military matters in the Anglo-Saxon kingdom. He tried to find appropriate Latin terms for the different types of ship, such as *lembus* for an Irish-style sailing (sewn) ship, and used the term *dromon*, derived from the term for Byzantine warships, to refer to a longship. It seems that he used the term "keels" (*carinae*) to refer to those drawn up on the shore, in this case differentiating ships by their situation rather than by their shape or purpose. Æthelweard's chronicle reveals an awareness of different ship types and functions in the tenth century, perhaps reflecting an English knowledge of seafaring and capabilities that increased as a consequence of a century of contact with the Vikings.

In some cases the heriot wills of late Anglo-Saxon England include ships. In one of these Bishop Ælfwold of Crediton willed a sixty-four oar *scegð* to the king. This tells us that the *scegð* could be a large ship, not necessarily a small one as suggested by Hollister. The name was of Scandinavian origin, and probably meant simply "longship," therefore referring to shape rather than size. The confusion arises from the 1008 entry in the *ASC*, discussed in the next chapter. From the rates of pay given to the Scandinavian *lithsmen* just before Edward paid them off in 1050, it can be calculated that there was an average of eighty men per ship, but this does not mean that ships were of uniform size or design.

As well as being troop-carriers, ships could also be status symbols. Whereas ships like Skuldelev 5 were probably representative of the majority, the Gokstad ship and perhaps Skuldelev 2 were vessels that belonged to people of high status. Even those of lower status may well have been painted or otherwise decorated in some way, just as many of the shields of the ordinary soldiers were. However, the ships of the chieftains and nobles, and especially of kings, were clearly decorated to show their wealth and power. The *Encomium Emmae Reginae* ("[Tract] In Praise of Queen Emma") gives the most dramatic description of Cnut's ships: "So great also was the ornamentation of the ships that the eyes of the beholders were dazzled, and to those looking from afar they seemed more of flame than of wood."[59] The *Encomium's* account is clearly rhetorical, among other things claiming that Cnut's warriors were "all of such speed that the swiftness of riding would be contemptible to them." Nevertheless, ships were ornamented. Several of high value are mentioned as given as gifts, for instance by Earl Godwine to King Edward the Confessor.[60] According to William of Malmesbury, the Norwegian king Harald Fairhair had earlier given one to King Æthelstan.[61]

Dragon heads probably adorned the prows (and sometimes the sterns) of ships, and gave them the name "dragon (ship)" (ON *dreki*). The well-known carving of Norwegian ship prows from Bergen, which dates from the thirteenth century, shows both dragon heads and weather vanes on the prows of ships in the center of the fleet, almost certainly representing the leaders' ships.[62] The dragon may have had protective and cultic functions in the pagan era, although the Icelandic law collection *Grágás* prohibited ships from entering harbors with these heads on the prows for fear that they would disturb the land spirits (*landvættir*), a law that reflected the unpredictable nature of Iceland, which we now know is a consequence of geothermal activity.[63] The Norse sagas also claim that the wind vanes of gilded bronze that were placed in the prows were symbols of power. A dragon head was found with the Oseberg burial. Although it is unlikely that many ships had as intricately carved sterns or bows as the Oseberg ship, it is probable that any ship of status had some form of decoration to the stem and stern posts.

Chapter 3
Military Organization and Training

Learning to command

How did a military commander of the Viking Era learn his trade? There is a general lack of discussion on strategy and tactics in the annals and chronicles, and the only military manuals or histories to learn from were Roman, unless the student was able to read Greek. Logistics, construction of camps, training of men, leadership in the field and deployment, and perhaps construction of siege equipment were all among the skills required of a military commander. Did generals of the Viking Era simply learn by trial and error, if they survived long enough? The answer to this must be no, as they had the opportunity to learn from those who had previously fought and led men on campaigns and there were instructive texts available.

Full-scale battles with several hundred men or more on each side were relatively infrequent, albeit more frequent than they were in the High Middle Ages, which makes it likely that commanders and even armies sometimes went into battle with no experience of mass combat. But even in this case, we must assume that there was some oral tradition of "battle wisdom." Even in the Christian realms of the ninth, tenth, and eleventh centuries society was still very much governed by oral tradition and ritual. Because it provides our main source of evidence for historical events, written material may appear more important than it actually was in the society of the day. Most everyday problems were handled within the local community using customary methods, and ritual was an important tool to ensure that custom was maintained. We should not be surprised if warfare was conducted to some extent in a ritualized manner as well. Until they came under the influence of the Christian realms they raided or settled, Viking kingdoms and communities were governed almost wholly by oral custom. Viking, Slav, and Magyar armies caused severe problems to their enemies, while the reduction of Slavic fortresses often presented major difficulties—none of these peoples had a written culture until the end of the period.

Having emphasized the role of oral tradition and ritual in the British Isles and the Frankish and German realms, it is also the case that the influence of written culture on military education has frequently been underestimated, especially in the areas that were ruled or formerly ruled by the Carolingians. The so-called "Carolingian Renaissance," encouraged by Charlemagne himself, led to an enormous increase in the number of scriptoria and copying of Latin works, and this expansion of learning continued in Ottonian and Salian Germany and Capetian France. Many Frankish and German monasteries specialized in the copying of certain authors. Between the ages of 7 and 14 most noble children learned the seven liberal arts. The teachers were invariably clergy, who taught geography, astronomy (though not as we would know them), numeracy, chronology, and reading. Following his basic schooling and the preparatory work of the trivium (grammar, logic and rhetoric), a noble might learn the quadrivium: arithmetic, geometry, music, and astronomy. The extent to which writing was taught is uncertain, but it was probably taught to most noblemen, at least to the extent that they were able to read simple Latin texts.[1] If young noblemen learned anything of military matters, we know little of their instruction. However, this general education was often followed by more training in specific fields relevant to the chosen path of the young nobleman. As will be seen, if he served in a secular capacity in the household of the king or a powerful landowner, he was likely to learn something of military matters. For this, a considerable range of Latin-language works was available. Almost all detailed texts of this nature known to have been available in several copies in the former Carolingian realms were classical or of classical derivation, although they were sometimes edited to bring them up to date. This contrasts with the situation in the half of the empire that had survived, known to us as Byzantium, where new military works were created alongside edited editions of old ones. These included the Strategikon, attributed to Emperor Maurice (r. 582–602), the Taktika of Emperor Leo VI (r. 886–912), the mid-tenth century Sylloge tacticorum, the Praecepta militaria of Emperor Nikephoros Phokas (r. 963–969), and the Taktika of Nikephoros Ouranos (*c.* 950–1011), as well as several shorter treatises.[2]

In Francia by far the most copied of the available Roman works was the *Epitoma rei militaris* by the fifth-century bureaucrat Vegetius. By the ninth century copies of this could be found in several monasteries, but it is uncertain how widely read it was. While it certainly cannot be assumed that every literate commander read Vegetius (and most among the Frank-ish elite were literate), it is also unlikely that it was not read, or was only read by monks, given the number of copies in circulation. In most cases, of course, it is impossible to know. It should be borne in mind that the copies possessed by rulers are likely to have been available to their courts, where many trained as future military commanders, not only to the rulers them-selves. Even if the *Epitoma* was read by only a few lay nobles, it is not a long text and much of it could have been passed on by word of mouth. Never-theless, how far Viking-Era commanders (or, for that matter, late imperial Roman commanders) actually attempted to follow the precepts of Vegetius, even if they knew them, is a matter for conjecture. Vegetius's work was not the only one available, as the *Strategemata* ("Stratagems") of the first-cen-tury Roman administrator and general Frontinus was also copied in the late ninth century

Although the most important underlying purpose of the histories and annals written during the Viking Era may have been to reveal the works of God, these writings were not totally devoid of material useful to the military commander. Description (and sometimes condemnation) of failures, such as dissension among commanders or neglect of scouting that led to disaster, was as relevant as tactical discussion. In order to do the work of God, lead-ership in all its forms had to be effective. Not only the works of medieval or classical authors made frequent passing mentions of leadership and train-ing, but so did the Bible itself. Other works also had a direct relevance to warfare, even if that had not been the main or only purpose in writing them. These included logistical and technical information. An example is Alcuin's *Propositiones ad acuendos juvenes* ("Propositions to sharpen the young"). Several concern difficulties in procuring food supplies, with detailed discus-sion of costs and seasonal markets, while others handle the capacity of var-ious containers used for transporting foodstuffs and drink and the weights of loaded wagons. Of direct value were the *prepositiones* that concerned the use of animals to transport supplies and how much the beasts themselves might consume, and how to get loaded wagons or carts across rivers.

Nor was Alcuin's the only work that dealt with logistical and technical matters which was available in Francia: among the practical manuals were those known as the *agrimensores*, which dealt with ancient theorems, field measurement, architectural methods, and so on. Among them was the *De munitionibus castrorum* ("On the Fortifications of Military Camps"), a

Roman work which probably dates to the third century AD.[3] Vitruvius's *De architectura* also included advanced mathematics for building, not to mention information and illustrations about the construction of siege engines. To this must be added the Mappae Clavicula, a compilation of recipes and processes of assorted nature, which included incendiaries and a battering ram.[4] Such technical knowledge had military applications, even if the work in question applied it to something else.

In the Anglo-Saxon realms education was also the responsibility of the Church, with schools linked to monasteries or located in the homes of bishops or priests. However, the ninth-century Viking invasions had a severe impact on the level of learning. King Alfred may have overstated matters when he lamented the dreadful state of it in the preface to his translation of Pope Gregory the Great's *Pastoral Care*, but there is no reason to doubt that it had declined. Following Charlemagne's example (perhaps consciously), he made a determined effort to revive learning, recruiting scholars from Mercia, Wales, and Francia to assist. Alfred set out to provide schooling in English for "all the free-born young men now in England who have the means to apply themselves to it."[5] He founded new monasteries, established a court school for his own children, the sons of his nobles, and intellectually promising boys of lesser birth, and either commissioned or completed himself a series of translations of Latin works into English. Although none of these was of direct military use, and basic schooling was in the vernacular, at the very least Alfred's use of ecclesiastical personnel in his administration and the generally higher level of literacy eventually achieved must have given many nobles the ability to acquire relevant knowledge. Alfred saw his educational reforms as equally essential to the defense of his realm as his military reforms.[6]

The preface to Alfred's English translation of Gregory the Great's *Pastoral Care* explains that kings who fail to obey their divine duty to promote learning can expect earthly punishments to befall their people.[7] Like the Frankish and German kings, Alfred represented the war against non-Christian invaders as a holy war, and like them he also believed that God had entrusted him with the spiritual as well as physical welfare of his people. From this point of view, all the works read during a noble's schooling contributed to success in war.

The Vikings must have had their own methods of measurement and assessing logistical requirements, just as they had effective navigation techniques, although we know little of them. We know that they were capable of laying out camps and assessing distances, but not exactly how they did it. Landmarks and time taken to move from one place to another on foot or horseback can be committed to memory, and this is much more easily done in a society unaccustomed to recording in writing. The inability of "barbarians" to capture walled cities by means other than treachery and starvation has often been noted, and this appears to have applied to the Vikings and the pagan Slavs and Magyars as much as any others. This is not surprising, as lack of technical skills is a corollary of the lack of a written culture and hence mathematical or scientific knowledge. Nevertheless, we might expect the Vikings and others to learn from their enemies, and on occasion they almost certainly employed (or forced) Frankish and English people to assist them.

Medieval military command differed from that of the modern era in several respects, but perhaps the most important was that the commander did not have to be a warrior or a soldier. The social elite was the military elite. For this reason, on occasion clerics and women could command, although we must assume that they had advice. Since churchmen were from the same aristocratic background as "fighting men," they must have known something of war, while some had been warriors before entering the church. Women are less likely to have had the same education as men, but those who had authority probably learned a lot from their menfolk. No female is known to have commanded Norsemen or Irishmen, although literature suggested that they could take the role of men if their menfolk failed to fulfill their duty to uphold the family honor. However, three women are mentioned as commanding armies in this period: Æthelflæd "Lady of the Mercians," Richilde of Hainault, and Matilda of Tuscany, but none of them is mentioned as engaging in combat. Women were accepted in the role of men because there were no adult male heirs to their lands and they were without a spouse, or, as in the case of Richilde, if they were widows of landowners. Æthelflæd fulfilled her role as heir to Mercia by expelling the Vikings, while Matilda successfully defended the Papacy and her own lands against the invasions of Emperor Henry IV. Æthelflæd took the position of a female character that sometimes appears in both Norse and Old English literature, who is able to adopt the role of a male ruler by repelling suitors. Similarly, in the *Primary Chronicle* Princess Olga of Kiev is said to have refused all offers of marriage after the death of her husband Prince

Igor at the hands of the Drevlians, beginning her rule by exacting a savage revenge for Igor's death. It is difficult to disentangle myth from history in the *Primary Chronicle* account of her rule, but there is probably a basis of truth in it.[8]

Training for combat

With a few exceptions, our sources are largely silent on how men who were expected to fight trained for action. However, there need be no doubt that those subject to the call-up to fight were trained. They were no less "soldiers" than modern military conscripts. Where "warrior" is used in this book it is not intended to imply that early medieval troops were more akin to the tribal warriors of New Guinea than they were to us, but to refer to people who went to war or had an ethos that required warlike behavior, something explored further in Chapter 7.[9] On the battlefield most infantry fought in a deep close-order line of several ranks, often referred to by the poetic name "shield-wall" in modern works, although, in deference to medieval authors who wrote in Latin, David Bachrach uses the term phalanx. Whether Viking-Age authors understood what the classical Greeks had in mind when they used this term ("roller") or not, this is an appropriate description of what seems to have been the most common battlefield infantry formation of the Franks, Germans, Anglo-Saxons, Vikings, and many Slavic tribes or early kingdoms as well.

Rabanus edited Vegetius's section on the training of men to use swords and retitled it "How they are exercised with wicker shields and clubs." The "clubs" were wooden swords. Vegetius had described how men were trained by using their swords against posts of man height, striking at the "head," the "side," the "knee" and the "lower leg," stepping back, lungeing forward and thrusting upwards, all the time covering their own bodies with their shields. In both the original and the revised text, training with double-weight weapons was recommended as a valuable method of making actual-weight weapons easier to handle when the time came. Evidence that these or very similar methods were actually used comes from Ekkehard of St. Gall, who described the training methods used by Abbot Engilbert for his military household. In this case they wore felt armor and the wicker shields had a heavy core of wooden boards, which is probably what Rabanus meant by "wicker shields"—in other words, they also were heavier than a combat shield would be. The emphasis placed on thrusting with the sword suggests that combat in close ranks was envisaged. However, Rabanus also mentioned that slashing was less effective against chain-mail, and was more likely to expose the soldier's side to attacks by opponents. Although it is not mentioned, similar training must have been provided for using spears.

We can be certain that very few, if any, Vikings, Picts, and Slavs ever read Vegetius. It is also unlikely that Anglo-Saxons or Irishmen were acquainted with the *Epitoma*, and improbable that the majority of literate Franks or Germans read it. Nevertheless, we can envisage that very similar methods to those used above were employed in training their warriors. There may have been less emphasis among the Irish and early Slavic tribes on fighting in dense formations, although this can only be conjecture. It is fairly certain that the Anglo-Saxons and Picts used such formations before the Viking Era, and the Vikings seem to have used them too. The battlefield formations used are discussed further in Chapter 5: suffice it to say here that some practice is needed to maintain close formation, particularly when moving forwards. As Vegetius suggested, mock battles were presumably fought, in which men became accustomed to forming under their standards and moving in lines and ranks.

An indication of the type of training given to mounted troops was given by Nithard, who had military experience himself. The exercises he describes were carried out in 842. Equal numbers of Gascons, Bretons, Austrasians (East Franks), and Saxons were organized into groups at opposite ends of a large field and charged each other at speed, wheeling round and feigning flight after slinging their shields on their backs to provide protection.[10] The instructions given by Henry I before the Battle of Riade in 933 and described by Liudprand of Cremona also give a good hint as to what was expected. He commanded his men to form an ordered line as they advanced against the Magyars, covering themselves with their shields in an effort to catch the first shower of arrows, before closing rapidly to prevent the enemy from reloading and getting off a second shot.[11] Liudprand says this is what occurred, referring to a painting he had seen at Merseburg, although the Hungarians fled the field before the German cavalry contacted them. He was at the court of Otto I, Henry's son, and it is unlikely that tactics had changed significantly. As in the case of infantry armed for close combat, heavy cavalry had to maintain line in a fairly dense formation.

Rabanus Maurus clearly regarded Vegetius's advice on training individuals to be horsemen as relevant to his own day. Vegetius describes the use of wooden horses, which men used to learn how to jump on and off their horses by stages, progressing from doing this unarmed to fully armed, then with drawn swords. Rabanus commented that this exercise "has flourished greatly among the Franks." Jumping on and off a horse may have been practiced in Rabanus's day, but it would have been much harder when the front of the saddle was raised to become a pommel and the back to a cantle. This appears to have occurred in the mid-eleventh century, as this type of saddle is first depicted in the Bayeux Tapestry. By that time it was more important that the horseman stayed firmly in his saddle than that he could quickly jump out of it.

The level of training for mounted combat available to any Viking (or even Anglo-Saxon) cannot be known, as there is simply not enough evidence. The horseman burials of the tenth century give a hint that the concept of mounted combat as practiced in Germany penetrated Denmark before the twelfth century, but it is very unlikely that it was practiced in any battle outside Scandinavia, if there. Our evidence from Scandinavia itself is so poor that we cannot establish whether there may have been any stud farms such as those in England.

It remains to be said that an important form of training for war was hunting. The same upper social groups that provided the trained soldiers in armies of the Viking Era regularly took part in it. For the elite, it gave good training in leadership skills. It also required mutual trust and cooperation between the members of the hunting party, whose members would frequently have been the same who fought together on campaign, as well as riding and weapon skills. Unlike the vast majority of hunting nowadays, ancient and medieval hunts involved considerable danger. The wielding and correct use of a spear while being charged by a wild boar required both courage and composure. A boar may have been responsible for the injury that the West Frankish king Carloman died from in 884, although there is some doubt as to whether it was one of his own men who accidentally wounded him.[12] Earlier, in 864, Louis the German had been seriously injured in a deer-hunting accident, but he survived.

The military household

Nineteenth-century investigation into how armies were raised in the early medieval kingdoms that emerged after the dissolution of the Roman Empire was based partly on preconceptions about early Germanic society and partly, whether consciously or unconsciously, on the demands of rising nationalism. According to these views, ancient Germanic society had been quite "democratic" and a form of universal military service was embodied in the Anglo-Saxon *fyrd* and the Frankish *landwehr.* These ideas survived well into the twentieth century, nor are they are entirely dead now. Historians like Sir Frank Stenton believed in the existence of the free *ceorl.* Warren Hollister realized that the core of the late Anglo-Saxon army was a select levy, termed by him the "select fyrd," but was unable to free himself of the old concepts, and thus devised the "great fyrd" as a representation of the nation in arms. His work of 1961 still has wide influence, particularly in nonacademic works on Anglo-Saxon armies and warfare. With far less evidence to get in their way, Scandinavian historians have been even freer to speculate about national levies, projecting the *leidang* of the High Medieval law-codes back into the Vendel and Viking periods. Some of them still believe that it was the basis of Viking military organization in the days of Sweyn and Cnut.

Arguably the most important single institution in the military strength of most of the rulers, chieftains, and magnates of the Viking Era was their personal following or household. The origin of the medieval military household is to be found in the war-band or *comitatus* (of which more in Chapter 7) of the Germanic chieftains and later kings. This personal following provided the rudimentary "administration" of the early petty kings of Germania and post-Roman England, and probably still of Scandinavia in the early Viking Era. The relationship between the leader and his following brought advantage to both. Besides a military force, the leader gained honor and prestige from having such a retinue, while the followers obtained the same advantages from association with him, and were rewarded with gifts from the tribute and plunder acquired. Even in the Migration Period (*c.* 400–550) the king's or chieftain's following probably included kinsmen and representatives (or hostages) of subject chieftains or sub-kings as well as adventurers. Once a ruler and his following established themselves in a specific region, it is also likely that some of them "owned" land which they farmed.[13] As realms expanded, followers received lands in exchange for service and acquired their own followings. Each noble had his own band, which would accompany him to the king when summoned to serve in a military enterprise. Some of the magnates of early medieval kingdoms were descended from successful associates of the kings, while others, if not themselves recently forced to submit, were descended from former rulers or chieftains who had been defeated and forced to submit, or were powerful ecclesiastical lords.[14]

The cohesion of the war-band or *comitatus* obviously depended on the success of its leader. Failure in war meant that neither honor nor wealth were to be gained by association with him. To some extent the same was still true in the kingdoms of England and Francia in the Viking Era, but by then possession of the kingship itself had begun to acquire a prestige that transcended mere military success, reinforced by sacral aspects. Although heredity seems to have played a part in pre-Christian rulership, descent from former rulers became increasingly important in selection of successors, even when they were, in theory, electable. The Slavic-speaking tribes had a similar rulership, although there is more evidence that a priestly caste continued to exist alongside chieftains who had primarily military functions, at least among the western Slavs, possibly even that the Wendish confederations became theocracies after the great revolt of 983.[15] Among the Scandinavians the kings and chieftains seem to have combined sacral and military functions even before the Viking Era.

Households enabled leaders to maintain contact with their greatest men and to forge bonds of loyalty and mutual dependence, or friendship in the medieval sense. The royal household was a permanent force that would form the core of any army mustered by the king and often its leadership, and enforce the king's will in all parts of his realm. There were strong similarities between all the kingdoms of Christian Europe and their military institutions, even between Frankish, German, or English kingdoms and the small Welsh and Irish kingdoms, frequently assumed to be "tribal" or "backward" in organization. Rulership remained essentially personal and rulers were designated rulers of peoples (*natio or gens*), not rulers of lands. Moreover, frontiers were more ill-defined than modern national borders. On a modern map, boundaries of known territorial regions where a single lord or family held sway (including both administrative regions such as the three hundred *pagi* into which Charlemagne's empire was divided, and regions inhabited by peoples who owed loyalty to a king) can be shown to have followed rivers, belts of forest, or mountain ranges. They can also be shown to have ancient origins, many being inherited from Roman administrative districts. However, it is improbable that medieval folk conceived of them as lines, or even as broad belts of territory, and certainly not on a map—for one thing, no maps that resembled modern ones in any way are known to have existed in the Viking Era. "Borders" were probably known places or landmarks recognized as being outside the jurisdiction of rulers on either side, the same places where those rulers tended to meet to discuss problems. Marchlands, on the other hand, were territories whose inhabitants were of disputed overlordship or under threat of invasion, perhaps conquest, by an alien *natio* or gens.

The military organization of the Carolingians and their French and German successors

Although the core of the East Frankish–German armies was provided by kings' military households and the trained warriors of their magnates, it was frequently necessary to raise a levy. Thietmar of Merseburg, writing in the early eleventh century, described the three basic elements of the military forces as the military households of both secular and ecclesiastical magnates, the select levies which could be used in expeditions beyond the frontiers of the realm, and a general levy used for defense. Thietmar himself and his father, uncles, and brother had served in the armies of the Ottonian kings and their successors. Other sources confirm his statement.

The Carolingian and Ottonian rulers built upon Merovingian and ultimately late Roman antecedents. Every able-bodied man was obliged to assist in local defense, an organization known as *Lantwehr*. This involved garrisoning forts and towns in time of war, but also labor services for the maintenance of these fortifications and other infrastructure essential for warfare, such as bridges. This obligation is described well in Charles the Bald's Edict of Pitres, issued in 864. Everyone who did not have the wealth to serve in the expeditionary levy was included, both free and unfree. Charles claimed this was done "according to ancient custom" (*antiqua consuetudo*). In East Francia exactly the same obligations were reiterated in a charter of King Arnulf to Count Heimo in 888. His dependents, both free and unfree, were granted immunity from the comital courts in return for their service. The Ottonians maintained this system, but transferred much of the obligation to mobilize the levies to abbots and bishops.[16] The latter were granted military immunity from the jurisdiction of local counts, but were obliged to exact the same services (*Burgbann*) from their dependents. Such levies could also serve in the field, but their equipment was often poor and their training for such an encounter was also probably very basic. An army of local levies, described by Regino of Prüm as an innumerable multitude, but lacking military training, not to mention armor and horses, took the field against a smaller army of Vikings in 882 and was slaughtered. Used in defense of fortifications and to block the routes of invading armies, they could be much more effective, and in this role probably played a major part in the destruction of the Magyar army after Lechfeld in 955.[17]

If the local levy was most effective in defending fortified sites, the more select troops were also occupied in capturing them. For any conquest to be effective, fortifications had to be captured, and their capture required considerable forces. It is in this context that the expeditionary levy most frequently appears in contemporary chronicles and annals. They are often designated as *exercitus* and by some general designation related to ethnicity or region, in contrast to the *milites*. Wealth, either of the individual or of an institution on whose land the individual resided, was the basis of qualification to serve in such an *exercitus*. The basis of the wealth measurement for most of the Viking Era was the *mansus*, which seems to have been a measure of income derived from property rather than the property itself by the early 800s.[18] In the late eighth century this service was required of everyone who had one *mansus* or equivalent income, but this was raised to three or four *mansi* early in the ninth century. The individual was supposed to appear equipped with a short sword and shield at the very least. Those with twelve mansi were supposed to have a coat of mail, helmet, shield, spear, long sword (*spatha*), and short sword, as well as a warhorse. Clearly there were those who did not fit either category, being poorer than the latter category and wealthier than the former. The Thuringian horsemen mentioned as present at Riade had no armor. Any individual or institution that possessed more than twelve *mansi* had to provide fighting men appropriate to his wealth—in other words, possession of thirty-six *mansi* entailed provision of three well-equipped men or nine with sword and shield, or a combination of the two.

There is evidence that this system remained in force in the ninth-century Carolingian realms that emerged from the empire of Charlemagne and Louis the Pious. It is likely that it was also used in Ottonian Germany, or at least, there is no evidence to the contrary. It is clear that men were still selected on the basis of wealth, as this is mentioned in surviving charters referring to tax obligations. In a charter of Otto III issued in 997, the recipient of a certain *mansus* was freed from the immunity held by the holder of this villa for judicial matters, but the man remained his senior, so Siggo probably still did military service as one of his armed men. Those ultimately responsible for mobilising the troops òf landowners were the counts in whose districts their property lay. Carolingian and Ottonian counts had to make lists of such property owners and keep them up to date. We know that many of them did this, as they were used in various court proceedings.

Obviously many property owners were not fit to serve in war, because of age, infirmity, gender, or religious vocation. They had to find a substitute to serve on their behalf or pay the *heribannum* fine. Others did not want to serve, and still other property owners had their separate military obligations that exempted them and their vassals from call-up by the magnates. An example was the bishopric of Halberstadt, which was given this privilege by Otto I. The bishops mobilized their men, and the counts did not have the right to do so. An increasing number of privileges of this type were issued to archbishops, bishops, and abbots (or abbesses) in tenth- and eleventh-century Germany. Carolingian legislation allowed groups of lesser property owners to pick one of their number, or even someone else, to serve on their behalf as a representative.

Many wealthier landowners chose to maintain men as a permanent military household rather than mobilizing men on an *ad hoc* basis as and when required. These *milites* were not necessarily aristocratic in origin: in fact some were unfree (*servi*) or semi-free throughout this period. Many were maintained directly by the magnate and ate and slept in his hall. Others were granted benefices by their lords. From the late Carolingian period onwards the military householders of lords received grants of land directly from the kings, partly in an effort to build up the strength of the households of loyal magnates, but often also as a reward for outstanding military service. This man was then able to recruit more soldiers from his property. The magnates also received direct grants so that they could increase the size of their households. In some cases the immediate purpose of the grant is clear: for instance, in 945 Otto I granted four *villae* to the brothers Folcmar and Richbert, in the vicinity of the fort of Zörbig, which was constructed on the site of a former Slav fortification.[19] They needed a force sufficient to garrison it and thus to strengthen the frontier defenses. Exchanges of property were also made to increase the size of magnates' properties in threatened areas. Otto I made a series of exchanges with Hermann Billung, who commanded the northern march facing the Slavic Obodrites and Redarii. Land was also borrowed from the Church (*precaria*) to establish benefices for household *milites*. Unsurprisingly, churchmen often saw this practice as an abuse.

Most important to the kings was their own military household. The fiscal property of the Carolingian kings and their Ottonian successors steadily expanded through conquest and confiscation of properties of rebels; they also acquired other property from the Church as described above, and they exacted tribute from polities beyond the frontiers of their kingdoms. By the eighth century the military following of the king, and also of the magnates, had expanded considerably. Nevertheless, despite this, and the undoubted influence of Roman institutions, the king maintained a contingent of *milites* that traveled with him, which Hincmar of Rheims referred to as expediti in the West Frankish kingdom—in other words, warriors prepared to travel with the king on his itinerary. From these was drawn a personal bodyguard. They were called antrustiones in the Merovingian period and Charlemagne's era, but there seems to have been no specific term for them in later periods. Widukind called the Ottonian kings' guard "faithful soldiers" (*fideles milites*) and in Henry II's reign Thietmar of Merseburg called them the royal household (*domestici regis*).

Among those who served in the household of Charlemagne and his royal descendants were young men being trained for future service, both those who would serve as officers of the household and others who returned to the households of magnates. This tradition was continued at the courts of both west and east Frankish and later German kings. They were educated in much the same way as young men destined for service in the Church, and some served in both capacities at court, such as Adalbero, nephew of Bishop Ulrich of Augsburg. However, his destiny was to command the bishop's troops. Magnates also "lent" troops to rulers for a given period, but continued to provide the necessary support for them.

All the troops referred to above constituted the king's immediate military household, who served close to the court, but a much larger number of *milites* served in garrisons scattered throughout the kingdom. Many of these held benefices, which enabled them to offer both payment and service for the fortification to which they were attached. The commander of the fortification was usually called its *praefectus*. By contrast, in the field commanders of units were commonly called *principes*, the overall commander of the force a *legatus*. Those who commanded sub-units of military households, both royal and magnate, were called officers, those who held an *officium*. In other sources they are called *principes militum*. Like the king, lay and ecclesiastical magnates employed many of their *milites* as garrison troops. Magnates held fortifications under licence from the king.

There remains the thorny question of the size of the field armies employed by Carolingian and Ottonian rulers. There is no question that the majority of forces raised by local magnates for raids and immediate defense would have ranged from the hundreds to low thousands, but the main disagreement has centered around the feasibility of fielding armies of tens of thousands. The largest armies were probably those raised in the later reign of Charlemagne. Karl Ferdinand Werner assessed the total number of cavalry that could be raised as thirty to thirty-five thousand. In her study of horse breeding in the Carolingian world Carroll Gillmor estimated that this number of warhorses could be maintained with the breeding programme in existence around the turn of the eighth and ninth centuries, even allowing for losses from disease and other wastage.[20] Obviously not all of these would be deployed in one army, and not everyone who was supposed to turn up did so when summoned. Willingness to turn up depended in part on the potential profitability of the upcoming campaign. The repeated campaigns against Saxon rebels probably became less and less profitable and it may have been difficult for Charlemagne to raise the armies he wished for in the 790s. On the other hand, he probably had considerably less difficulty in raising troops for the campaign against the Avars in 791, because of their fabled wealth. The argument against armies of tens of thousands is largely based on the (supposed) logistical impossibility of maintaining such armies in the field for several months. Horses were not the only requirement for the provisioning of an army, and more than one horse would probably be taken by most soldiers who might fight mounted. However, several routes were used to take armies over mountains and the armies of East Francia–Germany were clearly big enough to intimidate Slavic rulers into surrender on several occasions.

Anglo-Saxon England

As in Francia, the core of an army in Anglo-Saxon England was the king's military household, whose members served their lord in return for reward, by the seventh century increasingly given as landholdings. Nobles and royal officers had their own households, which could be summoned to the army. Young warriors served a form of apprenticeship in these households before they married and settled on their lands. In another parallel development with Francia, changes occurred in the methods of raising armies in England in the eighth and ninth centuries. At the time when the Viking "Great Army" appeared in England there may have been a problem with increasing amounts of land being donated to the Church, both by kings and by aristocratic families. In the late seventh century Bede had claimed that this was diminishing the amount of land providing warriors in Northumbria. It may be that ecclesiastical land was held by the family in perpetuity, rather than being dependent on good service to the king.[21] Alternatively, many earlier landholdings were also held in perpetuity, but the granting of them by charter, which made them "bookland," enabled a lord to bequeath it to a person or persons of his choice rather than being compelled to divide it amongst his inheritors.

Charters of late eighth-century Mercia and Kent make it clear that there were three common obligations to the king: fortress work, bridge work, and military service. Church lands were obliged to provide labor services such as repair of fortifications and bridges, even if they were exempt from military service.[22] Whether any were totally exempt is unclear. Kings like Offa of Mercia began to specify in their charters that Church lands were not exempt from military service, in order to maintain their military manpower. Offa used the obligations to create a network of forts and probably the Dyke on the frontier with Wales as well. By the ninth century these charter practices had spread to Wessex. It seems that it was around the end of the eighth and the beginning of the ninth centuries that kings began to specify the amount of military service required from a given amount of land: for instance, a Mercian charter of 801 says the owner of a thirty-hide estate should provide five men to the army, in other words one man per six hides, or more likely the owner and five men, one man per five hides. The five-hide unit is referred to in early eleventh-century tracts on social status as a designation of thegnhood. It also appears frequently in the listed military service requirements in the Domesday Book of 1086, but the variations it records in military obligation between shires tell us that this was not a universal standard throughout England. Notably, the five-hide shires largely correspond with those of Wessex and western Mercia. Given these variations, it seems unlikely that the obligations of Edward the Elder's time were identical to those of Edward the Confessor's, even if there was considerable continuity.

Many of the Wessex charters purporting to be ninth-century are forgeries. However, the reference made in many of these to two decimations of land by King Æthelwulf in 845 and 855 may have a basis in truth, as the *ASC* and Asser's *Life of Alfred* also refer to the 855 decimation. The object was to provide a tenth of his lands to the Church, but probably also to give lands to thegns, who were the mainstay of his army. He, Alfred and Edward the Elder almost certainly built upon the one man per five hide requirement when they reorganized the military defenses and forces of Wessex and Mercia. Both Asser and Hincmar of Reims say that Church lands were exempt from military service in Æthelwulf's kingdom.[23] It is likely that the increasing Viking threat brought about some of these changes in the Anglo-Saxon kingdoms. When they overran most of Northumbria, East Anglia, and a large part of Mercia, and almost defeated Wessex as well, the Vikings gave the impetus for even more far-reaching reforms by Alfred of Wessex. The basis was the construction of a series of burhs, so that no one lived more than a day's journey from one. Each had an administrative district that was to provide its garrison and maintain its defenses. The *Burghal Hidage*, a document which dates from the reign of Alfred's son Edward the Elder, indicates that each hide was responsible for defending and maintaining approximately 4 feet of wall. This appears to correspond well to the length of many of the known *burh* ramparts and their districts. In all likelihood the system, which Edward and his sister Æthelflæd extended into Mercia as they reconquered land from the Danes, was little changed from that instituted by Alfred after his victory at Edington (878).

Alfred also wished to have an army available at all times. According to the *ASC*: "The king had divided his army into two, so that there was always half at home and half out, except for those men who had to hold the *burhs*."[24] The entry is made under 894, but the reform, if it was more than a temporary arrangement, was presumably carried out before this and after Edington. It is more likely to mean a division of the army into three, rather than the two parts normally envisaged, in which case a man liable to service would spend a third of the year on his land, a third garrisoning the *burh* of his district and a third with the field army.[25] As Guy Halsall points out, apart from making a reasonable demand on the thegn's time, this would enable the assembly of the field army straight from the *burhs*, rather than from innumerable individual landholdings. This would save time and mean that the men of each district were already familiar with each other and had probably trained together in preparation for field service. The *ASC* entry of 917 mentions *burhs* as assembly points for armies. While garrisoning the burhs men could also carry out fortress and bridge work.[26] Both the *ASC* and Asser mention on several occasions that these men rode horses. This is additional evidence that these men were a select levy (*fyrd*). The levy of one man per hide of the *Burghal Hidage* must have been something else, perhaps called up in situations of imminent danger. Alternatively, they functioned as a "support force" for the real warriors, sequestered on the basis of the burghal system. Each man was supposed to provide twenty shillings for two months' maintenance in the event that he was called up: this was presumably the payment raised from the five hides for the support of the warrior (the 'man'), perhaps on the basis of one per hide. Æthelstan's Grately law-code states that "each man" should have two mounted men per plow (*sylh*). The latter would have been a heavy burden, even if the *sylh* referred to is equivalent to the Kentish *sulung* of the Domesday Book, which was two hides, rather than a single hide or even less. Again it may refer to the support for the "man" (warrior), who needed to be mobile to keep up with the army. Æthelstan needed to respond to threats further afield and more often than any of his Anglo-Saxon predecessors.

Even the warriors who remained "at home" might be called upon to fight if their lands were threatened. The Vikings were a mobile enemy who could strike at various points along the coast with little warning. In late 893 three ealdormen, Æthelred of Mercia, Æthelhelm of Wiltshire and Æthelnoth of Somerset, raised the garrisons and the "king's thegns who were at home near the *burhs*" to attack a Viking army encamped at Buttington by the River Severn. The problem is that the terminology used by those who wrote our records is rarely precise enough to tell us exactly who was being called up to fight—for instance, the *other folc* who joined the garrison of London to defend it in 895 need not be read as "common folk," but as men required to do service as soldiers who were not "on duty" at the time, or as commoners who aided in various capacities other than combat. London appears not to have been included in the Burghal Hidage, perhaps because it was on the boundary between former kingdoms. Despite the problems and uncertainties, we can be sure that it was the wealthier men who were expected to serve as warriors. Thus the military system required the service of a large proportion of the male population of England, but the fighting was (preferably) done by a minority. As in the case cited in Germany above, when "support troops" did encounter the enemy they were not up to the task. For instance, *ceorls* working on a fortification proved totally incapable of defending it against the Vikings in 893.[27]

Whatever the exact functioning of the system, what we do know of it does not suggest a mass peasant levy. There are no signs of exemption for harvesting periods and the like, which suggests that the levy was not primarily made up of those who labored on the farms. The need to cultivate the land cannot have been the primary reason for leaving some of the men subject to the levy at home for half the year, as this would still have seriously depleted the agricultural labor force when it was most needed. The idea was presumably that some thegns remained at home to keep order and ensure that normal farming activities could be maintained without internal disorder or external attack. At the same time the system ideally provided a fighting force that was sufficiently large as a field army, but not so large that it could not be provisioned for any length of time.

Alfred's (or Edward the Elder's) reforms represent an attempt to exact military service from a wide class of landowners. As in the case of the contemporary Franks, in the *burhs* and on campaign the troops are likely to have been commanded by officers of the royal household. The reform therefore represents a significant shift from a system in which the king was largely dependent on the highest nobility, who were summoned by him and then turned up with their households and any other men they chose to bring, which they then commanded. We know that there was some opposition to Alfred's reforms: in the 870s there had been some who preferred to submit to the Danes, and there must have been many landowners who were displeased with the measures he took after Edington. It was presumably the scale of the threat to Wessex that enabled Alfred to carry out his reforms, which may have involved seizure of Church property as well.

Alfred's reforms did not make the king less dependent on the nobility, but created a greater bond between many of them and his court. Those who served the household directly were provided for and in return would have owed service. Others may have been granted land in return for service. All this increased the status of the king. However, as Richard Abels made clear in his work on lordship and military obligation, many nobles were "sub-contracted" to raise fyrdmen in districts where they, and not the sheriff or other exactor of royal service, had jurisdiction. One such was the Bishop of Worcester, who held one hundred of three hundred hides at Oswaldslow in this way "by a constitution of ancient times" when the *Domesday Book* was compiled. Elsewhere abbots and other churchmen, as well as thegns, had similar rights, if generally over less lands and inhabitants.

There were thus two groups of fyrdmen: those who held their land of the king by book-right and had rights of jurisdiction by royal favor, and those who held land as a loan from another lord or under his seignory. The first category of fyrdman was heavily punished for not attending a summons by the king, usually with loss of his possessions. Although the word *fyrdwite* appears in the Laws of Ine, it is not clear what this means, and no reference to it as a fine for failure to perform *fyrd* service (or as a commutation of it) imposed by the king occurs before Cnut's time.[28] Thereafter the term appears only rarely, suggesting that its use was infrequent. The second category of fyrdmen was not directly the king's concern: all that concerned him was that the lord who was obliged to provide a certain number of men per hide fulfilled this provision one way or another. Abels emphasized that the situation in Worcestershire may not have been typical of England as a whole, but there are indications that it was similar to some other shires, if not necessarily the majority. There would have been important consequences of such a system—firstly, many of the king's most important lieutenants would have had to command their own contingents in the battle line and could not have stayed close to the king, and secondly, a considerable number of those provided by lords with their own jurisdictions may have been mercenaries, paid for to make up the quota for their hides, but not necessarily levies of the hides. Such commands would also have perpetuated the existence of regional contingents that had a distinct identity and perhaps ancient privileges as to position in the battle line. John of Salisbury claimed that the men of Kent held the right to strike the first blow, and the men of London the right to protect the king.

The "men of London" may in fact have been the housecarls. This group of warriors has attracted a great deal of attention, without any certainty as to who they actually were and how they served the king. They have been seen as a form of military brotherhood like the *Jomsvikings* (in any case of doubtful historicity) or as an early standing army. Alternatively, it has been suggested that there was little difference between them and other thegns.[29] There is no doubt that the term "housecarl" is of Scandinavian origin, and that Cnut's conquest altered the nature of the king's household. Even in *Domesday Book* sixteen of the eighteen thegns recorded as landowning housecarls had Scandinavian names, but this does not necessarily mean that that a new type of guard corps was imported wholesale to help Cnut maintain his rule over a conquered land. The question may simply be one of a change in terminology, as we know that previous English kings maintained royal thegns, for which "huskarl" may have been a translation. *Domesday Book* may similarly have used "housecarl" simply as a synonym for royal thegn.[30] Like Cnut, his predecessors as king had sometimes had to use their followings to enforce their rule, and some of these were Scandinavians, at least at the courts of Edgar and Æthelred II. If not quite to the same extent as in heroic poetry such as *The Battle of Maldon*, chroniclers such as Asser probably gave a somewhat idealized view of the relations between Anglo-Saxon kings such as Alfred and their followings, representing them in terms of gift exchange rather than the hiring of soldiers. The import of men from "outside" had advantages, as they had no link to vested interests in the kingdom.

Housecarls, perhaps like the royal thegns before them, appear to have had a special relationship with the king and his immediate entourage. For instance, the "housecarls of her son the king" protected Queen Emma in 1035, and they were used to impose taxes by King Harthacnut in Worcestershire in 1041.[31] As such they were provided with high-quality equipment, would have been well trained and must have lived within close proximity of the court. In this sense they were an elite and may have received a royal stipend, but their status need not have differed significantly from earlier royal household thegns who served as soldiers.

The English naval levy

Although nineteenth-and early twentieth-century British historians wrote quite a lot about Anglo-Saxon "naval forces," and even claimed that Alfred was the founder of the Royal Navy, very little has been written since. Finds of English ships from the pre-Norman period have also been rare, as noted in Chapter 2. It is inconceivable that early English kingdoms such as East Anglia, Kent, and Northumbria did not use ships to move their troops, given that they had long coastlines. Nevertheless, the ninth-century English kingdoms were utterly incapable of interfering with Viking fleets that penetrated far up navigable rivers. The impression is given that no fleets were available to block their entrance or exit from these rivers or estuaries. As N.A.M. Rodger points out, even in the 890s, after Alfred had begun to reorganize his forces and their logistics on land, the Vikings were able to sail up the Thames and the Lea and escape without difficulty.[32] One of the reasons Byrhtnoth accepted battle at *Maldon* may have been that he saw this as the one chance to defeat them, otherwise they would simply move away and land elsewhere. After his defeat the only method of getting rid of them appears to have been to pay them off.

If the English were unable to raise a fleet when Viking ships reappeared at the time of *Maldon*, the fleet had been allowed to deteriorate in the mid-tenth century, as Æthelstan certainly utilized one in his campaigns against enemies in northern England and Scotland in 934, and to assist Louis, the exiled Carolingian king of France, in 939.[33] Ann Williams noted the 992 entry of the *ASC*, which referred to the gathering of "all the ships that were any use."[34] The fleet was restored by Cnut's conquest, but as a primarily Scandinavian one, and was revived as an English fleet in Edward the Confessor's reign. Weather and other circumstances conspired to bring about its disbandment before William set out on his seaborne invasion. In 1069–70 William found himself in the position of Æthelred II before him, unable to prevent the Danes from moving up and down the English coast at will, and, like Æthelred, he paid them off. It was not a situation he wished to find himself in again, and he subsequently made full use of the English fleet, notably in his combined land and sea descent on Scotland in 1073, which compelled Malcolm to submit.

The probable reason for the decline of English fleets during the reigns of Eadred, Eadwig, and Edgar (946–75) was the relative lack of threat from outside England. Fleets were expensive to maintain and less useful for policing the kingdom than land forces. They were useful as symbols of royal prestige, but perhaps less necessary than conspicuous symbols on land. There is also a question as to how organized the fleet logistics of Alfred, Edward and Æthelstan were. There is no reference to a *scipfyrd* ("ship-force") in the 896 entry of the *ASC*, such as those which occur in eleventh-century entries. Nor does the 896 entry suggest fleets as large as the later ones. Alfred's fleets (if they deserve the name) may have been assembled through the burghal system at the string of coastal burhs on the coast of Wessex and Kent listed in the Burghal Hidage.[35] There are some problems with this: as Ryan Lavelle pointed out, there is no burh listed on the Isle of Wight, which would be an odd omission. He also observed that only two steersmen are listed in *Domesday Book* as living in urban centers, and one of these, Warwick, is landlocked. This hardly suggests a close link between coastal towns and fleet organization, although it is not wholly inconceivable that a system introduced by Alfred or Edward the Elder was completely overhauled during the late tenth century or Cnut's period.

Under 1008 the *ASC* E manuscript reads, "Here the king ordered that they should determinedly build ships all over England: that is, one *scægð* from three hundred and ten hides." It goes on to state under 1009 that: ". . . there were more of them than there had ever been seen in England in the days of any king. And they brought them all together to Sandwich, and should lie there and guard this country against every foreign raiding army." Unfortunately a dispute between two noblemen, Beorhtric and Wulfnoth, resulted in the latter being accused before the king, after which he went raiding. Beorhtric took eighty ships to intercept him, which were severely damaged and forced to put ashore in a storm, whereupon Wulfnoth burned them all.

The evidence for the raising and equipping of fleets in the late tenth and eleventh centuries is much better. Many wills survive in which *heriot* (from OE *heregeat*, "war-gear") bequeathed to the king was recorded. When he died a noble was obliged to leave a specified set of military equipment to the king, which often included swords, shields, spears, helmets, and horses. In some cases in this later period ships were included. Archbishop Aelfric of Canterbury left two ships, one of which was for the people of Wiltshire, a county without a coast. Other prelates also willed ships to the king. This suggests a levy obligation on all counties. At the same time the bequeathing of ships by magnates may mean that the *scipfyrd* was similar to the land *fyrd*, partly assembled from lands held of the king and partly as a quota from the lands of other lords.

There is a significant difference between the wording of the 1008 entries in the *ASC* D and E manuscripts: E, which is quoted above, says "from three hundred hides and from ten hides a *scægð*," whereas the D manuscript says "from three hundred [hides] a ship and from ten a *scægð*." As we have seen, a *scægð* could be a large ship, so Ryan Lavelle is almost certainly right in suggesting that the D scribe has transcribed the first *hidum* wrongly as *scipum* and that E is right in mentioning a levy of one large ship (or the necessary labor and materials to build one) per 310 hides, a reasonable demand.[36] He calculates that this would give a potential fleet of two hundred ships for the whole of England south of the Tees. It appears that all or most of them were assembled at Sandwich, a port which was to retain its place throughout the Middle Ages, presumably in preparation for the expected Danish attack. This presented a logistical problem, as the fleet could only be maintained offshore in one place for a certain time, perhaps usually for a few weeks. As Harold discovered again in 1066, if the enemy did not appear at the anticipated time, the fleet had to disperse again, running the risk that the enemy would appear off the coast when it was not ready. In 1066 the fleet maintained its station for four months until 8 September, when all provisions had been used up. William crossed to England after this and established a base in Kent. As we have seen, in Æthelred's case one of his own nobles destroyed half the fleet and Thorkell the Tall subsequently attacked Sandwich and Canterbury. Although there was a weakness in the fleet levy system, just as we have seen with the land army levy, in 1009 the greatest damage was done because of internal feuding between English nobles, a problem that bedeviled the Anglo-Saxon state until its end.

Cnut retained forty of his own ships in 1018. The number fell to sixteen, but Harthacnut brought sixty when he took the throne in 1040, retaining thirty-two in 1041. By 1050 Edward the Confessor had paid the last of these crews off, after which he abolished the *heregeld*, a tax that had been used to pay hired Scandinavian crews and their ships since 1012–13, when Æthelred had hired Thorkell the Tall's ships.[37] Nicholas Hooper made the point that the crews of the ships maintained from 1016 to 1051, referred to as *lithsmen*, were paid, not rewarded with land like the housecarls. These crews were not sailors as in a modern navy, but soldiers who also traveled by ship. A group frequently referred to after the disappearance of the *lithsmen* is the *butsecarls* ("boatmen"). There is no way of knowing whether they existed before 1051, but they appear to have close links with the ports of Sussex and Kent, the later Cinque ports, and were probably inhabitants of them owing a special ship service.[38]

It was also in Edward the Confessor's reign that the ship-levy reappears in the sources, after a long absence since 1009. In Edward's reign Earl Godwine is twice mentioned as commanding fleets that must have been the levy of Wessex ("the ships of the people of the land"), forty-two of them in 1046, and there is reference to a Mercian section of the fleet at Sandwich in 1049. *ASC* C and D refer to a fleet of forty *snacca* (probably small ships) at Sandwich in 1052, perhaps part of the general levy as *ASC* E mentions that they needed to return to London to get relief crews.

When the levy in this form was established is uncertain. If the levies of Edward and Æthelred before him were organized in the same way, the organization may have originated in the reign of Edgar or early in

Æthelred's reign. The *ASC* entry of 1008 mentions that uniformly sized districts had the responsibility to build the ships. The later Laws of Henry I (r. 1100–1135) say the same, calling them "ship-sokes." Since it says the counties were divided into ship-sokes, it is possible that they corresponded to the six groups of three into which the hundreds of Buckinghamshire were divided in the *Domesday Book*, each group of three being three hundred hides, which provided a ship. However, only a few of these ship-sokes can be traced in the sources.[39] In the Pipe Rolls of the twelfth century there appears no clear relationship between three hundred or three hundred ten hides and ship-sokes, nor did the hundreds necessarily consist of a hundred hides. As in Edward the Confessor's time, it seems that some towns had made their own arrangements. To complicate matters even further there seems to have been a tax to build ships, referred to (as existing in King Edward's time) in a writ of William I. This suggests that money was often provided instead of actual ships. The ship-scot that appears in several eleventh-century sources must have been raised either as a contribution to this tax or as a contribution to the building of ships.[40] The scattered eleventh-century evidence referring to ship service almost all comes from a few ecclesiastical lordships, and none of it from the former Northumbria (England north of the Humber). One of the sources, a letter of Bishop Æthelric of Sherborne to (Ealdorman?) Æthelmær, refers to a *scir* ("share" or possibly "shire") as the district that provided a ship, and there is no indication that this had anything to do with three hundred hides. This allows the possibility that there was more than one system of levying ships and crews, this perhaps being one used by lords to fulfill their quota of ships.

Although the lack of a fleet that could interfere with Viking fleets in the late tenth century was referred to above, it is important to realize that "interfere" does not mean "intercept at sea" as it did in the modern period. Fleets could be attacked while on shore, or perhaps trapped in rivers and estuaries, but no polity of the Viking Era possessed the methods that could enable its fleet to prevent a foreign fleet from landing on its shores. The fleets assembled in case of invasion at Sandwich or the Isle of Wight may have been demonstrations of power, but they were disbanded after using up their provisions without engaging the enemy. The invasions of Cnut, Harthacnut and William of Normandy were not prevented, nor were the depredations of Viking fleets or renegade English nobles. As Nicholas Hooper noted, English fleets were more effective used in an offensive role.

The Welsh

Despite the great outpouring of material that stresses supposedly pan-Celtic traits in warfare, religion and culture generally, it is debatable whether the remaining Celtic-speaking regions of the Viking Era—Ireland, the Pictish and Scottish kingdoms, Strathclyde, Wales, and Brittany—had much more in common with each other than they did with their Germanic neighbors, except their linguistic affinity. The evidence for military organization in all these regions in the early Middle Ages is sparse, but there is enough to show that there were many similarities with Frankish and English kingdoms.

The military household of the Welsh kings was the *teulu*, rendered *familia* in Latin, like the households of their English and later Norman neighbors. In early sources such as the *Triads* and the *Gododdin*, we also find *gosgordd*: if not the same as the *teulu*, it may have been the household generally as opposed to the personal bodyguard.[41] Here the term *teulu* will be used to mean "household." As in the case of other early medieval households, the size of the *teulu* must have varied. Literary references sometimes give numbers in the hundreds, while the *Brut* says that Gruffudd ap Llywelyn lost 140 men of his *teulu* in 1047, clearly not all of them.[42] However, even if this was not an exaggeration, it must be noted that he was a ruler of exceptional power (in Wales) at this time. Earlier sources give lower numbers—for instance, the *ASC* mentions that Brocmail of Powys fled the field at Chester with his fifty men. At Mynydd Carn in 1081 Trahaearn ap Caradog was killed alongside twenty-five of his *teulu* when many had already died in the battle, which indicates a similar strength.[43]

Like the households of other Viking Age rulers, the *teulu* could include men of all ages and social rank, including leading nobles, with the probable exception of unfree bondmen. The members had horses, although their equipment may have varied according to wealth, and many had "squires," such as the *daryanogyon* (shield-bearers) who attended *uchelwyr*, the aristocracy. These positions became offices, and were certainly of pre-Norman period origin.[44] The teulu could also include foreigners, hostages from the households of other nobles or rivals, and, like the Frankish households, sons of nobles sent to receive training. Gruffudd ap Cynan seems to have employed an exceptional number of Irishmen, but it is not certain that these were thought of as *teulu* members: for instance, they are probably the "pirates" blamed for excessive ravaging in the *Life of St. Gwynllyw*.[45]

The person responsible for mustering the *teulu* was the penteulu (head of the *teulu*), who was supposed to accompany the king at all times except when sent on a specific errand. Naturally, the office of *penteulu* had great prestige and the laws list many privileges, including a larger dwelling than others and a share of the proceeds from judicial proceedings paid to the king. Other members were appointed subordinate commanders of the *llu*, the military levy, should it be summoned. The teulu maintained the tradition of the *comitatus*, and Welsh poetry reflects the same traditions as Old English "heroic" poetry—it was supposed to stand by its lord to the last, as indeed Trahaearn's seems to have done at Mynydd Carn. On the other hand the Triads describe the two war-bands which abandoned their leaders on the eve of battle as earning everlasting infamy.[46] Since the *teulu* was also supposed to follow its lord even if he rebelled, this gave any lord the power to mount a rebellion, with consequent disruptive effects on Welsh society. A Welsh ruler had to secure the support of his nobles (*uchelwyr*)—as elsewhere in Europe, whatever the laws said about a king's rights to summon his nobles and their followings, their support had to be earned. Many Welsh rulers ran into trouble while trying to impose their will on their subject lords. In 984 Einion ab Owain of Deheubarth was killed trying to do so.

As noted, the usual word for the general levy was *llu*, but a variety of other terms were used for "army," such as *byddin*. Usually the levy was drawn only from certain districts, but Gruffudd ap Llywelyn may have been able to assemble a host from the whole of Wales at the height of his power, if this is what John of Worcester meant by "his whole realm." Numbers are almost impossible to assess. *Historia Gruffudd vab kenan* gives figures that appear realistic, the highest being in the hundreds. Davies estimates his army as something under 1,000 in 1075, as he is said to have had 160 men of Gwynedd and numerous foreigners (perhaps 500), especially Irish and Danes, and suggests that the rival armies at Mynydd Carn were each over 1,000 men. Earlier, at the height of his power in 1055, Gruffudd ap Llywelyn had enough men to trouble the English and to force Edward to assemble the host of all England.

Although Wales was never unified, it did undergo a process of reduction of the number of kingdoms in the early medieval period, as happened everywhere in Europe. Several scholars have found evidence of a change in military organization around the beginning of the Viking Period: for instance, the abandonment of some political centers, including hill-forts. In poetry of this period there are hints that free men (*eillion*) were being called up for service. In the laws supposedly codifed by Hywel Dda (d. 950) freemen have to attend musters and pay duties. Not all the codes imposed this duty on free men, and while some spoke of a "levy of the land," this must in practice have been selective, as in Anglo-Saxon England. Presumably the king called up those he needed. The *Brutiau* claim that Maredudd ap Bleddyn gathered "about four hundred kinsmen and comrades and a *teulu* of theirs" for a campaign in 1118.[47] The same source makes one of the very rare references to a general levy (of Meirionnydd) in 1110, which may even have included bondmen. With the exception of one referred to in the *Life of St. Cadog* (a fifth-century saint), all general levies are recorded as meeting with defeat. Bondmen had certain duties to construct encampments for the king's men and to provide pack-horses (and supplies?), but it is unclear whether they were expected to fight or not.

In Wales mercenaries (*alltud*—"aliens") were certainly used in many armies. Apart from the Irish mentioned above, John of Worcester mentions Viking mercenaries employed by Gruffudd ap Llywelyn in his attack on England in 1055. The laws also mention the billeting of armed foreigners on the local populace.

There is little evidence that Church lands were exempt from military service in Wales. There are hints that the early medieval *clas* church functioned in a similar way to the Church in Ireland, its senior men maintaining retinues and providing military service. Given the amount of land owned by the Church and the limited resources available to any ruler, exempting it would have made the raising of forces almost impossible. Most claims to exemption are made in later saints' lives and many of these are dubious.

Brittany

The successes achieved by Breton armies in the ninth century, and the more general success of Brittany in maintaining an effective independence from Frankish control, even when its rulers submitted to Frankish kings, demonstrate that Brittany was able to raise highly effective armies. Moreover, Breton troops were in high demand as contingents of the contenders in the Frankish civil wars. Sadly, we know very little of their organization. The limited sources suggest an increasingly powerful influence from Carolingian Francia, and at the beginning of the tenth century Brittany was more or less overrun by the Vikings. We cannot be certain that this did not mark the end of some specifically Breton traits in military organization and methods of campaigning. In light of this, it seems risky to conclude that the Breton forces in William the Bastard's army at Hastings, which comprised his left wing, had inherited the evasive tactics of their armies of two centuries earlier.[48] The Breton polity was restored by Alan Barbetorte in 936, although it was smaller than its predecessor of the ninth century. Although, as duke, Alan was treated as an equal by his neighbors, including even Hugh the Great, the most powerful noble in France and ancestor of the Capetian kings, after the reign of his successor Drogo internal disorder and external interference weakened Brittany.

What little evidence we have suggests that even in the ninth century Breton military organization had many similarities with Frankish practice. It is arguable that until the ninth century there was no Brittany, only Bretons. Early resistance to Carolingian expansion seems to have been regional, but despite, or perhaps because of, this fragmentation, the Franks had great difficulty in imposing rule over the region. Paradoxically, a more united Brittany was created by Nomenoë (r. 831–851) asprotégé of Louis the Pious.[49] The most powerful nobles after the princeps were the counts, and a link beween these and the plebs, a community centerd on a settlement named a *bourg*, was the *machtiern*, who possessed hereditary landed wealth in one or more plebes, but also held limited "public" authority in one or several *plebes*, receiving some dues and guaranteeing deals struck by others.[50] Their position, probably an inheritance from an early age, was undermined by growing Carolingian influence and ecclesiastical and secular aristocratic usurpation of local judicial and administrative rights.[51] A few of the usurpers may, of course, have been *machtierns* themselves, although they generally represented a second-level aristocracy. We know very little of local forces in Brittany, except that they were ineffective against the Vikings.

The military households of the kings and nobles formed the core of armies and also the environment in which noble youths, *pueri*, acquired their military education. The term encountered most often for those who committed themselves to serve another was *fideles*, although the term *vassus* also occurs, increasingly so in the eleventh century. This was not a permanent bond, but a lord–client agreement on the basis of service in exchange for reward. The Breton rulers themselves were usually *fideles* of the Carolingian kings, but some of those who served Breton lords, such as

Catworet who was Nominoë's *fideles*, were undoubtedly warriors.[52] Along-side aristocrats, important religious establishments provided military con-tingents: in fact, they may have been the most reliable source of troops in the early period, as many abbots and senior churchmen were members of the ruling house. As in Francia, aristocrats made gifts in exchange for equipment. The Redon Cartulary records that a certain Risweten, killed at Jengland in 851, surrendered his claim on an estate of Reden Monastery in return for a horse and a mail shirt, refusing the alternative offer of money. We know that service was required of the free people, "works," taxes, and carriage duties, but not how this was organized or whether some of this was rendered as a form of rent, as suggested plausibly by Wendy Davies. Nor is it clear who performed military service or precisely what part (if any) the *plebes* may have played in raising troops. Referring to the summons by the princeps Erispoë that preceded the Jengland campaign, the *Acts of the Saints of Redon* states, "at once all the Bretons rose from their seats." Seats (*sedes*) could mean either "homes" or "estates," in the sense of seats of power; the former interpretation would imply a general levy, the latter a raising of nobles and their followings. Given the nature of other armies in this period, the latter seems more likely. Since the judicial and other admin-istrative functions of the *plebes* appear to have been largely free of central control in the ninth century, a highly developed levy system is unlikely.

There is evidence that in the eleventh century aristocrats began to gain control over land that had previously belonged to the Church and the counts. Around the turn of the century Rivallon the Vicar treated land that had previously been invested to him as a servant of the count as his private property, and his family subsequently owned it as such, while the younger brothers of Archbishop Junguéne of Dol (d. *c.* 1037) seized ecclesiastical estates under his administration. By the mid-eleventh century they were erecting motte and bailey castles throughout the region, although it is not certain how they acquired the land and the rights to do so, whether through force or endowment. The idea of knighthood also took hold during this century, but there is little evidence of any clear link between knights' fees and military service until the later twelfth century. By 1050 Brittany was a land of castellanies and knights, resembling its neighboring dukedoms in many respects, but more fragmented. Given these similarities and the cultural influence from Francia, it seems likely that the Breton dukes of the tenth and eleventh centuries relied on nobles turning up with their followings if they wished to assemble an army. However the pattern of landholding changed, and however much local communities fell under the control of castellans, in this respect the fundamental character of Breton armies probably remained unchanged.

Ireland

We know a considerable amount about Irish law, social groupings, and obligations in the early Christian and Viking Eras, but the many overlapping rules of kinship and clientship, which worked on many levels, make it difficult to know precisely what the military obligations of kin, neighbors, and clients were. Even kinship functioned on different levels. The basis of inheritance was agnatic kinship, and the law functioned in such a way that land was partitioned as equitably as possible. Land was also distributed to neighbors, which thus became a community similar to a kindred. Excessive fragmentation of land was avoided by resharing and collateral inheritance of the property of extinct lines. The third community was the *túath*, the people of a small kingdom, which included many groups of neighbors, often living within a single territory of cultivated land. Each king had a retinue of men who owed allegiance to him, but the degree of obligation differed. Some of these were the so-called base clients, freemen who paid a fixed annual food-render in return for a grant from their overlord. They were expected to accompany him to war and to defend him, or avenge him if necessary. They also owed him hospitality, especially in the coshering season between 1 January and Ash Wednesday. Although the client relationship was personal, clients were usually forced back into a client relationship with a successor when an overking died, probably because the hospitality and the render they had been expected to provide put them into a position where, in addition to their own cattle, they needed his grant of cattle (sometimes called a "cattle fief"). This made them a client. Free clients had fewer obligations to perform service, but were still obliged to give a degree of hospitality and support.

The great dynasties were overlords of several client kings, who were rulers of small kingdoms. There was often tension between the branches of the great dynasties, which were rivals for the overkingship. One method of (hopefully) defusing this was for the overking to award the branches kingdoms of their own, albeit as client kings. Kings controlled churches and often used them and their patrons (saints) as a focus of unity if their territories or kingdoms were scattered. Thus different kingdoms could be linked by dispersed peoples and fragmented kindreds. Overkings toured their clients' territories and enjoyed their hospitality. Although it appears that the overkingships were resting on shaky foundations, supporting an edifice held together by royal clientship and personal loyalty, there were in fact other bonds of tradition, loyalty, and law that maintained the existing kingdoms for centuries. The Irish showed a remarkable resilience in the face of external influences from Scandinavia and England.

External to this society were the *fian* bands, partly made up of young men sent out to make their way in the wild, as discussed in Chapter 7. In the Viking Era they probably also attracted outright brigands or men deprived of their livelihood by Viking raids. The bands of legend may have been admired, but those of the Christian era were condemned by the Church as equivalent to the pagans. Some of them may have been of substantial size, perhaps several hundred strong. Although it is not mentioned in the sources, they may have been able to act as mercenaries or allies on occasions.

Scotland

For the most part the way in which the forces of the Pictish kingdoms and Dál Riata were organized is obscure. As in the early Anglo-Saxon kingdoms, it seems that the kings and chieftains had their personal households (referred to as *comitatus* or *familia* in Latin sources), which were supplemented by the retinues and free men, or even the half-free, of lesser chieftains who owed them allegiance to raise an army (*exercitus*). Adomnán (abbot of Iona 679–704) also used the word *cohors* to refer to a contingent in an army. Kings often awarded districts to their kinsmen to govern when they had the opportunity to remove rivals, but some of the powerful kingroups of the eleventh century probably had early origins. Behind the titles lay kinship groups or clanns, whose head (Lat. *capitalis*, Gael. *cenn*) might also hold a lordship or royal office.

Some of the titles that appear in tenth and eleventh-century Scotland are also recorded in references to the period before the union of Pictland and Dál Riata. In the later period the *mormaers* were territorial magnates equivalent in power to the earls of late Anglo-Saxon England, but the term *toísech* also denoted a landowner, perhaps of thegnly status, as the title *thanus* appears to displace it during the tenth century. *Óchtigern* denoted the highest ranking non-noble freeman, presumably a farm- or cattle-owner. The title *mormaer* is probably of Pictish origin, perhaps meaning "great officer," although it is first recorded only in 918. As in later Viking-Age Scotland, they may have been the senior magnates responsible for raising military contingents to support the king in battles such as Corbridge. The rank of *toísech* is the only other noble rank recorded in the tenth-century *Book of Deer* (*Leabhar Dhèir*), which includes the earliest writing in Gaelic.[53] The title probably goes back to Dál Riata, but it is not entirely clear what rank he may have held there or whether he was a royal official, as sources that record people of this rank sometimes seem to refer to princes and sometimes to lower landowners. As with the use of the Latin terms *comes* and *nobilis*, the terms *mormaer* and *toísech* may not be used to denote any specific office or rank when referring to a period before that when they were written, and if they do the author or copier may be imposing a later social/ military structure on an earlier polity.

Of particular interest is a document known as the *Senchus fer nAlban* ("History of the Men of Alba"), which has survived in several late medieval manuscripts varying only slightly in content. Its editor, John Bannerman, argues that these derive from a single mid-tenth-century source, and, more controversially, that this in turn is derived from a seventh-century original. The work includes a survey of the three principal kin-groups of Dál Riata— Cenél Loairn, CenélnÓ engusa, and Cenél nGabráin—and their military organization, claiming that they could raise a total of 141 ships, which Bannerman interpreted as sevenbenchers. The text as we have it is obviously corrupt, as the assessment of total numbers of houses (land units) for the Cenél nÓengusa as 430 does not correspond to the number of houses in the listed septs, which total 350, while the relative number of houses for the three Cenélá do not correspond to the numbers of men listed for them in the hostings. These errors are in all the extant manuscripts, so they probably derive from the tenth-century source, which was therefore based either on several conflicting earlier sources, or a single inaccurate or incomplete one.

By the tenth century Dál Riata was under the control of the Vikings: even if the Cenélá maintained their identity then, any pre-Norse organization is unlikely to have survived. In fact, the word *sess* or *sese*, translated as rowing bench by Banner-man, almost certainly derives from Old Norse *sessa*, meaning the same. Furthermore, the name Alba was used for the Pictish kingdoms before the ninth-century union of the Scots and Picts, and for the united kingdom afterwards, but not for Dál Riata.⁵⁴ The argument that the *Senchus* is an accurate reflection of the military obligations of pre-Norse Dál Riata rests on very shaky ground. However, corrupt as it is, there may well have been an agreement between the three Cenéla of Dál Riata on levies for service on land and sea based on "houses." There are sufficient mentions of Dál Riatan and Pictish fleets and even sea battles in the sources for them to have a strong basis in reality. We may doubt whether ships were of a standard size, but seven benches may be close to a realistic size for their sewn or hide boats. Unfortunately, whatever naval resources the Picts and Scots possessed were hopelessly inadequate to face the Vikings. The people of the Isles and Hebrides subsequently adopted a small version of the Viking longship, the *birlinn*.

Scandinavia

There has been considerable controversy over the raising of fleets and armies by the Scandinavians in the Viking Era. All three of the Scandinavian kingdoms (as known from the Viking Period onwards) preserve law-codes that provide for service on board ship, but the preserved versions do not date to the Viking Age: the Norwegian and Danish regional codes belong to the thirteenth century and the Swedish from the very late thirteenth and early fourteenth centuries. Under the name *leiðangr* (Old Norse *leiðangr*, Dan. *leding*, Nor. *leidang*, Sw. *ledung*) they all provide for service at sea, but also for payment in place of military service, in effect taxes in money or produce. Although they are broadly similar, the earliest law-codes are regional and there are differences between them even within one kingdom. Even in the High Middle Ages (1100–1300) the regions of each kingdom still had considerable autonomy. Many scholars have wanted to push these laws or those that formed the basis of them back into the Viking Era or beyond, to the Vendel Period (*c.* 550–800), or further still, to the sixth-century Chlochilaich raid of Gregory of Tours and *Beowulf*.⁵⁵ Until recently, in Denmark it was assumed that there was an organization of provincial defense, the *leding*, which developed as the kingdom of Denmark took shape, and an even older organization of local defense, the *landeværn*.⁵⁶

In recent decades the idea that a *leidang* resembling that of the law-codes originated earlier than the Viking Era has fallen out of favor. The term was not recorded before the Viking Era, but nor was much else. More important is the commonly accepted link between military service obligations and state formation, since it is generally assumed that they were imposed on the populace by the king. Without evidence that kings had sufficient power and authority to impose these obligations, their existence is unlikely. Frankish sources mention that King Godfred had a powerful fleet at the beginning of the ninth century, and even before him the earliest phases of the Dane-virke were built and the 500-meter Kanhave canal was constructed across the narrowest part of Samsø island. Many have also seen the construction of the "Trelleborg"-type circular forts built during the reign of Harald Bluetooth as evidence of royal authority in Denmark,[57] while the Danish ability to send fleets and armies to England year after year and ultimately conquer it is perceived as requiring a high degree of organization, created by an increasingly centralized and powerful kingship. However, none of these projects, impressive as they are, is evidence in itself of military work obligations or levy organizations of Carolingian or late Anglo-Saxon type, although they do indicate authority beyond the imposition of tribute by a king and his war-band.

As with so much medieval terminology, it is not easy to determine precisely what is meant by the term *leiðangr* in different sources. In its most general sense it meant any military expedition, but in later kings' sagas such as *Hákonar saga hákonarsonar* (the *Saga of King Håkon Håkonson*, 1217–1263) it sometimes appears to refer to the fleet, which could be equated with the military levy, and on occasion it could also refer to defensive forces. In a skaldic poem Harald Hardrada (king of Norway 1046–1066) was called *king of the leiðangr*, itself described as the duty and right of all men (*almen-ningr*). He was praised for summoning the *leiðangr* to attack Denmark. Over a century earlier, in *c.* 985, the skaldic courtly poets of Jarl Häkon of Lade (now in east Trondheim) and his son Erik praised their lords for summoning the ships of the *leiðangr* to the Battle of Hjorungavagr against a Danish fleet. The term *leiðangr* also appears in the *Encomium Emmae* (*c.* 1040). The problems with dating skaldic verse have been mentioned, although it is highly unlikely that all early references to *leiðangr* are spurious.

Other terminology from Viking-Age runestones and skaldic verse, such as references to *styrsimaðr* (steersman, captain), *þegn* (thegn or man of status), and *dreng* (retinue soldier or young man), are associated with ships and social status, and may have military connotations, but tell us nothing of any military organization and need not have the same associations as they do in later law-codes. Place-names often include *snekke* or *skib*, and therefore probably denote harbors or sites of boathouses for fast ships, but they may have belonged to the *liðs* of chieftains as well as to the king's fleet.

Archaeological remains of boathouses large enough to house long-ships exist only in Norway. In Scandinavia the majority of these were probably built entirely of wood, similar to the shelters used for church boats in Finland and Sweden in more recent times, or more akin to large halls. These have not survived, but Norway's boathouses were characterized by a depression in the ground with stone foundations to the structures. Datings are approximate, but the boathouses from the eleventh century onwards are scattered more evenly along the coast, which does suggest a systematic division of Norway into *skipreider*, at least in the north (Rogaland and Horda-land), where more boathouses have been discovered. Earlier boathouses, of the late Iron Age and Viking Period, are distributed in groups which were probably close to the central places of the petty kingdoms and chiefdoms of the era. Evidence for this is that many are close to grave mounds, although it has to be said that there are fewer dated to this early period than to the post-Viking period.[58] The post-Viking medieval Norwegian laws state that boats should be kept in boathouses, which should be built on the king's land, while sails were taken to churches. Many of the later boathouses are close to churches.

Ole Crumlin-Pederson argues that the much-repaired Skuldelev 5 (*c.* 1050), raised in Roskilde Fjord, Denmark, was a levy ship. His argument seems to be that no self-respecting noble would command such a patched-up ship, while its size and repairs are suggestive of the *leidang* ships described in the Norwegian *Gulatingslov*, which specifies fines for failure to maintain and equip warships, but also specified the amount of wear before a ship had to be replaced.[59] However, it does not follow that the ship belonged to a *leidang* fleet like that of the law-codes, as it could easily have belonged to the private fleet of a powerful magnate. Ships were expensive to build, and magnates as well as kings would have kept them afloat as long as possible. The rules of *Gulatingslov* might be applicable to any warship of the eleventh, twelfth or thirteenth century, as ships of similar size and construction were used for a very long period in the Baltic region, even up to the fifteenth century, and continuity in ship technology does not necessarily imply continuity in military organization.

It is questionable whether powerful centralized kingship is a prerequisite for the raising of large forces, as there is too much evidence, whatever the problems of our sources and however scarce they may be, for large armies numbering tens of thousands during the Migration Period.[60] If confederations of tribes and groups led by kings or chieftains could combine under certain circumstances to raise armies capable of confronting the Romans, it is not too much to imagine that chieftains or magnates of Scandinavia could combine their forces to form armies of several thousands. A king might still be electable, as Scandinavian kings were for most of the Middle Ages. In a sense he was first among equals, but the authority he obtained from the office of kingship enabled him to summon the chieftains in his polity to join him with their followings. In this scenario the king need not have statutory authority, but may have authority bestowed on him by the fame and powers of his ancestors, sacral authority and power acquired by virtue of his own successful exploits.

The Great Army was formed in a similar way, although some of its chieftains ("jarls") may have owed their authority almost entirely to their record of success, associated with *hamingja* ("good fortune" or "luck," regarded as an inherent quality of the person or his lineage) in the Old Norse sources. Like most of the Viking forces that ravaged Europe, the Great Army was a short-term arrangement. Fortunately for Wessex, parts of it, notably the army led by Ívarr, had already gone north when it invaded the kingdom. During the ninth and early tenth centuries Viking forces frequently combined and then separated again under their respective leaders. Some of the forces that attacked England in the 890s may also have been led by "jarls," such as the army at *Maldon*. In the subsequent Danish campaigns in England, Sweyn Forkbeard relied on trusted "jarls," both to maintain his authority in parts of Scandinavia, as Erik of Lade did in Norway, and to lead some of the expeditions. Thorkell the Tall led the invasion of 1010, but he changed sides in 1013, taking his *lið* with him. In 1006 the Danish army was led by a trusted chieftain, in this case probably the Toste referred to on the Swedish runestone (U 344) of Ulf of Borresta, who shared in three gelds paid by Skagul Toste, Thorkell the Tall, and Cnut. Little else is known of Toste, although Ian Howard suggests that he may have been a kinsman of Cnut. The runestone also demonstrates that there were contingents from the present-day region of Sweden. It is very unlikely that Sweyn or Cnut could compel anyone from Svealand or Småland to accompany them to England; their armies attracted smaller chieftains and their followings because their ventures were profitable. Sweyn ruled a land recently unified by Harald Bluetooth. The army may have been generally more united in purpose under his ultimate direction than the earlier Great Army, but it was probably composed from the forces of chieftains and their followings.

The *leding* rules of thirteenth-century Denmark provide for a four-yearly service as an imposition on the *hafnae*, responsible for providing one man for the leding ship. A number of *hafnae* belonged to a *skipæn*, the district responsible for raising and manning a ship under the direction of the steersman. The system is first described in the law-code of Scania, from the early decades of the thirteenth century, and then in the law of Jutland of 1241. There are some differences between them, but the latter was probably intended to be a national system, as proposed most recently by Michael Gelting: in other words, it was meant to supplement the Scanian law rather than provide a western Danish law that corresponded to the eastern one. Saxo mentions the introduction of a rotational patrol fleet in 1169, after the fall of Arkona on Rügen (off the coast of north Germany, then a Wendish fortress and pagan cult center), and although he does not mention *expeditio* at this point, Niels Lund has argued that this marks the introduction of the rotational *leding* of the Danish law-codes. He also argues that the Danish armies that plagued England in the late tenth and early eleventh centuries were assembled followings of chieftains summoned to serve the king.

In Danish sources references to the *leding* begin in the twelfth century, in various Old Danish forms and the Latin equivalent *expeditio*, alongside a fine or commutation for military service known as the *quærsæt*, similar to the English *fyrdwite*. The first securely dateable reference to *expeditio* is in a charter of Cnut (IV) granting lands with all their royal dues to the church of St Lawrence in Lund in 1185, payment for neglect of military service being one of the excepted dues.[61] As Lund suggests, this is almost certainly linked to Cnut's plans for an invasion of England, which caused him to introduce new taxes.[62] The fleet for the invasion was assembled but disbanded again after delays prevented it from sailing, after which Cnut attempted to introduce a tax in lieu of the unperformed service and based on the provisions. Saxo and Sven Aggesen refer to a fine for failure to perform service, but the earlier Chronicle of Roskilde calls the same imposition *nesgjald* (nose-tax). In the following year this resulted in a rebellion and Cnut's death. This may be the first attempt to introduce *leding* on the same principle as the later law-codes, as Lund suggests it is, but it is conceivable that there were also earlier references to *expeditio* in charters that have not survived. It is also possible that the magnates or *þegns* of the Danish provinces who owed Sweyn Forkbeard and Cnut the Great allegiance were required to raise troops on a similar basis to the Bishop of Worcester for Edward the Confessor—in other words to provide a number of men and ships appropriate to their wealth for a given period or for the duration of a campaign. In 1085 the problem may have been that impositions were more acceptable in defense of the kingdom, the primary purpose of the 1169 reform, than for an overseas expedition. If this was the case, the old "Viking" appetite for long-distance expeditions had gone.

Heimskringla and *Fagrskinna* give us the only accounts of the origin of a leidang system, in this case of Norway, but they date from the early thirteenth century. The accounts are similar, except that the former says it originated in the law district of Gulaþing and the latter of Frostaþing. Both say that it was introduced by Håkon the Good (935–961), a king who was fostered at the court of Æthelstan, where he may have got the inspiration. During the late Viking Period and Middle Ages there were four law-districts in Norway, each of which had a regional assembly (*thing*), Gulaþing, Frostaþing, Eidsivaþing and Borgarþing, but the law-codes of only two of these have survived, *Gulatingslov* and *Frostatingslov*, both of which have *leidang* rules. As in Denmark, the lands were divided into districts, in this case *skipreiður*, each responsible for equipping and manning a ship. Although the versions of the Norwegian law-codes we possess date from the twelfth century, it is often thought that the "Older Gulating Law" dates to the eleventh century, but if it does, it is not certain that it was the same as our extant version. Many of its rules could apply to any century from the tenth to the fourteenth.

Gulatingslov requires every man to arm himself with an axe or a sword in addition to spear and shield, and for every bench to have a bow and twenty-four arrows—again a stipulation that would be equally applicable to the eleventh or the twelfth century, and does not tell us when the law was created. Later twelfth- to thirteenth-century changes to this law-code list more extensive equipment for the more affluent freemen, with helmet, mail hauberk, shield, spear and sword demanded of the well-to-do farmer or burgher.

In *Gulatingslov* only the king has the right to call out the *leidang*, whereas in *Frostatingslov* it is emphasized that the law is paramount and the king must follow it. Its district, Trøndelag, had a long record of revolt against kings who, in the eyes of its inhabitants, set themselves above the law, and its law probably reflects this.[63] In these regional law-codes the call-out is made on the basis of *manntal*, a count of men, rather than property. The rules of *Gulatingslov* are more detailed. As observed by Kjergaard and Ersland, there are two separate ordinances, concerned with different matters: the first concerns the summoning of a force of free men according to *manntal*, at the king's behest, with clear rules on its organization, financing and maintenance, whereas the second concerns the duty of all sectors of society, "both tegn and træl (thegn and thrall)," to defend the realm against external foes and internal disturbance.[64] They define these as rules for the *"utbods leidang"* (expeditionary levy) and *"landevernet"* (a form of general levy) respectively. In *Frostatingslov* this division is more apparent, as the *"landevern"* rules are in a separate section. In line with the traditional opinion mentioned above, Ersland suggests that the latter have an older origin, in an era when the king had limited control over chieftains. This is possible, but the two ordinances may also be separate because the *landevern* section is concerned with emergency situations when the king did not have time to summon the *leidang* and bring it to the threatened region. Neither in these regional codes nor in the later *Landslov* (Land law) is there any indication as to the numbers that should be assembled, a possible reflection of their "emergency" nature. Nor do the rules restricting the right to build ships without permission necessarily belong to an early period when the king had limited control,[65] as suggested by some, as medieval kings never had full control over their aristocracy and were always threatened with rebellion and their kingdoms with brigandage.

The fines for neglect of duty on watch were considerably heavier in Viken (southeast Norway), a probable reflection of the threat from Denmark. As a defensive instrument the *leidang* was complemented by a watch system, the institution of which *Heimskringla* similarly attributes to Håkon the Good. As told in both *Heimskringla* and *Fagrskinna*, this institution is specifically linked to Håkon's conflict with the Erikssons, which gives a ring of truth to it that their claim of Håkon's establishment of the *leidang* does not have. Snorri tells us that watchmen were to maintain guard on a string of high fells with line of sight from each one to the next and that the system extended from the land's end to the northernmost *þingslag* in Hålagoland, although Håkon's realm in west Norway at the time of his conflict with the Erikssons corresponded roughly to the later *Gulatingslov*. The system was still in effect in Snorri's own time, and certainly extended throughout the realm by 1274, when Magnus Lagabøter's law-code (*Landslov*) was written down. It is likely that it originated in Vestland, Håkon the Good's territory, and was extended later to Trøndelag and subsequently Håligoland in the north, as well southwards and eastwards to Båhuslan (then part of Norway). Place-names with *vete-* as their first element are found all along the coast of Norway as far as northern Håligoland, and other place-names with the later component *vard-*, also suggesting a watch site, may have been named *vete-* earlier and so could date to the pre-1300 era. If we can judge by the fact that only *vard-* names exist in Finnmark, the watch system must have been extended to this region only in the later Middle Ages.

A very similar watch (*vakt*) system was provided for in the Swedish law-codes of Svealand. These were clearly associated with the rules for *ledung* and its associate taxes. In *Upplandslagen ledung* organization was tied to the *hundare*, the equivalent of the English hundred, which equipped four ships. The *hundare* was divided into *hälfter* (halfs), *fjärdingar* (fourths), and *åttingar* or *hamnor* (sing. *åtting, hamna*).[66] Rodén and Hälsingland differed, being divided into *skeppslag*, each of which equipped one ship. Västmanland was divided into eight *hundare*, each split into two *skeppslag*, in turn divided into *hälfter* (halfs), *fjärdingar* and *hamnor*. Each *skeppslag* provided a ship. Södermannalagen has a similar ledung to these other Svealand law-codes, but places more emphasis on the levy than its tax substitute. In the regions of Norrland (Hälsingland, Medelpad and Ångermanland) the administrative divisions were *skeppslag* and *har*.[67] There was also a levy from Gotland and eastern (coastal) Götaland. *Guta saga*, the saga of Gotland, provides what appears to be evidence of an early origin to the system, as it tells us that the king and jarl of the *Svear* could levy their taxes in Gotland before Christianization, and call on seven warships for their military expeditions.[68] It is quite possible that the *Svear* extracted tribute from Gotland in the Viking Era, but no jarl of the *Svear* is recorded before Birger Brosa in the late twelfth century ("dei gracia rex sveorum et guttorum"—it is not clear whether the latter refers to the *Götar* or the Gotlanders). Other figures must be later than the Viking Era: for instance, the number of ships specified for the town of Visby clearly belongs to the High Middle Ages, as the town was not large enough to supply them before this.

The lack of written evidence for Sweden before 1250 has led to assorted attempts to identify the origin of the *ledung* by study of place-names and the origins of administrative districts, but the problem is that none of the names associated with the law-code *ledung*, such as *hamna* or *hundare*, need have been associated with it when the settlements or districts were named as such, and even if they were associated with ships and levies, we cannot know what form these took.[69] The same applies to Norwegian attempts to date the Norwegian *leidang* by assessing the age of the *skipreider*. Attempts have also been made to link sites called Husby, Huseby, or Husaby with the *leidang* fleet. Sites with these names exist in all three Scandinavian kingdoms, but especially in Norway and Sweden. In medieval written sources many are royal estates, and the Norwegian law-codes say that the fleet levy should assemble on the king's land. The sites are on waterways, but this is not surprising, as virtually every place of importance was. They are often in strategic locations, but a location on trade routes or by natural harbors need not have purely military implications. Some seem to have had other uses, such as storage places for gathered tribute or even centers of industry or crafts, so they were probably used for various purposes. As usual their date of origin is obscure.[70]

All the Scandinavian law-codes provide for a rotational system that required some of the men of a district to man a fleet for part of the year while others remained at home. This is essentially a system designed for defense of the realm, similar to the levy systems of Francia and Anglo-Saxon England in the Viking Era. Certain scholars have argued that such systems are the product of polities that have ceased to expand, as nobles and their followings could no longer be relied on to turn up when summoned, as defensive war provided less opportunity for wealth acquisition. This is the basis of Niels Lund's argument that the Danish *leding* developed after the Viking Era, and more or less what Thomas Lindkvist argued in 1988 for the development of the Swedish *ledung*—that the term originally applied to overseas plundering expeditions, but was later transformed into a tax system (we might add a system of defense against Wendish and Estonian raiding) as the opportunities for wealth acquisition abroad declined. In other words, even had they wanted to, or been able to, Sweyn and Cnut did not have to levy fleets as their successors did two hundred years later, when they were making profitable expeditions to England.

The surviving medieval Scandinavian law-codes also include provision for payment of taxes in place of military service. It is frequently assumed that military service was transformed into taxes as royal administrations found it expedient and possible to replace an inefficient levy system with payments, which they could then use to hire more professional troops, later granting immunity from taxes to landowners in return for service as heavily armed horsemen. It is certainly the case that payment of taxes became more common, or at least more systematically organized, as royal administration developed. However, in the case of the Norwegian and Danish law-codes this is no more than an assumption based on analogy from elsewhere, as there is no clear indication that the *leidang* ever existed without payment in some form as an alternative to military service. In *Gulatingslov, Frostating-slov* and *Sverris saga* these substitute taxes already existed, suggesting that in Norway they were in place by the mid-twelfth century.

King Niels of Denmark (1104–1134) followed the example set by Cnut IV in 1085, but with less disastrous results, when he donated privileges to St Knud in Odense. In this case the payment is called *lethang withe*. It seems that these freemen are the equivalent of the *herræ mæn* in the 1241 Law of Jutland, which lists men exempt from the *utgerdsleding* (the service on a *leding* ship once in four years).[71] They were exempt because they were men commended to the king, bishops or lay magnates, and they served when called up. However, there is no reason to assume that the fine or the service was the same in 1241 as it was in 1104. In the case of Sweden, there is evidence that many of the taxes that were substituted for military service in the fleet were introduced into parts of Svealand quickly in 1250, after Birger Jarl's suppression of a rebellion, but we have no clear indication that the military ship levy was introduced much before this.[72] Given the threat of Slavic and Estonian raiders in the previous century, and the example of Denmark and Norway, it probably was, but again, this is "evidence" on the basis of analogy. It is therefore impossible to say with any certainty that the leidang without these taxes ever existed in Norway and Denmark, and even in Sweden outside the rebellious region of eastern Svealand. Conversely, even if the tax *leidang* came increasingly to replace the fleet levy, the latter was never abolished. However, the numbers of ships mentioned by the sagas as raised in the twelfth century are well below the numbers demanded by the law-codes. This may be due to a simple failure to fulfill duties, but another possibility is that the ideal numbers are related more to the demand for equivalent taxes than to an actual military levy.

It is possible that some of the components of the *leidang* systems of the law-codes were introduced in the late Viking Era. The use of fires to give warning signals is likely to have existed not long after man learned to make fire, and it is only a small step to establish a string of several such fires to carry warnings across larger distances once bigger polities developed, as long as the necessary topographical conditions existed. This type of watch system is known to have existed throughout the North Sea and Baltic coastal regions in the Viking Period. Ships and men, in the form of *lið*s summoned by kings, may have been levied in the Viking Era. However, the ship levy rules of the Norwegian and Danish law-codes imply a kingdom-wide organization of resources and taxation that is unlikely to have existed in the eleventh century, when the realms had been recently unified (or re-unified). The Swedish law-codes have more regional variation, suggesting input from local interests, but the law of Uppland probably provided the basis for the *ledung* rules of the other Svealand law-codes, at least in the form we have them. All are still designed to provide ships and men for the whole realm, and it is doubtful that any king of the *Svear* and *Götar* had sufficient authority over both peoples to impose these rules before the late twelfth century.

One of the many problems in estimating sizes of Viking armies is our lack of knowledge of ship sizes. The suggested size of thirty men per ship (above) is based on only two ship finds. Even in the era of the law-codes there is no strong evidence that ships were of a standard size. The Norwegian law-codes appear to suggest two sizes, twenty- and twenty-five oars, but this may be an ideal, designed partly to fit the equivalent in tax revenue. There is in fact a variety of evidence that earlier levy ships were not standardized. For all its dubious aspects (such as possible exaggeration of the enemy's numbers and suspect pre-battle speeches by the leaders), there is no need to doubt the author of *Sverris saga* when he describes ships of different sizes.[73] In the case of Denmark, the Halland list of *Kong Valdemars jordebog* (King Valdemar's Land Register, thirteenth century) refers specifically to all sizes of ship, varying from sixteen oars to forty-two. The discovered eleventh-century ships also vary in size.

The accounts of naval battles in the sagas give some large numbers of ships, such as two hundred at the Battle of Hafrsfjord in *c.* 872. *Gulatingslov* allows for a total ship levy of 309, whereas the naval battles of the wars of succession in Norway during the twelfth century, much closer to the time of the sagas' composition, appear to have involved fifty ships or fewer. Some of them supposedly involved the levies of most of Norway. Even if the average ship size was bigger, this gives reason to doubt the fleet sizes of the saga accounts. As noted in the last chapter, there is also reason to suspect that saga descriptions of individual ships of the Viking Era are anachronistic, which should make us wary of other aspects of the saga accounts of naval warfare. Danish fleets, on the other hand, may have been relatively large, and some of the fleet sizes given for combined Viking fleets or those of Sweyn and Cnut are believable. Given that they dominated large areas of Scandinavia and even some of Wendland in the period of their wars in England, their armies may have been larger than the Great Army. In composition they probably did not differ significantly, except that they were led by a king or a loyal subordinate.

Chapter 4

Campaigning

Logistics and numbers

As mentioned in the previous chapter, estimating the size of forces involved in early medieval warfare is often impossible. Numbers given in the sources can never be regarded as reliable without corroborating evidence, which can rarely be found. There is no dispute that the majority of campaigns were on a small scale, conducted as large-scale raids or attempts to intercept raiders, and possibly with the limited objective of capturing a camp or fort of limited defensive strength. In the Christianized kingdoms many of these would have been carried out by local forces and might have numbered anything from a few hundred to a couple of thousand men. On a general level, there is more dispute about the maximum size of army that could be put into the field by different polities. In the Viking Era, on the basis of territory controlled alone, the largest armies were probably raised by Charlemagne in his later years and his son Louis the Pious, although his authority does not seem to have been as great and his sons led intermittent rebellions. In the tenth century the ruler with the greatest authority over his subjects and the largest territories was unquestionably Otto I.

Until recent years the general tendency was to assume that medieval armies must have been small, as the inefficient, not to say primitive, infrastructures of European kingdoms were simply incapable of supporting large armies of tens of thousands in the field for a campaigning season. This view ultimately derived from Hans Delbrück, who argued that large figures in the sources must be exaggerated, while small numbers were much more likely to be correct. However, he did not present any good evidence for this assumption, nor was he particularly interested in the culture, methods and purposes of the people who recorded these figures. Even in recent years various historians have argued for small armies, including Philippe Contamine, Timothy Reuter, and most recently Guy Halsall. On the other side Karl Leyser and Bernard and David Bachrach have argued that the Carolingians and Ottonians could raise armies in the tens of thousands. In the kingdoms established after the disintegration of the Western Roman Empire, maintaining logistical support for their armies absorbed a large part of their resources and affected all aspects of social and political organization. If these aspects of military organization are considered at all in works on warfare, they are often dismissed with subjective statements or handled by comparisons with modern armies that may be entirely inappropriate. The best that can be done here is to make observations from what we do know and point out some of the problems.

It is certain that the armies raised after the collapse of central imperial authority in the fifth century were smaller than their Roman predecessors, which we can estimate better on the basis of the number of legions or other named units listed, making allowance for them being understrength, if the level of wastage was anything like that of early modern armies. Whereas estimates of twenty to thirty thousand do not seem unreasonable for many Roman armies, even most armies of the relatively well-organized Byzantine Empire seem to have fallen to between four thousand and ten thousand in our era. In exceptional circumstances Byzantine armies and those of the Caliphate may have numbered as many as their Roman predecessors'.[1]

There are many variables involved, however. In the period 750–1100 there was probably a steady increase in population, but that may have been greater in central and western Europe than in the Balkans and Anatolia. Manpower resources are obviously important, but so too is its productive capacity, which in this period meant essentially agrarian production. This in turn is dependent on climate, season, crop types, soil fertility, and agricultural technology. Movement and effectiveness of armies were dependent on the animals available for transportation and the infrastructure of communication, especially roads. Climate is variable, and the effect on agrarian production of repeated military campaigns in the same areas could be severe, with a possible knock-on effect on population. It is obvious from this list that there are so many variables involved that making any estimates based on them would be difficult, and it becomes almost impossible when we have virtually no accurate data to work with. This means that we have to fall back on comparable material, but it is rarely directly comparable. In Jonathan Roth's valuable work on the Roman army, he used nineteenth-century U.S. Army manuals to estimate the carrying capacity of pack animals, but the U.S. Army used specially bred mules with greater load-bearing capacities than the smaller Eurasian mules. Similarly, after the collapse of the Western Empire new species of "hard" wheat were introduced, which produced better bread with higher protein content than Roman wheats.

A clear difference between the logistical capacity of the Roman Empire at its height and its successors was the state of the roads, which declined rapidly after the mid-fourth century, even in the Eastern Empire. Nevertheless, the routes of Roman roads were known and used by Carolingian, Ottonian and Anglo-Saxon armies, as well as by enemies invading their territory. As mentioned earlier, bridge and road maintenance was a service demanded of local communities, but the roads were maintained as unpaved, which meant that they were more vulnerable to weather damage and needed more frequent repair. With the possible exception of a few paved Roman roads that survived in usable condition, in the Viking Era there was little significant difference between the roads of established Christian kingdoms and those in Scandinavia or eastern Europe, except that there were probably more of them. Pre-industrial revolution roads are extremely difficult to date. They tended to follow the contours of the land and are often marked by sunken lanes as they became deeper from use and tended to act as channels for run-off water. Many became wider as people avoided the rutted and potholed track by moving alongside it. Wooden trackways were often constructed to provide passage over waterlogged ground, but varied in length and quality from short stretches of brushwood to timber causeways covering several kilometers, sometimes supported on a foundation of stakes driven into the ground, possibly with additional foundations.

The lack of good roads meant a much higher dependence on pack animals as opposed to wheeled transport. Wheeled vehicles could move more easily along the wider roads in relatively flat or hilly terrain, but winter weather would have made this more difficult or wholly impractical, which is one reason for the rarity of winter campaigning. Many of the routes followed by armies were probably little more than tracks, especially those over mountains. On inclines in central Europe roads often had shallow steps, which were negotiable by pack animals but obviously not carts or wagons. However, wheeled transport was essential for the movement of some materials.

Anglo-Saxon and Carolingian roads linked settlements and sites of political and military strategic significance like *burhs* or other fortifications, settlements and monasteries, and were sometimes marked by marker stones, shrines, or crosses where they crossed moors or other inhospitable terrain. Western sources give little information on the difficulties of moving armies, but Byzantine military manuals contain some that must have been roughly comparable. The tenth-century emperor Nikephoros Phokas thought 24 kilometers (16 Byzantine *milia*) in the Tauros Mountains a difficult and tiring march for both men and horses. Vegetius gave a rate of 30 kilometers (20 Roman *milia*) in five hours on good road surfaces, although a faster pace of 24 *milia* in the same time was also practiced.[2] This might be increased further with a forced march, but this would always involve heavy loss of men and animals from fatigue. His rates were based on those for which the Imperial Roman army was trained, each man carrying his own basic equipment. On broken or hilly ground such as the Tauros troops on foot could march at approximately 3.2 kilometers (2 miles) per hour, as compared with (3) per hour on even ground. These are average speeds, but troops without encumbrance could be marched faster if necessary, while poor weather might make the going much more difficult. An average day's march might be some 20 kilometers or less, assuming that there was also a baggage train.[3]

Small forces moved faster than large ones, as there was a delay in each file setting off. The longer the column, the greater the delay in the rearmost starting and finishing the day's march. To take a simple example, if six thousand infantry traveled three abreast (on a road with a width of perhaps 3 meters) and there was a gap of 2 meters between each row, the column would be 4 kilometers long and even a short delay of five seconds between each row setting off would mean that it would take almost three hours for the whole column to pass a given spot on the route. Obviously the presence of animals and wagons in the army would make the column much longer, there would be delays for passing bottlenecks like bridges or crossing fords, and periodic rests would need to be taken.

Horses or mules needed at least one day in six as rest, to prevent injury to backs and feet. By comparison with men, in proportion to their carrying capacity they needed more in provisions and fodder. Even at rest Roman cavalry mounts probably required 6.8–9kg of fodder, approximately a quarter to a third barley, and the rest hay or grazing.[4] Modern horses are larger and bred differently from those in the Viking Era, and need more hard fodder. Ancient and early medieval horses needed to get about two-thirds of their nutrition requirements from grazing. The downside of this was that four to five hours' grazing was required every twenty-four hours. In addition, horses were vulnerable to regional and seasonal variations that affected grazing conditions. In wartime conditions horses could survive on

1.5kg of hard fodder per day, as opposed to perhaps 2.5kg in normal conditions, but they still needed some 7kg of dry fodder or 10kg of grazing.

Mules required at least as much hard fodder as horses, but about 25 percent less fodder in all, perhaps 6kg of dry fodder, usually hay. However, mules have the advantage that they can live on less rations and poor-quality grass and thistles. By comparison, donkeys carried 25 percent less, but needed slightly less feed. Whereas oxen converted protein more efficiently than equines, comparative figures suggest that they ate 7kg of hay and 11kg of mash. All of these animals needed large quantities of water: 22.75–36.4 liters per day for horses, depending on conditions,[5] at least 20 liters for mules and up to 30 liters for oxen.

Table 1 represents the feed requirements per day based on Jonathan Roth's estimates, which he made on the basis of Emperor Diocletian's *Edict of Prices*, Egyptian papyri, and modern data, and the carrying capacity of animals based on John Haldon's figures, for which he used Byzantine sources and the figures of other researchers. Roth estimated that donkeys and mules could carry about 25 percent more weight in total than the figures show.

Bernard Bachrach estimated the carrying capacity of a two-wheeled cart as 500kg and a four-wheeled wagon as 650kg.[6] Roman sources, Emperor Maurice and Leo VI recommended that each tent-group (*contubernium*) of eight men had one pack-animal, although Leo wrote that there should be an absolute minimum of one pack-animal for every thirty-two soldiers, usually for each group of sixteen, if soldiers were sent ahead of the main column.[7] John Haldon calculated that this would have allowed only a meagre ration

Table 1. Estimated feed requirements and carrying capacities of animals.

	Feed requirements of animals			Carrying capacities of animals			
	hard fodder (kg)	dry or greenfodder/ pasturage (kg)	water (liters)	man and equipment (kg)	military saddle (kg)	pack saddle (kg)	food (kg)
Donkeys	1.5	5.0/10.0	20			16–19	56.8
Mules	2.0	6.0/12.0	20			16–19	85
Oxen	7.0	11.0/22.0	30				
Horses	2.5	7.0/14.0	30	70	12		30
Pack-horses						16–19	85
Pack-animals*	2.0	5.5/11.0	20				

*as listed by Roth.

for each soldier, which suggests that the soldiers were probably expected to forage as well. In this case Leo was assuming that they would carry ten days' supplies. In his late sixth-century *Strategikon* Maurice recommended that cavalry carry four days' supplies. The rations of the tenth-century Byzantine soldiers consisted of bread, dried and salted meat, or alternatively cheese. The bread was baked in two forms, as ordinary bread and hard tack. This is not dissimilar from the state-provided rations of rank and file soldiers in Europe for most of the period up to the twentieth century, although gruel or porridge was also a staple food in barracks. Ancient and early medieval strains of wheat and barley had a higher protein content than modern strains, so that the bread ration alone would be sufficient to sustain men for the campaigning season, which it probably did on many occasions. As we will see, in Anglo-Saxon England and the Carolingian or Ottonian realms soldiers were required to bring their own rations for specified periods, which may have included other foodstuffs. Since water was often contaminated, beer was probably a staple drink. Anglo-Saxon food renders include ale, and Charlemagne demanded the transport of wine in the army's supply train.

An anonymous tenth-century Byzantine treatise on campaigning gives an estimate of the maximum amount of provisions that could be carried for a three-week cavalry march, adding that it was not possible for an army to transport more than twenty-four days' supply of barley for horses from its own country.[8] This treatise envisaged a force of 8,200 horsemen. As Haldon has estimated, with at least one thousand remounts and with each animal carrying 68kg of barley as feed for four to five days, as stipulated in a treatise of Constantine VII (905–959), 6,460 extra pack animals would be required to maintain the army in the field for a further eighteen days without a re-supply of hard fodder. The number of pack-animals could be reduced by taking more remounts and loading them, but each of them would carry half or less of the amount a pack-mule or donkey could carry. The solution must have been to accompany the force with a supply train including wagons and carts.

Vegetius specified a maximum load of just under 20kg per man (60 Roman pounds). On the weights of food calculated by Haldon, this would last about three weeks. In the tenth-century Byzantine army and under normal conditions most supplies were transported by pack animal or wagon. The total weight for an army of fifteen thousand would have been 288,400kg to last between two and three weeks. If the rate of march was some 20 kilometers per hour, which is optimistic, the army could cover 400–475 kilometers in three weeks. Supplies would have to be ready in advance at intervals of this distance. The problems of any army that transported plundered goods, cattle or slaves on its route home would obviously be increased, as even more transport would be required and slaves probably had to travel on foot, slowing down the rate of march, making the column longer and the whole force more vulnerable to attack.

Transport of armies and equipment by sea was obviously a major logistical exercise because of the number of ships required. The Vikings used their long-ships as troop transports and fighting vessels if necessary, and seized most of what they needed when they reached their destination, but the problem became much greater if an expedition required warhorses, which were very prone to seasickness, or even prefabricated defenses. Despite the relatively short crossing, William was faced with a major logistical problem in 1066, not least because the Normans possessed only a small fleet and had to acquire vessels from Flanders and elsewhere to raise a fleet that must have consisted of several hundred vessels.[9] The Bayeux Tapestry depicted transports that carried three, four, eight and ten horses. Clearly these were wider vessels than the Danish Ladby ship, and different from the Mediterranean horse transports, both suggested as a model for William's ships. Use of horse transports by the Scandinavians did not occur until 1135–1136, during the Danish king Erik Emune's expedition to Rügen.[10]

If we return to the start of this chapter, behind the discrepancy between attitudes to the capabilities of early medieval kingdoms and ancient kingdoms of similar size lies an assumption that has been noted before, that the medieval kingdoms of Europe were "more primitive" and less sophisticated than their ancient forebears. The latter, it is assumed, could raise large armies from citizens and peasants by much more efficient methods. As noted in the last chapter, there is a degree of truth in this, but medieval rulers certainly could raise large armies. It is to the way in which they were employed that we turn next.

Campaigning

As in the case of all medieval warfare, early medieval campaigning has frequently been represented as amateurish and unprofessional. In fact, virtually every "people" of Europe conducted warfare along similar principles.

These involved avoidance of battle in most circumstances and a concentration on relatively risk-free small-scale actions, attempts to secure strategic points, recognition of the value of surprise and cunning, and persistent ravaging of enemy territory. In Chapter 7 it is suggested that the ethos of the European aristocracy of Viking-Age Europe encouraged raiding and combat, whether it was feud or warfare. However, there were also sound military reasons for the strategy employed in campaigns. Battles were fought, and could decide the outcome of a campaign or a war, but this was usually only the case when leaders were killed or captured. The initial survival of Wessex when endangered by Viking conquest was probably as much a result of Alfred's survival as anything else. The risk of the leader being killed or taken, and of losing a substantial number of valuable troops, perhaps part of a military household, was considerable. At Hastings Harold lost both, and many of his family too. A strong case can be made that he should have employed a more attritional strategy against William, rather than opting for the lottery of battle without any clear advantage such as that he had achieved by surprising Harald Hardrada. Fighting a battle was a high-risk strategy precisely because it put the leader in much greater danger than other military actions.

Until very recently military historiography over-emphasized the importance of achieving a decisive victory in the field—largely a product of nineteenth-century military thinking, which demanded 'total war' with the object of complete victory over the enemy.[11] Complete victory was very difficult to achieve in medieval Europe. Charlemagne had to launch repeated destructive campaigns against the Saxons. The Wendish tribes of the south Baltic coast were eventually conquered and absorbed by colonization in the twelfth and thirteenth centuries, but 450 years of intermittent warfare and repeated attempts to force them into tributary status by successive German rulers, not to mention Poland and Denmark, had failed to do this earlier. Similarly, the English and subsequently the Anglo-Norman realm, one of the most centralized and organized kingdoms of Europe, had severe difficulties in bringing small Welsh kingdoms (later princedoms) to heel, and the last of them was finally conquered only after an enormous and very expensive effort by Edward I. They may not have written down their strategies and military thinking, but medieval commanders were well aware of the limitations on their military capability. These were organizational, logistical, and political.

Religious support

In the early Middle Ages it was essential for Christians to perform the correct religious preparations for war. Thus the *Consilium Germanicum* of 742 begins by emphasising that priests cannot serve in an army as fighting men, but also says that two or three bishops and a selected group of priests can serve with the army to provide pastoral care.[12] Not only were clergy expected to participate in ensuring the success of Charlemagne's campaigns when they accompanied the army, but also when they were at home. Prayers, special intercessory masses, public liturgical rites, and fasts throughout the realm were organized in support of the army.[13] Senior clerics such as Abbot Alcuin of York (d. 807), who acted as adviser to Charlemagne, were in no doubt of their value: as he set out to join the emperor on his campaign against the Saxons in 794, he assured Archbishop Riculf of Mainz that the Lord's angel would accompany the army if the proper religious preparations were made.

At home preparations such as those listed above helped to mobilize support for Carolingian campaigns from the people as a whole. For the army they were arguably even more important, as they represented a way of coming to terms with the sins that warfare inevitably involved, particularly homicide. By the mid-eighth century methods of regular cleansing of sin had been developed in Ireland and then England, from where they spread to the continent. Penitential manuals, often termed "tariff books" nowadays, listed sins and the penances required for them. Forms of homicide could then be differentiated, and that committed in the course of publicly or royally sanctioned warfare was regarded as less serious than other forms, hence requiring a lesser penance. The accompaniment of armies by large numbers of clerics enabled individuals to confess their sins before battle, thus ensuring that they would be cleansed of sin if they should die, and do penance after it. This was vital to the morale of the soldiers.

The pattern of clerical aid to armies established by Charlemagne was continued with minor modifications in the armies of the Carolingian, Capetian, Ottonian and Salian dynasties after his death. For instance, the clergy and people of the kingdom of Germany underwent penitential rites and prayed to God on behalf of Conrad II and his army before a campaign against the Slavic Liutici in 1035.[14] Increasingly kings made donations to monasteries and churches as a form of investment: in return the priests, monks, and nuns prayed for the king, the army, and the kingdom. The penitential aspect of rites before and after battle received more emphasis as Charlemagne's empire broke up and Christians frequently found themselves fighting other Christians. After Fontenoy in 841 a mass was said for the dead of both sides. The bishops of the victors, Charles the Bald and Louis the German, claimed the victory as a judgement of God that their cause was righteous, but held a three-day fast to mourn the fallen of both sides rather than a triumphal procession.[15]

The beliefs and rituals of the pagan Vikings and Slavs are obscure, as we are dependent on a mixture of place-name evidence, archaeological remains and accounts written by Christian authors, most of them produced some time after the conversion of the Scandinavians to Christianity. There was no "pagan religion" with a claim to universality like that of the monotheistic religions, but rather a large number of localized deities and cults. Even deities that were powerful throughout Scandinavia, such as Odin, Frey, and Thor, may have had a different relative importance in different regions and the rituals and cults surrounding them may have varied. Nevertheless, what we might call superstition certainly played a large part in battle. There may not have been any absolute morality such as that of Christianity or Islam, sanctioned by a higher power, but there were nevertheless supernatural powers that could be encouraged or even ensnared to favor one side in a struggle, and spells and rituals such as sacrifices would have been conducted to ensure their support. Thietmar of Merseburg mentions that the Slavic Liutizi tribal confederation practiced divination by lot-casting and walking a sacred horse over two crossed spears to ascertain whether a campaign would be successful or not.[16] As they were for the Greeks and Romans, forms of divination were no doubt practiced by all pagans. Christian scribes may have regarded pagan practices as magic or sorcery and their prayers as attempts to bend nature to the human will rather than appeals to the True God, but to pagans the prayers or other actions of the Christians must have seemed a form of magic. Although Christian authors sometimes ridiculed pagan superstitions, this does not mean they did not believe their sorcery could be effective. As Thietmar said of a Slav campaign in the reign of Otto II, "Without sustaining any losses and aided by their gods, they did not hesitate to ravage the rest of the [Saxony-Anhalt] region . . . ."[17] Clerical writers interpreted it as enlisting the aid of demons, in effect the power of the devil. God had greater power, but He did not favor those "Christians" who were not true to Him and He could use pagans to show His disfavor.

Attrition

Disease, starvation, and desertion were serious problems for medieval armies. The level of desertion is impossible to measure in the Viking Period, but we can be sure that it was high. Frankish laws stipulating the death penalty for this merely reinforce the point that it was a problem, as it continued to be in armies up to the nineteenth century. No commander was unaware of these problems, and accordingly they played their part in strategy: as noted elsewhere, one method of defending territory was to shut yourself up in fortresses and wait for them to take their toll. Small forces might be able to live off the land, but even that was dangerous. Water was often contaminated—hence the reason why so many armies carried alcoholic drink for their armies.

Examples of armies devastated by disease are common in the sources, particularly among forces fighting in the summer heat of Italy. The *Annals of Fulda* record the deaths of many of Carloman's army from a "terrible malady" in 877, and several Frankish armies besieging the Vikings were ravaged by disease. So too was the Magyar army in 923, according to Flodoard of Reims. Disease was no respecter of rank, as it took both Lothar II of Lotharingia and Charles the Bald (although, in a conspiracy theory typical of the age, the latter's death was also attributed to poison administered by his doctor). Armies were also dependent on their animals. The loss of the bulk of Charlemagne's horses during his campaign against the Avars in 791 has already been mentioned. In the same year a combined Frankish (in fact Saxon–Frisian) army in Bohemia "lost more horses than any mortal can remember."[18] In 896 King Arnulf's horses were apparently almost wiped out in Italy, so that most supplies had to be transported by oxen.[19] It is easy for us to underestimate the difficulties that relatively short marches could cause in the Middle Ages, if exceptionally bad weather or other misfortunes occurred.

Campaigning seasons

In western Europe the usual campaigning season appears to have been summer. There are repeated entries concerning Charlemagne's campaigns beginning in spring in the *Royal Frankish Annals*. Food had to be gathered for the men and fodder for horses and transport animals. The *RFA* specifically mentions that the Saxons rebelled when spring was approaching in 798, but the Frankish army was still in winter quarters because of lack of fodder. The date of the Frankish king's summons to assemble at the Marchfield marked the beginning of the regular campaigning season. This was originally 1 March, but changed to 1 May in the mid-eighth century, according to the continuation of Fredegar. This was probably because more long-distance campaigns were being made, requiring more supplies and more horses, if not more men.

However, although summer was the preferred season for campaigning, there were many occasions when it occurred earlier or later in the year. For instance, in 791 Charlemagne did not invade the Avar khaganate until 1 September. In winter proper, defeat was likely to result in disaster and foraging was difficult, although winter stores could be raided if all went well. In certain areas there were advantages to be gained from frozen ground. Rivers were crossed more easily and could even be used as highways, and marshes sometimes became passable. Nevertheless, the cold and the dangers of running out of supplies generally made winter campaigning high-risk, and for this reason it was rarely carried out unless a quick victory could be achieved. In January 859 Charles the Bald caught Louis the German by surprise and regained his kingdom. The sources give few details, but we can guess that Charles had raised forces and Louis was forced to retreat as his own were dispersed and wholly unprepared for a winter campaign.[20] At the same time of year Earl Harold Godwinesson's attack on the Welsh king Gruffydd ap Llywelyn in his palace at Rhuddlan in 1063 achieved total surprise, not least because Gruffydd believed he was at peace with England. Harold left Gloucester immediately after Christmas. He probably knew that the Welsh king's *teulu* had the right to leave him for a circuit of his townships after Christmas, and was therefore likely to be absent. His attack almost finished the campaign at a stroke, but Gruffydd escaped at the last minute. Nevertheless, it was the beginning of the end for him.[21]

Almost sixty years earlier, after what was apparently an indecisive campaign in which an army led by some of Sweyn Forkbeard's chieftains was shadowed by the English army (it is not quite clear which army was avoiding battle, if not both), the English army dispersed, King Æthelred II and his entourage went to Shropshire and the Viking army went to the Isle of Wight, but it then launched an unexpected winter campaign throughout Hampshire and Berkshire. Much plunder was gathered, and an army levied to oppose it was defeated on the way back to Wight. This led the king to make a truce with the Danes, pay tribute, and give further provisions to them. It seems that the Danes were no respecters of convention. On occasion campaigns continued throughout most of the winter. In the winter of 871 a campaign was fought in Wessex, in which the *ASC* claims nine battles were fought.[22] At this stage of the war for Wessex it seems that both King Æthelred of Wessex and his brother Alfred were attacking the Vikings whenever they raised sufficient forces to do so.

Routes and campaigning strategy

No scaled maps or anything resembling them were available to military commanders of the Viking Era. In all probability campaigning armies followed established routes, like the *herepaths* of England, or old Roman roads. Many of these would still have had milestones, although distances would often have been measured in time, like the times for travel round Norway given to Alfred by the merchant Othere.[23] We know that maintenance of roads and bridges was important to the Anglo-Saxons, Carolingians, and Ottonians, and measures were taken to ensure that local communities did the work. Many of the main routes were well known, preserved either orally or in writing and used for trade and the itineraries of kings and magnates around their lands as well as by armies. Landmarks would have been important for both land and sea travel. The importance of waterways as conduits for logistical support for armies is emphasized by Charlemagne's attempt to build a canal between the Danube and the Main–Rhine watershed in 792, as part of his preparations for a second massive invasion of Avar territory. The task proved beyond Carolingian capabilities or resources and it was abandoned at the end of 793. In the same year he ordered the construction of portable bridges that could be assembled and disassembled as required. Clearly navigable waterways were at the center of Viking strategy, as they were their main highways to the interior of the kingdoms they attacked.

One clue that Carolingian and Ottonian armies were often large is the strategy they adopted for crossing mountainous terrain. This strategy was employed by Charlemagne against the Avars in 791,[24] and was continued by his successors. Armies would usually muster at royal centers, whence they set out for the frontier region. Not only fortified centers but monasteries had a duty to supply the king and his entourage; many of them, of course, owed their existence to royal patronage. Once the army set out for enemy-controlled territory, routes that allowed resupply of the army or its contingents for as much of the journey as possible were chosen. In addition, maintaining contact with friendly settlements made easier the gathering of intelligence about the condition of routes and possible enemy activity. This was one reason for the establishment of landowners loyal to the king in the frontier districts. As an example, Louis the German is known to have been at the royal *palatium* of Aibling in March 855, perhaps his and his army's starting point for his campaign into Great Moravia. At least three routes to the River Drava were available from southeastern Bavaria, some following old Roman roads and crossing passes at over 1,000 meters. All would have utilized small settlements along the way, while use of more than one route would have reduced the strain on them and prevented the columns from becoming too strung out. Progress would have been slow, perhaps 10 kilometers per day.[25]

The multi-route invasion strategy had to be executed properly, either so that the different forces were capable of taking on the enemy alone, as Pippin did in 791, or so that they combined before they were likely to meet a substantial enemy army. After the Prˇemyslid duke Boleslav I ceased tribute payments to Germany in 935, and in response to an appeal for help from his Bohemian opponents, two armies were sent into Bohemia in 936, under the overall command of Count Asik. However, they failed to combine before Boleslav defeated each in turn. Only in 950 was the situation restored, when Otto I himself led an army comprising an "innumerable multitude" into Bohemia and intimidated Boleslav into submission.[26] In this case, as in the case of Charlemagne before him, not only the size of the army but the reputation of Otto probably played a part in Boleslav's submission.

Except for the fact that most armies moved as one body, the procedure used by the Carolingians was used by all armies of the period: gathering of supplies and assembly of the army at a central place, often a royal center, and then movement by established routes to the target area. Raids into enemy territory would also follow known routes such as old roads or rivers, but it would be hoped that the army could send out parties to cut a swathe of destruction around its path. If the object was simply to ravage, the army would preferably return by a different route to avoid passing through devastated territory on the return march. Such expeditions involved considerable expense and logistic planning, as armies could not rely on foraging alone, even if the distance covered was shorter than many of the Carolingian expeditions. Even if battle were avoided, a campaign was a high-risk enterprise. Once the Vikings adopted the strategy of overwintering in enemy territory, they created their own bases of operation, such as an island or easily fortified coastal or riverside site, often someone else's royal center, a monastery, or even a town. These places functioned as "anchorages" for their fleet while they traveled across land on their plundering expeditions, after seizing horses for the purpose.

Scouts (*exploratores*) are occasionally mentioned and must have been employed, but there is no clear evidence as to how efficiently scouting was carried out. Small parties and even armies were sometimes ambushed, but this has occurred in all wars and all ages. Moreover, even with scouting parties information had to be gathered from local people, and was not necessarily reliable. There may not have been specialist scouts in the modern sense, but experienced men with local knowledge would have been chosen whenever possible.

Destruction, plunder and slave-taking

"Never before has such terror appeared in Britain as we have now suffered from a pagan race. . . . Behold, the church of St. Cuthbert, spattered with the blood of the priests of God, despoiled of all its ornaments; a place more venerable than all in Britain is given as a prey to pagan peoples."[27] These are the well-known words of the late eighth-century religious scholar Alcuin of York, part of a letter to Æthelred, king of Northumbria. A century later and far to the east, the Baghdad-born traveler Al-Mas'ūd-ī reported Rus raids on the shores of the Caspian: "The Rus spilled rivers of blood, seized women and children and property, raided and everywhere destroyed and burned."[28] Whereas attacks in a family feud were conducted with strict objectives, usually regarded as commensurate with the injury done, raids needed no such provocation and almost invariably involved destruction. To peoples who had the means to raid others and to reach targets that were sufficiently "soft" not to be too costly to attack, this represented an extension of the hunting culture, which was also part wealth and food acquisition and part proof of prowess. The ship technology of the Viking Era gave the Vikings, and to a lesser extent the Wends, Kuronians, and Estonians, the opportunity to conduct long-distance raids, which reduced the chance of retaliatory invasion.

It was impossible to intercept fleets at sea or defend long coastlines or frontiers, which was why attempts to defend territory against the Vikings usually involved the construction of fortifications inland. However, the only coherent and successful attempt was Alfred's burghal system of the late ninth century. This is examined in more detail in Chapter 6. Charles the Bald also adopted a strategy of blocking rivers by fortified bridges. However, neither West Francia in the ninth century nor England in the late tenth century was able to adopt a sufficiently coherent strategy or maintain enough fortified sites to defend all their territory in depth. The attempts of Charles and his successors and Æthelred II to do so were undermined by lack of unity and support among their subjects. In West Francia many nobles were only too willing to hire the Vikings to attack their enemies, while many people in northern England were only too willing to make an accommodation with Sweyn.

By their nature raids had restricted objectives, although they might form part of a wider military strategy to weaken the enemy's economic base and possibly to show enemy rulers as powerless to protect their wealth or people. In effect, in an age when successful leadership in war was regarded as essential for any ruler, this meant that the ruler was incapable of ruling well. However, the immediate object of raiding was invariably the seizure of portable wealth, which might then be converted into status and even lead to the acquisition of landed wealth. If carried out by an army of an established ruler, a raid might increase his wealth at the expense of his enemy, or at the very least help to defray the cost of campaigning. Wealth was obtained through plunder, ransoming of valuable objects or captured people, sale of captives (slaves), or extraction of tribute such as the danegeld.[29] For this reason plundering and destruction were a matter of deliberate policy, but much of it must also have been carried out on an *ad hoc* basis by troops whose own supplies of food were often intermittent and also as a means of attacking the enemy whom they no doubt resented. When an enemy force approached, people living in the area often went into hiding in remote places or defended sites, which might save their lives, but did not guarantee their long-term survival if their crops and livestock were destroyed or taken.

Ravaging, however, was more than a consequence of plundering raids or a by-product of inadequate logistics or discipline. It was a central component of medieval warfare. "The main and principal point in war is to secure plenty of provisions and to destroy the enemy by famine." So says Vegetius, writing at a time when the object of strategy in the Roman Empire was to keep its frontiers intact. Despite the apparent differences, the later Roman Empire employed strategies that were not dissimilar to those of the developing states of Viking-Age Europe, at least after the period of Carolingian expansion was over: notably defense in depth and incapacitating hostile tribal confederations beyond the frontier by campaigns of destruction. How far Viking-Era commanders (or, for that matter, late Imperial Roman commanders) actually followed the precepts of Vegetius is a matter for conjecture. Ravaging was an attack on the economic infrastructure of an opposing lordship's strength and an attempt to weaken him psychologically. Land was the main component of a lordship's wealth, with its associated crops, livestock, and peasantry, and the seizure or destruction of these was therefore a relatively risk-free method of attack. In addition, crops and animals could be utilized to supply the army, both men and horses. Although the general level of plundering may have been exceptional during the periods when Viking, Magyar, or Saracen raiding was at its worst, the acquisition of plunder was one of the main motivations for offensive campaigns throughout the Middle Ages, and in this respect nothing changed. These attacks may be classed as raids, but many were carried out on a very large scale, especially by the Magyars.

Harrying alone might bring about the submission of the enemy, particularly if the demand was for payment of tribute or the surrender of disputed frontier territory; if the intent was conquest or the removal of the opposing prince, he was more likely to resist. However, in such cases harrying could also put pressure on subordinates or potential rivals to remove the reigning leader, particularly if they thought there was little prospect of success in the war. Persistent harrying might also compel an enemy to offer battle. In 1066 William's harrying of Kent, where Harold held land, was a contributing factor in bringing about the battle that did more than anything else to enable his conquest of England. Although Harold may have been unwise to offer battle so hurriedly, a factor working in William's favor was that Harold may not have felt entirely secure on the throne of England—not that any of the English nobility favored William as king, but any sign of failure on Harold's part might provoke rebellion. On the Slavic frontier the Carolingian and Ottonian kings frequently used rivals to the existing tribal rulership in their campaigns.

The safest strategy when defending against ravaging was to maintain a force in the field while shadowing and harassing the enemy, thus forcing him to keep his troops together as smaller ravaging parties were at risk, which made it difficult to supply the army. At the same time chattels, people, and perhaps animals could be moved out of the invader's way, either to the wilderness or into fortifications. Indeed, fortifications began to play an increasingly large part in this strategy as their number increased in the eleventh century. The construction or capture of castles became the key to controlling territory. If an attempt was made to take a castle by siege, the "low-risk" method of preventing this was to maintain an army in the vicinity of the besiegers, thus making it impossible for them to supply their army effectively or ravage the surrounding area. Thus castles were most effective for blocking an enemy advance when there was an army within striking distance of the threat. At the same time attempts would be made by both armies to harass the other, whilst keeping an eye on a possible ambush or surprise attack on a fortification. This is precisely the sort of warfare conducted around the frontier districts of their lands by the magnates of France in the eleventh century, such as Geoffrey Martel of Anjou and William of Normandy in their struggle for Maine in the 1050s.[30]

A more drastic defensive policy was scorched earth, which obviously did more damage to the defender's own resources. Even if this was not employed to its fullest extent, it was preferable to destroy resources that could not be moved out of the enemy's reach, such as crops. These strategies often produced favorable results, as long as a leader remained secure at home. However, the longer a leader holed up in a fortification and waited for the enemy to go away, the more likely this strategy was to annul his authority as a leader in war.

Faced with the formidable armies of the Carolingians and Ottonians, the Slavic princes often adopted an attritional strategy. Louis the German's invasion of 855 was a failure, probably considerably worse than the *Annals of Fulda* let on, but even they admit that "he returned home without victory . . . ." Rastislav shut his forces and as much material as he could gather in his fortresses, whence they sometimes sallied out to harass the enemy. Louis devastated the surrounding territory, but obviously supplies ran short and losses mounted. He had no choice but to retreat, harassed by the Slavs on the way. They followed the routes of his army into the marcher lands, destroying many settlements along the Danube. This suggests that while it is probable that he had entered Pannonia and Moravia by the southern routes described below, he retreated via the northern route.

In 805 three armies invaded Bohemia from different directions: Saxony in the north, Bavaria in the south, and the main army along the Upper Main through the Bohemian Forest. They reunited in the Bohemian basin, but failed to take the fortress of Carnburg. The Bohemians hid in inaccessible places, according to the RFA, refusing to do battle with the enemy host. After forty days of harrying, the *Annals of Metz* explained, the invaders were forced to return, as they lacked fodder for the horses and food for the army.[31] The next year another campaign took place, but the annalist's statement that this occurred "without serious incident" indicates that it too achieved little. These campaigns set the pattern for many subsequent invasions of Bohemia, in which the defenders retreated to their strongholds, presumably removing as many chattels and people as they could from the countryside, and attempted to "outstarve" the attackers.

During ravaging and shadowing operations there would have been clashes between small groups of opposing troops, as one force tried to harry the territory or acquire supplies and plunder and their opponents tried to stop them. On occasions this strategy escalated to more or less systematic harassment of an army or repeated small-scale attacks, which might even be remembered as a single "battle." The most famous "battle" of this type occurred before our period, in the Teutoberg Forest in 9 AD, when Varus's Roman legions were destroyed in a series of ambushes. Fighting of this type, if perhaps on a smaller scale, must have occurred often in the Viking Era. After the Lechfeld in 955 the Magyar army was destroyed in a prolonged pursuit. In their campaign of 938 in Saxony they failed to make any headway against fortifications and suffered from attritional skirmishes as small parties of foragers and raiders were attacked. The Vikings themselves used these tactics during King Arnulf of East Francia's first campaign in 891, targeting his supply trains and ambushing them from the forests, forcing him to retire and reorganize. Invading armies were very vulnerable when returning laden with plunder. The same King Arnulf suffered serious losses in ambushes when withdrawing from Moravia after a raid in 893. According to Snorri, in one of Olaf Haraldsson's (the later St. Olaf's) early expeditions the Vikings were on the receiving end. He describes a day-long series of ambushes as occurring during the return from a raid into "Finnland" (here almost certainly the south of present-day Finland or Karelia):

> The day wore on, and the king [Olaf] returned towards his ships. But when they passed through the forest, they were attacked on all sides with arrow fire. The king bade his men protect themselves as best they could and advance against the enemy, but that was diffi-

cult because the Finns hid behind trees. And before the king left the forest behind, he had lost many men, and many were wounded before he reached the ships late in the evening.[32]

An added ingredient in medieval campaigns of ravaging was terror. The infliction of what we would call atrocities on the general population was a commonplace of ancient, medieval, and renaissance warfare, but it could also be carried out as a matter of policy, or alternatively reduced in return for support. Rough treatment could lead to depopulation through flight. Movement of people to safer places was acceptable to a defender, but uncontrolled flight could cause problems. Flodoard of Reims mentions that the mere rumor of an attack by the Magyars was enough to cause panic and mass flight across Lotharingia and northern France in 927, which must have seriously disrupted the local economy.[33] For local lords or rural communities brutality was also an added incentive to come to terms with the invader, either by payment or provision of supplies.

The failure of a lord to protect his people undermined his standing, both with them and with his men; apart from being unable to prevent losses in possessions or even lives, he was failing in one of his chief tasks: as a leader in war. In loose political structures such as confederations of tribes or petty kingships, often brought together by the force of one leader, any failure on his part was liable to lead to the disintegration of his authority and the melting away of his military forces. After a long and successful career (certainly by Welsh standards) as king of most of Wales, Gruffydd ap Llywelyn was brought down by Harold and Tostig in 1062–1064 as he failed to prevent them from devastating or threatening to devastate territories belonging to those who owed him allegiance, and they pursued him even into his mountain fastnesses. It was Gruffydd's former tributary kings who bought themselves peace and thus brought the English campaign to a successful conclusion by murdering him. Even when their power base was more secure, lords were supposed to protect their subjects. Not only were they supposed to defend the interests of those who owed them service, but also to reward them with riches or land and gain them prestige. So important was it to demonstrate this capacity that some newly appointed kings conducted a harrying campaign soon after their accession. For the Irish kings of the southern Ui'Neill, ravaging Leinster immediately after succession seems to have become such a strong tradition that it was almost part of the succession ritual.[34] In this case, however, there were other motives, as the kings of Leinster were unwilling clients of the Uí'Neill high kings, and had to be "encouraged" to renew their client status with the new king, as the relationship was with the former king, not with his polity or his kindred.

Destruction was not only meted out on enemy territory. There was probably always a certain amount of this as many of the troops who passed through "friendly" territory did not necessarily feel any affinity to the people there, even when they were subject to the same overlord. For instance, in the kingdom of Scotland, with its diverse languages and ethnicities in this period, there is no particular reason why Galwegians should have felt any sympathy towards the people of Lothian (former northern Northumbria), or the latter towards the people of the northern highlands. They even spoke different languages. Similarly, although a mutually intelligible language may have been spoken, in Germany the people of Bavaria may have felt little affinity with the people of Saxony, or even of neighboring Swabia. If there were supply problems the soldiers would have been compelled to pillage wherever they were. The *Annals of St. Bertin* record that in 868: 'the squadron which King Charles [the Bald] sent with Carloman across the Seine laid waste some territory, it is true, but did nothing of any use as far as resisting the Northmen was concerned—and that after all was the purpose for which they had been sent.'[35] The squadron (*scara*) was a detachment of household troops, commanded by the king's son. Similarly, in 1006 "the campaign caused the people of the country [England] every kind of harm, so that neither the native raiding army nor the foreign [Danish] raiding army did them any good."[36] It is not easy to distinguish the actions of poorly disciplined or controlled soldiery from deliberate destruction or robbery, but when this occurred among subject peoples who were not in rebellion it is unlikely that the ruler endorsed it: he may not have been concerned about the welfare of peasants, but they were an economic resource and kings were supposed to protect their people. However, there were occasions when a scorched earth policy was deemed a military necessity to deny resources to an invading enemy.

One of the best known campaigns of destruction of our era was carried out by William the Bastard/Conqueror in 1069: the infamous "harrying of the north." Other campaigns may have been equally destructive, Charlemagne's invasions of Saxony and the Avar khanate among them, but there are fewer sources for them and those that do exist are heavily partisan. Orderic Vitalis claimed that William's harrying caused the death of 100,000 people, mainly from famine and disease: no doubt he exaggerated, but it is probable that a large number died in terms of the contemporary population of England.[37] In fact, the 1069–1071 campaigns in northern England involved the English and three invading armies: the Normans, the Danes, and the Scots.

William's rule in England was not fully secure in 1069, so it is debatable whether the north of England was friendly or enemy territory; one motive for his harrying may have been to weaken potential rebel landowners by destroying their resources of food and manpower. However, another motive, perhaps the most important, was to deny the Danish army the resources to conduct a campaign there in the following year. In northern England there had been continual dissatisfaction with existing lords and consequent disorder for four years, beginning well before William's invasion of England. A succession of earls had been removed, including Tostig Godwineson, but then the northerners went too far and called in a foreign army, which was a major threat to William's newly won kingdom. If correct, William of Malmesbury's claim that William ordered his troops to hit the coastal districts of Yorkshire particularly hard after the Danes had left is an indication of William's priorities.[38] The Danes were the greatest threat to William, and it was they who had brought about the annihilation of his substantial garrison in York. William paid them off, just as his Anglo-Saxon predecessors had done, and allowed them to subsist on the resources of the coastal districts in return for a promise to leave for home. They did not do this, but William bought time to make sure they could not return to Yorkshire.

In 1069 the Danes were not the only foreign army in England: the Scots had also intervened and were not far to the north. A traditional interpretation of Malcolm Canmore's invasion is that he was taking advantage of the problems in England to launch a plundering raid, and there is no doubt that the Scots plundered northern England for loot, cattle and slaves throughout the Middle Ages, but there is also a good case to make that he too was supporting the rebels, or hoping to detach northern Northumbria (to which the King of Scots had a traditional claim) from England. Edgar Atheling and his sister Margaret, grandchildren of King Edmund Ironside, had both been at Malcolm's court and Edgar returned to England twice, the second time joining the Danes, in abortive attempts to re-establish his claim to the throne. To William, the Scottish invasion may have appeared a further demonstration that his kingdom was in danger of disintegration. The Scots retired after the harrying of southern Northumbria and the departure of the Danes, and no doubt, as reported, they did lots of damage on the way, probably a combination of a deliberate attempt to make something out of the expedition and the traditional behavior of medieval troops in foreign lands. The reckoning with Malcolm was delayed until 1073, when he was forced to submit to William.

Viking strategy

The Vikings presented new problems to those they attacked. Throughout their campaigns they took fleets far inland on navigable rivers, and at no time in their 250-year rampage were their enemies able to stop them doing this, even though some well thought-out attempts were made, notably by Charles the Bald, and during a temporary period of successful warfare by the Wessex kings Alfred and Edward the Elder. The early raids were carried out by small bands, but from the mid-ninth century onwards these increased in size to become substantial armies of several thousand. Although their leaders were often called kings or jarls by their enemies, it is usually not clear what status they had in Scandinavia. In general the ninth-century campaigns do not appear to have been led by those who held power in Scandinavia itself—on the other hand, Scandinavian kings may well have had a hand in the sacking of many of the trading emporia of northern Europe, as they had an interest in transferring the trade to sites they controlled. According to the *Royal Frankish Annals*, in 808 King Godfred destroyed the Slavic center Reric and transferred the merchants to Hedeby. His son Horik I (d. 854) seems to have attempted to curb the activities of some Viking leaders, presumably because success in wealth-gathering by raiding could make them potential rivals for the kingship, and claimed that he had nothing to do with attacks on Frisia.[39]

From 865 to 880 a series of campaigns was made year after year by the "great army" (*micel here*) in England. In the *Anglo-Saxon Chronicle* the movements of this army usually appear as the first entry in each year, which began on 24 September. The Vikings seem to have attacked East Anglia after this, as Edmund is recorded as having been killed in winter. His feast day was on 20 November. John of Worcester claimed that the Danes attacked York on 1 November 866, and they invaded Wessex in January 878. The timing was no accident, as this was the period when wealth and food renders such as churchscot were stockpiled after harvest time. Furthermore the targets of the Viking attacks were invariably secular and ecclesiastical centers such as royal vills or monasteries, or towns that still had some Roman walls: York in 866, London in 870, Reading in 870–871 and Chippenham in 878. They were easily adapted to become fortifications. Most armies dispersed for winter at precisely the time when the Vikings made these attacks, so that the English kings were faced with the prospect of raising forces with difficulty and attempting an assault on a fortified site if they wanted to remove the menace. Several such assaults were made in the spring, with conspicuous lack of success. The most notable disaster was the Northumbrian attack on York in March 867, which resulted in the death of two kings.

Although the different Viking forces were not necessarily on good terms with one another, there was sufficient contact and movement across the seas for them to be aware of political developments in different realms. In general they aimed for "soft targets." Any sign of failure to resist their attacks led to the appearance of more predators. All the important centers of Brittany were overrun within the space of a decade in the early tenth century after the success of initial attacks. Conversely, when resistance stiffened and wealth acquisition (or land acquisition, in the case of England) became difficult, the Viking bands moved elsewhere. After Alfred's victories and Guthrum's submission in 879, a new army arrived to overwinter at Fulham, but it went to Francia. The Frankish annals note the sudden upturn in Viking activity there. The Vikings concentrated on the weakest point, northern Lotharingia (now the Low Countries), but their activities spread southwards into West Francia. The heavy defeat at the Dyle in 891 seems to have caused many to move back to England. As in the 860s, they arrived in several groups and camped at different places before combining into one army. However, their campaign in Wessex achieved little, faced with its revamped defenses. Many of these Vikings returned to Francia. They were joined by newcomers, but it is likely that some of these were from Ireland, where their presence had been virtually eliminated by 902. Some of their leaders were granted settlements on the Loire and in Normandy, but Brittany was the main sufferer. From 914 on the Vikings returned to Ireland and re-established themselves in their old *longphorts*.

It is no accident that attacks on West Francia intensified in the 840s, when strife between the sons of Louis the Pious tore the Carolingian Empire apart. Nevertheless, for all the limitations on the power of kings such as Charles the Bald, West Francia was never in danger of being conquered, as it remained one kingdom and it was simply too large. The strategy of the Vikings there appears to have been to plunder an area until it was exhausted or they were bought off. Nor were their wealth-acquiring activities limited to plunder, as rival magnates were more than willing to employ them as mercenaries or pay them to attack a rival's land. In England the Vikings were faced with smaller kingdoms and regularly retired from one kingdom to a more pacified neighbor to recoup or spend the winter. The kingdoms of Anglo-Saxon England were in a sense "ideal targets," as they were relatively stable, wealthy, and centralized by the ninth century, but also quite small.

The situation in Ireland was different again. West Francia was too large to make an assault on one political or ecclesiastical center a serious threat to the kingdom, while in Ireland there were no vills or urban political centers. The nominal centers of kingship, such as Tara, were ancient places possibly retained for reasons of tradition and as "neutral" centers of high kingship that did not deprive rival or client kings of any site important to their kindred.[40] The sociopolitical structures of Ireland may have had their own internal logic, and indeed were based on a body of widely accepted law, but the intricacies of client relationships and the sheer proliferation of "kings" of varying client status may have been beyond the Vikings. Removal of one king did not lead to the collapse of a polity, but his replacement by someone from his extensive kindred or a neighbor, even if it led to a power struggle first. Alliance with one king usually entailed enmity with another, or several others, and the instalment of puppet kings was unlikely to succeed as it did in England with the likes of Ceolwulf II of Mercia. Unlike in England and Francia, the Scandinavians in Ireland were not paid to agree to a truce or go away, as Irish kings did not have the resources to raise gelds repeatedly. The Vikings found out soon enough where the centers of wealth were in Ireland, and there were plenty of monasteries and nunneries to plunder, but they may have had difficulty in assessing the potential strength that kings could muster against them. It was in Ireland that the Vikings met their first serious defeats in battle, beginning in 848 with Máel Sechnaill's victory in Meath.

In the late tenth century the unification (or reunification) of Denmark under one king stabilized the situation, although the new dynasty still hoped to gather wealth by plunder. Ian Howard has argued that the development of heavy cavalry armies persuaded the Vikings that they had little chance of success in any attack on Germany, whereas England, without such an army, was a more feasible target. This seems highly unlikely, although it is certainly the case that the defeat suffered in 990 would not have encouraged any attack on Germany. However, there were two other reasons for desisting from attacks on Germany. The first was that it was a large and powerful neighbor, which could easily retaliate with an invasion of Denmark. The second, a problem that applied equally to West Francia, was the proliferation of fortifications. As will be seen, there was an element of planning in this, in Germany at least, but the steadily increasing number of private fortifications made raiding much more difficult. Although the level of planning was not the same, the Vikings were increasingly faced with the same problem in Francia and Germany that they had met in Wessex in the 790s. Without capturing key fortifications, they were unable to secure much plunder and their foragers were under threat from the garrisons.

There was also a positive reason for Sweyn to attack England—he and his chieftains may have expected some support in England, where they must have known there had been Danish settlement. If this was a hope, it turned out that it was not unfounded, as a kind of hybrid English–Danish culture seems to have developed there.[41] In the event, the victory at *Maldon*, whoever commanded the Vikings there, was sufficient to encourage further attacks. Moreover, the best route to profit for Norwegian and Swedish Vikings was to join Sweyn's armies. The Viking threat of the late tenth century thus became largely concentrated on England, although the Vikings of the Irish Sea, Western Isles, and Orkney (no doubt with support from Norwegian friends) continued to cause problems for Scottish kings and *mormaers* in the west and north of Scotland.

In the late tenth century the aims of Sweyn Forkbeard developed from extracting large payments from England to outright conquest, which he achieved in 1013–1014. The former could be achieved by causing widespread damage, or even, perhaps, by simply avoiding defeat, as Æthelred paid for truces to buy time, rather than to persuade the Danes to leave the kingdom. Conquest required submission from all of England and the removal of Æthelred. As the Great Army had done before him, Sweyn used royal centers and monasteries as bases and targeted them to extract wealth. However, during his campaign for the kingship he needed to obtain the submission and support of key centers. Ian Howard has shown that his marches often followed the routes of old Roman roads. He endeavored to keep London within a week's march but often struck out at other targets such as Oxford. The English forces had to attempt to prevent a descent on London, but could not be sure of Sweyn's intentions. One by one the other large towns submitted: York, Lincoln, Norwich, Thetford, and Winchester, two under threat of the destruction that had already been meted out to much of the countryside, three without much difficulty.[42] Whether the *burh* defenses had fallen into disrepair or not, Æthelred was faced with a lack of will to resist on his behalf. The Danish army had inspired fear, and clearly some of the towns that were well defended did not believe any English army would come to their aid. There is no evidence that Oxford and Winchester, or the smaller towns of Bath and Wallingford, were not well fortified, but they surrendered nonetheless. Only London resisted successfully, but even it submitted in the end.

The road to battle

How was a battle brought about? With or without scouts, the likelihood of armies accidentally running into each other was not high, even if higher than might be thought given that armies tended to use a limited number of routes when campaigning. This made ambushes a possibility, particularly in hostile territory. Whatever happened at Stamford Bridge, all sources agree that the Norwegian army was caught unprepared, which represents a total failure to gather intelligence, for which Harald Hardrada has to be held culpable. Generally, information from scouts could be used as effectively to avoid battle as to bring it about. A number of battles and assaults on fortified sites resulted from attempted surprise attacks. Despite the image of medieval warfare as unsophisticated, army commanders were always on the lookout for this type of opportunity, as it gave them the chance to inflict losses and possibly even a severe defeat without the risks that a battle between two prepared armies entailed to them and their armies.

Passes and river crossings on these routes were good places to await the enemy, either blocking his path or in ambush. It was possible for a commander to nominate a battlefield and challenge the enemy to meet his army there, as Håkon the Good is said to have done when he fought the sons of Erik Bloodaxe in 955. In 1006 the Viking army in England camped at Cuckhamsley Barrow, Berkshire, and challenged the English to give battle there, as they had said that no enemy who reached it would see the sea again. The English failed to turn up. The nomination of the field had something in common with the restricted area in which single combats took place—indeed, *Egils saga* uses the fanciful image of a field marked out by hazel twigs at *Brunanburh*, a reference to a method used for judicial combat among the Vikings, thus taking the idea of battle as a duel one step further. Even when a challenge was not delivered by messenger, there were other ways of issuing one. Occupation of a site important to the enemy, such as a royal estate or an estate owned by the king's or chieftain's family or otherwise important to them was also an indirect challenge. Later in the period besieging a fortified site of this type became one way of attempting to provoke a battle, although shadowing the besiegers could be equally effective.

Chapter 5

Battle

Battles were often climactic events in which one or both sides might lose a substantial proportion of their armies in one day, sometimes within the space of a few hours. They were also seen as important events by many ancient and medieval authors, but their idea of a battle was not necessarily ours, nor were battles necessarily decisive. As Ryan Lavelle notes, to the chroniclers of Alfred's 871 campaign a battle was an encounter which involved the king and his ealdormen.[1] In earlier times, when armies often seem to have met by arrangement at a predetermined place, frequently a landmark, it may have been the location that determined whether an encounter was regarded as a battle. Then and later, the set-piece nature of an encounter, in which both sides prepared and carried out certain preliminaries before the fighting started, may have been important.

In the Viking Era many army commanders died in battle. In a period when political bonds were personal, when the loyalty of an army's rank and file was usually to its leader, and political and military command were usually held by the same person, the death or capture of one of the army commanders would be more decisive than the numbers lost. This is reflected in medieval accounts of battles, in which deaths of important men were recounted but no attempt was made to give realistic casualty numbers. In 871 an encounter in the field without king or ealdormen, no matter how many men were involved, could not be "decisive," perhaps not even significant, such was their importance to the army.

It may be asked why the early medieval idea of battle matters, since we can make our own decisions as to whether an action was a battle or not, but the problem relates to the sources, as what was perceived as a battle in 800 may be reinterpreted later according to later concepts. For instance, a battle, so defined because the king was present, is later assumed to have involved thousands of men, because it was called a battle. Whether an encounter is given a name may determine whether it is later perceived as important, or even remembered at all. The size of contending forces that distinguished a battle from any other clash is also relative to the size or population of the polities involved: battles in pre-Viking Ireland may have involved a few hundred men at most, but this may have represented a substantial proportion of those eligible to fight and possibly the entire force of seasoned warriors led by a king or kings on each side. In any case the numbers involved in a medieval battle are usually uncertain: those given by the sources mean very little beyond conveying the idea that a battle or losses were large or small. We should also be wary of claims of victory. Apart from the problem of how this is defined, commanders and their servants from Ramesses II to Kutuzov and Saddam Hussein have been economical with the truth.

The modern image of a "Viking battle" is often one created by the movie industry, by "historical" novels, and even comics, and more recently by re-enactors and wargamers. There may be some reality in this image; for instance, the term "shield-wall" is familiar to most people who have any interest in the Vikings, whether fictional or historical, and as the authors of heroic poetry intended, it conjures up an image of warriors lined up shield-to-shield (or shield-rim against the boss of the shield next to it) to face the enemy. Unfortunately, we can never be certain about the reality of a Viking Era battle. Most of the stresses of a medieval campaign were likely to be caused by fatigue, hunger and disease, sometimes interspersed with skirmishes. Large-scale conflict was largely confined to sieges. A battle, should it have occurred, must have represented an intense concentration of energy, emotion and horror in a short space of time.

As mentioned in Chapter 1, many of our accounts of warfare in the Viking Age are colored by classical terminology or borrowings of whole passages from classical authors. In descriptions of formations we encounter the *phalanx, cohort, testudo, cuneus,* and *turma.* When he wrote about the Battle of Sherston in 1016, Richard Abels realized that John of Worcester's account of formations and tactics, the most detailed we have, was adapted from Sallust. However, various scholars have argued that this account drew on lost versions of the *ASC* or other earlier texts, and Bernard Bachrach has argued that much more of the Roman tradition of war, like other Roman institutions, was inherited by the Germanic kingdoms of the early medieval west than was once thought. To some extent it is a question of what medieval authors understood of the Latin texts they used and what they were trying to do when they wrote. It seems reasonable to conclude that they knew a *phalanx* and a *testudo* were close-order infantry formations, but turma was used more loosely by the Romans, not always for a cavalry unit. Perhaps Bachrach was right, and John consciously used appropriate phrases for what he was trying to describe, but this requires a leap of faith. If we accept that John was not trying to write history in the modern sense, and accuracy as regards detail of events often took second place to moral discourse, demonstration of knowledge of classical texts and style, and sometimes entertainment, we must have severe doubts. But should we then discard the *cuneus* (wedge), which has been widely accepted as a formation used by Viking armies?

In the Viking Era battles involving all or a high proportion of contending forces were uncommon, but more common than in the High Middle Ages. The change in the pattern of warfare was in part a cultural change, but it also came about through a steady increase in the number of fortifications. This pattern was already evident in Francia in the late tenth and eleventh centuries. Fulk Nerra was count of Anjou for fifty years and for much of that period he was at war, but he fought only two battles, both in the early period of his rule.

Preparation for battle

In the ancient and medieval eras the period immediately before a battle opened was vital. It was then that a commander could carry out actions that would influence the progress of the battle and its outcome, whereas once battle was joined his power to alter its course was very limited. If one army awaited another the commander could choose his ground. The only tactical decision recorded in Asser's account of Ashdown (871) is the Vikings' positioning of their army on high ground. Standing on higher ground than the enemy gave a morale advantage. Should the enemy choose to attack uphill the advance was slowed, the troops tired more rapidly and their formation might break up, particularly if they had many cavalry. Harold knew this well when he chose to await William on Senlac Ridge.[2] Positioning behind marshland or other terrain difficult to cross could give similar advantages. On occasion these were augmented by man-made obstacles, which could be hidden from the enemy. It has even been argued that the Bayeux Tapestry shows stakes placed in front of the English army, although they may be representations of vegetation. The Vikings were adept at using defenses, regularly digging banks round their camps on shores and riverbanks as a precaution, or improving existing structures with improvised defenses. Structures such as these, marsh, forest, watercourses, or inaccessible hills also provided useful obstacles on which to rest the flank of an army.

Since the routes used by armies were limited, it was also possible to lay an ambush for an approaching enemy, using uneven ground or forest for cover. Other methods of surprise attack included night approaches and dawn attacks, but this ran the risk of the approaching army falling into confusion. An attempt to do this at Andernach in 876 resulted in disaster for Charles the Bald.[3] As will be seen, however, armies sometimes chose to meet on even terms, on suitable ground for a battle that favored neither side. Even then there were advantages to be had if one army could attack with the wind or the setting or rising sun behind it.

Whether the combatants were pagan, Christian or Moslem, there was a strong ritual as well as practical element to preparation for battle. This might take the form of religious rituals such as prayers and masses. For Christians and Moslems, if it was helpful to form up on higher ground than the enemy, it was perhaps even more important to secure the moral high ground. The troops would be assured that their cause was justified, which meant righteous. Conversely, the enemy would be denigrated and shown to be unrighteous.

Just as pagans enlisted the support of supernatural forces for a raid or a campaign, perhaps even more so they would have done so before battle. The role of Odin as warrior-god is explored further in Chapter 7. In the poems of *Hávamál* a series of spells are listed, designed to aid in battle.[4] Neil Price lists the functions of war-spells as follows: to instil fear or confusion; to confer courage and clarity of mind; to instil physical strength or weakness (on enemies); to hinder the body's movements; to break or strengthen weapons and armor; to make warriors invulnerable in battle; to kill people; to resurrect dead warriors to fight again; to provide protection from enemy sorcerers; to combat and kill sorcerers.[5] For the pagan Norsemen it was necessary to achieve magical mastery of the battlefield before the fighting began. Leaders may have been accompanied by sorcerers, but in many of the literary examples that have come down to us the leaders themselves had these abilities. An example is Queen Skuld in *Hrólfs saga kraka* (and *Gesta Danorum*), who deceives Hró lf's army so that it remains in camp, its warriors unaware of the approach of her army and preoccupied in sexual activity with their women. There is no evidence that women ever led Viking armies, but it is generally accepted that Viking kings and chieftains had combined military, legal and sacral functions, and may have been believed to have magical powers also.

The forms of Christian, Moslem or pagan rituals may have differed, but the object of all of them was to secure divine favor. Although it may have been clear to Christians that heathen opponents did not have God's favor, they themselves could not expect His help if they did not show due humility and respect. Asser gives the following account of the preliminaries to Ashdown:

> But Alfred arrived at the place of the battle more quickly and more readily with his men, just as we heard from those witnesses who saw it. For doubtless his brother, King Æthelred, was as yet in his tent hearing mass, having been at prayer, and strongly declaring that he would not depart thence alive before the priest had finished mass and not to desert service of God for man. And he did thus. Thereby the faith of the Christian king was of great value to the lord [Alfred], just as will be revealed more clearly by the following account.

Asser goes on to say that the pagans might have attacked Alfred's division alone, as they were ready before Æthelred's arrival. However, despite the risk taken, he is in no doubt that the king's decision to hear mass was correct and reaped benefits. Conversely, in his (and no doubt Æthelred's) eyes, to do otherwise would have been courting disaster, more so than taking the tactical risk.

Christianity introduced a moral dimension into warfare that had not previously existed. Evidence for Christian ritual in Scandinavian armies before battle is almost nonexistent before the twelfth century, as our accounts of their activities in the Viking Era are either written by their enemies or dubious tales from later sources such as the sagas, Saxo, or the *Russian Primary Chronicle*. Undoubtedly they adopted many of the practices of their already Christianized neighbors. How they perceived what they were doing is another matter. For instance, it may well be that when Scandinavian warriors new to the faith offered prayers and made donations to churches (or even of churches), they perceived it as a form of gift exchange, a reciprocal arrangement similar to those made with other powerful men or pagan gods—in other words, when they gave something to God, he was more or less obliged to give something in exchange.

The celebration of mass involved the reception of the eucharist, accompanied by confession to a priest. Chroniclers mention confession by kings and princes relatively frequently, but we also know that the whole army did this: for instance, Widukind describes it in his account of the early morning preliminaries to the Battle of Lenzen in 929, when a German army faced the Slavs.[6] The rite could signify the giving of health to the sick, or a last confession for those about to die. Either way, it gave peace of mind to those about to enter battle. A common practice was also to fast before battle: a demonstration of penitence and thus worthiness of God's support. This might be accompanied by explicit requests for aid from God, or from those who could intervene with Him, the saints. Failure in battle was commonly interpreted as failure to please God beforehand, perhaps in the immediate preparation, perhaps in the general conduct of the army of its commander prior to the battle. Whereas victory for an opposing Christian army might be interpreted as a sign that God favored it in preference, victory for an opposing pagan army was a sign that He was punishing the losers.

In addition to religious rituals, shows of bravado might be made, designed to demonstrate prowess to both sides and perhaps intimidate the enemy. On occasion challenges to combat were also issued, either from commanders to the opposing leader, or by champions as a call for any of their foes to come out and face them. Sometimes a challenge was issued to decide the matter by battle between the rival armies. In Christianized societies they were in effect accepting trial by battle, to decide who was favored by God. Such a consideration may well have played a part in Byrhtnoth's decision to allow the Viking army to cross the Blackwater unmolested at *Maldon*: we cannot simply assume that he was stupid or arrogant, or misjudged the tactical situation, as if he were a modern commander.

Mounted and foot

An important aspect of early medieval armies was the "multi-purpose" nature of their troops, insofar as their equipment allowed: there was no concept of "cavalry," "infantry" and "mounted infantry" as troop types, a point made strongly by Guy Halsall.[7] Ownership of a riding horse was clearly a status symbol long before the Viking Era, in Scandinavia and in England as well as elsewhere, although this does not necessarily mean that it was ridden into battle. It does seem that the Vikings rarely used horses in combat. However, one reason why they used horses mainly for transporting the army may be that many of those they commandeered would not have been suitable for mounted combat. To be effective in mounted combat both horses and riders need considerable training. In 851, during the Danish campaign in Germany, King Arnulf's army was attacked in the flank by mounted Viking warriors while attempting to assault a defended camp on the river Geule.[8] In this case the horsemen appear to have arrived just after the Franks had been repulsed from the camp during the battle and the quality of their mounts would not have been of any great importance. The attack may have been no more than a pursuit if the enemy fled as they approached.

As noted in Chapter 2, Saxo stated that the Danes had not yet adopted the use of mounted troops outside their own land in the early twelfth century, implying that they did use them within the kingdom, but without telling us how they used them.[9] It is often assumed that the impact of German mercenary knights at Fotevik in 1134 marked the point at which the Danes began to adopt their equipment and tactics, but this is a quite different matter from adopting mounted combat in general. The earlier situation is similar to that in Anglo-Saxon England, as we know from the tenth-century Danish "horseman burials" that there were military horses ridden by warriors, but not whether they were ridden into battle. In Norway the terrain does not favor mounted combat, while we have no description of any battles in Sweden apart from their results and the deaths of important men before the late thirteenth century. There is no evidence that horses were ridden in land battles in Scandinavia during the Viking Era, but there is no good evidence against this either: with the exception of much later accounts of a few of them in Norway, we know virtually nothing of these battles.

In the regions around Kiev and Chernigov there was suitable terrain for mounted combat. Indeed, the steppe peoples the Rus had to face, first the Khazars and then the Pechenegs and Polovtsy (Cumans, Kipchaks), used large numbers of horsemen. For this reason the *družina* (household) troops of the princes of southern Rus seem to have taken to mounted combat. Nevertheless, this probably did not occur until the late tenth century at the earliest. To John Skylitzes, writing of the Byzantine campaign against Sviatoslav in 970–971, it was obvious that the Rus were not familiar with the methods of mounted combat. Sviatoslav had managed to defeat both the Khazars and the Pechenegs before this. Unfortunately we know only the general outlines of these campaigns and nothing of any battles. An army on foot crossing the steppe would have been very vulnerable to mounted armies with numbers of horse archers, but it seems that Sviatoslav employed Pecheneg and perhaps Oghuz horsemen against the Khazars, and Khazar and Oghuz horsemen against the Pechenegs.[10] In Bulgaria he had both Pecheneg and Magyar horsemen at the Battle of Arcadiopolis (970), where the Byzantine general Bardas Sclerus conducted a withdrawal with some of his cavalry and led many of them into an ambush before turning on the Rus foot.[11] Referring to the garrisons of the forts of Sviatoslav's son Vladimir's rampart defenses south of Kiev, Simon Franklin and Jonathan Shephard make the point that they must have included mounted men, as they would have needed to pursue mounted foes, primarily the Pechenegs.

Varangians continued to be employed by the princes as household troops and especially as mercenaries after 1000, at least until mid-century, and it should not be assumed that these were always the ones who fought on foot, or that they fought only for the princes in northern cities such as Novgorod. Without any evidence, Yaroslav's defeat at Listven has been attributed to a failure of Scandinavian foot faced by mounted troops.[12] It is very likely that a large portion of his army was made up of Scandinavian mercenaries, and also probable that these preferred to fight on foot. It is also very probable that the bulk of Mstislav's army was recruited in the south, in which case a large number might have been horsemen from the steppe, but here we have a succession of probabilities and possibilities, rather than evidence. In the words attributed to Mstislav (quoted below), only the Slavic tribe that lived in the Chernigov area, the Severians, and Varangians are mentioned. All we know is what the Russian *Primary Chronicle* tells us, and the detail of its account of the conflict between Yaroslav and Mstislav is suspect. Mstislav is associated with "Khazars," because his father Vladimir allegedly placed him in Tmutorokan, where the ruler was known as "ruler of the Khazar country" (i.e. what used to be a part of the Khazar Empire). In fact he may also have been ruler of Chernigov before Listven.[13]

Anglo-Saxon armies were heavily influenced by Scandinavian practice, particularly after the Danish conquest of 1017. Harold's army fought on foot at Hastings, but this was not necessarily because the English habitually did this or because they could not field effective cavalry. There were good reasons for Harold to take up a defensive position on a ridge. Not only did he know that the Normans had high-quality armored cavalry, but they could probably field more of them than the English. Earlier in the year, when the English faced Harald Hardrada's army at Fulford, they probably had even fewer troops capable of fighting mounted, as the army was raised from northern England only. Such troops may have been available only from the households of Earls Morcar and Edwin, one reason for the decision, as it appears from the much later Icelandic sources, to fight on foot with secure flanks and behind a beck. These were the same considerations, in fact, that had come into play at *Maldon*, where local forces were the mainstay of Byrhtnoth's army.

The accounts of *Maldon* also suggest that one reason for fighting on foot was that the dense formation of men on foot had more solidity than a mounted force, or, to put it another way, mounted troops were more likely to flee. This may be what happened at Hereford in 1055, the battle often cited in support of the argument that the English could not fight effectively from horseback, despite the fact that John of Worcester says the Normans led the rout. It is he who claims that fighting on horseback was contrary to the English custom, writing during the reign of Henry I, when the English troops in the Anglo-Norman army certainly did fight on foot, whereas the *ASC* says nothing of custom, simply that the army "fled because it was mounted"—does this mean that it "was able to flee because it was mounted," or that it 'fled because it did not wish to fight mounted', or that it "fled because was it was mounted in terrain more suited to foot combat?" The army may have been caught by the Welsh in unfavorable circumstances. Halsall also points out that the term *pedestre*, used by the author of the *Encomium Emmae* when referring to the army at Assundun, can mean "on foot," but also "on land," as it was used elsewhere in the same work.

The accounts of *Maldon* and Hastings are better than those of other battles, and these happened to be battles in which the English fought defensively on foot. Other accounts of Anglo-Saxon battles give little information on the mode of fighting, although mounted warriors in pursuit are mentioned in the *Brunanburh* poem.[14] We also have accounts of a battle fought in this era which do claim that the English fought mounted, namely the Icelandic–Norwegian *Heimskringla* and *Morkinskinna* versions of the Battle of Stamford Bridge (1066). The problem is that these were written nearly two hundred years after the battle. This does not mean they should be dismissed out of hand, but it is a better reason to dismiss them than the usual one, that they cannot be correct "because the English did not fight mounted," the assumption being that they were colored by accounts of the Battle of Hastings. All accounts of Stamford Bridge agree that the Norwegians were taken by surprise and that many did not have time to don their armor. These would be suitable circumstances for a mounted attack, as the English would not be facing the problem of breaking a prepared and solid phalanx of infantry, which, as William found, was not easy to do. That the pre-Conquest English were familiar with mounted combat is suggested by a number of pictorial sources produced in England, such as the Viking-Era sculptures at Gosforth in Cumbria, Gainford in Durham, Neston in Cheshire, and Baldersby in Yorkshire, and the early eleventh-century Canterbury version of the Utrecht Psalter. Others show mounted and armed men, like the depiction of Abraham's army in the Old English version of the Hexateuch (also eleventh century), and Old English versions of earlier Latin works.[15] This is not clear evidence that the English fought mounted, but both art and written works were usually adapted to suit the taste and habits of the expected audience.

The question of whether Vikings and Anglo-Saxons fought mounted or not is part of a wider debate, concerning the extent to which their armies differed from others on the European continent. It has often been claimed that the elite of Frankish armies always fought mounted when possible. It may be that they preferred to fight on horseback when the terrain was relatively flat, but they certainly fought dismounted on several occasions. In the River Geule battle referred to above, they were faced with the prospect of crossing a marsh before assaulting the fortified Viking camp. Any attempt to do this mounted would have had no chance whatever of succeeding, although in the event they still suffered a defeat.[16] Faced with a similar situation at the Dyle later in the year, they managed to storm the camp. On that occasion mounted contingents were left at the rear to guard against a repeat of their earlier experience.

Most have argued that Franks preferred to fight mounted in the Carolingian period, but Bernard Bachrach has argued that although there was an effort to maintain large numbers of mounted men, they were used only for hunting down small groups of relatively untrained enemies and in a supporting role in sieges. In battle the men were more likely to dismount to fight.[17] His conclusion is echoed by Charles Bowlus in his book on the Battle of Lechfeld: "There was never a 'cavalry revolution' during the age of Charlemagne. The few accounts that we possess of heavy cavalry in action indicate that this arm was used sparingly and sometimes poorly deployed."[18] Like the argument that Anglo-Saxons must have fought on foot, the argument that Charlemagne's armies rarely fought mounted is based on very limited sources: there is no evidence that there was a cavalry revolution, but there is no clear evidence that Charlemagne did not employ cavalry in a similar way to Henry I of Germany either. We know hardly anything of Charlemagne's battle tactics. There is no way of telling whether the Carolingian pictorial sources that portray mounted troops represent them as if in a full-scale battle or a skirmish, or simply as they wanted to be represented. The *RFA* account of the battle cited by Bachrach, in the foothills of the Süntel Mountains in 782, does not tell us that the Frankish horsemen were defeated because they attacked mounted or because they were only used to attacking small groups while on horseback, but because they attacked rashly, without order, and without waiting for the main part of the army. Nor does Henry I's supposed creation of a battlefield cavalry force between 924 and 933 tell us that the East Franks had never had any effective battlefield cavalry earlier. Nevertheless, as a corrective to the common perception that the mainstay of Carolingian armies in battle was their cavalry, Bachrach and Bowlus have a point—just as the Anglo-Saxons may well have fought mounted on occasion, so the nobility of Charlemagne and Louis the Pious may often have fought on foot during the hard initial stages of a battle and mounted to finish off the enemy once he wavered or broke, or a small mounted reserve may have been kept back for this purpose. In other words, the methods of eighth-and ninth-century Anglo-Saxon and Frankish armies may have been much more alike than previously accepted.

In the case of Northumbria's near neighbors, the Picts, we are almost entirely dependent on pictures on carved stones or cross-slabs. There are many depictions of men on horseback, but only one clearly shows them in battle: the Aberlemno Stone, usually taken to represent the Battle of Dunnichen/Nechtansmere, fought two hundred years before the arrival of the Vikings. The general consensus is that horsemen were used in battle, but we have no idea how they were used. Neil Aitchison draws the conclusion that they formed in front of the battle-line and opened the battle with a charge, but it is difficult to see how he reaches this conclusion. The horsemen on the stone are "in front" of the foot, but this need not be an accurate representation of battle. He is probably right that cavalry in this era was of limited effectiveness, but a tactic such as this would run the risk of horsemen stampeding back towards or into their infantry and disrupting their battle-line. Classical Greek cavalry (also of limited effectiveness) often formed up in front of the phalanx and Xenophon mentions precisely this happening to the Spartans at Leuctra in 371 BC.[19] As for the Scots of Dál

Riata and the Irish, we know even less of their armies. Irish sources refer to chariot-warriors long after the chariot must have disappeared from the battlefield, and the name may refer to the small band surrounding the king, which may or may not have used horses in battle. After the Anglo-Norman invasion in the twelfth century, they did have lightly armed horsemen, but this may have been a response to the new invaders, as their few more heavily armored cavalry undoubtedly were.

Command and army division on the battlefield

Armies commonly formed up in a series of divisions, each one composed of either mounted or foot. These divisions, later called "battles," incorporated the various leaders with the troops they had brought. Leaders were usually aristocracy of some degree. Their social rank was usually their military rank. It is arguable that in ancient and medieval warfare the most important single function of a commander was to inspire his men. With a sufficiently good record, a commander could also instill fear in the enemy. We may call it charisma or reputation: contemporary people knew of these, but must have thought success indicated the favor of God, or, as the Scandinavian sagas frequently mention, luck. This is a concept that almost certainly goes back to pagan times—certain men were favored by luck, a characteristic that was often apparent in their physical appearance. This is a subject beyond the scope of the discussion here, but the understanding medieval folk had of mental faculties and emotions and how they worked, whether they were pagan or Christian, was very different from ours. It follows from the above that a commander who familiarized himself with those under him was more likely to be effective. This applied to all leaders, both the overall commander and the secondary commanders. Since most armies were small, it is possible that even the man at the top had a chance to address all his men, as our (literary) accounts imply. An address like that of the *Maldon* poem or the *Heimskringla* account of Stiklestad (below) probably had more to do with reassurance that the general was in control than it did with actually telling the men how to hold their spears and shields.

There were basically two styles of overall command, what Philip Sabin calls "the leader" and "the commander." The first led by example and often fought in the front rank. This was inspiring to the men (as long as he remained in action), but meant that the leader had little chance to influence the outcome once battle was joined, other than by helping to bring about a breakthrough or preventing flight at the point where he was fighting. The "commander," on the other hand, had less direct influence on the fighting, but could change position to intervene at a point of danger, perhaps to encourage wavering men to hold fast. As far as we can tell, this was more often than not the practice of Roman and Byzantine commanders and it was to become the pattern for command in the modern era. It is clear that many leaders in the Viking Era felt obliged to lead from the front. This obviously had its dangers, as the commander was more likely to be killed, just as Byrhtnoth was at *Maldon*. In these circumstances it was all the more important to be surrounded by hardened warriors. Known examples of commanders who adopted the "Roman" approach in the Viking period are rare.

Sources rarely state explicitly where the overall commander was, but it is clear from many anecdotes and passing remarks, particularly in the Scandinavian sagas, that he was at the front or in the middle of the phalanx in many battles. A commander, of course, was not visible to everyone, and he was symbolized by his standard, which served as a vital rallying point for all those under his command. Both standards and trumpets or horns were used for signaling. All are frequently mentioned in contemporary sources. Just as there were many leaders at varying levels of command, so there were many standards. Just like the commander himself, a standard could inspire those who fought under it, but also demoralize them if it was lost. For this reason it was with the associated leader, surrounded by the best warriors among those who fought under it. The carrying of the standard was an important, not to say vital, task, which was therefore allotted to an experienced warrior. Viking standards were named, a practice that continued long after the Viking Era. In 878 Ealdorman Odda captured a standard called *Raven* from the Vikings at the Battle of Cynwit in Devon.[20] The raven was, of course, a totemic animal associated with the battlefield, and the Raven Banner makes several appearances as a magical object in later sagas. It is probable that this reflects its status in the era of Viking expansion, even after Christianization. Thietmar of Merseburg mentions standards stored in the Slavic (Liutitian) temple at Riedegost, taken out only for war, and a standard with an image of a war goddess carried on a campaign against the Poles in 1017.[21] In his account of the Danish attack on Arkona in 1168—9, Saxo ridicules the pagan Slavs for believing that their standards had magical or protective powers: it is unlikely that they had changed their habits since the Viking Era. Probably other banners were also "followed" by the group of warriors they represented.

As modern experience has shown, even without magical powers a standard could become a powerful icon. In the Viking Era, of course, each banner would have been strongly associated with a certain leader. In Carolingian manuscript illustrations of the ninth century flag types are carried, but also the dragon windsock, known to have been used by late Roman armies and many of their Germanic foes and successors. We know very little of the symbols used on standards in this period. Christian armies used banners with Christian symbolism, as this too had a quasi-magical nature, some being associated with religious relics, which were also carried into battle. Such *vexilli* could be blessed to aid against enemies and inspire those who trusted in God. At the Battle of Riade Henry I's army was preceded by a large banner carrying the image of St. Michael, which, according to Widukind, gave great comfort and resolve to the troops.[22] Others might have had something associated with the commanders they accompanied, rather like the later heraldic devices. Evidence of their importance, and perhaps their power, was the significance attached to their capture. In accounts of victories over the Vikings they feature prominently. Among other things, they functioned as "proof" of victory, like the sixteen sent to Bavaria by Arnulf after the Battle of the Dyle (891). Among the Vikings it was not just standards that had quasi-magical properties, but the war-horns. These too had names, well into the Christian era and after the Viking Period.

The number of divisions in an army normally varied from two to four, but could be more. The number was often related as much to the number of sufficiently senior nobles and their relative status as to battlefield necessity, especially when the army formed in one line. At Ashdown (871) the Wessex army had two divisions, one commanded by the king and the other by the atheling, and its opponents also formed in two divisions. In this case the Wessex and Viking divisions were clearly organized according to the number of commanders of sufficient rank to command their own division, named as two kings with lesser "jarls" on the Viking side. However, it is probable that the Viking divisions, as well as reflecting loyalty to a certain king, also reflected geographical or "ethnic" origins, of which Asser was unaware or not concerned. Most of them were probably Danes, but Denmark's different regions were not yet integrated into a state; we know from Saxo that even in the twelfth century forces from Jutland, Funen, Zealand, Scania, Lolland, and Halland still operated as individual contingents, not always harmoniously. In his description of Stiklestad

(1031–1030) Snorri Sturluson notes that the anti-Olaf coalition formed in this way:

> Kálf [Árnason] setup the standard and stationed his house carls under it, and with them Hárek of Thjótta and his company. Thórir the Hound and his men stood in front of the standards at the head of the formation. And a chosen band of farmers was on both sides of Thó rir, men who were the keenest and best armed. This [the center of the army] was both long and deep, and in it were men from Trondheim and Hálogaland. To the right of this formation there was placed another, and at the left side of the center stood the men from Rogaland, Horthaland, Sogn, and the Fjords, and there was set up the third standard.[23]

We have no way of knowing whether this battle-line was actually the one used at Stiklestad, given the date when this was written, but, as noted above, little had changed on the battlefields of Norway. It seems that Snorri is describing the battlefield formation planned by Kálf once he was appointed overall commander, rather than an order of march, as Thórir and his men are subsequently found behind the army when it proceeds to Stiklestad, but then form up in front of Kálf's standard for the attack.

It is hardly surprising that armies formed by regional contingents when their organization reflected existing social and political divisions and the social and political elite were also the military leaders. The weakness of this organization was that regional loyalties often took priority over "national" (kingdom- or empire-wide) loyalty, and the personal nature of rulership often meant that loyalty to the local lord was greater than loyalty to the overall army commander. In order for one leader to be accepted as senior to another, even temporarily, he had to have at least equal and preferably superior social status. In all armies, if called upon to fight, men would be with their companions and following leaders and standards they were familiar with. Their sense of solidarity was the medieval equivalent of "regimental pride," but in the modern era pride in the regiment, even if regiments were largely drawn from specific districts, supersedes pride in the district as the army is regarded as something distinct from "civilian" society. In the Middle Ages only those who had more-or-less permanent warrior status, the households (or *comitati*) of rulers, warrior fraternities, or mercenary or raiding bands that operated for long periods under the same leader can have had a similar military ethos and a sense that they were people apart, warriors, as opposed to the bulk of (free) society. This would have been one of the strengths of the Viking bands, who often campaigned together and operated for years in the territory of their enemies.

Inevitably, the contingents will often have varied in quality. It has frequently been assumed that those with better armor or more experience formed in the front ranks and those with lesser experience and poorer equipment behind, the system employed in Roman Republican armies (in this case with veterans at the rear as well), and also, at least as far as experience was concerned, in Classical Greek armies. However, the limited evidence suggests that this was not necessarily the case in the early medieval era. In many cases, when armies were levied from poorer freemen such as the Scandinavian *bøndur*, they seem to have fought separately from the wealthier and better armed, albeit perhaps with a leader and his bodyguard of superior standing. Not only is this the impression of Scandinavian armies throughout the Viking and High Medieval Periods given by the kings' sagas, but it is also how the English army is depicted in the Bayeux Tapestry. This shows men armored in mail hauberks banded together and unarmored men together. There is even a distinction between armored men with round shields and those with kite shields, although this may be for artistic effect. To place the better troops among (or in front of) their social inferiors might have strengthened the resolve of the latter, but it weakened the *esprit de corps* among the elite troops. The best troops, those who made up the comitatus or personal household troops, were kept with their leader and around his standard. They were supposed to remain with their leader, to die with him if necessary, like Byrhtnoth's companions at *Maldon* or Harold's housecarls at Hastings, or to avenge his death. Conversely, the leader tried to preserve his household or *comitatus*, without which he must have felt very vulnerable. In many polities the household was not just a warrior elite or bodyguard, but an advisory council and administration as well. Hence the reported statement of Prince Mstislav after his victory at Listven (1024): "Who would not rejoice in this? Here lies a Severian, and here a Varangian, but the *družina* is intact."[24]

Tactics and battlefield formations in Scandinavia, Britain and the Carolingian world

We have very little information about battlefield formations below the "divisional level" discussed above, either on foot or mounted, or how they were deployed relative to each other. Many still hold the view of Charles Oman, that after the classical era battle degenerated into a mindless and brutal slogging match, devoid of manoeuvre or tactics. Similarly, naval battles consisted of two lines of ships tied together and closing with each other—in other words, creating a situation as close as possible to that on land so that the troops could engage in a brutal slogging match at sea. In part this view of early medieval warfare is a product of the lack of information on tactics in the sources. There is an element of truth in the stereotype, but commanders could and did make decisions that could alter the course of battle, and within the limitations of the troops available, there were variations in tactics.

More than any other, the idea of the "shield-wall" has penetrated the public consciousness as an infantry formation used by Vikings and Anglo-Saxons. From them its use has been extended to other contemporary peoples, such as the Picts.[25] The "shield-wall" appears in modern English translations of *The Battle of Maldon* and Asser's account of Edington (878).[26] Among the non-Latin terms that appear in poetic sources alongside shield-wall are spear-hedge, war-hedge, shield-fort, and battle-enclosure. It is important to realize that these terms, like "shield-wall," were not intended to refer to tactical formations, but were imagery designed to convey the appearance of troops arrayed for battle. In other words, there was no infantry formation special to the Viking Era called a "shield-wall." This and the other terms listed would be appropriate not only for Viking or English infantry in close order during this period, but for many others drawn up in similar fashion, such as Frankish, Ottonian, or even Slav infantry, and equally appropriate for formations used by medieval infantry in a later period, late Roman and Byzantine close order infantry, or, for that matter, the classical Greek phalanx. Indeed, contemporary authors who wrote in Latin often used the term "phalanx."

While the word phalanx is applicable to the single line of multiple ranks employed by most armies in this period, it is by no means certain that the authors who wrote in Latin had a clear idea of the meaning of other Latin terms for formations, or simply employed them for effect. The most appropriate use for a *testudo* would have been in assaults on defenses, but Asser uses the term in his accounts of Ashdown, suggesting that he was referring to a close order body of infantry. Classical terminology was so familiar to those who understood Latin that it conveyed both an image and evidence of the author's learning. Most of the audience or readership would have known the classical sources of the pieces of text used as exemplars. However, all the Latin and vernacular terms listed above indicate a fairly dense formation, while some of them suggest a single long linear formation. This must have been in several ranks, but we have no idea how many. Once again taking the Aberlemno Stone as a representation of actual battle practice, Aitcheson concludes that Pictish infantry probably formed in three ranks, but this seems too few. In his account of a battle fought on the ice just west of Oslo in 1161, in which both armies were apparently drawn up in similar fashion, Snorri Sturluson mentions that King Inge's men were arranged in five ranks, but the clear implication here is that this was less than the norm, as he had to do this to extend his line to the same frontage as his opponents'. According to Snorri, a similar procedure was adopted at more than one battle in the Viking Era. At the battle on Rastarkalv plain in *c.* 955, King Håkon the Good is supposed to have said, "We shall have an extended line of battle so they cannot surround us, even though they have more men," whilst disguising this from his enemies by setting up ten standards to make his army look bigger than it was. It is also implied that King Olaf thinned his ranks at the Battle of Stiklestad, in which he faced a larger opposing army, as he refers to his army as having fewer men behind the front ranks and says they must hope to win quickly through the ferocity of their onslaught. Only by this means could they avoid an attritional "slogging match" that would wear both sides down and thus result in his line breaking first.[27] Unlike Håkon's army at Rastarkalv, they failed to break the enemy formation and Olaf lost both the battle and his life.

Snorri's account of Inge's formation draws attention to the compromise a commander had to make: his line had to be long enough to avoid outflanking by the enemy and deep enough to prevent him from breaking through easily. Rear ranks were able to use their weapons to some extent, as Snorri claims in his description of Stiklestad: "Those who stood foremost slashed with their swords, those standing behind them thrust with their spears, whilst all those in the rear let fly both with javelins or arrows or threw stones or hand-axes or shafts with pointed stones."[28] Although Snorri was writing some two hundred years after the event, the way battles were fought in Norway in his time did not differ significantly from the Viking Period. The main function of the majority of rear ranks will have been to act as replacements for those who fell in front of them and to add "weight" to any attempt to push the enemy back or hold the line if it was buckling. This "weight" may have been both physical and moral. Greek sources mention the action of "pushing" (*othismos*) by rear ranks, but the Greek hoplite shield was much more suited to this purpose than the bossed shields of the Viking Period, as it could be placed against the back of the man in front. Even in this case there has been much argument about the extent to which *othismos* was a literal or metaphorical description of what occurred.[29]

Five must have been close to the minimum number of ranks that would still give some solidity. To return to ancient analogy again, Herodotus tells us that the Athenians extended their line at Marathon by reducing its center to four ranks. However, the Persians broke through the center, only to be defeated by the wings, which were twice as deep. Accounts of Greek hoplite battles are almost the only ones that mention the number of ranks used. Vegetius recommends at least nine ranks, although, as so often with his advice, it is not certain whether he based this on actual practice of his day. The army of the later Roman Empire, which many consider the precursor to armies in early medieval Europe, probably formed in eight ranks, but possibly six or ten.[30] The Byzantine army of the tenth century formed in seven ranks, but the three middle ranks were archers. This became eight ranks to repulse heavy cavalry, with four ranks of spearmen in front of the archers, but the depth was increased to fourteen after Nikephoros Phokas' death.[31] When the enemy approached, Nikephoros envisaged that this infantry would act primarily on the defensive as a shield for the main arm, the cavalry, to fall back upon if necessary.[32] Its deepest formation was designed to repulse heavily armored Arab cavalry. Nevertheless, it was this infantry that fought with the Rus in Bulgaria in the 970s. There is no reason why any given army, even in the same era, need have used a standard depth in the Viking Era, and the best that can be said is that the favored depth is likely to have been between five and ten ranks.

A reason why the depth of formation is likely to have varied is that, as in the case of Inge's army in 1161, armies usually seem to have squared up against one another. Sources rarely mention any attempt at outflanking when armies formed up for battle. In most cases one of the armies must have conformed to the other, which had assembled first. Although this appears to be evidence of lack of imagination or excessive adherence to convention, there was good reason for it. Commanders were aware of the danger of being outflanked, as those who prepared to receive an attack frequently formed their lines of battle with the ends anchored on a terrain feature such as a wood, marsh, or river. Secondly, many of the opposing armies that faced each other in battle were approximately equal in size or unaware of the opponents' exact strength, and any attempt to extend the line beyond the opposing line entailed the risk of having less depth than the opposing formation, which might lead to a collapse of the line before any advantage was gained from having a longer line. Thirdly, commanders were probably aware that any attempt to form up with a greater frontage would be noted by the enemy, who would respond in kind, thus resulting in a fruitless jockeying for position. Since the objective, in the minds of the majority of the troops, would have been to get to grips with the enemy, there may also have been a danger that any part of the formation beyond the enemy's line would edge towards the enemy during the advance, resulting in excessive bunching, slowing the advance of that part of the army and possibly throwing the line into confusion. Such conscious or unconscious considerations contributed to what had undoubtedly become a convention long before the Vikings descended on their neighbors, which was also followed in the knowledge that in any case the outcome of the battle was actually determined by God, or perhaps, in the eyes of pagans, by fate or more powerful magic.

This is not to suggest that on occasion the front of one army did not extend beyond its opponent's. Outflanking may have occurred on the rare occasions when armies encountered one another unexpectedly, or during ambushes, or when a force faced a much larger opposing army and could not conform to its front without thinning its ranks too much. However, wheeling a section of a long line several ranks deep would have been next to impossible. When part of a line disintegrated the enemy could attack the flank and/or rear of the troops on either side of it, but they did not necessarily have to be in good order to achieve the desired effect. This may possibly have happened when one division of an army was defeated and those pursuing were reformed to face the flank of another division, which would have taken some time. This appears to have happened in some ancient battles, but there is no known example of it from Europe in the

Viking period. In the Middle Ages deliberate flank attacks were rare and invariably carried out by small units of troops from concealed positions, much as the Black Prince did at Poitiers in 1356. The attack of Thietmar's fifty horsemen against the Wiltzi (Slavs) at Lenzen (929) may have been such an attack, although on that occasion the Slavs were first worn down by repeated attacks from the front. Small groups were more easily manoeuvred and easier to conceal during the flanking movement or when placed in ambush. Again, there is no known example of a similar attack during a battle in Viking-Age Europe. At the River Geule the Vikings did attack the rear of Arnulf's army at an opportune moment, but it is not clear whether this was planned or the horsemen just happened to approach the battlefield at the right time and seized their opportunity.

It is also impossible to know what frontage per man was used. Vegetius recommended that men lined up at 3-foot intervals and that 6-foot space was maintained between ranks.[33] Even in one army and one era file spacing and rank depth may have varied to some extent, although less experienced troops probably felt more security in being more densely packed. However, as Vegetius pointed out, if men were too closely packed together they lost the ability to fight effectively. It is frequently assumed that the usual infantry formation entailed forming up as close to the next man as possible with overlapping shields, thus presenting the enemy with an intimidating wall of shields. This is the formation portrayed in the Bayeux Tapestry. Like the Greek hoplites, the infantry wield their spears overarm, which would have been much more effective than underarm when the men were this close together with each shield rim touching the boss of the next. In the case of the English, it would also have allowed the possibility of throwing them. There is no reason to doubt the accuracy of this portrayal of their line at Hastings. There is also an emphasis on spears in the poetic account of *Maldon*. However, this does not mean that English infantry always formed up in this fashion. At Hastings they were facing an opponent with formidable armored cavalry, and it was essential to form a solid front which prevented any of them from breaking into the line. In this case the English line was also stationary throughout the day (apart from those which broke formation to pursue fleeing or apparently fleeing enemy), although, once again, the Greek hoplite experience demonstrates that it was possible to advance in a similar formation.[34]

The writer of the *Strategikon*, supposedly Emperor Maurice, describes two formations which he calls *foulkon*. The word is undoubtedly of Germanic derivation, and Michael Speidel, who is keen to emphasize continuity in Germanic warfare throughout the Iron Age and even into the Christian period, has argued that these formations were derived from Germanic practice.[35] Although there were certainly changes in armament, organization and even tactics between Maurice's reign and the Viking Era, none of these was significant enough to change the essential nature of warfare. The first *foulkon* is described as follows:

> They move in a foulkon when the two lines, ours and the enemy's, are getting close, and the archers are about to open fire, and the front-rank men are not wearing coats of mail or knee-guards. The command is: "Form foulkon." The men in the front ranks close in until their shields are touching, completely covering their midsections almost to their ankles, The men standing behind them hold their shields above their heads, interlocking them with those of the men in front of them, covering their breasts and faces, and in this way move to attack.[36]

In the same book Maurice describes a different *foulkon*:

> The first, second, and third men in each file form a foulkon, interlocking their shields, fix their spears firmly in the ground, holding them inclined forward and straight outside their shields, so that anyone who dares come too close will quickly experience them. They also lean their shoulders and put their weight against the shields to resist any pressure from the enemy. The third man, who is standing nearly upright, and the fourth man hold their spears like javelins, so that when the foe gets close they can use them either for thrusting or for throwing and then draw their swords.[37]

The Byzantines or their late Roman predecessors presumably adopted the term *foulkon* for a formation they thought similar to one used by Germanic warriors, but a problem with Spiedel's attempt to identify the Byzantine *foulkon* with specific "Germanic" formations is that Maurice is probably using the term to mean no more than "close order foot formation." *Foulkon* is also used in this same sense in an anonymous tenth-century Byzantine treatise on skirmishing.[38] Along with the first *foulkon* Maurice describes ranks of archers behind the shield-men and firing overhead, a characteristic of late Roman and Byzantine formations throughout the early Middle Ages, but one for which there is no evidence in Germanic armies. However, it is not implausible that this use of shields during the advance to the attack, designed to protect the advancing troops as much as possible from missiles, was employed by them, and continued to be employed by them into the Viking Era. If so, we have no representations of it, but it is conceivable that a formation with similar use of two rows of interlocking shields was what Asser referred to as a *testudo* when Alfred advanced against the Vikings at Ashdown.

Maurice makes clear that the second *foulkon* is for defense against cavalry, and in the sixth-century context the greatest threat to the Byzantines was posed by the heavily armed and armored cavalry of the Sassanian Persians. Speidel notes that Ammianus described Alemannic warriors fighting on their knees in the front rank of a formation in the fourth century. Again, it cannot be ruled out that Germanic armies used a similar formation in the early Middle Ages, but we have no evidence of it. Nevertheless, late evidence from northern Europe of a similar practice is provided by the account of the Battle of Nakło in 1109, in the *Deeds of the Princes of the Poles*. The author states that the Slavic Pomeranians "were not drawn up for battle in Christian fashion" and describes them as sticking the butts of their spears in the ground with points turned towards the enemy and crouching behind their shields in a tight formation. In this case their infantry was routed by the Poles attacking from two directions, but it is not clear whether they were on horseback or not. Specific mention is made of the fact that the Pomeranians had no horsemen on this occasion (probably because they had just emerged from the woods), and the Polish groups were led by Boleslaw himself and his standard bearer, the latter circling round to the flank, which suggests that some or all of the Poles were cavalry.[39] The account also suggests that its author thought of the phalanx/shieldwall of standing men as the "Christian" way to fight on foot, probably because it was learned from those who converted the Poles to Christianity, the Germans.

Our limited sources also suggest that Viking and English warriors threw spears and other missiles before close contact, incidentally something that Maurice also describes shortly after the first passage quoted above. To

Aerial view of Northey Island and the site of the Battle of Maldon, looking from the east. The outskirts of the modern town of Maldon are just visible on the right. (*Photograph by Terry Joyce. © Terry Joyce*)

A Viking-Age spearhead, shield-boss, ring, and buckle from Vestre Slidre, Oppland, Norway. (*Photographer unknown, © Museum of Cultural History—University of Oslo, Norway*)

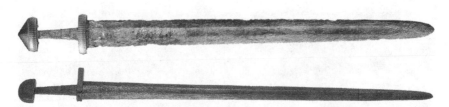

Two Viking Period swords inscribed with names. Top is an +VLFBEHRT+ sword, of lower quality than the +VLFBERH+T swords made with steel from central Asia. It was found in the River Meuse at Lith and its hilt suggests Viking manufacture, although the blade may well be Frankish. The other sword was found at Wijk bij Duurstede in the River Lek, and has the inscription ATABALD.

(© *Rijksmuseum van Oudheden, Leiden, The Netherlands*)

Two Viking Period iron axeheads from Norway, one from Marker, Sambøl, Østfold, and the other from Ringsaker, Grefsheim, Hedmark.

(*Photographer unknown, © Museum of Cultural History—University of Oslo, Norway*)

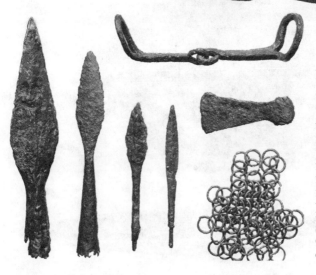

An arrowhead, two spearheads, a fragment of ring-mail, a bit, a dagger, and an axehead. All Iron Age/Viking Period, found in Hedmark in Norway: in Elverum, Bjølset; Elverum; Elverum, Prestmyra; Trysil, and Elverum, Heradsbygd, respectively. (*Photographer nknown, © Museum of Cultural History—University of Oslo, Norway*)

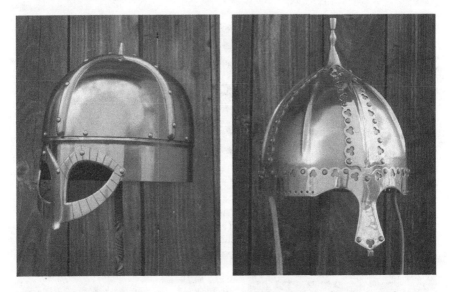

(*Above left*) Replica of the tenth-century helmet found at Gjermundbu, Norway, by Grzegorz Kulig (aka Thorkil). (© *Grzegorz Kulig, www.thorkil.pl*)

(*Above right*) Replica of one of two ninth- or tenth-century helmets found at Gnezdovo, Russia, by Grzegorz Kulig. The original helmet had an aventail. (© *Grzegorz Kulig*)

(*Below left*) Replica of the so-called "Wenceslas helmet": tenth-century, Bohemia, by Grzegorz Kulig. (© *Grzegorz Kulig*)

(*Below right*) Replica of a helmet of segmented and riveted construction, probably eleventh century. The site where the original was found is uncertain. This type of riveted helmet may be that represented on the Bayeux Tapestry, although the type with bands of metal similar to the spangenhelm is an alternative possibility. Helmet by Grzegorz Kulig. (© *Grzegorz Kulig*)

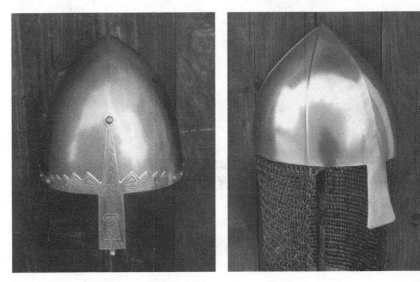

(*Above*) Picture stone from Lärbro socken, at Tängelgårda, Fånggården, Gotland, showing a fully manned Viking ship. The stern and stem posts resemble those of the Oseberg ship.
Photograph by Christer Åhlin, © Historical Museum, Stockholm, Sweden.
http://kulturarvsdata.se/shm/media/museumdat/211523)

(*Left*) Picture stone of the late Vendel or early Viking Period, Lärbro socken, Stora hammars, Gotland. The scenes may be from the tale of Hildr Högnado´ttir, alluded to or related in three sources. The warriors and the hero falling from his horse may well reflect contemporary experience of combat.
(*Photograph Statens historiska museer 2004-12-30, © Historical Museum, Stockholm, Sweden*)

(*Below*) The Gokstad ship, early Viking Period. Excavated in Sandefjord, Gokstad, Vestfold, Norway. (*Unknown photographer, © Museum of Cultural History—University of Oslo, Norway*)

The runestone U344, found at Yttergärde, which commemorates Ulf of Borresta's expeditions to England. Transcribed into Old Norse, the text reads: **En UlfR hafiR a Ænglandi þry giald takit. Þet vas fyrsta þet's Tosti ga[l]t. Þa (galt) Þorkætill. Þa galt Knutr. ("And Ulfr has taken three payments in England. That was the first that Tosti paid. Then Þorketill paid. Then Knútr paid.")** The stone is now in the churchyard of Orkesta, Uppland, Sweden. (*Author's photograph*)

(*Below & right*) Two examples of late Anglo-Saxon stone sculpture showing armed and mounted men, one with a shield, which was unlikely to be carried on a hunt. Sockburn 14, a hogback cist of yellow sandstone, and Chester-le-Street 01, a cross-shaft in pale yellow sandstone, both from Co. Durham. (© *Corpus of Anglo-Saxon Stone Sculpture, photographer T. Middlemass*)

Carolingian horsemen of the late ninth century, Golden Psalter (*Psalterium aureum*) of St Gallen—St Gallen, Stiftsbibliotek, Cod. Sang. 22, f.140. The horsemen are carrying "winged lances" and the standard is of the Late Roman "dragon windsock" variety, which was probably carried by all armies of its Germanic successor kingdoms at least until the ninth century, alongside other types of standard. It is also shown carried by the English in the Bayeux Tapestry. (*Source: Gettyimages*)

A scene from the Bayeux Tapestry, showing Norman cavalry attacking armoured English infantry, one of whom is carrying a two-handed axe. (*Source: Gettyimages*)

Aerial view of Harald Bluetooth's circular fort at Trelleborg, Jutland, Denmark. Outlines of the interior and exterior longhouses are marked. (*Photograph by Knud Erik Christensen. Source: Colourbox*)

View of the rampart and ditch of the Bullcroft area (north flank) of the burh at Wallingford, Oxfordshire. (*Image courtesy of the Wallingford Burh to Borough Research Project*)

The reconstructed inner gateway of the late tenth- or eleventh-century imperial palatine fort at Tilleda, Saxony-Anhalt, near the contemporary frontier with the Slavs. This form of construction would have been common in the Viking Period. (*Photograph by Gabriele Roeder-Campbell. © Gabriele Roeder-Campbell*)

The reconstructed ninth-century Slavic fortified site of Groß Raden, in Mecklenburg-Vorpommern, Germany, the land of the Slavic Obodrites in the Viking Period. The photograph is taken from the outer fortified enclosure and shows the smaller main fort, which was surrounded by water in the ninth and tenth centuries. (*Photograph by Ronny Krüger*)

throw a spear any distance would have been quite difficult in a very dense formation, unless the thrower stepped out of it to cast his missile. Nevertheless, *The Battle of Maldon* and the Bayeux Tapestry both suggest a dense formation and the throwing of spears. Some of the close combat weapons used also required more space than others to be used to maximum effect, such as two-handed axes. These are depicted on the Bayeux Tapestry in the hands of armored English warriors. Only one man with a two-handed axe is clearly portrayed in an unbroken battle line and all are shown together with spearmen or swordsmen. If the Tapestry can be taken as an accurate representation of their use, two-handed axes appear to be carried by only some of the men, backed by others with spears and swords, perhaps so that they could step out of the line to attack when the opportunity presented itself. With the one exception, long axes are shown in the hands of Harold's brothers and other armored men in what appear to be the last stages of the battle, when the English line had been broken.

The idea has been perpetrated, particularly by wargames rule writers, that early medieval (and other) close order infantry operated on a fairly rigid frontage per man and became less effective on broken ground. There seems no reason to assume that Viking, Anglo-Saxon or other contemporary infantry, in particular those who were experienced or practiced warriors, could not move across broken terrain and fight on it in a slightly more open formation, without overlapping shields, but still maintain a line. They may not have been drilled as Imperial Roman or Spartan troops were, but they could certainly be taught by veteran members of their household and learn by experience or example. Some of the Viking-Era European troops were "regular" in the sense that they were standing units. In addition, they had to adapt to fighting in different circumstances, which required different techniques, a known example being on the decks of ships. It may have been difficult or impossible for rear ranks to use "weight" or push effectively in a formation that was not densely packed, but they would still have provided moral support, replacements for the fallen in front of them and the means to dispatch wounded enemy on the ground. In his *Strategikon* Maurice describes the opening and closing of files as appropriate to the situation. He was discussing the Byzantine army, perhaps better trained than its "barbarian" counterparts. Nevertheless, there is no reason to assume that English, Carolingian, Ottonian or Viking troops that practiced for war could not close files and form a closer wall of shields to defend against missiles or cavalry, like that depicted in the Bayeux Tapestry, or open files to move to the attack or cross uneven ground.

However closely ordered a line was, it cannot have remained straight once battle was joined, as parts of it would have been pushed forward or back as more pressure was applied at some points than others by each side. It was important for the line to maintain cohesion if this occurred. If opposing lines separated completely from time to time, they could be reordered to some extent. In his study of the Greek phalanx, but equally relevant in many ways to the long line of several ranks that appears to have been the most common battlefield formation in our era, Alan Pittman suggested that if the integrity of a line was broken the gap might be difficult to exploit without reserves, and that the lines in the disrupted section might "reform" in looser formation to continue the struggle as a more fluid battle.[40] This might occur if the line being pushed back was severely disrupted but did not flee, the advancing line being disrupted as well. Once a section of the line broke and fled it was almost impossible to remedy the situation. If it were possible at all, any transfer of rear ranks from the phalanx to the flanks of the "hole" in an attempt to close it would have to be done very quickly and would likely result in total confusion. It would weaken the phalanx on either side of the gap, besides running the risk of causing those in the front ranks to collapse if they misinterpreted the movement as flight, bearing in mind that many of their line had already fled. There was a much stronger possibility that the collapse and flight of one section of a battle line would lead to disaster for the whole line, what Pittman calls the "snowball effect," as panic spread outwards from the broken section. For troops trained and accustomed to fighting in a phalanx, this formation gave them security and solidity, and its breaking must have severely weakened their morale. Only the highest quality or most dedicated troops might have continued to fight in knots or attempted to halt an enemy that had broken through a line.

A battlefield formation that appears in almost every modern work on Viking warfare is the wedge, but the evidence for its use is thin. The authority most frequently cited in this context is Saxo, yet the wedge (*cuneus* or *caput porcinum*, "boar's head") is mentioned only in the early books of his *History of the Danes*, which are constructed from a mixture of tradition and mythology and woven into a tale ("history") by the author himself. His detailed description of the *cuneus*, given in Book VII, is difficult to interpret, although there is little doubt that he describes a wedge of sorts.[41] Odin instructs Harald to use a formation headed by a triangle of twenty men with two men at the front. Three further units of twenty men are arranged behind this to complete the triangle. On each flank of the triangular head is a wing composed of young men with veterans behind them, but it is not clear whether these wings are positioned as files on the flanks of a block or column of lesser men, which Saxo describes as following the pyramid, or as lines extending to either flank facing the enemy with the lesser folk behind them. Behind this formation are another three units of twenty men formed like those at the front. Saxo appears to suggest that these could form a wedge facing the rear if necessary. The wings are supported by slingers, but again, it is difficult to understand precisely where they are, as at one point he seems to indicate that they could give support from behind the wings. Even allowing for difficulties of interpretation, there are strange elements in this formation. The suggestion is that the elite troops at the rear would guard against an attack to flank or rear, but it is difficult to understand why they too would form a wedge, while the description of skirmishing slingers supporting the flanking lines suggests classical influence. It is difficult to know how much of the detail might be Saxo's own invention or that of his source. In any case, it is improbable that all wedges, if used by Germanic armies, would have been identical in size and structure. Saxo himself describes a simpler but shallower and broader wedge in Book II, with each rank double the length of the one in front.

There is sufficient evidence that the Roman army used a wedge formation, even though the term *cuneus* was also used as a term for a cavalry unit in the fourth century. Both Livy and Caesar mention it as an infantry formation, as does Ammianus in the fourth century, when he calls it caput porci (boar's head) as well as cuneus.[42] Vegetius also describes the *caput porci* used as a formation by a Germanic unit, but he is a suspect source for late Roman tactics, since he used passages from earlier Roman authors.[43] The Norse wedge, the *svinfylking* ("swine-array"), appears in a number of Icelandic sources as well as Saxo's history, probably sufficient to suggest that such a formation was used, even allowing for borrowing of themes from each other. If we accept this, was the *svinfylking* a memory of a past method of fighting, or was it a formation used closer to Saxo's own time and transposed back into the mythological past, as many other elements of his first nine books certainly are? Given its antiquity and the relative ease of using such a formation (though not Saxo's version), it is unlikely that it was developed independently in Scandinavia after the Viking Era. On the other hand, in the era when Scandinavian written sources appeared, its authors were well aware of classical literature, none more than Saxo. In his Book VIII Odin instructs another to use a concave line to defeat Harald, a formation that would have been a suitable response to an attack in wedge, and again one recommended by a Roman author.[44]

Use of a wedge formation would certainly have been feasible, and in certain circumstances advantageous. Ian Stephenson suggested that the "boar's head" would probably have had a wide "boar's snout" of a number of warriors, rather than the one-or two-warrior "snout" often suggested, usually with Saxo in mind. Rather than being a strictly triangular formation, the "wide snout" wedge would have been a column wider at its base than its head. It should have been easier and faster to launch an attack in such a formation (or more than one wedge) than in line, and it would have been an effective method of putting the main weight of the attack at a certain point, possibly a vital point such as the place occupied by an opposing commander. A wedge formation would also have given a greater opportunity of breaking an enemy line relatively quickly, which could well end the battle. An army so inferior in strength that it could not avoid being overlapped on its flanks might have been well advised to use it rather than contacting the enemy in a long line that would either be overlapped or prove too thin.

In his tenth-century military treatise Emperor Nikephoros Phokas described a wedge used by the Byzantine army, in this case formed of heavily armored cavalrymen on armored horses (*kataphraktoi*).[45] He envisaged it as operating in the center of the Byzantine front line with its flanks protected by other cavalry. Its purpose was to smash through the enemy formation, if possible where the enemy commander was stationed. This is exactly the way in which western European armies might use an infantry wedge. Unlike their western contemporaries, the Byzantines saw their infantry as adopting a defensive role on the battlefield, probably because their most dangerous enemies had always used horsemen as their main striking arm. Nikephoros had the Hamdanids in mind when he wrote his treatise. Notably, although he is describing formations used by an army that probably had more tactical flexibility and more formal training than contemporary western European armies, his wedge formation is less complicated than Saxo's. It is also a "wide snout" wedge like that suggested by Stephenson. Where Saxo and Nikephoros agree is on the use of elite troops. We know from

Leo the Deacon that Nikephoros's successor John Tzimiskes used the heavy cavalry wedge in a way Nikephoros had not envisaged against the Rus in the first battle at Dorostolon. After a prolonged series of clashes throughout the day, the Emperor introduced his heavy cavalry wedges on each flank. Their attack broke the enemy line and caused a flight back to Dorostolon. If Skylitzes's account of their subsequent discussions is to be believed, it was not an experience the Rus wished to repeat too often.[46]

There is little evidence for the use of the wedge formation in western or northern European armies, but Richer of Saint-Rémi does mention the use of a *cuneus* in battle, ironically by the Franks against the Vikings. Richer was familiar with military matters. After the main Viking force had been routed at Montpensier (892), another approached from the flank, having apparently been sent "by side paths" to attack King Odo's army. If we disregard Richer's figure of 4,000 for the fresh Viking force, his description of the attack on them is plausible, as it was led by one Ingo carrying King Odo's standard, seemingly positioned at the apex of a wedge and among elite troops in close formation, probably, but not certainly, indicating an attack on foot.[47] Stephenson also noted that Asser described Alfred as advancing on the battlefield of Ashdown "in the manner of a wild boar," which might be a reference to the use of a wedge.[48] However, in the same passage Asser describes his division as having "closed ranks in proper order as a *testudo*," and the wild boar may simply be a reference to Alfred's courage and determination.[49]

If the infantry wedge was widely used by western and Scandinavian armies in the Viking Era, its use probably declined soon after. Although Charles Oman's thesis of the era of cavalry dominance has long since been demolished and it has been shown that motivated, cohesive and dense infantry formations generally had the advantage in a head-on battle with medieval heavy cavalry, a better argument can be made that the role of infantry became more defensive, rather as it had been in the Byzantine army, as effective heavy cavalry became the main offensive strike force. However, there are occasional references to use of a wedge (*cuneus*) by infantry that did act offensively against other infantry in the High Middle Ages, for instance the Italian communal infantry of Bergamo in 1156.[50] In Scandinavia its use may well have continued in Norway, where "Viking military tradition" lasted longer, and perhaps Sweden.

Although it seems that they made little use of cavalry in battle themselves, the Vikings had to contend with armies that did use it. In the armies of western and central Europe cavalry fought in dense formations on the battlefield, just as the infantry did. In the early ninth century Nithard described how Carolingian horsemen were trained. From what we know of battles in the period 750–1080, similar training would have been suitable throughout. The tenth-century poem *Waltharius* describes how cavalry formed into compact groups, approached the enemy and threw spears before (if) charging into contact, a form of attack not dissimilar from that used by infantry. More will be said of actual combat below. It is difficult to argue, as some have done, that the use of heavy cavalry developed in the Frankish realms only in this period, as we know so little about them beforehand. We know that in the High Middle Ages knights trained in groups of five to ten, referred to as *conrois* in much of western and central Europe, but in the period 750–1100 the actual operational units are obscured by use of classical terminology.[51] Nithard's descriptions of training for mounted combat suggest that similar groups were used even in practices organized on a regional level. The tactical units of both infantry and cavalry must have varied in size, as landowners had varying numbers of followers, but were probably somewhat larger than ten. In the Byzantine army the smallest tactical unit of cavalry was the *banda* of fifty. The ultimate object of cavalry training may have been to execute a massed charge, as many assume, but this was very difficult to execute in unison and only appropriate in certain circumstances. In a situation like that faced at Montpensier, Lenzen or Hastings, where infantry "walls" had to be broken down, smaller units must have been used in an attempt to disrupt them, like the group of fifty horsemen that finally routed the Slavs at Lenzen, allowing more control and avoiding the risk of wholesale flight if an attack was repulsed.

Missile men on foot

The role of missile men in battles of the Viking Era is very unclear. In the Byzantine army of the tenth century the archers formed whole ranks behind at least two ranks of spearmen, with one or two ranks of spearmen at the rear, but this was a primarily defensive formation designed especially to repel cavalry. In other European armies the only evidence that foot archers operated *en masse* comes from the Frankish realms, and these examples are so few before the late eleventh century that we have no idea how often this tactic was employed. The nature of the sources means that lack of mention does not imply lack of use. Only one English archer is depicted in the

Bayeux Tapestry, among the ranks of the heavy infantry. There has been a general assumption that dispersing archers around or amongst the "shield-wall," seeking targets of opportunity, was the predominant practice in the Viking Era, but we cannot be certain. There are representations of archers in Frankish illustrations, and archers were used in the defense of Paris in 857, but there is rarely any clue as to how they were employed on the battlefield.[52] With the exception of the nomad horse archers and Byzantine cavalry, there is little evidence of mounted use of the bow in battle. However, it was among the equipment demanded of noble Carolingian warriors in Frankish cartularies. The bow also appears in the St. Gall "Golden Psalter" in the hands of one armored cavalryman. This suggests that cavalrymen did use it in warfare. This may have been the practice only in skirmishes, when they were not expected to close with the enemy and fight it out hand-to-hand, but it cannot be ruled out that the bow was sometimes used in battle by men in the rear ranks, such as the mounted archer in this illustration. One mounted archer is shown in the Bayeux Tapestry, but during the pursuit.

It is from the Tapestry and from written accounts of Hastings that we have our best evidence for the use of massed infantry archers, by the Normans. The only reference to their use in Norman armies before then, in William's army at Varaville in 1157, comes from a dubious source, Wace's *Roman de Rou*, a poetic work in French written a century later. Nevertheless, it is clear that William was experienced in their use by 1066. William of Poitiers describes his army as approaching the enemy in three divisions, archers and crossbowmen first, followed by mailed infantry, followed by the horsemen. The archers opened the battle and then made way for the cavalry to attack. The Tapestry suggests that they did this in small groups, presumably corresponding to the later *conrois*. There may have been an attempt at a mass charge early in the battle, possibly the phase that led to the confusion when William was thought to have fallen and had to remove his helmet to show himself and rally his troops. The object of these "sting" attacks by cavalry, combined with feigned flights and probably alternating with attacks by foot spearmen and archery fire, was to break up the English line.

In the end, however, it was probably an unnamed archer who decided the Battle of Hastings, by hitting Harold. William's contemporary, Robert Guiscard, also used archers and horsemen in combination four years later at Dyrrachium against the Byzantines, which suggests that the practice was usual among the Normans, and probably the Franks. In fact, there is an account of an earlier battle in which similar tactics were used against the Vikings, at Montpensier in 892. Richer of St-Rémi tells us that Odo deployed his infantry and archers in a front line and his cavalry behind. The archers bombarded the enemy with arrows, then the infantry attacked, followed by the cavalry, which proved too much for the Norsemen.[53] The 'Norman' formations mentioned above differed from those of the tenth-century Byzantine army in that their foot divisions were not of combined arms but entirely of archers or of foot armed for close combat. They were able to do this when they knew the enemy was standing on the defensive. Neither Harold at Hastings nor Alexios Komnenos in the final stages of the battle at Dyrrachium had horsemen to challenge the Norman heavy cavalry.

The Normans probably derived their tactics from Frankish practice rather than their Viking forebears, as the settlers had been absorbed by the eleventh century. However, we do know that the Vikings used bowmen. On at least one occasion a Viking archer had an important influence on a battle, when he shot and badly wounded Count Ranulf of Poitiers at Brissarthe in 866, in this case shooting from a church tower. The evidence is mostly late, and archers are usually mentioned in naval battles. What does seem likely is that all household and mercenary warriors had the ability to use missile weapons. There are many records of Scandinavians of all classes using bows on board ship. Those referring to the Viking Era may be late sources, but there is good reason to assume that the housecarls and leaders of the twelfth century were following the example of their Viking forefathers. In 1098, during one of Magnus Barelegs's expeditions to the Irish Sea, his fleet approached Anglesey, where they were confronted by Hugh of Shrewsbury and a force of Normans. Despite being fully armored, Hugh was killed by an arrow which penetrated his brain through the eye socket, allegedly fired by King Magnus himself.[54] Other European aristocracy also used missile weapons when appropriate—William the Bastard/Conqueror and his son Robert, for instance, were known to be excellent archers, but again, they do not appear to have used bows or crossbows in field battles.

Slings and javelins were also used, but we have no idea what proportion of armies either they or the archers made up, or whether they were used to any extent on the battlefield. Given their tactics, the Wends of the south Baltic coast and the Irish must have used javelins in battle, but it is not certain that others did. In the Byzantine army they were used in support of cavalry and also brought into the action when enemy cavalry had been halted by the spearmen and archers. The Bulgarian tsar John Vladislav was killed by these light infantry in 1018, after being injured and knocked from his horse.[55] Again, it is possible that lightly armored men with lighter spears or javelins were sometimes used for similar purposes in western and Viking armies, if in a less organized way, dispersed among the ranks. Roman sources mention that Germanic tribesmen used them to support horsemen, but if the practice continued throughout the "Dark Ages," we have no evidence for it. Nor can we even make a guess as to how many archers, slingers or javelinmen there were in English, Pictish, Scottish, Viking, Frankish or any of the armies of the emerging Slavic states. Unlike the Byzantine army, there was no prescribed ratio (which even in this army cannot always have been fulfilled) of troop types: to a large extent western and northern European armies were *ad hoc* assemblies of troops, since lords or chieftains were summoned to bring their men, and what turned up with them was the army.

Reserves and rear support

A characteristic of most battlefield formations for the majority of this period (and in the previous three centuries) seems to be the lack of any reserves, although there are examples of one division of the army being kept back in a concealed position. On these occasions the troops held back were not kept behind the line, but on one flank and to the rear, the idea presumably being that their unexpected appearance as a reinforcement would demoralize the enemy. When confronting the Scots and Northumbrians at Corbridge (918) Ragnall, king of the Dublin Vikings and of York, is supposed have deployed in three divisions and kept a fourth, his own, hidden until an opportune stage in the battle. Its arrival seems to have saved the Viking army.[56] Earlier in the year, while campaigning against Niall Glú ndub in Ireland, Ragnall's division had snatched victory from impending defeat by arriving unexpectedly at Topar Glethrach near Clonmel.[57] It is not certain whether on this occasion he arrived late on the field ("from the camp of the foreigners") by chance or design. If the former, he may have devised the tactic after this experience. However, the convention in most European armies was clearly to commit all available troops on one front to break the enemy line. This meant that any collapse at one point of the line was likely to lead to defeat, as there was little chance of repairing the breach. Once an enemy line disintegrated, the victorious troops would also lose all cohesion, which theoretically left them vulnerable to any newly arrived enemy force.

The practice of forming in more than one line had been used by the Byzantine army for some centuries, in this case largely to prevent encirclement of the first line when facing opponents who often used fluid tactics, such as armies composed largely of horse archers, or to form a reserve should the first line be routed.[58] In his *Taktika* Leo VI argued that there was no advantage in deploying in only one line, save perhaps to impress the enemy. A problem that Byzantine commanders had to face less than their Latin counterparts, although they were not free of it, was jealousy between commanders of different contingents. This may have been one contributory factor in the tendency to deploy in one line in northern Europe, but a greater fear may have been, with less disciplined armies, that the rear line would flee on seeing the first line break. There was also a danger that quality troops would be "wasted" if placed in a rear line or reserve, unable to contribute to the battle at all. As always, such practical concerns easily became subsumed in convention. Even against the Magyars or the Saracens there is no evidence that other European armies followed the Byzantine practice. In 982 Otto II, the son of the victor of the Lechfeld, suffered a crushing defeat by the Saracens in southern Italy, and was only saved by swimming to a Byzantine ship lying offshore. Unfortunately we know virtually nothing of this battle other than Thietmar's brief account.[59] The account also suggests that initial success led the Imperial army into a rash and disorderly advance, but whether this was brought about by a "feint withdrawal" or not is unknown. There is no indication that there was any rear line, which the Byzantine army would certainly have used against such opponents, and if there was it too rushed forward. Among the fallen were six counts, four other nobles and the bearer of the holy lance, "and innumerable others whose names are known only to God," testimony to the severity of the defeat.

In the Frankish realms the practice of forming up in more than one line was used on some occasions, perhaps increasingly so as the period progressed. One example is the Battle of Montpensier mentioned above. Like William at Hastings, Odo may have known that the opposing army intended to fight on the defensive and deployed accordingly. Unlike the Byzantines, whose two lines were each of combined arms, their separate lines were each of one troop type. An exception to this rule in the west may be the Angevin count Fulk Nerra. In both of his battles he seems to have employed two divisions, but these were not deployed alongside one another. In the first instance, at Conquereuil in 991, in which he was faced by the army of Conan of Brittany, they were deployed one behind the other. Conan's army was waiting in position with secure flanks. The first division attacked rashly, the charge probably initiated by a part of the force without the count's orders, although he decided to commit the entire division in support. According to one account, they blundered into the series of pits, traps and ditches dug in front of the Breton force, which counter-attacked and caused serious losses among Fulk's men, Fulk himself being wounded. However, the entire Breton force was now in disorder and was overwhelmed by the attack of Fulk's second division. Both lines appear to have included cavalry. At Pontlevoy in 1016 the initial attack on Count Hugh's army was also repulsed, although it appears that the withdrawal was more orderly in this case. The attack by the second division took Hugh's army completely by surprise, particularly as it was launched with the evening sun behind it, and brought about the flight of Hugh's knights and the slaughter of much of his infantry. In these instances Fulk was deploying one division as a reserve, whereas his opponents were deploying in one line. The pattern of deployment used by him was to become much more common in the twelfth and thirteenth centuries, with two or three divisions ("battles") often drawn up one behind the other to deliver successive blows or cover a retreat.

Tactics on the periphery: Nomads, Slavs and Celts

So far the discussion has concentrated on the tactics used by the majority of armies in northern and central Europe. Battle was a set-piece "slogging-match" in which close-quarter combat ultimately determined who won or lost, unless both sides fought to a standstill. However, there were "peoples" who fought major engagements in a different manner, by using skirmishing tactics. In our "Viking Era" the most feared of these were the Magyars, although this fear was not necessarily created by their reputation in battle, but by the damage they caused and their speed of movement, which made it difficult to get to grips with them. In addition, unless they were confronted with their backs to a river, in unsuitable terrain for use of horses and bows, or when looting or loaded down with plunder, it was hard to prevent them from simply fleeing *en masse* and reassembling elsewhere. The tactics of other nomads such as the Pechenegs were very similar. Virtually all these warriors carried a bow with which they were able to shoot in any direction, including behind as they retreated, the so-called "Parthian shot."

The Magyars had a significant influence on the tactics and organization of the German armies that the Vikings faced. Both Leo VI in his *Taktika* and the western chronicler Regino of Prü m emphasize that surprise, encircling movements and feigned flight were their methods of warfare.[60] After initial disasters in the first decades of the tenth century, beginning with the reign of Henry I, the Ottonians learned not to be goaded into rash advances by arrow fire or drawn into them by feint retreats. Whatever formation horse archers were in, surprising and closing with them quickly gave their opponents a good chance of victory. In order to do this, the German cavalry had to maintain a close formation and advance steadily. When their evasive tactics failed and they were in danger of being forced into mêlée with more heavily armed opponents, the Magyars abandoned the field. In both of the famous victories won by the Ottonians most of them probably escaped, but after Lechfeld (955) their army was destroyed during the subsequent retreat.[61] Although any battle line of horse archers was a relatively loose formation, it had to be maintained at a suitable distance from the enemy, possibly while he was advancing or even withdrawing, in order to cause sufficient damage with volleys of arrows to break up his formation. Horse archer armies may have been loosely formed and well practiced in skirmishing tactics, but there was still a chain of command and a line (or successive lines) of battle.

Vikings must have come into contact with peoples using similar tactics to the Magyars in the east, the region that is now Russia. These would have included Khazars, Pechenegs, Kasogians and Alans (Yasi). Their main hostile contact was probably with the Pechenegs, which would have been encountered by independent Viking bands or mercenaries serving the Rus princes in the late tenth and eleventh centuries. Al Masudi, the Arab historian, describes how the Pechenegs detached troops of "one thousand horsemen" to left and right of the main army when fighting a Byzantine–Bulgar army, troops which proceeded to cross from right to left and vice versa while raining arrows onto their opponents until the latter charged out in a disorderly manner, whereupon they were surrounded by the main force and annihilated with arrow fire. Both Pechenegs and Magyars almost certainly formed command units in multiples of ten, like all known medieval Turco–Mongol armies.

In *c.* 1036 Yaroslav Vladimirovich inflicted a heavy defeat on the Pech-enegs with an army of Varangians and Slovenes and allies from the north. How was an army of mounted archers defeated by such a force? The answer is probably that the Pechenegs, who were besieging Kiev, allowed them-selves to be attacked, perhaps electing to defend their camp/s rather than choosing to lift the siege and fight elsewhere. The defeat of Kerbogah out-side Antioch in 1198 is a betterdocumented example of a besieging army with numbers of horse archers being defeated by an army that had very few mounted troops.[62] It is also possible that Yaroslav had learned from past difficulties and acquired more mounted troops. The nomad Polovtsy or Cumans replaced the Pechenegs on the steppe north of the Black Sea in the mid-eleventh century, and proved an even more destructive enemy. After our period, the Rus led by Vladimir Monomakh adopted a policy of striking deep into the steppe with the object of attacking the Polovtsy where they were vulnerable: the first such attack was in 1103, when "cattle and sheep and camels and tents with their contents and slaves" were taken and a number of Polovtsian princes were killed.[63] This tactic had been used suc-cessfully once against the Magyars in central Europe, in 946, but it must have been difficult to achieve as it entailed reaching the nomad camp before it could be moved and without interception by an enemy who should have been faster-moving.

As noted earlier, the nomads were not alone in using skirmishing tac-tics. Other armies that employed numbers of lightly armed horsemen on smallish horses (or ponies) also took a similar attitude to battle, notably the Bretons and the Wends. The comparison between Magyar and Bre-ton tactics was made explicitly by a contemporary chronicler, Regino of Prüm.[64] It is probably no coincidence that much of the terrain in Brittany and Wendland was uncultivated and difficult to move through, in the Bre-ton case forests and hills, and in the Wendish area forests and marshes. Like the nomads, among their horsemen only the princes and their bodyguards would have been armored, although there were probably more of them. Their missile weapons were primarily javelins rather than bows, so they had to take a greater risk of being contacted by enemy cavalry to inflict any damage. The explanation for the length of the Battle of Jengland in 851 (three days, if the sources are to be believed) is probably the tactics of the Bretons. Charles the Bald's army was unable to counter these tactics, and after two days he fled at night, causing his army to disintegrate on the next day and losing his baggage and a vast amount of treasure in the process.[65] In the ninth century Vikings served as both allies and enemies of the Bretons, and caused severe damage at times in the region around Nantes. They suffered some serious defeats in 890–891 at the hands of Alan of Broweroch ("the Great").

A curiosity of our accounts of early Breton forces is that they make no mention of infantry. It is inconceivable that no Bretons fought on foot before the eleventh century, given the terrain of Brittany, so this is probably an accident of the very limited sources. Breton raiding forces are likely to have consisted of mounted men, and their own sources, like many of the Frankish ones, may have been interested only in the elite of their armies. In the tenth century, presumably after the reconquest of Brittany from the Vikings, Breton armies probably became very similar to those of their neighbors in Francia, and they were virtually indistinguishable from the Normans and other heavily armed cavalry in William's invasion army in 1066. In addition, we have evidence of infantry when they fought Fulk Nerra at the end of the tenth century. It may, indeed, have been the Vikings that brought this change about, as Brittany suffered unparalleled devastation for thirty years after 907, and was all but overrun by the Norwegian Rognvaldr in 919, apparently with little serious resistance. Without a single recognized ruler, it seems that Brittany could not put an effective army into the field.

Our best accounts of Wendish tactics come from the twelfth century, but there is no reason to believe that they had changed significantly. The defeat of the Danes by harassing horsemen in *c.* 1113 has already been mentioned. Many Wendish warriors fought on foot, and, like their Frankish counterparts, those who owned horses probably fought on foot also when the occasion demanded. In Saxo's descriptions of battles with the Danes later in the twelfth century both infantry and cavalry often took to flight when faced with more heavily armed opponents, although, as in the case of his Frankish predecessors, what Saxo describes as terrified flight is often feigned flight. As noted above, the Pomeranian foot at Nakło (1109) adopted a dense formation, which the author of the *Deeds of the Princes of the Poles* clearly thought odd ("not Christian").[66] They were overwhelmed by the Poles, fighting in western style. However, on occasion Slavic foot did put up a stiff resistance, as against Henry I's troops at Lenzen in 929. Although Widukind says their infantry (the vast majority of their army) had poor morale and had to be driven forwards to fight by the whips of their own horsemen, this is belied by events, as they proceeded to hold out for most of the day and were only routed by an attack on their flank by some of Henry's armored cavalry. As suggested by David Bachrach, the Slavs may have learned this phalanx-method of forming up for battle from their western neighbors. Widukind says that the Polish duke Miesco used a phalanx against the Slavic tribe of the Wuloini, and they also used it after this.[67] The Moravians and the Rus also adopted this method of fighting on foot in dense lines, but there is some indication that the Wends nearer the Baltic coast fought more often in looser formations, as they generally did in the twelfth century.

It is possible that Irish armies fought in a similar fashion to the northern Wends, given the nature of the terrain and the equipment of the pre-Viking Irish warriors, which was ill-suited to close combat with the Vikings. Eventually the Irish adopted Viking weapons, longer swords and even two-handed axes, although armor remained very rare, but this does not mean they regularly fought in dense masses. At Clontarf in 1014, where it appears that the battle was a regular encounter between close order lines, if the early twelfth-century *Cogadh Gaedhel re Gallaibh* (*The War of the Irish with the Foreigners*) is at all accurate, the Irish forces in both armies had difficulty in resisting the onslaught of their Viking opponents. However, even in the ninth century the Vikings suffered a number of defeats in battle, and this at a time when their English and continental opponents were struggling to defeat them. Unfortunately Scandinavian sources tell us virtually nothing of Ireland and the Irish annals usually list the date, the place (name) and the casualties, naming the important people. Only rarely do they describe actions during battles, and then only if they were considered exceptional. Casualties are invariably listed in the hundreds, an indication of the small size of the forces involved.

The one action we have some detail of, albeit given in the late sagas, is the battle that ended Magnus Barelegs' forays into the region in 1103.[68] Magnus and King Muirchertach had been campaigning in the north of Ireland. When Muirchertach left with his army to go to Connaught, Magnus decided to return to Norway, leaving some forces to hold Dublin, but he first sent a small force to his ally to get provisions. Its return was delayed and Magnus took most of his army a short distance inland and met up with it. While strung out on tracks and stepping stones through bogs and thickets on their way back to his ships, his army was ambushed by a large number of Irish. Magnus attempted to gather his men and ordered some to occupy a knoll so they could shoot at the enemy, but they fled after crossing a ditch, leaving Magnus and his force on the other side to be overwhelmed, the king himself being killed. This battle may be typical of many the Irish had fought against Scandinavian forces. However they fought against each other, the Irish may have realized quite quickly that it was better to attack Viking forces in terrain favorable to their lightly armed and equipped troops. Viking raiders would have been particularly vulnerable to ambushes when returning to their ships laden with plunder. A comparison may be made with Welsh forces, which were capable of fighting battles but usually avoided them against better-equipped foes if circumstances were unfavorable. Many of their victories against the English may have been ambushes, like that which gave Gruffudd ap Llywelyn victory over the army of Ealdorman Edwin in 1039, if John of Worcester's account is reliable.[69]

Feigned flight

A tactic favored by all armies that used skirmishing horsemen was feigned flight, but these armies were not alone in using it. Those who suggest that Norman and Frankish (or German, after 900) horsemen were incapable of performing a feigned flight are underestimating their abilities, besides assuming that a large number of sources have falsified events.[70] In the early ninth century Nithard described how Carolingian horsemen were trained to execute this manoeuvre.[71] Feigned flight was a useful tactic for breaking up a close order formation, but it was also a risky one. Since the object was to draw out the enemy in pursuit, it was likely to be successful only when the enemy being enticed to pursue could not easily make contact. If there was any danger of contact other troops would need to be kept in reserve to exploit the undisciplined pursuit. Since those feigning flight would need time to halt and reform, this was probably the preferred option in any case. There is still dispute about whether the Normans deliberately employed this tactic at Hastings, or whether some of them actually fled and rallied. Possibly both occurred, a genuine but temporary flight first, which was followed by deliberate feigned flights after the first had inadvertently achieved positive results. Those depicted as pursing them in the Tapestry seem to be the unarmored *fyrd* troops. Although this may have resulted in some of them being cut down, there is no evidence that sufficient numbers were killed to win the battle; as noted, it was probably only Harold's death that brought this about. The danger with a feigned flight was that it would degenerate into a real flight. The troops conducting the withdrawal might panic, the pursuers might contact them with their backs turned, or those held in reserve might mistake the feint as a real flight and follow suit. In theory it was possible for a whole army to "flee" and reform once it had outdistanced the pursuing enemy, but without reserve troops this could all too easily become a wholesale flight from the battlefield.

Feigned flight could also be used to lure the enemy into an ambush, as it was by the Byzantines at Arcadiopolis, in this case with spectacular results, as it brought about the destruction of many of the opposing army's horsemen. In an account that was probably drawn from eyewitnesses to the battle, Liudprand of Cremona also tells us that Henry I sent lightly equipped Thuringian horsemen forward in front of the main imperial army at Riade (933). In this case it was an attempt to draw the Magyars forward within range of his heavy cavalry rather than to lead them into rash pursuit, as the nomad tactics would have been to shower them with arrows. Nevertheless, the Thuringians would have had to execute a rapid retreat in the face of the enemy to avoid heavy casualties. The tactic of feigned flight was also used by the Vikings on foot at Saucourt, although once again it is difficult to know whether it was planned or not. This was not an ambush, but the Vikings withdrew to a royal villa, before charging out again unexpectedly and almost reversing the course of the battle, as the Franks evidently believed that they had already won it. Louis managed to halt the flight of his own forces and turn the tide again. He did this by dismounting, which suggests that this was understood as a signal that there would be no flight. Any feigned flight by infantry, if this Viking retreat was such, could only be made into defenses or terrain which was inaccessible to the enemy.

Combat

As far as we can tell, with the exception of those who adopted skirmish tactics, both mounted and foot used fairly dense formations. This meant that the advance to combat had to be steady, rather than the mad rush of the movies. The portrayal of medieval battle in these films is probably correct in one respect, however—if troops *had* rushed towards the enemy in this way, as fast as they could, they would have been in no formation whatever when they made contact, which is precisely why they rarely did this. Snorri's description of the advance at Stiklestad is much more likely to reflect reality:

> Now when the battle order of the farmers was established, the
> landed men spoke to them, exhorting the troops to watch their
> position, where each one was stationed, beneath which standard
> was his place, how far from his banner and how near it. They asked
> the men to be alert and quick to take their places when the trum-
> pets sounded and they heard the signal, and then keep step; because
> they still had to advance their army a very long distance, and there
> was a chance that their lines might break during the march.[72]

There may have been a surge forward for the last few yards, but, as Guy
Halsall suggested, it is very probable that there was a halt (or hesitation)
immediately before this, as the troops steeled themselves. Either then or
during the final advance an assortment of missiles might be thrown at the
enemy, by both cavalry and infantry, but spears are most commonly mentioned. Since stones were available everywhere, it is likely that they were
widely used by infantry, as Snorri mentions in his accounts of battles. The
conversations reported in the kings' sagas are obviously not word-for-word
reports of what was said; even immediately after the battle speeches would
not be remembered entirely accurately, and they are too literary in style.
Nevertheless, there are realistic elements in them: it may well be that people
who had changed sides were taunted as turncoats, and people reminded
of their past failures or defeats, just as the Vikings at the Dyle are reported
to have reminded Arnulf's men of the Geule defeat. It is even possible that
this taunting phase, accompanied by boasts and threats, was customary
before formal battle in pagan societies. At some stage leaders and champions would urge their own army forward. Attacks were normally preceded
or accompanied by shouts or war cries, designed to raise morale and intimidate the enemy. The Magyars certainly made loud yells as they approached
or circled their opponents, and the animal-like howls of the Rus before
Dorostolon were recorded by Leo the Deacon. There were other methods,
however, as Nikephoros Phokas demanded that his *kataphraktoi* form up in
wedge to attack the enemy in absolute silence, which may have been equally
intimidating.

The preliminaries to combat suggested above would only occur, of
course, if both sides stood: there were certainly occasions when one side
simply fled at the approach of the enemy, as troops were seized by an
uncontrollable panic. It is probable that when ancient or medieval chroni-

clers had only the information that a battle was won, they resorted to a stock description of a hard struggle and the eventual triumph of the winner—no one wanted to relate, hear or read that one side fled without a fight, as this brought no glory to the winners, let alone the losers. As regards the men on the battlefield, those who were more accustomed to battle would have known, before and during the fighting, that the best chance of preserving themselves was to stand their ground, as flight made a man an unprotected target. Nithard records all three possible outcomes of a conventional confrontation at Fontenoy-en-Puisaye (841). Evidently each of the three divisions on each side squared up against an opposing division: of the defeated army, Lothar's division was driven back by Louis and broke after a stiff fight, and Charles' opponents fled when Lothar was defeated, but those opposing the seneschal Adalhard fought on even when the rest of their army had gone. In the end that division also left the field, but Nithard hints that it held either until nightfall, when it was able to leave the field unmolested, or until an agreement was made to let it do so. Apprehension need not have produced flight, of course. There was also a danger of an uncontrolled charge forward by inexperienced troops, in an effort to "get it over with," sometimes referred to as the "flight to the front," another reason for the advice to make a measured advance in Snorri's account above.

There has been much discussion about the use of the couched lance and when its utilization by western horsemen became general. It is certain that this did not happen until right at the end of our period, if then. It was a tactic that was most useful against opposing horsemen and relied on the weight of the horse's There has been much discussion about the use of the couched lance and when its utilization by western horsemen became general. It is certain that this did not happen until right at the end of our period, if then. It was a tactic that was most useful against opposing horsemen and relied on the weight of the horse's momentum. Some spears are used underarm in the Bayeux Tapestry, but most are wielded overarm or thrown. It is not clear from this that tactics had changed significantly from the early ninth century when Nithard wrote, although there were continual improvements through horse breeding and there must have been experimentation in fighting methods. In battle the noise made by hooves, armor and battle cries must have been frightening and horses had to be well trained to face it and close with the enemy.[73] It was also intimidating for infantry awaiting the approach. *Waltharius* describes cavalry as advancing steadily in close ranks. It is possible that the final charge became faster during the last 40 yards as our period progressed, but this cannot be certain either. Nevertheless, the impact of a confrontation between cavalry forces was considerable and could be horrifying, if the *Waltharius* poet's description is accurate: 'The chests of some horses are smashed by the chests of other horses and some of the men went down [with their horses while] others were unseated by the hard shield bosses of their adversaries."

An account of the consequences of an advance to battle made in the wrong way is given by the *RFA* under the year 782, concerning the battle at the foot of the Sü ntel Mountains referred to above. Certain Frankish nobles decided to attack the Saxons before the rest of their army under Count Theodoric had arrived, because "they feared that the honor of victory might be Theodoric's alone if they should fight by his side." To make matters worse:

> They took up their arms and, as if they were chasing runaways and going after booty instead of facing an enemy lined up for battle, everybody dashed as fast as his horse would carry him to the place outside the Saxon camp, where the Saxons were standing in battle array. As soon as the fighting began, they were surrounded by the Saxons and slain almost to a man.[74]

If such a textbook existed, this would be a textbook example of "what not to do"; instead of forming in closely ordered formations and employing controlled charges like those discussed above, they attacked rashly, too quickly, in complete disorder, and when they were heavily outnumbered.

Once battle was joined it is likely that many, probably most of the infantry levy troops, adopted a primarily defensive posture in an effort to preserve life and limb. This does not mean they could not advance, but envisages a situation in which it was possible to push forward in combat between phalanxes, making occasional attempts to strike at the opponent/s in front, but always trying to keep the shield up and head down. This is, of course, conjectural, as we have no good account of this experience from any era, so there is plenty of room for debate, similar to that which has occurred over Victor Hanson's suggestion that Greek hoplite battles were primarily pushing matches until one side broke.[75] As described earlier, early medieval levy infantry must have received some training. Re-enactors and others have suggested that it takes little training for infantry to form in ranks with spear and shield. This assumes that, unlike household troops, they were prepared for a limited task, which may sometimes have been the case. This is true even of infantry as they appear in the Byzantine military treatises. However, those who led forces in battle were well aware that levy troops needed the ability not only tostand in line, but to advance and maintain line, and they had to be capable of putting up a fight against any troops.

Pre-battle speeches probably reiterated what had already been taught at local musters, emphasising the duty of the men to their leaders, to each other and to the community. The example of men of experience would have been vital to urge them on, but in battle those in contact with the enemy would have had no choice but to fight if rear ranks pressed from behind. Although the mode of combat is very different nowadays, studies which have shown that the aggressive actions of relatively small numbers of men can sustain units in action may well be relevant to the medieval experience.[76] Once units closed to within striking distance, perhaps as close as a few meters from the enemy, leaders and elite troops may have led the assaults on the enemy line, or even made individual attacks as an example. These troops will have been those prepared to take risks that others did not, perhaps because they were more accustomed to battle or more regularly trained for it, more convinced of their own invincibility, or less concerned about their own safety. This is when troops such as berserkers would have come into their own, but even in the armies of Christianized peoples some troops probably went into a battle frenzy.

As Guy Halsall notes, if one side did not break, eventually the physical effort, accentuated by weight of equipment, would have caused more and more men to fall back into a defensive posture as tiredness set in, and this may have brought about a separation of the opposing lines.[77] This is a possible explanation for the reported length of many battles, as it is inconceivable that troops fought continuously for hours on end. If a battle consisted of repeated clashes, there would have been a need for water, replacement shields and so on. In some cases there may have been a tacit agreement to allow this before battle recommenced. Even with adequate re-supply of necessary equipment and sustenance, with each effort to close with the enemy or resist an attack the formation would probably have become more fragile, until one side broke or, a much rarer occurrence, the battle was ended by agreement. Under these circumstances it was possible for one force to give ground but come out victorious if it had more staying power than its foes,

who might finally succumb as tiredness and failure to break their opponents' will took their toll.

As for battles that are reported as lasting several days, of which are there
a considerable number in the *ASC*, if these are not exaggerated accounts
there may be several explanations. Some may have involved extended periods of skirmishing, while in others there may have been a long stand-off
before the armies actually clashed head on. It is also possible that some "battles" were a prolonged series of smaller actions, perhaps extending over a
wide area. Here we return to the start of the chapter, the discussion of what
constitutes a battle: even though there was no single "field of slaughter," a
series of clashes could be remembered as one action if it became associated
with a named place or terrain feature. These "battles" may in fact have been
a prolonged series of skirmishes, such as those mentioned in Chapter 4.

Naval battles

The heading of this section is somewhat misleading in that it conjures up
an image of the navies of modern times, but there was no such thing in the
medieval era. The point has been made that the main purpose of medieval fleets in war was to transport fighting men and equipment, not to seek
out other fleets to give battle. There was no concept of "control of the sea"
such as that of the seventeenth and eighteenth centuries. However, English, Frankish and Byzantine ships did make attempts to intercept Viking
or Arab raiding forces near the coast when ships were available for this. We
have records of clashes between Wessex and Viking fleets in 851 (Æthelstan, sub-king of Kent), 875 and 882 (both led by Alfred) and 885, but no
details of tactics.[78] All sixteen Danish ships engaged in the last action were
allegedly captured, but the Wessex fleet itself was subsequently defeated.
The other actions were smaller. Alfred is said to have built his new ships
in 896, and Edward the Elder deployed about a hundred ships in 910, but
there is no mention of any more battles until the eleventh century. Similarly, if Frankish fleets fought in large numbers in a single engagement in
the north we have no record of it. We do, however, have brief records of
Frankish battles against the Arabs in the Mediterranean between 799 and
813, after Charlemagne had ordered his son Louis to build a fleet there. This
was largely successful and Arab raids ceased, but they returned in mid-century, around the same time as the Viking raids intensified in the north.[79]
The Slavs, Kuronians and Estonians of the Baltic used ships for raiding, but

again, no major engagements with Scandinavian fleets such as those of the twelfth century are known of in this period. This does not mean there were none, as it is possible that battles went unrecorded by English or Frankish sources because there were no kings, earls or dukes present, or no place-name, landmark or memorial foundation to identify them by.

Of the known large-scale naval battles fought in the Viking Era, all those in northern waters were fought between Viking fleets. They are known mainly from later sagas, but it seems highly unlikely that all these battles were invented as back-projections of what occurred in the twelfth century. In addition, at least some of the Viking Era skaldic verse quoted in the sagas is likely to be authentic. There was clearly a tradition of fighting battles from shipboard in Scandinavia even before Harald Fairhair is said to have triumphed over his enemies at the Battle of Hafrsfjord in 872. All naval engagements were fought close to land, frequently in fjords, inlets or bays, where calmer waters could be found and the coast or islands could be used to advantage. In addition, information about the whereabouts of an enemy fleet was almost always acquired from people on land, living or working near the coast. The saga reports of conversations with named individuals in the Viking Era may be fictional, but this was undoubtedly the main method of information gathering and coming to grips with the enemy. As a result, just as on land, the fleet operating "in friendly territory" had an advantage. Fleets close to hostile territory either had difficulty gathering information, or worse, were misinformed, sometimes deliberately. Historical or not, the saga tradition was that the Jomsviking fleet on its way to attack Håkon Jarl was told that he was not far up the coast with only his own ship. They hurried north and succeeded in finding him, but he had 160 ships waiting to give battle.

The men who fought on board ship were the same who fought on land. Close combat on the decks of ships must have been every bit as grim an experience. Fallen men or severed body parts would have lain among stones and other debris of battle on decks slippery with blood. Space was limited, and men must have been pushed or forced to jump overboard even before one side lost heart. However, there were clearly differences between the fighting methods used on land and on board ship. In a fully fledged sea battle, both forces were on manoeuvrable platforms. Weather conditions, which obviously affected the surface of the water, were more likely to prevent battle from being joined or disrupt the fleets if they changed during an action.

Nevertheless, in one respect ship-to-ship engagements closely resembled land engagements in this period—the outcome was decided by close combat. After the demise of the ram used on the warships of the Mediterranean powers from *c.*700 BC to AD 300, and before the advent of shipboard cannon, there was no really effective "ship-killing" weapon available, and the only method of disabling enemy ships in warfare was to board them and overcome their defenders in hand-to-hand combat.[80] Ships, or at least their crews, could be burned, but the use of Greek fire or inflammatory substances was limited and potentially dangerous to those using them if conditions were not ideal. These weapons were not used in northern European waters, but a Rus fleet had a disastrous encounter with a Byzantine fleet using Greek fire in 1043. Some ships used by the Rus were of Viking type, but probably quite small as they had to negotiate the rivers to the Black Sea before approaching Constantinople. *Monoxyla* (dugouts) were also used, but neither was a match for the larger Byzantine *dromons*, even without fire siphons.

Almost all of our descriptions of Viking Age naval battles are to be found in the later kings' sagas, most of the remainder appearing in *Gesta Danorum*. None of the sagas gives a systematic description of how the various operations necessary for a naval battle were carried out, such as drawing the ships together into line, manoeuvring groups of several ships that were roped together, separating ships when trying to escape, and so on. However, most of these are explained in passing during accounts of battles or in the pre- or post-battle speeches attributed to commanders. It is necessary to draw analogies from later battles in Scandinavian and Baltic waters to assess the nature of naval warfare in the Viking Era. The accounts of mid-twelfth-century battles in the Icelandic–Norwegian sagas are more likely to be reliable as many were fought within one generation of people still living when they were written. Although the sagas drew on skaldic poetry for their tales of earlier battles, this rarely gives any insight into tactics, and we have no idea how reliable this or other oral tradition was. Accounts of the Viking-Era battles tend to be of the variety: "Immediately a great battle began, both vicious and long-lasting, until finally the king was victorious," usually including anecdotes of individuals or single ships, followed by a list of the fallen. Although the accounts of the battles of the Norwegian internal wars that lasted from 1130 to 1240 are similar in many ways, some of them give more revealing detail, particularly those in *Sverris saga*, which covers the wars of Sverre Sigurdsson from 1177 to 1202. It is valid to use these accounts because the ships and the nature of battles at sea seem to have changed very little, although Sverre adopted a slightly different approach to his predecessors. There were some changes: there is evidence that warships proper became wider and eventually larger, especially in Norway, as their primary purpose was no longer long-distance voyaging and penetrating the river systems of Europe, but fighting battles in home waters. In addition, the crossbow became a favored weapon on board ship, at least of the nobility. These changes had little effect on tactics, however, as the basic technology of shipbuilding and ship capabilities remained the same.

The different sizes of Viking ships have already been discussed. The traditional picture of a Viking sea battle is two lines of longships roped together side by side and facing each other head on. This is indeed the way virtually every Viking Age sea battle fought in the north is described in the sagas. This should act as a warning about their accounts: although it is possible that all the described battles were of this nature, there may be an element of convention in the descriptions; as will be seen, later battles were not all like this. As noted earlier, accounts of battles in the Norwegian internal wars also give cause for suspicion as to the numbers of ships said to have been engaged in the Viking Era. Having raised these doubts, the tactics described for the Viking Era are likely to be realistic, even if the specifics of the battle in the accounts were part fabrication, as they had to be believable to an audience that was familiar with similar ships and weapons in the twelfth and thirteenth centuries.

When ships were roped together some were left to act individually, as claimed at the Battle of Niså:

> Now King Harald [Hardråde] had the prows of his ships chained together, and the Danes rowed out while the trumpets blared to urge the men on.... But Håkon [Ivársson]'s ships, being unattached, had free range and ran among the ships attacking on both port and starboard.[81]

Håkon was apparently a freebooter, but considered himself Norwegian enough to want to serve Harald against the Danes. It was often the smaller vessels, less suitable for the battle-line, that were left free. Their task was to exploit any opportunity that might present itself, to intervene if the line was in trouble, or to prevent interference at the end or rear of the line. The sterns of the longships were as defensible as the bows, but no crew wanted their ship to be attacked from both ends. This was rarely possible unless, as in the case of a battle-line on land, a part of the line was overrun or driven off. There were advantages to roping the ships together, as it was easier for men to move from one ship to another and difficult for the enemy to cut out individual ships. It was obviously impossible to manoeuvre a long line of ships linked in this way, so it was a tactic more easily adopted by a fleet waiting to be attacked than vice versa. Nevertheless, a fleet could advance to a position close to the enemy, perhaps to hand-hurled missile range, before closing up and linking the ships. There are descriptions of two different methods of doing this, both in *Sverris saga*. At the Battle of Florvåg (1194) the fourteen ships of Sverre's enemies had a rope or cable laid across them and the ships were rowed forward in line abreast and then drawn together by pulling the rope in. Presumably they were pulled in towards the center ship, which would have been the fastest method. Ten years earlier, at Fimreite (1184), the fourteen large warships (still referred to as longships) of King Magnus Erlingsson were roped together further out in three groups, presumably two of five and one of four, and rowed forward by the oarsmen on the outer sides.

Whether ships in a linked line of battle were cut loose after being overrun must have depended on circumstances: whether it was the best way to disrupt the enemy line, how much danger the ship was in of being retaken, its size relative to those next to it, and so on. In his description of the Battle of Svoldr (1000), Snorri describes how those attacking Olaf Tryggvasson's fleet separated the ships surrounding it so they could isolate and surround Olaf's ship, the famous *Long Serpent*.[82] His and the other Icelandic accounts of the battle are suspect, not least because it is Erik Jarl's Norwegians that do most to defeat the Norwegian king Olaf, while Sweyn Forkbeard's Danes, the Swedes and the Jomsvikings show less inclination to fight. Nevertheless, the tactics used are believable and had to be so for the audience.

The commander's ship was normally in the center of the line, as Olaf Tryggvason's was, the most secure position and the easiest from which to communicate with the rest of the fleet. However, in several twelfth-century battles it was at the end, and it is possible that this was also the practice sometimes in the Viking Age. As it was imperative to protect the commander, he usually had the biggest ship, which carried his hirðmen. According to *Haraldskvæði* and later sources such as *Heimskringla*, those with Harald Fairhair at the Battle of Hafrsfjord (872) were berserkers and *ulfheðnar*.[83] Harald awaited the attack of his enemies in the fjord with his ships bound together. Although there would be a case for placing the commander's leading subordinates at various points along the line, many of them seem to have been concentrated around the commander's ship, thus helping to defend him but also putting the weight of attack at one point. This is what Sweyn Jarl is supposed to have done at Nesjar in 1016—17, when, as was often the case, the commander's ships faced each other. In the event it was his ship that was taken by Olaf (Haraldsson), who had about a hundred picked warriors on his ship.[84] Fleet commanders were also aware of the danger to the ends of their line. Since ships stationed there were more vulnerable, they too had to be of substantial size. There were also ways of securing the flanks. One or both ends of the line of ships might be so close to the shore or an island that it was difficult or dangerous to go round it. Other obstacles that could be used were man-made, such as piles or sunken ships placed earlier to restrict access to rivers or inlets. Just how dangerous it was to leave a ship vulnerable at the end of the line was demonstrated at Fimreite. Although it is not explicitly stated, Magnus's three floating platforms seem to have manoeuvred into line shortly before they contacted Sverre's flagship. He and his leading supporters were at one end of the line. While their line attacked the flagship, which was of exceptional size, Sverre's second largest ship pulled alongside and boarded the ship at the opposite end to Magnus's. As the attack gained momentum Magnus's ships were overrun one after the other, causing a crush of men at his end of the line. Many men had no choice but to jump into the water, two of his ships overturned and he and many of his *lendmenn* were drowned.

As in naval battles in the Mediterranean, it was necessary to take down the sails, awnings and masts before coming within missile range, because of the danger that these would fall on the ship. On occasion this happened, as at the battle off the island of Sekken in 1160, when one fleet came upon the other suddenly and the battle turned into a free-for-all.[85] It was possible for this to happen because fleets were always close to the coast when searching for the enemy. Not only did headlands and islands conceal approaching fleets, but they could be used as cover for ambushes. In the twelfth century the intention to fight was signaled by the raising of the commander's standard, presumably a time-honored practice. As the distance between the fleets closed, showers of missiles were hurled or fired at the enemy. These included arrows, spears and probably slingshot, but most of all stones. These were loaded onto the ships before the action. This may seem a primitive weapon, but stones were easily available and expendable should they land in the water. They were used not only by the Vikings, but on Byzantine and Arab ships in the Mediterranean. Ships carried grapples, just as they did to the end of the age of sail in the nineteenth century. These were thrown to hook onto the side or prow of the enemy ship so that they could close to contact and hold a ship fast for boarding. If two lines of ships approached each other contact would be made prow-on, so the prows of the ships were probably wedged between those of the opposition. This exposed only a limited part of the ship to boarding, and the highest part of the ship's bulwark at that, unless or until a neighboring ship was overrun. Although the difference in height of bulwark between different sizes of Viking ship may seem insignificant to us, it was sufficient to make a difference in ship-to-ship combats. Time and again in the sagas the higher-sided ship is said to have the advantage. It was almost invariably the case that bigger ships had higher bulwarks, which meant that they would usually have more men on board as well. Ships did not carry only oarsmen, but might be packed with additional warriors if expecting a battle.

The fate of Magnus's longships at Fimreite demonstrates how difficult it was to disengage when things were going wrong if the ships were roped together, although this was an unusual situation. Under more normal circumstances a crew that wished to disengage from close combat had to separate its ship from the enemy by removing any grapples, but the ship also had to be separated from its neighbors if they were roped together. This cutting of ropes is described in the *Sverris saga* account of the Battle of Nordnes (1179), in fact the only clue that the ships on Magnus's side were roped together in this battle. In its account of the Battle of Torsbjorg (1198) *Sverris saga* mentions that his crews used long poles to push their ships off from an enemy ship, thus separating them further.[86] These actions were virtually impossible with enemy on board, so any who had boarded had to be driven off the ship before the grapple(s) could be removed and the ships forced apart. Just how difficult this was in the midst of a battle is shown by the losses incurred by Magnus at Nordnes. It appears that his fleet had had the better of the action up to the point when he fell on the deck of his ship (his foot was hit by a sword thrown by an enemy), whereupon his ships began to abandon the fight, thinking him dead. Some managed to escape, but eighteen ships were lost, many because they were attached with grapples (their own, in many cases) and in the midst of combat. It may be noted in passing that the fleets using the "floating platform" tactic against Sverre suffered heavy defeats, but as far as we know no one in the Viking Era used his tactic of making his ships operate independently at all times.

In a battle in the Göta Älv in 1158 the fleet of Håkon the Broadshouldered took up a position with his fleet roped together and both ends anchored to piles on the river bank. Although it occurred some eighty years after what would generally be reckoned the end of the Viking Age, this action demonstrates difficulties caused by circumstances and the use of stratagems to overcome them by both sides, problems that must also have faced fleets in the Viking Era. In order to attack Håkon's fleet in this position the opposing fleet of King Inge would have had to approach upriver, rowing against the current. In the pre-battle discussion supposedly held by Inge and his leading advisers, it is pointed out that whereas the defending fleet can use all its manpower to hurl missiles, the attacking fleet will have to employ one-third of its men to row and another third to shield them, leaving only one-third to reply to the missile barrage. The stratagem used to force Håkon's fleet out of its position was to send smaller ships up the river by its other exit and round the island so that they passed Håkon on the way out to sea again. It was hoped that this would be interpreted as flight and his fleet would follow. Meanwhile Inge's larger ships were hidden behind a headland. The stratagem worked, but the "ambushing" longships were unable to prevent Håkon's fleet from evading them and taking up another position in an indent on the river bank, again side by side with the end ships anchored to the shore. To attack the fleet in this position it was necessary to row across the current, rather than rowing against it, but this still caused problems, with one ship belonging to one of the leading men in Inge's fleet running aground. Nevertheless, in the end Inge's fleet was victorious. It is obvious that when attacking in these circumstances it was not possible for Inge and his commanders to rope his ships together, even had they wanted to.

Inge's chief adviser and chieftain, Gregorius Dagsson, had also been faced with a similar problem in 1157, although it was not strictly a naval battle but an opposed landing. On this occasion Håkon's ships were defending the quays at Konungahelle on the same river, with the bulk of his army on the waterfront behind to repulse any landing. Rather than approach upriver, with the disadvantages mentioned above, Gregorius adopted the strategy of rowing past the defenses close to the opposite bank, then turning his ships and allowing them to drift downstream to attack the defending ships. By overcoming the necessity to row and employ men to shield the rowers, he freed more men to use missiles and clear the decks of the ships blocking his landing. Again, it must be assumed that such stratagems had to be used sometimes in the Viking Age, as not all its battles can have been straight fights in calm weather and calm waters with no current.

It has already been made clear that the land played a significant role in battles between ships, by securing flanks, hiding ships or providing a refuge for the defeated, but the fighting could also extend onto land. Time and again *Sverris saga* refers to ships being driven to land by enemy ships. This was obviously a tactic, using speed, superior numbers, weather and currents to force vessels to beach. If the odds were against them, just as they were for those in flight from a naval battle, this might be the best option for a crew to save their lives, even if they had been forced ashore and surrendered a valuable ship to the enemy in the process. In some cases the battle would then extend to land, as the pursuers too left their ships in an attempt to get to grips with their enemies. A fine analysis of an action in shallow waters, in which there was fighting on board ship as well as on the beach, was made by Magoun from a re-examination of a passage in the *Anglo-Saxon Chronicle*.[87] It may have received such a detailed entry precisely because it was one of the first tests of Alfred's new fleet, and it is evident that his crews were still inexperienced in their new ships as several of the English ships ran aground and allowed some of the Danes to escape their trap. The object seems to have been to force the Danes to abandon their ships in hostile territory. According to the *ASC*, the losses among the three crews that escaped forced two of their ships to beach later on, and their crews were captured and hanged. There were probably many unrecorded actions of this type on the coasts of the North Sea and the Baltic.

The "reality" of battle

Of all the difficulties in interpreting the nature of battle in the Viking Era, perhaps hardest for us to fathom is the way that those who fought in them perceived what was happening. To the pagans, nowhere can their reality of gods, spirits and shape-changers, of weather- and weapon-magic, sorcery that could weaken or strengthen muscles or render weapons and shields useless, and even perhaps revive the dead, have seemed more imminent than on the battlefield with all its traumas. Of those who were Christians, many would still have believed in the power of such forces, and even if they did accept that much of this was devilry or delusion, supernatural agency was still ever-present, for, whatever men might try to achieve, it was God who determined the outcome, and His saints constantly intervened to do His will, to protect those who fought for Him or destroy His enemies. Sometimes saints, like spirits, were actually seen on the battlefield. When the Vikings attacked the abbey of St. Germain-des-Prés at Paris in 846, a monk saw Germanus "in helmet and hauberk, and weary as though just coming from the field of battle." Notwithstanding the saint's famed humility, in a miracle text it was said that the local lord who defeated a force of Vikings approaching the abbey of Fleury had the help of St Benedict of Nursia, who "held the reins of my horse in his left hand and, holding a staff in his right, sent many of the enemy falling to their death."

Nowadays most of us (but not all) may understand visions as the product of extreme emotion, stress or pain, or even mind-altering substances, but in a world that already accepted them as reality that would not have been the case. The evidence of supernatural forces would be there for all to see: an army on the verge of victory is thrown into confusion by the sudden descent of a mist; dust, snow or hail is blown into the faces of one of the contending armies by a strengthening wind; an agile warrior stumbles and falls; a veteran of many wars is killed by a novice; a man felled by a blow that should have killed him rises to his feet again; as if from nowhere, an arrow strikes a leader in the eye. There may have been some Christian commanders who felt certain of victory, secure in their own conviction of the justice of their cause, or pagans who were certain that they had the most powerful magic, but for the vast majority of those present battle was a terrible trial whose outcome could never be certain, and even if their side was victorious they themselves might not survive to see it. It was not for nothing that magical protection or supernatural aid was solicited, or prayers uttered for God's favor.

Although any discussion of pagan Viking beliefs and their effect on battlefield behavior must be conjectural, echoes of it survive in the sagas of the late twelfth to fourteenth centuries. Perhaps the most dramatic account of a battle in which supernatural forces intervened is the *Jómsvíkinga saga* description of the Battle of Hjǫrungavágr, traditionally dated to 986, in which Jarl Håkon of Lade defeated a Danish-Jómsviking fleet. In this Håkon secures the help of his "patron deity" Þorgerðr by sacrificing his seven-year-old son. As the battle begins, the sky darkens and there are flashes of lightning and thunder. Having been too hot before the storm, the Jó msvikings are now chilled to the bone. Their ships have to be rowed into the teeth of the storm, hail and rain lash their faces and the stones and spears they hurl are turned back against them by the wind. Those with second sight see an ogress in the fleet of Håkon, from whose fingers arrows fly, and when the storm abates he summons another tempest, this time accompanied by two women who appear on his ship: "Then Sigvaldi said, 'Now I am going to flee, and let all my men do so. I did not vow to fight against trolls, and it is now worse than before, as there are two ogresses.'"[88] Sigvaldi himself cannot see Þorgerðr or the ogresses, but those who have the ability to see into other realms can. For him, the evidence that they speak the truth is there in the violence of the weather.

The above tale was written around the turn of the twelfth and thirteenth centuries. At the very least it has been elaborated during the two centuries after the event. However, there are some skaldic poems that are probably contemporary which appear to allude to the battle, so it probably occurred.[89] The slightly later *Heimskringla* and *Fagrskinna* versions of the battle agree on its outlines but make no mention of sorcery or the storm favoring one side, and accuse Sigvaldi of cowardice and treachery in abandoning the fight and leaving twenty-five of his ships to be overrun by the enemy.[90] It is impossible to know what sources were used as a basis for these accounts: whereas *Heimskringla* and *Fagrskinna* may represent "cleaned-up" versions of a traditional account, the *Jómsvíkinga saga* may equally have grafted fantastic elements onto what was originally, in our terms, a sober or very brief account. In all likelihood it is a deliberate construction of the twelfth century. Some elements of it are obviously suspect: for instance, Håkon, the last pagan ruler of Norway, is not only a sorcerer but has other characteristics attributed to pagan rulers by Christians, such as a predilection for human sacrifice and extraordinary promiscuity. Thirteenth-century sagas certainly included fantastic elements drawn from all sorts of sources, not all of them Scandinavian; on the other hand, it is generally accepted that the sorcery and supernatural forces of many Icelandic sagas have a long tradition and some of it represents an echo of pagan practices.

The *Saga* account of the battle is not history, but may serve as an example of how battle *might* have been perceived in the pagan period, since it is largely concocted from material inherited from the pagan past. Þorgerðr, elsewhere also named Hǫlgabrúðr or Hǫlðatroll, probably does originate as a supernatural being of destruction in the pagan Scandinavian tradition, although there is no way of knowing when or how she was associated with Hjǫrungavágr in the way that the saga describes. The effects (and one-sidedness) of the weather at Hjǫrungavágr may have been exaggerated, but weather could indeed have a dramatic effect on the outcome of a battle, and not only at sea. Army commanders could take account of the position of the sun, but weather was difficult to predict and thus easily interpreted as controlled by supernatural forces. In itself contrary weather would be disconcerting, the more so if it was believed to be controlled. The *Jómsvíkinga saga* tale of Sigvaldi's decision to abandon the fight, even if largely fictional, may be taken as a model for how things might have been seen by a pre-Christian commander of the ninth century. The modern reader might take his action as a rational decision to attempt an escape with at least part of the Jó msviking–Danish fleet because the weather had given the enemy a decisive advantage, or use of allegedly supernatural forces as an excuse not to carry out the oaths the Jó msvikings had earlier sworn because things were clearly going badly. But decisions may well have been taken because the balance of supernatural forces was seen to favor the other side, and panic and disorganized flight may well have been accelerated if warriors felt that this was so. The perception of battling warriors or their leaders when adverse events beyond their control occurred might be loosely compared to the demoralising feeling a modern competitor might get that luck is conspiring against him, but that feeling would be much more difficult to dispel if the "luck" were believed to have supernatural force behind it.

It is not suggested that warriors concentrating on survival in the maelstrom of battle, perhaps in the grip of fear or fury, exhausted or wounded, paused to consider the supernatural implications of what was happening around them, but as noted above, fighting need not have been continuous and deeply held beliefs do modify basic instincts and affect the way people act. What is important to recognize is that, whatever their precise nature, the reality of the pagan Vikings, Slavs and Magyars must have been very different from ours, and will have had a powerful influence on decision-making in battle.

Winners, losers, and memorialization

A variety of events could spark a mass flight. Men in battle were under severe stress and in an extremely volatile situation. As exhaustion or demoralization from losses or failure to make headway set in, some men might make their way to the rear and spark a mass exodus from the field. There was even a chance that a natural phenomenon could spark a panic. In an age when social and political bonds were personal, the general personified the fortunes and divine favor of the troops, so his fall was likely to cause a plunge in morale, or a simple loss of purpose. Even the Byzantine army was prone to this, as shown by a defeat seized from the jaws of victory at Apamea in 998, when a lone Kurdish horseman killed the general Damianos Dalassenos.[91] The fleeing Arabs rallied and the pursuing (and looting) Byzantine troops fled. At Brissarthe the Franks had the Vikings cornered in a church. Thinking that a siege would ensue, Robert the Strong removed his armor, but the Vikings made a desperate sortie, probably in an attempt to escape, and Robert was killed. With his co-commander Ranulf badly wounded by an arrow at the same time, the army had no leadership and left. Interestingly, although Cap Colonna appears to represent an exception to the rule, in that the Fatimid army won the battle despite the loss of its commander, the emir of Sicily Abu al-Qasim, his loss still caused the army to go home after its victory rather than advance further into Italy.

In cases of internal conflict, in which rivals fought for the kingship, the troops had little to fight for if the candidate who led their army fell: the war was over and divine favor had been shown to be on the other side. Awareness of the loss of their commander or the defeat of one part of their command may have caused spreading panic as the news was communicated by sight and sound to the rest of it. A key factor appears to have been the loss, or "fall," of the commander's standard. The reaction to any significant event during a battle was, of course, unpredictable: for instance, it was possible, if much less likely, that troops would fight with increased fury if their leader fell. That it actually happened at *Maldon* may be a poetic fiction, but the poem suggests that this is what *ought* to happen.

When was a battle won and lost? This may seem a stupid question, but it may not always have been clear. How could those on the side that was apparently winning be sure that all their enemies were in flight, or, even more problematic, if they knew some were not in flight, or had simply withdrawn a certain distance, how did they know they would not return to renew the struggle? In many cases they did not know, hence the possible cases of negotiation and agreement to end the fight. The rank and file, of course, would not have stopped to think about such matters when the enemy immediately to their front broke and fled. Even if the commanders wanted to be wary, once the enemy front line had broken it was very difficult to prevent uncontrolled pursuit. Loss of discipline on seeing enemy flee was a great weakness of all medieval armies, particularly when booty was to be had. Nikephoros Phokas railed against the soldiers' greed and recommended dire punishments for breaking the rules about plundering in battle, but booty made up a substantial portion of soldiers' income in any army, sometimes all of it. Booty was, after all, the main purpose of Viking expeditions. In non-raiding armies plunder was the chief benefit the troops had to look forward to. Thus it was both an incentive to fight and an incentive to stop fighting once the enemy baggage was in sight.

If the opposing army (or "navy") was in several divisions and one broke, it was not easy to persuade the pursuers to halt and assist in attacking the others. Some pursuers might spontaneously turn to attack the flank of a neighboring enemy force, especially if led by a local commander with a standard, but the overall commander had little control over this. Even if Egil's exploits are amplified, a credible account of such an attack is given in the *Egils saga* version of the Battle of Brunanburh. The battle line of the coalition army is fractured when the Scotsmen to Egil's front are defeated and flee, but he breaks off the pursuit to lead his men in an attack on the flank ("against their open shields") of Anlaf's Dublin Norsemen.[92] By contrast, at Fontenoy-en-Puisaye, where one division of the defeated army was able to continue the fight, it seems that each pair of opposing divisions was fighting its own battle.

For the commander to rally pursuing troops and persuade them to form up again and return to the battlefield was difficult and took time. If a commander was at the rear he had to make a choice of whether to abandon all influence over the battle as a whole in order to rally the pursuers, and if he led from the front he was too embroiled in his own part of the battle to do this, unless of course he himself was among those pursuing. A commander of a pursuing division may have been as caught up in the pursuit of those opposing his troops as they were, not to mention keen to take control of any plundering. For any commander on land, to become caught up in the pursuit was difficult and even dangerous, as his own followers could become dispersed and isolated enemy individuals or groups might turn and fight. This was the fate of Damianos.

Those who had long experience of fighting nomad armies must often have been wary of rash pursuit, but this was learned through bitter experience of their tactics—in a way, they had come to recognize a situation in which the temptation to slaughter the enemy and loot his baggage was outweighed by the dangers. If they halted after the enemy fled, they could at least claim the victory. The *Anglo-Saxon Chronicle* commonly refers to an army as having "control of the place of slaughter." Its concept of the battlefield may have something to do with the way in which battlefields were decided upon, as if an artificial arena had been created. The hazel field laid out before the contest at Brunanburh in *Egils saga* must be a fiction, but it is one that reflects this concept. The site itself became something to be won or lost. After the fighting was over at Hastings, William himself slept on the battlefield. Since this can hardly have been a pleasant experience (except insofar as he had won the battle), there was probably some ritual or at least symbolic significance in his act. Possession of the field of slaughter was important, a concept that still existed in the modern era. Some Viking Era battles recorded as victories were probably pyrrhic victories at most: for instance, whatever Asser and Æthelweard may say of the great slaughter of pagans after Ashdown, the West Saxons were to suffer two defeats at their hands in the same year, one only fourteen days afterwards. For all that, the memorialization of the battle as a victory was important for Alfred, the West Saxons and ultimately for England.

In the victories the Germans achieved over the Magyars, it is difficult for us to know whether their horsemen fled in panic, the interpretation Christian scribes wished to put on their flight, or simply abandoned the field to fight again another day once they perceived that their methods had failed. As nomads, to whom the concept of land ownership as understood by settled agricultural communities was alien, we can surmise that they probably also had a different concept of a battlefield—the idea of fencing off a space in which to fight would have been senseless. The same applies to the steppe nomads further east. Unfortunately, we have insufficient detail of the eleventh-century campaigns of the Rus and how they may have run down the Pechenegs and Polovtsy, as they too adopted the use of heavy cavalry as their main offensive arm, albeit supported by infantry and some light horsemen acquired from the steppe.

On occasion both sides in a battle fought to a standstill. Nightfall commonly led to a cessation of fighting, and this might happen before one or other side had fled. During a pause in the fighting, it was even possible to make an agreement to end the battle. There are many occasions where this *might* have happened, but we have few records of how armies separated without decisive result. At the start of our period, in 775, an agreement to end a struggle in which both sides would have been risking serious defeat had they continued was made by Franks and Saxons at Lübbecke.[93] This may have been an isolated incident, but that is unlikely. The opposing forces in this particular case had different beliefs and had been engaged in a war marked by atrocity and massacre: if such an agreement was possible in this case, it was surely possible between Christian commanders.

Unlike nomad horsemen faced with more heavily equipped opponents, who could often make their escape, for the vast majority of armies flight almost invariably resulted in heavy casualties. The heaviest bloodletting of a battle occurred at this stage. Fleeing troops threw away anything that might encumber them, including shields and often weapons, rendering them defenseless. Culturally induced feelings that overcame fear in the line of battle had gone, and with it the reassurance of knowing that their comrades would fight alongside them. Paradoxically, when the primeval urge to save life and limb was uppermost, there was a much greater likelihood that they would be killed. Their pursuers were unlikely to show mercy in these circumstances. An explosive mixture of feelings combined, which caused the victors to cut down any enemy in their path and carry on doing so until overcome by tiredness: pent-up emotion and the stress of hand-tohand combat were released, comrades had to be avenged, and the enemy had to be dispatched permanently now that the chance presented itself.

Although such discoveries are rare, evidence from burials of battle victims from the Middle Ages bears terrible witness to this release of energy and desire to remove a threat permanently. At Heronbridge fourteen skeletons were found, probably men killed at the Battle of Chester in 616. A man in his early twenties had five injuries to the head, four of which would have been fatal on their own.

Another in his forties had four head injuries from blade cuts and a stab wound in the abdomen, not to mention an unhealed wound on his thumb.[94] The men who cut them down had hacked at them repeatedly, sometimes when they were already dead or dying. The victims in three mass graves from the later Middle Ages suffered similar fates: those of an unknown battle of *c.* 1300–1350 in Denmark, from Visby on Gotland (1361) and Towton in Yorkshire (1461).[95] The fate of any wounded men of a defeated army lying on the field, even if they somehow escaped the attentions of the pursuers, was almost certain death as the victors "mopped up," unless they were valuable enough to be ransomed. If an agreement was made to end a battle both sides might be able to take their wounded as they withdrew. For men like these and the victors' wounded, whether they survived or not was a lottery. Treatment might be effective, but its rudimentary and sometimes dangerous nature is well known. Wounds easily became infected and even a minor one could lead to death.

The casualties suffered by the defeated side in a naval battle were likely to be even worse than those on land. When one side truly got the upper hand ships that managed to break loose might escape, but an undermanned ship was not easy to row away at speed. A common practice was to run the ship up on the shore and make off across land, probably because it was easier to hide or evade pursuit there. We read of crews trapped on islands after defeats, their best hope being that they could survive long enough for the enemy to lose some of his bloodlust. The situation was much worse if the defeated were on a ship that was being overrun by the enemy. There was no escape but to jump overboard. There are references to swimming, but that was not easy when tired, and possibly wounded and weighed down with armor. Moreover, men were not spared because they were in the water, and if they were lucky enough to reach the shore the enemy might be waiting for them.

Although the impulse to save one's own life is described above as a primeval urge, it was not seen in quite this way by Anglo-Saxons in the Viking Era: as represented in their writings, the decision to flee, like any other action likely to bring about defeat, is a rational choice.[96] Godric son of Offa chooses to steal his lord's horse and leave the battlefield of *Maldon*. In John of Worcester's account of Sherston, Eadric Streona holds up a severed head, claiming that it is King Edmund's.[97] Both are acts of betrayal, marking a contrast to the actions of the loyal subjects, who fight on. In addition, such betrayals provide a reason for the defeat other than superior valor or ability shown by the enemy, the underlying message being that the English will prevail only if everyone does his duty.[98] Heroic poetry and other material that refers to courage or cowardice may represent ideal rather than reality, but in this case it is the ideal that represents how people ought to behave, and probably how they wanted to behave.

Once the initial pursuit was over, uninjured survivors from the defeated army who escaped the enemy had more chance of survival. Many of the rank and file might make their way home, although travel through hostile territory could be risky. If captured, their fate was less likely to be a "return to normality." If large numbers of prisoners were taken their fate was uncertain. If they were peasants from lands the victor might take for his own they might be set free. Many others would be sold into slavery. If they were a liability they might simply be massacred, as happened to the Frankish prisoners after the Geule battle. It was not possible to retain large numbers of prisoners of no economic value: armies had enough difficulty feeding and supplying themselves. Prisoners had to be either released or massacred. This latter fate is not commonly recorded, but was probably more likely when enmity was compounded by religious animosity. Although there has been a recent tendency to attribute bitter animosity between Christians and Moslems to the behavior of Latin Christians in the "official Crusades" that began with Pope Urban's call to arms in 1097, there is plenty of evidence for it before this. As for the Christian attitude to pagans, Charlemagne had conducted regular massacres of Saxons during his eighth-century conquest and Slavs were treated little better by his successors in East Francia–Germany.[99] After Lenzen (929) and Recknitz (955) the captured Slavs were all beheaded, partly in revenge for the massacre of inhabitants of Walsleben not long before the former battle and Cocarescemier [*sic*] before the latter.

Many commanders died in the Viking Age, but the obscurity of our sources often makes it difficult to know whether they were killed during the fighting or afterwards. King Edmund of the East Angles was famously killed by the Vikings in 869, but tales of his death by torture belong to hagiography, not history. The *Anglo-Saxon Chronicle* entry merely says, ". . . and that winter King Edmund fought against them, and the Danish took the victory, and killed the king and conquered all that land."[100] Prisoners of higher status might be ransomed, a practice that was to become more entrenched in the "chivalric" culture of the High Middle Ages. The Vikings certainly ransomed some prisoners, although these were not necessarily captured in battle. Their primary interest in these cases was undoubtedly profit. Many high-ranking prisoners were not so lucky. After a Danish fleet achieved victory over a Norwegian fleet on Carlingford Lough (Ireland) in 853, one of the two Norwegian commanders, Iercne, was beheaded. According to the *Annals of Ulster*, in 845 Turgéis (Torgils), the scourge of central Ireland in the 840s, was captured and drowned in Lough Owel (Loch Úair) by Máel Sechnaill, king of Mide.[101] Torgils's family background is unknown, and in any case Ireland had a long tradition of killing rival kings, even when they were Christians.

In this period one event stands out: the hanging of the three Magyar leaders, Lél, Bulcsú and Sur, captured after Lechfeld. The Saxon chronicler Widukind thought they deserved nothing less, but captured Hungarian leaders had not always been treated in this way.[102] By 955 the Saxon dynasty and the Magyars were familiar neighbors and Otto I was well aware of the special Magyar regard for their leaders. The act of Otto and Duke Henry in executing the princes, particularly by a degrading method normally reserved for common criminals, was designed to demoralize the Magyars utterly, and it worked.[103] It is an indication that brutality was often calculated, just as the Vikings regularly weighed up the potential for profit against the desire for vengeance or the need to remove a dangerous enemy when they decided whether or not to kill an important prisoner. In his testament, the Rus prince Vladimir Monomakh claimed that he had freed more than a hundred captured Polovtsy princes, but had put to death and drowned in the rivers more than two hundred. In his dealings with other Rus princes, even with his cousin Oleg, who had made war against him in alliance with the Polovtsy and killed his son, his attitude was more conciliatory. There was more likely to be an element of mercy if both captors and captives were Christians, but even then there were no guarantees.

A wise precaution for a commander was to keep possible routes of escape open if a battle was to be fought. Even in defeat casualties might be limited if the army could retreat into a fortification or beyond impassable terrain. On a number of occasions, such as the Battle of the Dyle, some Vikings managed to escape in their ships, as their camps were usually on river banks or coasts. The Rus ventured out of Dorostolon to fight John Tzimiskes's army in 971 in the knowledge that they could retreat back into it. By contrast, at Andernach Charles the Bald's army suffered catastrophic losses and he only narrowly escaped with his own life because there was no route of escape. He had gambled on a night approach under cover of negotiations for peace, but neglected to provide for the possibility that things might not go to plan.

For the people of the Viking Era, whatever their beliefs, the fate of the dead was important, but the slain on the battlefield were left lying "to be eaten by worms and wolves, birds and dogs." The quote is from the *Carmen*, the earliest source for Hastings. Later sources such as Wace and William of Poitiers claim that the English were allowed to bury their dead, but this is probably an assumption or a deliberate distortion, based on what later became the practice. Orderic Vitalis recorded the pile of whitening bones at Stamford Bridge. As depicted in the Bayeux Tapestry, the practice was to strip the dead of everything of any value and leave the bodies, or their parts, naked on the field. The frequent reference to food for ravens and wolves in Germanic heroic poetry reflected reality. Noble dead were treated better, at least on the victors' side. Those on the losing side might be buried, eventually. Relatives usually tried to arrange for this, just as Harold's queen did after Hastings. Despite her offer of considerable wealth to William, he refused, probably because he did not want his opponent to receive a conspicuous burial and memorial that might become the focus of a cult later on. The body was later removed to an unknown location. According to William of Malmesbury, William deprived a knight of his knighthood for slashing at Harold's leg with his sword when he lay on the field during the last phase of the battle.[104] One wonders if he did something worse to the body. Bodies were regularly decapitated and limbs were removed after death, but throughout the Middle Ages we have occasional references to other mutilation such as removal of genitals. Such acts were an extension of the release of anger, vengeance and bloodlust, rendering the enemy impotent even after death.

The way in which battles were remembered has been touched on in the discussion of what a battle was. If, as may often have been the case, the battle was fought near a cross, thorn tree, mound or other symbol which already had a tradition behind it, that would also aid in remembering the battle. It was important for victorious Christian rulers to give credit to God and his saints for success. This was often declared publicly, as Henry I did after Riade, and frequently accompanied by more concrete acts, such as donations to churches or other religious institutions, or the foundation of new ones, sometimes on the site of their victory, as both Cnut and William did after *Assandun* and Hastings. This was a form of penance for taking part in the shedding of so much blood, but it also memorialized the battle for future generations.[105] The same purpose was served by battle literature and pictorial records such as the tapestry that portrayed Byrhtnoth's deeds, which his widow donated to Ely Monastery, and the Bayeux Tapestry. According to Ralph Glaber's *Historiarum*, Fulk Nerra founded the monastery at Beaulieu-lès-Loches in order to do penance because "he had shed blood in many battles in many places."[106] Bernard Bachrach argues that it was also intended as a memorial to his victory at Conquereuil in 992, as were the sculptures there that represent battle.[107] As at Ely, monasteries kept records of donations of land and other items, often in return for prayers on behalf of the dead person, and these too maintained the memory of them. Unfortunately for the modern historian, few of these methods of remembrance tell us where the site of the battle was. A battle had to become important, and only then would it acquire a name that stuck. In any case, the precise site of the battle need not have been the most important thing to remember, particularly if there was no other landmark of significance nearby. If Brunanburh, now recognized as one of the most important battles ever fought on English soil, is on the Wirral, the most favored area, this is a case in point. Memories of battle could fade, even without the accidental loss of documents and pictorial representations. Successive generations had to have an interest in preserving the memory. In an age when memories of battle were usually preserved as commemoration of the deeds of individuals, if their family line disappeared and their ecclesiastical foundations became dominated by an unconnected family, the motive had gone.

Chapter 6

Fortifications and Siegecraft

During the period 780–1100 large numbers of fortifications were constructed or continued in use throughout Europe, from Ireland to Russia. The sole region where they were not widespread was Scandinavia. A fortification may have many purposes: to obstruct a route of advance or retreat for an enemy, to guard or block access to a strategic point in the landscape, to provide a center for domination of a hostile or subject population, as an observation post, as a place for storage of valuables or supplies, as an assembly point for troops before a military campaign, as a refuge from attack for local population, or to enclose a population center. Since all have to be habitable to some degree, even refuges, and there is often an element of display in their appearance, there is always a compromise between defense and other requirements. In the past most attention has been given to tactical considerations such as the topography of the site and the design and construction of the defenses, but many fortifications also had a strategic function, related to the defense of the surrounding polity, "controlling" important routes, river crossings, passes, coastal landing places and so on, or as bases for attackers to threaten surrounding territory and disrupt communications. This assumes an element of planning in their placement in the landscape. Other fortifications were built primarily with the defense of one site in mind, or by a local landowner purely to defend himself, his family and the occupants of his estate, in which case tactical considerations came to the fore.

Opinions have varied on the strategic effectiveness of medieval fortifications. On the one hand medieval forts or castles are often mentioned as "controlling" or "dominating" surrounding areas, while on the other it has been said they were relatively ineffective in controlling them, as they were easily bypassed by an invader or raider. Medieval fortresses were not equipped with anything capable of hurling a projectile more than a few hundred meters, if that, so the garrison could not prevent any force from passing nearby without sallying out to do battle with them. However, fortifications do not have to form an impenetrable barrier to contribute to the defense of a territory. As noted earlier, frontiers were not conceived of as linear borders before the advent of accurate maps, but were probably identifiable locations recognized by neighboring rulers as between their jurisdictions, or as an ill-defined zone between two sites occupied by people of different allegiance. A frontier might approach our concept of a border where there were strings of fortresses close to one another or linear earthworks known to represent the limit of a ruler's authority, similar to the Roman Limes or Hadrian's Wall in function. The raising of forces to face invaders took time, and fortresses at strategic points slowed their advance and restricted the routesavailable. The fact that some fortifications may never have been attacked does not mean that their function was primarily non-military, as defenses are as much a deterrent to attack as a physical obstruction when actually attacked.

Obviously a fortification could function as a defended site for people and possessions, thus denying the invader the opportunity to capture or destroy them and denying him supplies, but it could also "dominate" the landscape by monitoring it. Castles were usually placed so that the maximum possible surrounding terrain was visible from them. Not only could they monitor enemy movement, but garrisons did not simply take a passive role, even when under siege. The enemy's messengers, foragers, and scouting parties were in danger and any attempt to move supplies in the castle's vicinity was fraught with risk. If the castle was not taken, it had to be blockaded, which used up resources. The greater the number of fortifications in the frontier belt, the greater the risk to any invader, and the more he was forced to concentrate his forces, slowing movement, reducing the capacity to devastate the countryside and increasing the risk of supply failure. Once an army was defeated and began to fragment into smaller groups, escape through such a region was also difficult.

The Carolingian and Ottonian world

In general, there is little evidence of change or advances in fortification in northern and central Europe during the period between the collapse of the Roman Empire and the ninth century. The infrastructure of the Roman world did not exist and many of the Roman city walls fell into disrepair. In places walls were deliberately demolished, either for a ready supply of dressed stone or to make way for new structures. Settlements often moved to sites near the former Roman towns but outside the walls, as in the cases of York and London. Nevertheless, many of these returned to the former

Roman sites in the ninth and tenth centuries, and in some places the Roman walls were still defensible. In 946 they proved too much for the combined armies of King Louis IV and King Otto I, who abandoned their siege of Senlis (defended by the troops of Hugh Capet, later the first Capetian king of France) after deciding that an assault would be too costly.[1] In 985 King Lothar (of France) had to use an arsenal of machines and a siege tower to overcome the third-century walls of Verdun. In the previous century the same walls had saved the city from sack by the Vikings.

During the Viking Era fortification became much more widespread and previously undefended trading emporia were given defenses. An obvious explanation for this might be the advent of large-scale raiding by the Vikings and later the Magyars. Italy was also part of the Frankish world after 774 and suffered heavily from Saracen raids and later invasion. Undoubtedly this was a contributory factor, but there is evidence of a change in attitude in the Frankish Empire before the ninth century. The Carolingians made a conscious effort to imitate Rome, and this included Roman architectural styles, and their conquests brought them into close contact with Byzantine fortifications in Italy, themselves descended from the Roman model.

The Franks needed new forts to secure their hold on conquered territories. In areas formerly controlled by the Romans, such as southern Germany, earlier fortifications were certainly reused and repaired, but the defenses of these sites have often been difficult to date, if they have been researched at all. Former Roman *villae* were also used both by the Agilolfing *dux* Tassilo (r. 747–788) and by his Frankish successors in Bavaria. Until very recently it was wrongly assumed that Frankish and Slavic fortifications could be differentiated on the basis of style, the assumption being that the Franks built more advanced defenses from stone. Many of the early fortifications on the eastern frontier with the Slavs were of similar type to their enemies'. The construction of what became a deep belt of fortresses began in the Carolingian period and continued under the Ottonians. In Germany during the tenth century a huge building programme was begun under the Saxon dynasty. This may have been initiated by Henry I's *Burgenordnung* of c. 925, although it has proved very difficult to link any known fortifications with it. The style of fortification on the eastern frontier varied. One object was certainly defense of rural settlements against raiders, particularly the Magyars, but also the Slavs. In the reign of Otto II similar defenses were organized on the comparatively short Danish frontier.

The Viking threat posed an altogether different problem than frontier raids by the Slavs, not least because the Vikings were capable of penetrating well inland up navigable rivers. An interesting solution to this problem was attempted by Charles the Bald. Carroll Gillmor suggests that the idea may have struck him when he built a bridge across the Marne to block the retreat of some raiders. When he held an assembly at Pitres in 864 he ordered the building of fortifications on the Seine to prevent the Northmen from passing further upriver.[2] The idea was a bridge with powerful fortifications of wood and stone at each end. The site was Pont-de-l'Arche. Excavation has revealed a square enclosure with 270 meter-long sides on the north bank. Originally there was a clay rampart, but this was cut away to place a line of 4.5-meter tree trunks, which were then faced with stone on the outer side. Unfortunately there is no way of knowing the height of the work, as it was leveled in the later Middle Ages. The earth and timber rampart with stone facing was no more advanced than many fortifications had been in the Iron Age, but a more serious problem may have been that it was built very slowly and not properly garrisoned, despite the king's demands. Another work was built at Les Ponts-de-Cé on the Loire, but that seems to have been ineffective as well. Elsewhere Charles did contribute to the defense of the realm. In his reign and those of his successors Carloman and Charles the Fat, many old walls of towns were repaired and new fortifications built round monasteries, including St. Bertin, which subsequently saw off a Viking attack in 891. However, it was not only the king who began to build forts, although this was supposed to be a royal prerogative. Although Charles had ordered the destruction of private fortifications at Pitres, he was unable to prevent unauthorized construction and a dangerous trend (from the royal point of view) had begun.

Similar measures against Viking attacks were taken on the Rhine and Meuse in East Francia after Danish attacks in 863, 880–881 and 884–885. Town defenses were strengthened, the royal palace at Nijmegen was given ramparts, and a castle was built by Duke Henry at Duisburg. In Flanders, more or less an independent polity at this time, Bruges and Ghent were fortified by Count Baldwin. Most interesting in this region, however, are five ninth-century circular earthworks with palisades on the islands off the coast of Zealand–Flanders. They had two roads across the site, meeting at the middle, and varied from 144 to 265 meters in diameter. Since no occupation layer was found, they were probably refuges. Only Middelburg on Walcheren survived this period to become a settlement. In the central Netherlands another unusual fortification was the Hunnenschans, a late Carolingian 4 meter-high horseshoe-shaped earthwork with a palisade, enclosing an area 100 meters in diameter. In 2007 a further earthwork was discovered at Appel, just to the west, while to the south is another, Duno, with a roughly semicircular series of banks and ditches. Both appear to have been tenth century. There are uncertainties about the excavation and recording of data at Duno and Hunnenschans, but Appel at least seems to have had links to the counts of Hamaland and bog-iron production.[3]

Fortifications also proliferated in the tenth century throughout the kingdom of Germany, and not only in the Slavic frontier zone, where there were hundreds of them. Many continued to resemble earlier Saxon, Frankish and Slav fortifications, while some were simple palisaded enclosures. Fortifications built by nobles often followed a similar pattern to royal ones, if on a smaller scale. There can be no doubt that there was a strategy of "defense in depth" on the eastern frontier. The East Frankish and German rulers were well aware that individual fortifications had a limited capacity to hinder the movement of enemy forces, just as they knew that it was difficult to stop enemy forces from "crossing the frontier." Periods of intense construction of fortifications on the frontier appear to coincide with preparation for or consolidation of advances into Slavic territory, especially by the Ottonian kings, or anticipated trouble from the east.[4] However, it has to be borne in mind that there were other reasons for fortification building. The kings of the Saxon Ottonian dynasty were keenly aware of the need to project their image and power as kings and emperors, and one way of doing this was to build imposing structures. Other powerful landowners also built fortifications for the same reasons; even if they were not able to compete with the German kings, they could still imitate them and compete with each other.

Many German scholars trace the origins of the "classic" medieval fortress types to the eleventh century, although the disappearance of many earlier fortifications has distorted the picture somewhat. The larger fortresses in Germany, often known as *hohenburgen*, had inner and one or more outer enclosures, not dissimilar in principle to many earlier German and Slavic fortifications. Whenever possible they were constructed on higher ground. However, a new development was the appearance of the *Bergfried*, a free-standing tower, either on the most vulnerable side of the main enclosure as an additional defense, or in the center of the enclosure and unattached to it. Usually the *Bergfried* was tall and slender and lacked windows; it was not designed for permanent habitation, but as a last resort if the main or outer defenses were overrun. Increasingly these fortifications were built or rebuilt of stone. According to Adam of Bremen, the archbishop of Hamburg planned to encompass the entire town of Hamburg with stone walls, but he died having built only a fortified stone structure with towers and battlements.[5] This was certainly a response to the threat from the Slavs, which had increased after the revolt of 983. In 1008 Henry II also fortified Bamberg with walls, outworks and a strong tower. By contrast, the defenses at Meissen were probably made of wood, as the Slavs attempted to set light to them in 1015. Others were smaller, ringforts or square palisaded enclosures with or without a ditch. They too frequently included a *Bergfried*. Alternatively, towers could be built entirely on their own. Most were built of wood in this era, but stone towers were constructed on similar principles both before and after 1100. These towers were more common in low-lying areas, where they also fulfilled the function of watchtower.

The most significant change in fortification style in the eleventh century was the development of what we now call the motte-and-bailey castle, which originated in West Francia.[6] It consisted of two elements, a mound (motte) surrounded by a ditch, on which some form of tower or fortified house was usually built, often with a palisade around its base, and an outer yard (bailey) enclosed by a palisade and ditch. The bailey was usually large enough to enclose several buildings and animals if necessary. Sometimes there was more than one bailey. In our period the defenses were almost invariably of wood. The main strength of these castles was their earthworks and ditches with their steep banks: the wooden fortifications alone would not have presented a serious obstacle, but the whole structure was very difficult to assault, although the wood was obviously vulnerable to fire in the right conditions. In addition, the castles were relatively cheap and easy to build and did not require a skilled labor force. However, medieval accounts suggesting that mottes could be thrown up in a few days either exaggerate the ease of building or refer to very small mottes. Larger ones may have taken many months to build.

Various reasons have been suggested for the spread of motte-and-bailey castles in the eleventh century: for instance, that they were used widely by the Angevin counts as defense against Vikings, that they arose as a result of "feudalization" (the fragmentation of power and the growth of fiefdoms), and even that the design may have been Viking in origin, hence its wide-spread use in the territory they were granted, Normandy. Since there is no evidence whatever for such a design in Viking Scandinavia, the last explanation is improbable. Even if correct, the argument that motte-and-bailey castles appeared precisely where fiefdoms did in the feudalization process, in northern Europe, gives a reason for the spread of castles, but not the appearance of a new type of castle. According to D.J. Cathcart King, the earliest known example of the motte-and-bailey design was at Les Rues-des-Vignes (medieval Vinchy), Nord-Pas-de-Calais, known of from 979. Fulk Nerra and Geoffrey Martel, who reigned as counts of Anjou 987–1040 and 1040–1060, used various types of fortification, as often to secure control of territory they had gained as much as to defend their frontiers against Vikings and neighboring lords. They constructed stone towers as well as ringforts and mottes. The deciding factor was probably the speed at which they had to be constructed. The strategy of constructing forts rapidly after an initial advance into enemy territory and then improving them later was used by the Normans in England. Nevertheless, on the continent the simple ringfort continued in use, although some were converted with the addition of a motte. During the Norman conquest of England it seems that ring-works were often built first and converted to motte-and-bailey castles later.[7]

Bernard Bachrach has highlighted Fulk Nerra's strategy of building each castle no more than 35 kilometers from the nearest—in other words, within a day's ride.[8] In England and Wales this strategy was particularly useful to Duke William for securing control of a hostile territory. Each motte-and-bailey castle built by the Normans after their invasion was designed so that a small number of occupants could control the immediate district or estate and be safe from attack, but were also within reach of relief from neighboring castles. In addition, the appearance of the castle would have had a powerful intimidating effect on the English. An interesting aspect of William's castle-building is that most of the sites were new, and in many regions such as Somerset it seems that the old Anglo-Saxon *burhs* were initially avoided.[9] The most likely reason is the Norman perception of them as centers of resistance, where large concentrations of hostile people were available to attack any garrison. This was not unreasonable, as the fate of the garrison at York in 1069 showed, although there the English had Danish help. The break-up of old estates and the creation of new ones also meant that central locations for control of estates changed, to places where castles were needed by the new landowners.

The Slavic regions of central Europe

The Viking Era is the period to which the origins of the Polish, Bohemian and Rus states are usually traced, when there are signs of economic and population growth and the appearance of a wealthy aristocracy. The early Slavic-speaking people of the regions that later became Moravia, Bohemia, Poland and Rus must have been able to build strongholds if they had wanted to, but few of them did until the eighth century.

East of the Frankish domains and Italy, existing terrain features were utilized, usually reinforced with man-made ramparts and wooden palisades or walls, occasionally dressed with stone. These construction methods were used by the first Slavic polity, the Moravian Empire of the ninth and early tenth centuries, by the emerging states of Poland and Bohemia in the tenth century and by the tribal confederations of the so-called Wends. Most frequently they were hill-forts, but promontories, islands, and sites surrounded by marshland were also widely utilized. These were old traditions of fortification, less dependent on manpower or widespread economic and administrative infrastructure than the Roman model. In the Slavic-speaking areas defenses varied in style, even within one domain or tribal region. Some had earthen ramparts with palisades of upright timbers or wattle, others had two rows of vertical timbers filled with earth and stones, sometimes with transverse beams to strengthen the structure, and still others were of timbers laid horizontally, each layer at right angles to the one below, the so-called "grill technique." The so-called "box" or "caisson" ramparts with timbers set horizontally, both longitudinally and transversally to form "boxes" within the rampart, which were then infilled with clay, rubble or other detritus, was particularly effective, and firing of such structures with clay soil infills could make them almost impervious to subsequent burning. Earth and timber defenses were sometimes faced with dry-stone built walls. Very similar techniques had been used for centuries in "barbarian Europe," being particularly widespread in the Iron Age before the Roman conquests north of the Alps, and some even went back to the Neolithic.[10]

The most common plan was oval or circular, but any basic shape was possible, although sharp corners were always avoided. Many fortresses consisted of two enclosures, a lower one that enclosed a town or village, or the houses of artisans and warriors of the prince's retinue, and an upper one or citadel. At the larger defended sites, like Mikulčice in Great Moravia, there were often more lower enclosures, as many as three. In this region stone facings were often added to the earth and timber walls. The principle of these Slavic fortifications was the same as the Carolingian and the better known motte-and-bailey castles of northwestern Europe: any attacker would first have to take the lower or outer fortress before he could attack the upper or inner citadel. The weakness of these defenses was that timber was vulnerable to fire. Even though reinforcement with packed earth and stone facings often made the main walls less likely to burn, the ramparts, which sometimes had timber roofs, were entirely of wood.

Some sites were not fully enclosed because inaccessible approaches did not have to be defended, such as Arkona on Rügen, where the north and east sides of the site ended in sheer cliffs. In the Wendish area sites that housed temples were also fortified. It is difficult to know whether the main motivation in fortifying so many places was provided by the threat from Christian states to the west, Vikings from the north, or rival tribal confederations. A shift in the pattern of fortification from large forts to smaller round ones with moats in the mid-ninth century appears to suggest a breakdown into smaller chieftaincies, which was reversed in the second half of the tenth century when larger sites were once again fortified, as at Kolobrzeg (Kolberg) and Santok. In the eleventh century the pagan Wends were faced with an increasing threat from Christian Poland, but they also launched their own seaborne raids against Denmark.

Poland has an extraordinary variety of fortress types from the pre-Piast period. Our earliest knowledge of Slavic communities in Poland comes from the *Bavarian Geographer*, who gave a list of peoples inhabiting the regions east of the Elbe and north of the Danube. The names cannot all be identified with those of peoples known from other sources, and no names of peoples are listed for some regions known to have been inhabited in the ninth century, such as eastern Pomerania or Mazovia (around the Rivers Wkra and the Bug further east). Nor is it certain what the geographer meant by *civitas*, whether he was referring to fortified sites or settlements. The late eighth, ninth and tenth centuries are also marked by the general appearance of fortified sites, but there were some in certain regions before this.[11] In Pomerania many early strongholds are thought to have originated in the late seventh or early eighth century, but in the late ninth century smaller and stronger forts appeared, more widespread and more evenly spread across the region, largely concentrated on the river routes. This region had clearly benefited from trade in the ninth century, as witnessed by the growth of Wolin, Szczecin, and Kolobrzeg, where grave goods have clearly indicated the settlement of Scandinavians.

Also in Little Poland there are other fortified enclosures of 3–5 hectares in area or even larger, known as the "Great strongholds of the Vislane." They are considerably larger than fortresses in neighboring areas and are also exceptional in being built on the slopes of hills in upland areas, but it is not known why they were so large, possibly too large to mount a defense of the whole rampart with the available warriors. This raises the possibility that they had other uses, or were perhaps intended to be large enough to accommodate livestock as well as people in times of danger. In addition, it is unlikely that it was necessary to man the entire length of the rampart if the potential enemies did not have the capacity to attack at numerous points simultaneously. The sites have been compared with those of Moravia, but are comparable only in size and date (although they were in use after the collapse of Great Moravia), not in structure. Stradó w was a multi-enclosure structure during its heyday, with walls of the caisson type. However, the whole site was in use only for about a century (c. 970–1070), although the main stronghold continued in use for another century. Others, such as Naszacowice, continued in use into the eleventh century, after the Piast domination began. Krakow was later the most important city of the region, but the history of the fort that preceded it on Wawel Hill is very unclear.[12]

In Poland there are also a number of linear earthworks, usually several kilometers long, the most famous being the "Silesian Ramparts" that run along the River Bó br, with three parallel embankments and ditches, the width of the whole being almost 50 meters in places. These have been linked to the expansion of the Dziadoszanie towards Lusatia, just as similar earthworks have been linked to the Goplanie tribe in Kuiavia, but there have been few finds of dateable material.

Fortifications in Rus

When Viking bands started to establish trading posts at important points on the river routes in the future region of Russia they encountered no fortified sites of any strength. As far as we can tell, the Slav- and Finnic-speaking tribes used islands and hills, or dug a single rampart and ditch if no natural defense was available, to which they added a fence. In this respect the fortified hill-top sites of the eighth- to tenth-century Romny–Borshevo culture were an exception, not just in Rus but in the early Slavic-speaking world as a whole.[13] They were situated at the edge of the forest zone bordering on the steppe, on the left bank of the Dnieper.

There is no way of knowing what structures made solely of timber existed in the eighth and early ninth centuries. Early Viking posts were probably also simple fenced enclosures, but more substantial fortifications were constructed as the Kievan principality began to emerge. The increasing concentration of wealth made tempting targets for the nomads of the steppe. The *Primary Chronicle* attributes the construction of "stockaded towns" to Prince Oleg in 880.[14] It is well known that Byzantium exerted a powerful influence on Kievan Rus through trading relations and cultural contacts. Its architectural influence is often emphasized, and is clear in Kievan ecclesiastical architecture, but the majority of building work was done in wood, including fortifications. The nearest comparable fortifications are in the Slavic-speaking lands to the west.

Around the turn of the tenth century Kiev began to expand from the original settlement on a hill on the right bank of the Dniepr. The hill-top became the princely residence and the lower town, Podil, the market and craft center. An earthwork rampart was constructed around the whole site. Vladimir rebuilt the fort on the hill with a 6-meter-high clay rampart, topped with earth and timber walls and a stone gate, and provided the whole settlement with a moat. The town thus took a form similar to Slavic fortified settlements elsewhere.

Other towns were similarly fortified in the early tenth century, such as Novgorod, which developed from several settlements. Pskov and Staraya Ladoga had early ramparts too, but these places became substantial only in the eleventh century. Other sites remained hill-top forts strategically placed. Archaeology, for once, confirms the picture given in the later *Eymunds saga*, that Yaroslav the Wise was largely responsible for the expansion of Novgorod, as the timber defenses of the citadel (*kremlin*) have been dated to 1044. In his reign the ramparts of the city of Kiev extended for 3.5 kilometers, 20 meters thick at the base and 12 meters at the top. In the mid-eleventh century the ramparts of Chernigov extended for 2.5 kilometers and were 4 meters high. On the whole this type of fortress served its purpose until the Mongol invasion in the mid-thirteenth century.

The Rus princes also attempted to strengthen fortifications when they expanded into areas further west. Vladimir did this at Przemyśl in Ruthenia, and Yaroslav at Tartu ("Yuryev" in the Primary Chronicle, in Estonia) in *c.* 1030. Both places fell to enemies when the Rus princes fought amongst themselves, Tartu to the Estonians in *c.* 1060 and Przemyśl to Boleslaw II of Poland in 1071. We know from accounts of this attack that it had deep ditches and a citadel with a tower. The outer fortification was taken by assault, but the citadel was starved into submission. Other sites captured by Boleslaw are also listed as *castra*, but appear to have been palisaded and presented no major obstacle. By contrast, the unidentified site of Wohdin took six months to take and was captured only when it surrendered through hunger, so it presumably had powerful defenses, as no others had prevented the Polish prince from storming the outer defenses.[15]

No survey of Rus fortifications would be complete without mentioning the extraordinary series of earthworks constructed around Kiev, known as the "snake ramparts." It is now known that much of this work was carried out during the reign of Vladimir (980–1015), who was obviously well aware that Kiev was dangerously exposed to raids from the steppe. The *Primary Chronicle* understates the scale of his work, but the German missionary bishop Bruno of Querfurt was impressed in 1008, describing "the most firm and long fence with which Vladimir has everywhere enclosed his realm."[16] Vladimir was able to move people south from the forest zone to his new settlements around Kiev, many of which enclosed 7 hectares or more, and must have mobilized almost every male (perhaps females too) to build the ramparts. In total some 500 kilometers were constructed during the twenty-five years after Vladimir's conversion.[17] The ramparts ran in loops around the region to the south and west of Kiev and along the left bank of the River Dniepr and the lower Sula. Where the rivers met there was a fortified settlement enclosing 27 hectares with a harbor. To the south of Kiev a rampart blocked access from the steppe between the Rivers Irpen and Dniepr. Further south, another was constructed between the lower Stugna and the Irpen and ran northwestwards to the Teterev. This rampart was 100 kilometers long. Beyond all these ramparts were further lines of outer ramparts, which were obviously purely obstructions, but they met at the fortified port of Vitichev.

The earthworks incorporated rows of logs or box-rampart style "fences" as reinforcement and in some forts with unfired brick, the knowledge of which was acquired from the Byzantines. These outer ramparts were 3.5–4 meters high, but had ditches up to 12 meters wide outside them. In places, such as around Belgorod, the ramparts were over 5 meters high, and their height was increased still further in the 990s. With the exception of the forts, these ramparts were not intended to be manned, but they were obstructions that slowed down nomad horsemen. If raiders did cross them, their retreat with captured livestock, slaves, and plunder was more difficult, and they were vulnerable to attack from the forts.

Scandinavia

Scandinavia appears to have been the region of Europe with least fortifications in the Viking Period, although they had been widespread in certain areas during the earlier Migration Period (400–550).[18] The reasons for this are not entirely clear. To some extent it may have been a cultural phenomenon: in other words, it may simply have been customary to seek a decision by battle in internal conflicts between tribes or petty kingdoms. A comparison may be drawn with early Anglo-Saxon England and medieval Ireland, where fortifications existed but only on a small scale, and played little part in wars as defended sites. Nevertheless, certain coastal trading centers were fortified, such as Birka in Lake Mälar, Hedeby in Schleswig, and Århus on the eastern coast of Jutland. The Scandinavians who controlled them were well aware of the risk from seaborne raiders, not least other Vikings, to places such as these.

In view of the general lack of fortifications it may seem surprising that two substantial linear earthworks were constructed in Scandinavia. The Danevirke joined the defensive rampart of Hedeby and ran across the neck of the Jutland peninsula to the marshes in the west. The total length of its sections is some 30 kilometers. Many modern archaeologists now think that its origin was as protection for the trade route from Hedeby to the Rivers Treene and Eider. There can be no certainty about this as we have very little knowledge of tribal or political divisions in 737, the date of the timber at the front of the rampart found by dendrochronology, but the earliest phases of construction, the so-called Hovedvolden, Nordvolden, and Østervolden (Main-, North-, and East-walls) and the somewhat later Kovirke (Cowwork), do not function well as defense from the south. Among other things, the ditch of the Kovirke is on its northern side. This is probably the wall referred to in the *Royal Frankish Annals* as built by King Godfred in 808, "against Saxony" (then ruled by Charlemagne), but it may have been built as late as the reign of Harald Bluetooth (r. *c.* 958–987). The *RFA* refers to a single gate, which seems to have remained the only one thereafter. The *RFA* interpretation of its purpose may simply be an assumption based on its view of Godfred as a king who was hostile to the Franks, as hostile he certainly was.

In the tenth century there was a third construction phase, in which the Hovedvolden was rebuilt to a height of 10 meters and the wall connecting it to Hedeby was rebuilt. This last wall has given dendrochronological dates of 968 and 951–961, which suggests that it is the work of Harald Bluetooth. The Danevirke certainly did have a palisade in the Viking Period. It was later strengthened still further, being heightened and given a brick wall in the early twelfth century and the reign of Valdemar I (1157–1184).

A similar work was constructed in Sweden, the Götavirke, consisting of two parallel defensive walls running north to south between the villages of Västra Husby and Hylinge in Ö stergö tland. The ramparts cover the distance between the lakes Asplången and Lillsjön. South of Lillsjön, the terrain is virtually impassable, while north of Asplången there are remains of several Migration Period hill-forts that may have been incorporated into the defenses. Archaeological excavations have revealed carbon-14 datings from various eras, including several from the Viking Era, from the ninth century and *c.* 1000. We can only speculate on the reason for the construction, but the siting suggests defense against attacks from the east (the Baltic) on the most fertile and settled areas of central Östergö tland. In the opinion of most Swedish scholars, those most likely to be the perpetrators of such attacks are the *Svear* from the Mälar region, who probably also raided and enforced tribute in Gotland and coastal parts of Latvia and Poland during the Vendel and Viking Periods.[19] However, the culprits may also have been raiders from Scania and the islands of eastern Denmark, and possibly the Wendish lands to the south and Estonia and Livonia to the east, although we have no records of raiding from there before the eleventh century. Defensive constructions were also built along the 20-kilometer Slätbaken, a narrow inlet that stretches from the Baltic Sea to Gö tavirke. Like the Danevirke, the wall had a palisade and a road behind.

Hedeby was arguably the most important trading center of Viking-Age Scandinavia, which became the seat of a bishop in 948. It is first mentioned in Einhard's Frankish chronicle (804), but was probably founded around some thirty or forty years earlier. Another nearby port, Sliasthorp, was also mentioned at the same time, and this may be the site recently excavated just to the north on the water route to Hedeby.[20] In 808 King Godfred increased Hedeby's importance by destroying Reric, the competing Slavic trade center, and moving its merchants to Hedeby.[21] The town was surrounded on its northern, western, and southern (the three landward) sides by earthworks. On its eastern side the town was bounded by the Schlei inlet and the bay of Haddebyer Noor. At the end of the ninth century the northern and southern parts of the town were abandoned, and in the tenth century a semi-circular earthwork 1300 meters long was built to guard the western approaches to the town. The rampart underwent as many as nine phases of alteration and grew from about 2 meters high and 4 meters wide to a substantial 8 meters high and 25 meters wide.[22] The Hedeby defenses were incorporated into the Danevirke system several decades after the original town rampart was built. It is also possible that a nearby hillfort was used as a refuge in the period before the town defenses were constructed.[23]

Despite its defenses, Hedeby changed hands several times. Adam of Bremen was even informed (by the eleventh-century king Sweyn Estridson) that a Swedish family had controlled it at the end of the ninth and the beginning of the tenth century. The Germans occupied it in 974, but it was re-occupied by the Danes nine years later. Harald Hardrada destroyed it in 1050 during his war with Sweyn Estridson, when he sent burning ships into the harbor. The remains of burned ships were found in the excavations of 2005. Its final destruction came at the hands of the Wends in 1066, after which it was slowly abandoned in favor of Schleswig on the opposite side of the Schlei. By northern European standards it was obviously a prize, although Ibrāhim ibn Ya'qūb was not impressed with it. His worst condemnation was reserved for the singing of its inhabitants, which he thought worse than the baying of hounds.[24]

The effectiveness of Harald's attack emphasizes how vulnerable medieval towns were to fire. Although many settlements or towns were small by today's standards and many houses had plots of land for growing food, much of the building material was wood or thatch and towns were congested enough for fire to spread easily. Containers of water relayed to the scene of a spreading fire were of limited use once it caught hold, so that the only solution was often to demolish houses in its path in the hope of preventing its spread.

Århus—or Aros as the town was called in the Viking Age—emerged around the tenth century, although it is now known that there was a small settlement there previously. It was ideally placed as a trading port on the east coast of Jutland, which means that it was also a useful port for longships. Ramparts were constructed around Århus as early as the tenth century. As far as possible, these were placed alongside natural watercourses which then functioned as moats. In this case they encircled the town on an island with natural watercourses on three sides and the sea on the east. It is estimated that the town inside the Viking ramparts covered about 6 hectares. That this was a high-status center is indicated by finds of six runestones, erected only by the aristocracy, from the turn of the eleventh century. Århus, Hedeby, and Birka were all by the sea, but an exception as a defended town in the Viking Age was Ribe, mentioned earlier than any other Danish town. Its earliest enclosing ditch was probably a demarcation of the settlement, as it can hardly have functioned as a defense. However, later in the ninth century this was replaced by an 8-meter-wide moat with a rampart on the inner side.

The settlement on the Swedish island of Björkö was probably established at about the same time as Hedeby, in the middle of the eighth century. It is usually identified as the Birka of Rimbert's "Life of Ansgar" (*Vita Ansgari*), a monk and early ninth-century missionary to somewhere in present-day Sweden, and mentioned in Adam of Bremen's "The Deeds of Bishops of the Hamburg Church" (*Gesta Hammaburgensis ecclesiae pontificum*), which appeared in 1075—6. Neither tells us precisely where the place is, but it was clearly important and the Björkö site is by far the biggest of its type in Sweden.[25] Björkö is one of the earliest urban settlements in Scandinavia, at its height probably the main Baltic trading center connected to the river and portage routes into Russia and hence to the Byzantine Empire and the Abbasid Caliphate. Approximately seven hundred people lived there when it was at its largest. "Borgen," literally "the fort," is in the south of this area, consisting of a hill with a 700 meter-long semi-circular rampart that encloses an area of about 13 hectares. The bank was 1.8 meters high and 6–12 meters wide with a palisade and had six gaps for defensive towers or access. It was often rebuilt. At its northern end the rampart connects with defensive piles in the harbor which defended the seaward approach to the town.[26] This may have been the home of a garrison and functioned as a refuge, although the site at Hovgården on a nearby island (Adelsö) was probably the site of an estate which was used by the king's retinue when he visited.

There are large burial mounds on this site, one of which was a Viking-Age boat burial. The Björkö site was abandoned in favor of Sigtuna in the late tenth century, but it is not clear whether this was a result of a change in the water level of Lake Mälar, enemy attack, change of ruler, or something else.

The most famous Viking fortifications are the circular forts at Trelleborg (Zealand), Nonnebakken (Funen), Fyrkat and Aggersborg (Jutland), and Trelleborg (Scania).[27] Unlike the earlier Danevirke, which must also have required mobilization of considerable resources, they are distributed across the whole of the medieval kingdom. There are no similar monuments attributed to one king from Norway or Sweden, but (as mentioned above) there are ring castles with some points of resemblance in the Low Countries. The largest of the Danish forts, Aggersborg, is 240 meters in diameter, Trelleborg in Zealand is 137 meters, and Nonnebakken 120 meters. All had four gates with two roads crossing at the center. In the four quadrants were identical longhouses laid out on a geometric pattern. The ramparts of Trelleborg were 17.5 meters wide at the base and 5 meters high, with outer walling of oak. The whole structure was surrounded by a dry ditch which also had a palisade in it. Alone among these fortresses this one had a bailey with a graveyard, almost all of its occupants young men. The forts were clearly garrisons, and their period of use appears to have been very short, as there is no sign of any maintenance or long-term occupation layers at the excavated sites. Their purpose is uncertain. Originally it was thought that they were garrisons or boot-camps built by Sweyn Forkbeard in preparation for his invasion of England, but they turned out to belong to the reign of his predecessor. Although four are on the coast, Nonnebakken is in the center of the island of Funen. Military preparation for a war with Germany is more likely in the reign of Harald, but the forts are curiously positioned for this eventuality, given that a German attack was almost certain to come overland from Saxony, as indeed it did in 974. The spacing of the forts around the realm has led many to the conclusion that they were built to control it.

Some of the Viking settlements outside Scandinavia also had defenses of earthwork banks, notably those in Ireland. The Vikings built *longphorts* (the Irish term meaning "longship-port") as protection for their ships and bases for raids inland. These camps were usually at a tributary where both sides were protected, providing shelter and access to the sea as well. Many such camps were abandoned after one or two seasons, but others became towns in Ireland. Suburbs grew up outside the original enclosed area and defenses were built to enclose them, taking the form of ditch and bank enclosures that appear to have completely encircled the towns. At Dublin, defensive earthwork banks replaced earlier lower ones that have been interpreted as flood defenses. Some of these early defenses were burned in the mid-tenth century. The annals record that early in that century all the Viking bases in Ireland were overrun by the Irish, to be re-occupied by new settlers later in the century. This corresponds to the archaeological datings of new banks that seem to have been built in two phases. Some of these banks had post and wattle reinforcing as well as a wattle palisade, and later ones were built on top of a foundation of logs, wattle and brushwood. The latter survived to a height of 2.30 meters and 6.40 meters wide and had a ditch with a palisade in it.

At Wexford no remains of Viking-Age defenses have been found, although it seems that the Anglo-Norman invaders had to besiege it in 1177, so there must have been some form of defense by then. There has been less excavation here, but the town was also smaller than the other Hiberno-Norse settlements and the early defenses are either undiscovered or buried directly beneath the later Anglo-Norman walls. Waterford appears to have been a *longphort* site in the ninth century. Like Dublin, it had a ditch and bank that would have been 3 meters high with a timber breastwork in the eleventh century. According to the fourteenth-century *Caithreim Cellachain Caisil*, in the mid-tenth century the defenses were overrun by the warriors of Cellachán, king of Munster.

Cork and Limerick were situated on islands, a fairly common arrangement for "overwintering" in the ninth century. Similar bases were set up in Kent, at Thanet and the Isle of Sheppy, and on an island in the Rhine at Neuss in 863, in this case fortified with a bank. Otherwise, the rivers may have been considered sufficient defense. The use of islands mainly occurred in the ninth century, but Cork and Limerick grew into permanent settlements. The *Caithreim* account of the capture of Limerick by the Irish of Munster in *c.* 950 gives the impression that it had defenses involving the use of stone, but claims that they followed some fleeing Vikings in through the gates before they could close them.[28] All the Norse towns in Ireland were periodically sacked.

Despite the apparent lack of fortified sites in Viking Age Scandinavia itself, the Vikings were adept at using fortifications on their campaigns. In the mid-ninth century Viking forces began to overwinter in the territories of the lands they had been raiding. They regularly selected defensible places to camp, or at least places that could easily be made defensible, such as towns, royal villas, churches, monasteries, and nunneries. In 880 they wintered in Nimwegen, using the royal palace as their quarters and throwing up a rampart and palisade around the town, sufficient to deter Louis the Younger from attacking them.[29] In Francia the Vikings occasionally also occupied towns with Roman walls, such as Angers and Verdun, both of which had to be besieged to drive them out. York must also have had surviving Roman walls, and possibly Anglo-Saxon defenses as well. Asser tells us that the Danes fortified Reading in 870–871 by constructing a rampart between the two rivers that joined there. At Wareham, which also lay on a narrow strip of land between two rivers, they made the church and its perimeter wall the center of their defenses.

The most striking and extensively excavated example of a semi-circular fortification is Repton in Derbyshire. This site was occupied by the "Great Heathen Army" in the winter of 873—4. The camp at Repton consisted of a large ditch and bank which formed a D-shaped earthwork with the River Trent protecting its open end, incorporating an Anglo-Saxon church into the line of the earthwork, perhaps as a gateway or strongpoint. Later Viking defenses in England appear to have been similar to the Anglo-Saxon *burhs*, but proved inadequate to halt the advance of their enemies in the early tenth century. However, this was no network of defenses like that of the burghal hidage. The Viking armies that opposed Edward and Æthelflæd still moved around and built or improved defensible sites as bases for raiding. We know that one at least, Tempsford in Bedfordshire, was stormed by Edward the Elder in 921, in what seems to have been a major defeat for the Vikings.[30]

Two other fortifications that may have been occupied for several years by the Vikings were constructed in Brittany. At Camp de Peran, near Plédran and Saint-Brieuc, a more or less circular earthwork with a single 3 meter-high rampart and 4 meter-wide ditch dominated the valleys of the Urne and Gonet. The rampart is thought to have been 4 meters high and 5 meters wide at the base originally, and its roughly circular shape led its excavator, Jean-Pierre Nicolardot, to compare it to the Trelleborg forts.[31] It was built from large stone blocks resting on a clay bank, with timber bracing on a vertical and horizontal lattice. Finds date it to the early tenth century, but at some point the whole site was engulfed by fire. It may have been the Vikings themselves that burned a Breton fort, or Alan Barbetorte burning a Viking fort, as sources record him as landing at Dol and fighting a battle with the Vikings near Saint-Brieuc.[32] There are also two earthworks at Trans, Ille et Vilaine. One, an 80 by 90-meter trapezoid fort with double banks and multiple wide ditches, is known as Vieux M'Na, but it has not yet been properly excavated. The fort is similar in shape to two other Breton forts, at Saint-Suliac near La Ranee and Lanlerf near Saint-Brieuc. Some 500 meters away is the Camp des Haies, a circular double-ditched enclosure on the crest of a hill, which was excavated in 1979. Pottery found there was dated to 920–980. Vieux M'Na may have been a Viking fort occupied after their retreat from the north. The rough and ready nature of the ditches at Camp des Haies has led some to the conclusion that it was hastily constructed and briefly occupied, perhaps by Alan Barbetorte as a siege fort in 939.

The Viking use of these defenses was fluid: there is some suggestion that when the Northumbrian army attempted to retake York in 867, they were allowed to "break in" before being hemmed in inside and slaughtered, both kings being killed. At Nottingham in 868 the Wessex and Mercian attack was probably repelled at the defenses, but on other occasions the Vikings came out to fight in the open. Asser describes them as doing so ("in the manner of wolves") at Reading in 870, when Æthelred and Alfred reached the gate. The sudden counterattack may have taken the Wessex army by surprise, as they had just been pursuing fugitives. Similarly, Flodoard of Reims notes that the Vikings sallied out from their defenses by the banks of the Seine to fight the army of King Raoul in 925.[33] In this case the Vikings succeeded again, although Flodoard attempts to play down their victory. A very similar attitude to defense was taken by Sviatoslav in his defense of Dorostolon against the Byzantine army in 971, when he sallied out with his army twice to fight full-scale battles. It would be stretching the point to attribute this to his (probable) Viking ancestry, however, as in this case he had no hope of assistance from allies and little hope of escape from Bulgaria without either a victory that would enable him to break out or a negotiated settlement involving evacuation of the region.

Anglo-Saxon England

The Viking period saw some of the most dramatic developments in fortification in England's history, but they have left few remains to compare with the later medieval castles or even with Roman fortifications. However, contrary to the impression sometimes given, defensible structures were not unknown to the Anglo-Saxons before the reign of Alfred. The *ASC* records a battle involving a *byrig* at Meretun, presumably a fortification of some kind, between Cynewulf and Cyneheard, two rivals for the kingship of Wessex. In question is a hall, a building for the retinue to sleep in, and gates that were presumably part of a palisade or wall. Such relatively small enclosures for lords and their immediate followers may have been common, and continued to be so.

To English-speaking people, Offa's Dyke is probably the best known pre-Viking "fortification," besides being the most familiar long earthwork bank. About 80 miles of it survive, the lack of it on some areas of the frontier of western Mercia probably being due to erosion and removal. It may have been 8 meters high and had a ditch. It can be fairly securely dated to the reign of Offa (757–796), not just on the basis of its name, but on statements recorded in the *ASC* and Asser. It was not the first such linear earthwork in England, as there are a number of others, notably Wat's Dyke on the Welsh border, the Wansdyke and Bokerley Dyke in Wessex and the Devil's Dyke in East Anglia. They are much more difficult to date, perhaps belonging to the sixth and seventh centuries. They cannot have been defended along their full length and there are no forts, although they may have functioned as frontier markers and obstructions to retiring raiders. The construction of a linear frontier marker not only defines the land behind it as the constructors', but the land beyond it as someone else's, in the same way that Imperial Roman linear frontier defenses marked an intention to limit their *imperium*.

After Offa's reign the chief threat came from the sea and, with the coastline largely indefensible, a strategy of defense in depth was eventually adopted. The frontier with the Danelaw existed for only a few years and never solidified. The Viking assault on Wessex provided the catalyst for a more systematic organization of defenses than anything seen in northern Europe since the Roman Empire, albeit in only a small kingdom. Alfred's victory at Edington and the subsequent peace bought him the time to construct them. Fortifications had to be of a sufficient size to withstand attack, but with limited resources and a limited time within which to construct them, compromises had to be made. The end result was remarkably successful. As noted earlier, the main evidence for Alfred's fortification network is the *Burghal Hidage*, either late ninth or early tenth century in date. It lists the number of hides involved in the provision of defenders for each of thirty-three burhs. The sites are approximately 32 kilometers apart, and many were on *herepaths*, "army routes." There is no uniformity in size between the burhs, nor were they always settlements or towns, as is sometimes assumed. The shape and size of their ramparts was determined by existing fortifications that could be repaired, such as the Roman walls of Bath or Exeter, the terrain, or the extent of existing settlements. Some *burhs*, such as the substantial earthwork defenses of Wallingford, were new constructions, intended to defend important strategic sites such as river crossings and population centers. At Wallingford the ramparts are just over 2,800 meters long, 8 meters high and surrounded by a 3-meter-wide ditch. The number of hides allocated to a *burh* in the *Burghal Hidage* should correspond to the length of the walls, sixteen hides to one acre's width of wall foundation, as listed in the *Burghal Hidage* appendix. Where the line of the walls is known this has been shown to correspond closely in some cases, such as Wallingford mentioned above, and even more closely with the Roman walls of Winchester, but in other cases, such as Wareham, it equates to the length of only three of the four walls.

Roman walls were probably repaired with stone, at least when time allowed. Some of the new fortifications, such as Cricklade and Wallingford, were built on the Roman plan, although probably of turf and wood. Excavations have suggested that there was at least one tower on the ramparts of Cricklade. The interior layout of the larger *burhs* presumably allowed for rapid movement of men from one side of the fortification perimeter to another, and wooden walkways were probably laid on top of earthen ramparts. Other *burhs* were smaller and located on promontories or earlier hill-forts, such as Lydford, which has the gorge created by the River Lyd on three sides, or Malmesbury, which is almost encircled by the Avon. The smallest forts located on heights are more likely to have been refuges or links in the network, and were probably the first to be abandoned in more peaceful conditions, as they were expensive to maintain and had no function as centers of trade, crafts, or population.

Although the burh network in Wessex was constructed much more rapidly and under more royal control than the East Frankish–German fortifications on the Slav frontier, partly because Wessex was a smaller region and under threat of extinction, the principles behind the network were the same. Viking incursions into Wessex could not be prevented, as it had a long coastline and a fairly long land frontier as well. Once they invaded, however, they could be denied provisions, which would be concentrated in the *burhs*, and if they dispersed to forage they were at risk from the garrisons, which could emerge to attack smaller forces or insufficiently guarded ships. If they were badly defeated in the interior of Wessex, they had to run the gauntlet of the *burhs* and their garrisons to escape to their own territory or ships.

When Alfred's son Edward and his daughter Æthelflæd began the recovery of the Mercian Danelaw, they constructed new *burhs* to consolidate their gains, just as the Ottonian kings later did when they pushed their frontier eastwards. These included Hertford and Witham by Edward and Tamworth, Stafford, Eddisbury, and Warwick by Æthelflæd. At Buckingham Edward ordered his men to construct fortifications on both banks.[34] Such double *burhs* were presumably intended to block a river entirely, a measure reminiscent of Charles the Bald's fortified bridges, but the origin of the one at Hertford may have been a camp opposite the enemy one. However, there is no doubt that the importance of river crossings was perceived: twenty-two of the thirty-three *burhs* listed in the *Burghal Hidage* were built round them. Both Alfred and Edward had to construct the *burhs* quickly, the one during the period immediately after his victory of 878 and the other during their advance into the Danelaw. They must have been built with wooden palisades of some variety, perhaps being strengthened later. The bank of the *burh* at Cricklade, for instance, was built in 878–879, but reinforced with a stone wall in front some ten years later.

Not surprisingly, given that many of the *burhs* were built at strategic points and routes across the landscape, and were places where supplies were gathered, many became focal points for trade and grew to become population centers even where there had been none earlier. As frequently happens, it seems that their defenses were often neglected once the Viking threat had passed (or rather, once it seemed that it had passed) in the tenth century, presumably partly because it was expensive to maintain. When the Vikings returned in the reign of Æthelred II, they did not encounter as much difficulty as they might have. However, it has to be remembered that the strategic aims of Sweyn Forkbeard and his army were not necessarily the same as the Viking armies of the ninth century. Furthermore, it is likely that many of the *burhs* did still function, if only as a deterrent to attack. The *ASC* implies that the inhabitants of Winchester were lucky when the Danish army bypassed their town in 914, but it may have been too strong to attack. Richard Abels, however, argues that the towns functioned as refuges for the population rather than as a system of defense in depth as they had in the previous century.[35] Many towns were taken and sacked by the invaders, but others, even small ones such as Watchet and *Maldon*, survived assaults.[36] Although some earlier sites such as South Cadbury hill-fort were refortified in Æthelred's reign, the *burh* system was not reconstructed.

It has already been mentioned that the Normans may have been anticipating resistance from the towns when they invaded England, and they did meet some during the years 1066–1070. The relatively easy passage of the conquest after Hastings is attributable more to the lack of any coherent English leadership after the destruction of Harold's close family in that battle than to a lack of fortifications. It has often been stated that the establishment of the burghal system had inhibited the construction of private fortifications in England and that this made things easier for the Normans. Nevertheless, there were some, as indicated by the statement of Archbishop Wulfstan of York's eleventh-century tract *Geþyncðo*, that a man was entitled to the rights of a thegn if he had "fully five hides of his own land, church and kitchen, bell and *burh*-gate, seat and special office in the king's hall . . . ." "*Burh*-gate" can be taken to stand for the whole manor. One site, at Goltho in Lincolnshire, has been been extensively researched, and in this case is a site that had been in continuous occupation from early Saxon times.[37] As Ann Williams emphasized, it cannot have been unique. In this case it had an earthen bank and ditch. Many such habitations were probably palisaded enclosures, perhaps with a small wooden or stone tower. They would not have differed significantly, in fact, from the lesser "fortifications" of the same period in Germany. Before the Norman castle was constructed in one corner of the Roman fort at Portchester, there was a thegn's residence there, suggesting that some former *burhs* belonged to thegns after they ceased to function in the burghal system. It has also been pointed out that many churches formed parts of thegnly manors, and some were defensible.[38]

Ireland, Scotland, and Wales

There are very few references to defense or assaults on fortifications in the Irish annals, although these increase as the Viking Era progresses, but the fortifications in question are usually Viking settlements. By far the most common fortification when the Vikings first appeared in Ireland was the ringfort. They are distinguished by name according to the material used to build them, the *castel* being built of dry stone and the *rath* of earth. Many were bivallate, with ditches outside each bank, but some had only one bank and a few had three. They varied in diameter from 15 meters to about 80 meters, the smallest being too small even to include residences. Almost all were built for an extended family, and some had souterrains as underground refuges. It might be concluded from the above that the so-called ringforts were not in fact forts at all, and indeed, this has been argued by several archaeologists, who make the now-familiar claim that they had more to do with status than with defense. James Mallory and Tom McNeill, for instance, claim that they were highly defective as defenses: a single family could not have defended the length of rampart of the average ringfort (some 100 meters), their gates were weak, and the inner banks were often lower than the outer ones in bivallate forts. Matthew Stout, on the other hand, says he has not seen any evidence of the last "defect." Moreover, the other criticisms are only defects from a certain point of view—that of someone accustomed to think of fortifications as able to withstand siege and assault from a well-equipped force numbering hundreds or more. It may well be the case that every self-respecting land- or cattle-owning family had to have a ringfort like their neighbor, but the ringforts were defensible against the most common threat in early medieval Ireland: the small-scale raid, often in search of cattle. They were not designed to withstand sieges. In addition, although little of the surrounding terrain was visible from most of them, neighboring ringforts were. A mapping of the ring-forts in the Braid valley of Antrim revealed that as many as seventeen were visible from each. It would thus be quite easy for neighboring families to come to the aid of one under attack. This was defense in depth against raids. An individual ringfort or crannog would have been little help against substantial Viking raids, or even a full-scale raid by an Irish king, but given the sheer number of these forts in areas where they were densest, if nothing else they could have functioned as a "communication chain" to warn of enemy approach. Many continued in use into the Viking Era and beyond.

Other forts in Ireland were of types used for many centuries, such as promontory forts, in which a settlement on a height or a coastal spur that was approachable from only one direction was defended by a stone wall on that side, and crannogs, lake settlements on stilts and usually surrounded by a fence. Almost all of these were also small. In Scotland and Wales both types of fort also existed alongside hill-forts. Promontory forts were also common in Cornwall, although it is not certain how many were in use in the Viking

Era. Many of the possible Welsh pre-Norman sites are under later structures. However, a few of these forts are mentioned in *Brut* as destroyed by the Mercians, such as Degannwy in 823 and the crannog on Llangors Lake in 916.[39]

A new phenomenon that appeared in Ireland in the Viking Era was the tall round tower. Most of these were associated with ecclesiastical properties and certainly functioned as bell towers and places to keep valuable property. It has been remarked that the sole useful defensive feature in them is the door raised from ground level, and that otherwise they would have been death traps, as their narrow windows and timber floors would have soon led to asphyxiation had any attacker managed to start a fire inside the door. They were only suited to defense in the most passive sense.[40] However, this would also be true of the *Bergfried* in Germany. Those that were in sites which were clearly fortifications were certainly last lines of defense, and also "passive" in the sense that many were as ill-suited to the use of missiles by the defenders as the round towers were. The difference, of course, is that people would hope that such a refuge was not necessary and that the main defenses would hold. If the main defenses were breached, there was no place to escape to but the tower. In the case of Ireland's round towers, there was no main defense, and O'Keeffe is probably right that flight into the countryside was a safer bet for local people than crowding into a cramped tower, but they needed good warning of enemy approach if they were to escape. If the towers were used for defense, the hope can only have been that the attackers would give up rather than expend the effort needed to take the tower. We can at least envisage that they may have been used as such by local monks or clergy, but this need not have been their main function.

The eleventh-century *Cogadh Gaedhel re Gallaibh* (*The War of the Irish with the Foreigners*) claims that Brian Boru built the fortification of Cashel and the royal forts of Munster, and strengthened the existing duns and fortresses in the same region. This may be an exaggeration, but the *Annals of Ulster* also credit him with a building campaign. Cashel may have had stone defenses, as later, but the form of the forts is unknown. Since there is no sign of any significant advance in Irish fort-building, they were probably built on the former pattern. Strengthening of forts may simply mean "repairing." Nevertheless, it may be that Brian tried to increase the number of forts to make it more difficult for an enemy to ravage Munster. It has to be borne in mind that his most likely enemies were still other Irish kings, albeit sometimes with Norse aid.

The siege

Sieges were by far the most common direct confrontations between substantial opposing forces in continental Europe. The siege warfare of the period 750–1000 has often been considered crude, in line with the other methods of making war. This is certainly the impression given by the sources on Anglo-Saxon England, Ireland, Scotland, Wales, and, at the other end of Europe, Rus. If a besieger succeeded in taking a fortified place, it was either through blockade or assault, or less commonly, by treachery. We can assume that everyday tools, battering rams, scaling ladders, and fire were sometimes used, but there is no indication of much else.

The Irish *Fragmentary Annals* provide one of the few detailed accounts of a determined attack on Chester in 909, when the Vikings attempted to overcome the old Roman walls. Having suffered one reverse, when many of them were enticed into the town and ambushed, the Vikings attacked again, using propped-up hurdles for cover as they tried to make a hole in the wall, but the hurdles were crushed by "huge rocks and beams" and many were killed. Columns were then placed under the hurdles, which were covered in hides after boiling ale and water was hurled over them. The Vikings finally gave up after beehives were dumped on them.[41] This account indicates that the Vikings had some experience of attacking fortifications, but neither they nor the English employed siege engines or towers. Nor is there any indication elsewhere that these were introduced into England before the coming of the Normans.

Long sieges carried out by the English, Irish, or Vikings were rare. The Vikings are mentioned as using siege machines at Paris, one of the few long sieges they conducted, but not elsewhere. Writing at the end of the twelfth century, Saxo mentioned that the Danes had to enlist the help of German settlers to build engines in 1134. Despite being in constant contact with Germany to the south and having had repeated experience of defending fortifications against siege engines and towers during their expeditions, it seems that the Danes had still not adopted their military methods. By contrast, the Bohemians and Poles had begun to adopt "German" siege methods and to use machines in the eleventh century. It is difficult to avoid the conclusion that Vikings had little interest in conducting long sieges involving technical expertise and extensive construction work, the attitude that fortifications were often best defended by coming out and fighting a battle in the open probably being another aspect of this culture. Their attempt on

Paris was an exception, a failure (in military terms, if not necessarily profit) that may have discouraged further such efforts.

No systematic treatments of the techniques and technology involved in sieges were put into writing in northern Europe, although there was Roman material available, including Vegetius and the *Agrimensores*, the latter texts available in a late fifth- or early sixth-century compilation. In Byzantium military treatises did refer to siegecraft: in particular, we have two anonymous tenth-century Byzantine treatises, known as *Parangelmata Poliorcetica* and *Geodesia*.[42] Knowledge of Greek may not have been widespread in northern Europe, but there were numerous contacts between the Franks (later Germans) and Byzantium, and there is no reason why many of the techniques used by the latter should not have become familiar and used by the former. The Geodesia gives methods of measuring devices used in warfare to ensure the correct dimensions, including the necessary mathematical formulae, and is based heavily on Heron of Alexandria's *Dioptra*.

The image of a siege that comes most readily to mind is that of a city or fortress cut off from the surrounding world, but this was very difficult to achieve without building fortified lines around it. A rare example is Charles the Bald's siege of Viking-held Angers in 873, when he built a ring of earthworks around the town.[43] Nevertheless, the siege was lengthy and difficult, because the Vikings were fighting for their lives, as Regino of Prüm tells us. The fighting men had also moved their families into the town after the inhabitants had fled. Regino also says that the Breton force supporting Charles diverted the River Mayenne. This threatened to leave the Viking ships moored at the city high and dry, which persuaded them to negotiate their departure. According to the *Annals* of St. Bertin they gave hostages and a promise that those who remained pagan would never return. These annals give a favorable slant to Charles's success, emphasising his determination and the terms extracted from the Vikings, although they were also permitted to set up a market on an island in the Loire. However, Regino says Charles was "overcome by base lust" and accepted payment from the Vikings, who broke their promises and continued to plunder the district once he had retired. Despite this accusation, he himself gives us the real reasons for Charles's leniency, namely that his own army was nearing exhaustion, was short of supplies and suffering from a pestilence.

The siege of Angers demonstrates the problems that might be encountered in a prolonged siege. Any attempt to starve out a besieged garrison or population was difficult and time-consuming, and ate up much of the resources of the surrounding area, not just livestock and crops, but timber and other materials. If there were several thousand beseigers the camp would have been huge, resembling a small town of tents, markets, horse lines, and an inner camp for the leaders. They tried to take as many comforts as possible, including servants and entertainers such as grooms, valets, cooks, priests, and musicians. Even lesser nobility would have had many followers. Obviously numerous craftsmen such as smiths, carters, ferriers, and fletchers accompanied the army, as well as the wives of many of the men. The troops were expected to find or purchase their own food to supplement their diet, so siege camps attracted sellers of all sorts, not to mention prostitutes and beggars. Although tents would have been provided for many, others were billeted in local villages or manufactured lean-tos or sheds from locally found or looted materials. Naturally, the presence of so many people in such a small area increased the likelihood of disease. The risk of starvation in a siege camp may not have been as great as it was for the besieged, as sieges were abandoned if provisions ran very short, but otherwise the besiegers faced the same risks if they were detained there for any length of time, because of the makeshift nature of many of their camps and the rudimentary hygiene. Numerous sieges were abandoned because of disease. Charles the Bald's 873 siege of Angers was at most a qualified success, for this reason. We do not know the nature of all these diseases, but dysentery, typhus, and pneumonia were certainly some of the most common, along with malaria in southern Europe. Food poisoning must also have been prevalent.

Invariably there were truces and negotiations, as besiegers and besieged were within shouting distance and both usually had an interest in avoiding the risks that increased as time wore on. This is also the explanation for many of the campaigns that simply ended in promises of tribute and hostage-giving. To the modern mind, a campaign without a "decisive engagement" being sought may seem unsatisfactory, especially given the number of times such agreements were broken, but the medieval commander knew that the risks of a long campaign involving a siege were greater. For instance, in 929, despite the extensive and powerful defenses of Prague, Wenceslaus of Bohemia agreed to Henry I's terms immediately upon his arrival. Widukind says this was a miracle, but he also tells us that Henry had his entire army with him. In other words, Wenceslaus was not prepared to risk a siege that might end in disaster, while Henry preferred a bloodless and relatively risk-free 'conquest'. Usually there was no calculation that mass bloodletting was essential to teach the enemy a lesson, as the submission was enough. No doubt considerable damage had been done to the countryside in any case. Boleslav made the same decision as his predecessor when Otto I invaded Bohemia in 950, and elected not to defend Prague.

Although assaults on fortifications were risky, they were frequently made, no doubt because the risks of long sieges were greater. Commanders were well aware that advantage could be gained by launching an assault when the enemy was unprepared. In 954 Count Heribert of Vermandois captured Roucy from its count, Reginald, in what Flodoard calls a sneak attack. Later in the same year Reginald captured Heribert's castle at Montfélix in a surprise attack. On occasions, presumably both to achieve surprise and hinder defensive fire, fortress walls were scaled at night. In 949 King Louis captured the outer defenses of Laon in this way, but failed to take the citadel.[44] Most long sieges involved periodic assaults in any case, as well as sallies by the garrison, designed to demoralize the attackers or destroy their equipment. On occasion this could even result in a battle outside the walls. The *Parangelmata* author warns against the danger of heavy objects being rolled down from above if attacking a hill-top fortress, suggesting the use of wooden stakes placed three or four deep and ditches and banks to prevent them from hitting the besieging troops. The heavy objects include roundish stones, building columns, wheels, column drums, loaded four-wheeled wagons, plaited containers full of gravel or compacted earth, and barrels. In order to face the dangers at the wall, all troops assaulting a fortification had to cross a killing ground to reach it, under missile fire from the defenders. They would have been in range of stone and spear-shooting engines at perhaps 350 meters, slingshot and arrows within 200 meters, and spears and stones at close range. Apart from a slow approach involving the digging of ditches and erection of fences as described above, various structures could be used to protect them, but however an assault was conducted it was necessary to attempt to clear the defenders from the battlements with missile fire from the besiegers' army.

The usual method of scaling walls was with the use of ladders. The *Parangelmata* describes these in detail, including attaching a drop-bridge to the end and a dubious method of extending their height with inflatable leather ladders based on a third-century work by Philo Mechanicus. Hooks were often fixed at the top of the ladders, or to whatever extension they had, to hold them fast to the wall, and sometimes they had spikes at their foot to secure them to the ground. The *Parangelmata* author is correct that ladders had to be reasonably light, but they also needed to be strong. More often than not they were made of wood, but rope ladders are also mentioned. During the siege of Antioch in the First Crusade a ladder collapsed under the weight of armored men. This form of assault must have required some practice. Modern firemen have considerably better boots and stronger and more stable ladders, but need extensive training to climb them while carrying equipment and anticipating danger. In their case it is improbable that anyone would be trying to throw the ladder down or push it away with a pole as it was being put in place, or injure them when they were at the top.

Troops at the walls were obviously exposed to objects dropped from the battlements. Apart from stones and other heavy objects, burning materials could be dropped and hot sand, lime, or boiling liquids tipped out of containers. In 1004, at the siege of Bautzen in the land of the Slavic Milzeni, Hemuzo, "a warrior noble in lineage," was killed when half a millstone dropped from the fortress wall hit him on the head.[45] In Arnulf's siege of Bergamo in 894 the defenders even pushed sections of the battlements onto the heads of assaulting troops, who had adopted the simple procedure of hacking and digging into the walls whilst using their shields to protect their heads from missiles. As the *Annals of Fulda* do in this account, Liudprand of Cremona also describes the troops using their shields above their heads at Rome. Neither uses the term *testudo*, but they appear to be describing a similar formation to that employed by imperial Roman troops in similar circumstances. In his history, Richer of Saint-Rémi does use this term when describing a similar technique used by Conrad the Red's troops withdrawing under fire from an assault on Senlis in 949. He also mentions the use of shields (*clipei*) specially constructed for this purpose at Lothar's (of France) siege of Verdun in 985.[46] They may have been similar to the cane or wicker screens described by Liudprand as used at Rome. Richer seems to have understood *testudo* in the way that the Romans used it. This was not a formation that could be used by untrained troops, as the shields had to be held in specific ways and positions whilst moving forward.

Artillery

There is much confusion around the types of artillery used in Europe during the Middle Ages, deriving largely from the wide variety of terms used for it. For all the variations in size and shape of these engines, there were basically three methods of missile propulsion. The most familiar to us is tension, the pulling force exerted by a string, rope or cable on another object, in this case the missile, as used in bows, crossbows, and their larger cousins, usually referred to as ballistas.[47] The last come into the category of siege artillery, as their size made them generally unsuitable for the battlefield. A strong frame was required, with some mechanical means to wind back the cord. In the Middle Ages these were used largely to fire bolts. With a range of some 350 meters, although inaccurate at this range, they could be used both to clear defenders from the parapets of fortresses and by the defenders to inflict damage and casualties on besieging troops operating their own machines. The second widely employed force was torsion, the twisting of ropes by an applied torque. The release of this stress provides the energy to propel the missile, either a stone or bolt. In the Hellenistic kingdoms and late Republican and early Imperial Rome a device similar to a crossbow but with the arms fixed into vertically held frames containing coiled sinews or ropes was used. These weapons fell out of use in the later empire, but they were replaced by the bow ballista as bolt-firer and *onager* (mule or wild ass) as stone-thrower.

In many modern works it has been assumed that the same artillery used in the later Roman Empire continued in use in the Byzantine Empire, but ceased to be used in "barbarian" Europe before reappearing in the Carolingian era, but there is no compelling evidence for this. It is possible that the artillery that did remain in use in the eastern part of the empire was adopted by the Lombards, who are mentioned as using siege engines by Paul the Deacon (writing two hundred years after the Lombard conquest of northern Italy), and then by the Franks, but this is guesswork. Often the sources that mention artillery used by the Frankish kingdoms and their successors simply refer to *machinae*, rather as many Byzantine texts use the term *magganika*. Later the term *tormenta* became common. The main controversy surrounds the *onager*, which appears in many modern works on medieval siegecraft under the name *mangonel*, although there is no way of knowing which machine is meant when the term *mangana* or similar is used in Latin sources. The onager was a single-armed vertically mounted torsion-powered stone-thrower. The arm, which had a cup at the end to hold the missile, was held in a twisted skein of horsehair or sinew. It was held flat to load and then released so that it struck a crossbeam with great force, propelling the stone or other missile from the cup. The Roman name presumably derived from the kick when the beam was struck. Naturally the whole frame had to be of very robust construction to withstand this.

Although the *Parangelmata* refers to torsion artillery, the lack of reference to this elsewhere suggests that the twin-armed type of artillery utilising torsion and used by the Romans fell out of use even in the Byzantine Empire, possibly in the fifth century, whereas the tension-powered bolt-throwing ballista continued in use. Procopius certainly describes the *onager* in Justinian's wars, and the references to artillery in Maurice's *Strategikon* do not exclude it. Once again, the only source to refer to the single-armed torsion engine after the sixth century is the *Parangelmata*. There are no descriptions of torsion engines in other Byzantine military manuals, whereas there are clear references to traction artillery. Torsion artillery was more powerful but more difficult to use and maintain, at least in a technical sense. In the twin-armed torsion machines the skein in each arm had to be maintained at the same level. If the ropes or sinews became wet in any torsion machine the tension went from the skein and drying out was a lengthy process. The massive construction required of the *onager* made it heavier than a traction engine throwing a stone of similar size, but it required less space, which meant that it could be deployed on defensive structures such as towers. However, an *onager* of any size would have required a very solid platform, as the movement of the whole frame engendered by its action could damage stonework.

In view of the above evidence it seems that the *onager* was largely or wholly replaced by the traction counterweight lever engine. This machine originated in China and was introduced into Europe by the Avars in the late sixth century. A beam acting as a lever was secured in a frame so that it rotated on a pivot through a vertical plane. The ropes on the shorter end of the lever were pulled on by a team of men, and its release hurled a stone from a sling attached to the longer end.[48] The men would have required some training to coordinate their movement, and the machines would have to have been of considerable size to damage stone walls. Nevertheless, it did not have to be of such massive construction as the *onager* and was easier to build or assemble from parts. As usual, the terminology for these machines is not always clear. The Byzantines called them *petrobolos*, meaning "stone-thrower," and *petrarea* (also the usual term in later medieval Latin sources) or *tetrarea* and *labdarea*. The last two terms may have designated two types, as represented in illustrations to one manuscript of John Skylitzes's history. The second of these was used at the siege of Dorostolon in 971. It is likely that these machines were employed north and west of the Byzantine Empire, but there is no clear reference to them before the siege of Lisbon in 1147. Unlike the torsion-powered *onager*, at least in its smaller varieties, they could not be deployed on battlements.

There is no doubt that the tension-powered ballista was used by the Byzantines throughout their history. Tenth-century Byzantine lists of artillery mention the *cheirotoxobolistra* and the *toxobolistra*. John Haldon suggests that the former was manually spanned, whereas the latter term referred to all types of windlass-spanned *ballistae*. Whether the Byzantines used wagon-mounted artillery is debatable, but the *alakation* referred to in Leo's *Taktika* appears to have been a tension-powered weapon that could fire stones and arrows, light enough to be used from wheeled transport. If such a weapon was employed further north there is absolutely no evidence for it. The ballista, or great crossbow as it came to be known in High Medieval Europe, was a powerful weapon. It is often stated that it was very accurate up to 350 meters or so: this might have been the case if medieval machines had possessed more than the most elementary sights. This restricted all long-ranged anti-personnel weapons, whatever their potential, to more or less the same range: that within which they could be aimed, unless they were fired at mass targets, or at battlements simply in the hope of keeping people's heads down.

Siege machines were certainly used by the Franks and their enemies in the eighth century, as there are a number of references to them being used by Charles Martel and Pippin in their campaigns against enemies within Francia itself. According to the *RFA*, they were also used by the Saxons besieging Syburg in 776, but "the catapults did more damage to them than [to] those inside." In general, references to siege engines increase as the period progresses. In his siege of Angers in 873, Charles the Bald employed "new and high-quality types of siege-machines," according to Regino of Prüm. Abbo's account of the Siege of Paris frequently mentions *ballistae* deployed by the defenders, and *catapultae* on the towers. If these were stone-throwers, as seems likely, in all probability they would have been torsion machines. Although the term *ballista* was later used of the crossbow as well, the context here indicates that these were larger bolt-shooters. The Vikings themselves are said to have used *catapultae* and *mangana*, which could throw heavier stones. Doubt has been cast on this, but even if the Vikings knew little of these machines, which is not certain, they could have enlisted or compelled the help of Franks. Nor can we be certain whether the *mangana* were large torsion engines or traction machines. Abbo clearly knew of different types of machine, whatever they were, and he is not the only source for the use of siege machines at Paris.

There are numerous references to the use of siege machines from tenth-century France and Germany, but they are very difficult to identify. Among the other weapons used in 962 by Otto I at Montefeltro (San Leo) in Italy is listed *fundibalus*, "sling." The context suggests a reference to the traction engine rather than a staff sling. The "*machinis arcem*" used by his grandson Otto III at Rome in 998 were probably ballistas.[49] Widukind also notes that attackers and defenders exchanged missiles "stone for stone and spear for spear" when Henry I besieged Laer. Again, in 1008 the defenders of the archiepiscopal palace at Trier used stone-throwers against Henry II's assaulting troops. Assuming these accounts of stones fired by defenders are accurate, we have no way of knowing what type of engines the defenders were using, or whether they were firing from the fortifications or over them.

Rams, towers, and other devices

Little is known of the construction of rams and other structures designed to protect troops attacking fortress walls in the west. Rams are certainly attested in the Frankish realms, in both Merovingian and Carolingian eras, including the huge one described by Abbo as used by the Vikings at Paris. Even if its size is exaggerated, the structure, a wheeled wooden housing, resembles closely that recommended by Vegetius and the *Mappae clavicula*.[50] Most rams were probably single tree trunks with iron heads, suspended from a beam in a housing on wheels.

In the *Parangelmata* the author describes an assortment of tortoises, movable covered structures for attacking fortifications, both for excavating and filling ditches and for protection against heavy rolling objects. The latter were light wedge-shaped beak tortoises with roofs made of curved vines, which were recently invented.[51] He describes single-log and composite rams, portable wooden towers, different forms of scaling ladders, structures designed to protect against objects and incendiaries dropped from above, tools for digging through walls, drop-bridges to cross ditches, machines for mounting walls without the use of ladders and scout-ladders for viewing over a defensive wall. These should be lightweight, simple enough for any craftsman to make or repair, easily assembled and disassembled, difficult to damage, and easy to transport. With the probable exception of the wall-mounting machines, these structures may well have been used in the Viking Era by western armies, as well as by the Byzantine army, even if the materials used to make them differed.

The anonymous Byzantine author recommends many small wedge-shaped tortoises (the shape of upturned ships) for the assault on the walls, made of wicker, unless moving uphill, in which case they should be stronger to deflect objects rolling downhill. For the tortoises the protection of hides or canvas is necessary, preferably slack so they absorb the force of any striking missiles, and soaked with water to offer protection from fire. It is suggested that these structures are carried uphill by the troops protected within them, but wheeled if on level ground. The approach avenues should be fortified with stakes and boards as they are prepared. The filler tortoises were used to fill in boggy ground and ditches, but even for them the way had to be prepared by men probing with iron-pointed lances and wearing wooden soles supported under their boots because the enemy could bury caltrops and clay pots or other disguised holes that would cause the ground to collapse under the weight of the machine. At the wall both ramming and excavating were used to weaken it. The *Parangelmata* indicates that the height of the ram-bearing tortoises should be twice their length, with a roof sloping down to the back. It should have four wheels and be compact enough to maneuver, with a ram suspended from ropes inside. Other tortoises should be positioned behind to make a covered way of approach for the men. The point is made that the ram should be directed higher up a stone wall than the base, as this part was usually exceptionally strong.

Virtually all the methods described in the *Parangelmata* were probably used in western Christendom, with the exception of the wedge-shaped tortoises. Some of its functions would have been fulfilled by wheeled sheds, but the most common method of covering troops approaching defended walls seems to have been use of the mantlet (the structures named as vinea or plutei). This was a large wooden screen covered in matting or leather and moved on wheels. They are described by Vegetius, and were used by the Vikings at Paris and by Louis IV (king of Francia 920–954) at the siege of Laon in 938, among others.[52] Their use was probably widespread at sieges in the Carolingian realms and their successor kingdoms, although they are only identifiable in sources from West Francia. To deflect objects rolled downhill the same purpose as the wedge-tortoise would have been served by constructing the mantlet with an apex at the front, as some certainly were later in the Middle Ages.

One structure for which we do have definite evidence is the siege tower. The tower could serve two purposes: to overlook the ramparts of a besieged fortification and enable troops stationed on the upper level to shoot down on them, and to assault the ramparts, for which purpose a drop-bridge was usually necessary. In 985 King Lothar of France attacked Verdun, defended by supporters of Otto III, then an infant. For once, we have a detailed description of the siege tower constructed, penned by Richer of Saint-Rémi.[53] The base was made from four 30-feet beams, fastened together to create an internal space of 100 square feet (10 × 10 feet). Four 40-foot beams were fixed perpendicularly at each base corner, and reinforced with eight 10-foot cross beams, four at the mid-point and four at the top. Four beams were also attached from the apex to the base, to steady the structure. Two planked floors were added, with wickerwork sides or defensive screens to cover the men. The tower was moved to the wall with a pulley system and ropes pulled by oxen. Pulleys were attached to the tower. The ropes passed through them, and also through metal fittings on four large posts driven into the ground near the fortress wall, so that the oxen could move away from the fortress while pulling the tower towards it. This was a more sophisticated system than that used at Castel Sant' Angelo, when the towers were pushed forwards.

It is obvious that the expertise of a craftsman was required to build towers and the sheds used as cover for men attempting to damage the wall or gates. Although there were probably many who could construct the timber structures with wheels, more specialized knowledge was needed to install a ram and make it work properly. The same applied to drop-bridges. Since it was quite impossible to move them with the army, large structures were made on site when the siege was already in progress, although they were sometimes transported in parts for assembly on site.

The other method of assault on the wall described by the anonymous author is undermining, either by boring at the wall from the cover of tortoises or by digging a tunnel. The excavated part of the wall needed to be propped up by timbers and filled with inflammable material, after which a fire could be lit under the stone wall to crack the stones or cause the wall to collapse. Similarly, if a tunnel was dug under the wall the chamber excavated directly under it was filled with combustibles which were then fired. Mining was used widely in western and central Europe during the High Middle Ages, but evidence for it is lacking in the Viking Era. Although undermining of walls is frequently referred to in some sources, for instance by the tenth-century annalist Flodoard of Reims, it is not clear that this does not mean attacking the base of the wall rather than digging a mine under it. However, the mine was certainly a known method at the beginning of the twelfth century. Bohemond's Normans used it at Dyrrachium in 1108, when his miners were intercepted by the Byzantine defenders, who had dug a countermine.

Aftermath of the siege

The fate of any garrison or the population of a town or settlement that was taken by siege was in the hands of the besieging commanders, unless it was taken by storm, in which case controlling the attacking soldiers was virtually impossible and, as far as we know, rarely attempted. Usually a negotiated surrender that enabled the besieger to avoid a prolonged siege and heavy casualties would preserve the lives of the inhabitants at the probable cost of tribute and after ritual acts of subordination. In 1001 Otto III besieged Tivoli, near Rome, building siege machines and constructing earthworks to interrupt the city's water supply. However, Bishop Bernwald and the Pope were allowed to enter the city and persuaded the citizens to submit. Once this was agreed, the delegation of bishops left the city, followed by all the leading citizens, naked except for loincloths, carrying in their right hands a sword and in their left a rod. They surrendered themselves and their possessions to the emperor to do with as he wished.[54] He was entitled to execute by the sword any he found guilty, or show mercy by whipping them with the rod, and could also instruct them to destroy the walls of the city. He showed mercy, pardoned the guilty, and decided not to destroy their city. The ritual was a public display including prescribed acts for such a submission (*deditio*), such as acknowledgement that the rebels merited punishment, while the bare feet and garments signified penitence.

A prolonged siege was more likely to result in reprisals against the garrison and inhabitants of a fortress when it was eventually forced to surrender. It was therefore important, if a garrison was expected to hold out, that it had hope of relief, hence the siting of many of the forts within a day's march of the next. Like political relationships in general, any act of surrender, whether of a fortress or a district, had to be accompanied by the appropriate gestures, after which a victor of superior status might accept a former enemy or rebellious vassal as a friend (in the medieval sense of the word). There were accepted rules of behavior in Christian Europe, and, as far as we can tell, among pagan peoples as well. At the same time a lord was allowed a certain unpredictability—he was not obliged, for instance, to forgive rebels who threw themselves on his mercy.

Treatment of prisoners varied. Without a surrender on terms, there was a greater risk of severe treatment. After Arnulf's assault on Bergamo in 894, its commander, Count Ambrosius, was hanged from the tower where he made his last stand. The pro-Arnulf *Annals of Fulda* claim this was brought about by the demands of the army, but Liudprand of Cremona holds Arnulf responsible. In 933, during fighting between noble factions in France, Count Heribert of Vermandois took the *castrum* at St. Quentin by force, but released the prisoners of Count Hugh the Great's garrison after they made oaths not to take up arms again, installing a garrison of his own. Hugh reacted quickly and retook the *castrum*, but he chose to hang many of the defenders, including a noble cleric, and mutilated many others by cutting off various limbs. It was probably as a result of this treatment that Heribert's garrison at Roye surrendered to Hugh without a fight shortly afterwards.[55]

Savage treatment of prisoners was usually calculated rather than simple mindless violence. Various considerations came into play when a commander decided how to treat them. The victorious commander might consider whether it was necessary to set an example that might discourage others from defying him, or encourage other enemies to give in without a struggle. The examples of Arnulf and Hugh come into this category, as both incidents were followed by the surrender of other fortresses without a fight. A commander might also be constrained by political factors or kinship ties, or alternatively, there might be political pressure to eliminate someone. In 870 the Viking kings of Dublin, Olaf and Ívarr, captured Alt Clut (Dumbarton Rock), the main fortress of the British kingdom of Strathclyde, after a four-month siege, in this case a matter of patrolling the sea around it with their longships. They took the king, Arthgal ap Dynwal, as a prisoner to Dublin, but murdered him two years later, allegedly as a political favor to Constantine, the king of Scots.[56] However, the Vikings were known to ransom prisoners on occasions. Noble prisoners often had a high value, or might be useful as hostages, but even lesser folk had a value as slaves, either to be sold or as a workforce.

If a place was taken by storm, pillage, rape, and massacre would almost invariably follow. In part this was a result of the same pent-up emotions that caused victors in battle to cut down fleeing enemies, but it was also generally accepted that the whole community was responsible for any defiance. For Christians, the Laws of the Book of Deuteronomy offered a guide as to how the inhabitants of a defiant city should be treated:

> But if it [the city] makes no peace with you, but makes war against you, then you shall besiege it; and when the Lord your God gives it into your hand you shall put all its males to the sword, but the women and the little ones, the cattle, and everything else in the city, all its spoil, you shall take as booty for yourselves; and you shall enjoy the spoil of your enemies, which the Lord your God has given you.[57]

In fact, leaders often preferred not to capture towns by storm, as it led to uncontrolled looting and a consequent reduction in their proportion of the spoils. In 852, when the king of Italy and future emperor Louis II was besieging Arab-held Bari, he hesitated to launch an assault after breaching the walls for precisely this reason, and the respite allowed the defenders to repair the gap with timber. He subsequently abandoned the siege.

Chapter 7

The Way of the Warrior

There are many explanations for warfare and warlike behavior: sociobiological, such as male competition for women; environmental and economic, perhaps competition for limited resources due to population pressure or declining productivity; political, motivated by the need to reinforce personal authority or status; and cultural, encompassing moral ideals and norms that sanction violent behavior, with methods of socialization such as ritual practices that reinforce such behavior and may lead to the formation of a warrior society. In general, it is not all that difficult for us to understand economic motives for the actions of our ancestors, in their case sometimes a matter of survival as they lived in subsistence or near-subsistence economies, nor do political motivations seem unfamiliar, even if the methods of political interaction between communities may vary with time. Here, however, we are largely concerned with cultural factors that might make violence and warfare inherent in society.

We can understand that there were ideological motives for warfare, but many of our ideologies, such as modern nationalism, belief in an economic system (capitalism), or belief in a system of government, would have been totally alien to people in the Viking Era. To the vast majority of those who were not Christians or Moslems the idea of enforced conversion to another religion would also have been alien; in fact, they did not have any conception of a religion in this sense. More familiar would have been the warrior ethos and cultural motives for aggrandisement and/or defense of the home community. They may not have sparked wars without additional political and economic incentives, but they played a major part in determining the nature of war in the Viking Era. With a few possible exceptions, usually regarded as outcasts from society or criminals by the majority, no one nowadays believes that being a warrior *is in itself* something to aspire to, or perhaps, to be more accurate, something that you *must* be. Yet it is arguable that this was what the male elite of the Viking Era felt, with certain (qualified) exceptions in Christianized societies. Furthermore, glory as a warrior and respect as a member of the social elite was not simply earned by killing enemy warriors, the "heroism" still widely respected nowadays, but by rapine and enslavement.

It is largely with the elite or landless men turned warrior that this chapter is concerned. They were not professional warriors in the modern sense, nor can they have spent most of their time fighting, but their lives were dominated by warrior imagery and warrior rituals. They probably spent a good deal of time practising for war, not to mention hunting, which was closely related, and even some of the clothes and accoutrements they used will have had associations with war. However, it was often necessary to raise larger armies than these could provide. This had been true in the Migration Period when tribal confederations wished to migrate, conquer territory or confront the Roman Empire. Once more settled kingdoms of substantial size began to emerge on the European mainland, and later in Britain, the raising of large armies was still necessary on occasion. The bulk of these armies, particularly those employed for defense against raids and invasion, were made up of free men summoned by their lords. Their main occupation was farming or herding, not fighting, preparing to fight, or acting as enforcers on behalf of their lords. They are barely visible in the sources, which were almost invariably written by members of the elite, and they left little behind when they died. As mentioned elsewhere, they almost certainly received some training for the eventuality of combat, and, like most people of their age, they will have been used to a certain level of violence and no doubt were capable of it themselves, but for the vast majority of them war will have been an unwelcome and thoroughly nasty business, a threat to their own lives and those of their families, which was unlikely to bring them much profit.

Kinship and vengeance

In the Viking Era a man's status and honor were intrinsically connected to that of his family or to a *familia* such as a warrior fraternity. Germanic lawcodes, which were often preoccupied with procedures for the curtailing of feuding by setting compensation tariffs, tell us that status and honor were matters for all free men. The primary unit of social organization in northern Europe in the early Middle Ages was the kin-group, and it is in this sense that "family" is used here. The medieval meaning of *familia* was the household, the smallest social unit of that period. A household, as the word suggests, was the group of people settled within an enclosed space, which might be a house, but might equally be a settlement enclosed by a defensive wall, palisade or ditch, or a monastery—the residents of a monastery or nunnery were also regarded as a *familia*. The people within a small settlement were normally blood-relatives, although the *familia* also included the slaves and servants. However, the household was part of a larger network, or "extended family," which included other households linked by shared ancestry, even if located elsewhere. The monastery is one example of a household that often cut across kinship bonds and involved the creation of a new *familia* based on shared commitment, reinforced by oaths and religious ties; another was the military household or *comitatus*, whose origin extended far back into the pre-Christian era. Initiation into it involved oath-taking and ritual, but there was also a pragmatic side in that it involved reciprocal gift-giving and acquisition of honor. Some warrior fraternities (or warrior-bands) had a similar structure outside the kin-group, but the kin-group probably also had a part to play in the formation of many warrior-bands, particularly the smaller raiding bands of the Vikings, Slavs, Balts, and Estonians.

Ties between kin involved obligation. Systems of inheritance and kinship structures from the Viking Era and the earlier Middle Ages are often obscure, but we know they were complex.[1] The level of integration achieved through marriage varied between different peoples, and so did the level of obligation to assist. In cognatic kinship societies marriage extended the kin, whereas in an agnatic system such as that of Ireland and the Pictish kingdom, later Scotland, it created a bond of friendship, what we might call an alliance.[2] In certain societies the network created by marriage and friendship ties could result in the formation of a clan, usually organized on the basis of a mythical or mythologized common ancestor, who functioned as the symbol of unity and gave the clan its name.[3] Clans were characteristic of Ireland in the Viking Era, and on that basis probably of Scotland too. In Ireland these collectives functioned in a hierarchical territorial arrangement, wherein subgroups and individuals were linked to superiors through cattle clientship, tribute or service.

In Viking-Age Scandinavia, although an agnatic system, no clans were formed and marriage implied an extension of the kin-group. Although cognatic kinship was characteristic of the Germanic polities, in most of them the family into which the woman married subsequently became the primary kin of any offspring. In Scandinavia kinship remained "bilateral" well into the Middle Ages, with both families retaining an equal status as the next generation's kin. This meant that a kin-group could become very large, giving the alliance maker a choice of "friends." In addition, the most important kin unit, the ætt (ancestral family line), could be extended through marriage, foster relationship and blood brotherhood. Fostership was an important institution throughout Europe, but it was also tied to clientship. Fostering another's child might be an honor, but it also implied an inferior status. The family took precedence over the individual, which is reflected in the saga practice of nominating the most promising member to manage its wealth and the odal rights (referring to the patrimony) that made alienation of a dead member's property to someone outside the family very difficult.

All kin-based social units owed their origins to the need for mutual support in pre-state societies, and involved some obligation to maintain the honor of the kin-group or clan. A prime motivator in the creation of extended kin networks was the establishment of a power structure, which implied the ability to muster a sufficient armed force to defend the group's interests. When family honor was at stake, it was the duty of the kin to maintain it, while members had obligations to involve their kin (particularly the powerful members) in any decisions that would extend the family or create ties to other kin-groups. An example of someone who went too far even for his own family is Sweyn Godwineson, who was declared a *niðing*, a non-person, of no worth whatsoever, by the king and the *here* ("host") in 1046. He subsequently murdered his cousin Bjorn.[4] Perceived injustices and disputes over inheritance could also lead to splits within families, as occurred between Harold and Tostig in the same family, with serious consequences for the whole realm.

Paradoxically, the larger a kin network became, the greater the chance of splits within it, particularly if there were inheritance disputes. Families of lesser means were tied to those with greater resources through the bond of lordship, the lord–man relationship being characteristic of all the Germanic kingdoms and the larger polities of Slavic Europe that developed on the same model, which could require them to provide military service. When disputes arose within powerful kin-groups, there was a serious danger that this would erupt into warfare, as they could call upon considerable resources. These disputes were more likely among wealthy kin, because the Europe-wide practice of powerful men of keeping as many concubines as possible, not to mention repudiating and replacing wives, led to numerous offspring with no certainty as to precedence in inheritance. When bonds between rulers and lesser magnates were largely personal there existed an inherent potential for political fragmentation, which invariably resulted in warfare as sons battled for supremacy. The two most spectacular examples of this in the Viking Era were the warring between the sons of Louis the Pious in the ninth century, which caused the break-up of the empire Charlemagne had created, and in a polity with even less bureaucratic structure, the sons and grandsons of Sviatoslav in eleventh-century Rus. In both cases internal strife brought misery and destruction to the populace, but opportunity for predatory neighboring rulers, bands of mercenaries, plunderers, and slave-traders. The Viking bands that infested northern Europe from the late ninth to the early eleventh century had an eye for any of these methods of acquiring wealth.

Internal strife between rulers also, of course, created opportunity for other powerful kin-groups or their leading representatives to increase their power, either by extracting concessions from rival princes in exchange for support, or by naked aggrandizement that could not be checked by more powerful rulers. They were represented by client kings and client kindreds in Ireland and probably Pictland, later Scotland, and the magnates and magnate kin-groups (sometimes sub-kings) of England and Carolingian Europe. In Rus there were no magnates or established landowners in the eleventh century and the prince's "administration" was his *družina*. However, the land was not unpopulated and the local tribes probably had a hierarchy of kindred groups.

Behind the tendency for strife to break out whenever governmental authority was perceived to be weak, if it existed at all, was the culture of feud, tied to the preservation of the family's or *familia's* honor. Conflicts known as feuds or vendettas, or sometimes as private wars, were a part of political life in every part of medieval Europe.[5] Feuds could take different forms in the Viking Era, even within one polity. In general, feud was a state of mutual hostility between two groups that arose when one had suffered injury from the other and sought retaliation, which could in turn lead to further reciprocal actions. Nevertheless, these hostile relations were conducted within rules and could end in peaceful settlement. When discussing the early medieval blood-feud of the Franks, J.M. Wallace-Hadrill defined feud as a three-stage process: "We may call it first the threat of hostility between kins; then the state of hostility between them; and finally the satisfaction of their differences and a settlement on terms acceptable to both."[6]

This is a definition that could be applied throughout the Viking Era. The Germanic law-codes that attempted to provide means of resolving feuds by setting prices to be paid as recompense for injury were a first step towards substituting legal procedures for use of private force, but the time when kings had sufficient authority and control over the procedures to enforce settlements lay in the future. Richard Fletcher has given an example of a bloodfeud in England that resulted from political machination and the murder of Earl Uhtred of Northumbria in 1016, although he sometimes has difficulty in relating it directly to the politics of late Anglo-Saxon England after that.[7] What he does do is demonstrate that such behavior was integral to English noble behavior in that era.

Few would define low-level feuds, defined as above, in which low numbers of people died in tit-for-tat killings, as warfare. However, the mentality that brought feuds about was common to all nobles in every part of Europe: it was not an aberrant form of behavior, and it was integral to politics. Even if family feuds rarely escalated into warfare that engulfed whole societies, the actions of powerful individuals may have been wholly or partly conditioned by the need to avenge insult or injury. Seen in this light, the actions of Sweyn Forkbeard after the St. Brice's Day Massacre (in which his sister was killed), or of Tostig Godwineson in 1066, were not made on the basis of political calculation and desire for wealth or power alone. Warfare could also engender feuds as relatives sought revenge for slain men or injury to their reputation.[8] Nor is it beyond the realms of possibility that feuds led to large-scale warfare.

Warrior-bands and the acquisition of honor

As part of his interpretation of mythology, Georges Dumézil argued that there was a tripartite structure of functions in the Indo-European social hierarchy: chieftains and priests, representing sovereign and supernatural authority; warriors, the second function of physical force; and farmers and herders, the third function of fecundity. Warrior ideology seems typical of the societies of many other language groups, but the suggestion is that this division was formally recognized as a basis for social stratification in Indo-European society, at least in the early stages of its development, so that warriors were a distinct social group. However, violence and warfare have been valued as aspects of masculinity in most preindustrial societies. The groups associated most with this behavior are usually young men, who have learned the rules and values of the warrior as boys. However, they have less vested interest in the general rules of social behavior as they do not have possessions or a family. Their image is ambivalent, as they are seen as heroic and sometimes chivalric, but also as brutal and cruel. They are often excluded from decision-making within the community because their behavior is suspect, what might nowadays be termed "anti-social," yet their activities sometimes defend and enrich the community. Hence they are often employed "outside the community," herding cattle or raiding communities foreign to the clan, tribe or other polity they belong to.[9] In this capacity, and with their own shared values, they often form warrior fraternities that cut across social and kinship bonds of the community. Characteristic of these fraternities is a religious association and some form of initiation rite for entry, almost invariably one that emphasizes bravery and masculine prowess. Often the community actually organizes the separation of youths from women and all the trappings of everyday social life, sending them to the wilderness to act in a manner contrary to the norm, perhaps like animals. In this case, return to normal society may also require a cleansing ritual.

In preserved poetry and narrative in the Indo-European languages warfare and fame won in battle are common themes. This includes not only the Germanic heroic poetry mentioned in Chapter 1 but Irish and Welsh, Serbian and Russian material, not to mention earlier Greek and Indian epics. Indo-European scholars in general accept that the second Indo-European function of force was institutionalized in the warrior-band often referred to as the *comitatus*, organized around a leader. The evidence suggests that all of the northern European Indo-European language groups, Celtic, Germanic, Slavic, and Baltic, continued to maintain the *comitatus* institution throughout the Iron Age. The replacement of Imperial Roman rule with rule by Germanic kings ensured that it survived in a modified form throughout the former Western Empire, and even after Christianization in the form of knighthood, most obviously as orders of knights.

It may well have been the young men living on the margins of society that formed most of the war-bands of pre-state Indo-European societies.[10] They were ideal material for the *comitatus*, which had its own "community spirit" and owed more to the leader than to the rest of society. Some have chosen to distinguish a *comitatus* from a military household (e.g. Ger. *Gesinde*) by its inter-tribal nature, sought out by young men seeking success in war, which meant wealth and honor.[11] By contrast, the household was restricted by kin or tribe, chosen from a warrior class that became increasingly hereditary. It is not suggested that the armies of late Anglo-Saxon England or Ottonian Germany were raised and organized in the same way as the armies of the Germanic Migration period, but it is suggested that the mentality and ethos of the early Germanic warrior-bands survived in the aristocracy that formed the core of the later armies.

The military household of the Anglo-Saxon and Frankish kingdoms of Viking Era Europe had grown well beyond the *comitatus* of the Migration Period and changed in character to the extent that it was based more on clientship and patronage relationships and included fewer adventurers from outside the king's realm, while some of its members might be scattered across the realm on the king's lands.[12] Nevertheless, the nature of the relationship within the household was essentially the same, one of mutual benefit and, for the warrior, prestige and reward gained from association with the lord. It was no accident that heroic poetry which gave a simplified picture of the king or lord as "giver of rings" and his immediate followers in their hall or in battle, as in the *Maldon* poem, still found an audience among the aristocracy of Anglo-Saxon England or Ottonian Germany. In its ideal world, the same personal loyalty was expected of the household as of the *comitatus* of old. The ideal of the *comitatus* was thus preserved in the Viking Era, although bonds between lord and follower related to the granting of land had gained increasing importance in western and southern Europe.[13] This was the bond that enabled the assembly of the bulk of Frankish and Anglo-Saxon armies in the Viking Era, often referred to as some variant of *heri* (the OHG word, cf. ON *herr*, OE *here*). The armies of the Vikings, however, were arguably much closer to the earlier Migration Period model, particularly in the early Viking era.

The relationship within the *comitatus* was reciprocal: the followers offered loyalty and protection to the leader, whilst assisting him to increase his wealth and status by pillage, tribute or tax gathering, trade, or any other means, and he in turn offered them a route to advancement. Among his obligations was the redistribution of wealth to them. Failure to fulfil the obligations of the warrior fraternity by one or other party constituted a reason for dissolution of the bond. Honor and wealth were inseparable in the Viking world. For a leader to gain one he had to have the other, but there was no honor in piling up wealth for himself—he had to be generous with it.

This is a recurring theme in the sagas and Saxo's *History of the Danes*. Those who are not generous and fail to redistribute their wealth invariably come to a sticky end, because their followers abandon them. In *Gesta Danorum* Hialte tells of King Rorik, "rich in capital but not in worth," who "has grudged to give rings": when attacked, he has no followers to help him and his attempt to bribe his enemies comes to nothing, as they kill him and steal his treasure.[14]

Material wealth was not the only reward for members of the *comitatus*, as they also increased their standing both from proximity to the leader, who might have some sacral status himself, and from the acquisition of glory. This combination of glory and standing, partly deriving from wealth and power, was also embodied in their concept of "honor." The ancient Germanic word for this still exists as modern German *Ehre* (cf. Old English *ár*, Old Norse *æra*, Old High German *êre*), but the modern German word has more or less the same meaning as modern English "honor" and corresponds to the pagan Germanic conception only in certain respects. The latter was centerd on external approval (by others among the warrior class) of meritorious acts, which involved courageous deeds on behalf of one's king or lord, rather than anything involving internal soul searching that derived from an acceptance of man's sinfulness, the basis of Christian morality. No paradise awaited the dead Viking warrior, but, as we shall see below, the idea of Valhǫll embodied the concept of honor: selection by Odin as one of his *einherjar*, chosen warriors, reflected the status achieved during life. Moreover, a preoccupation of the heroes of the Icelandic sagas, even in a (partially) Christianized society, was their reputation after death.

The Germanic idea of honor survived Christianization and although some members of the nobility chose to reject worldly goods by joining a monastic community or taking the individual path of the hermit, the majority did not. Nevertheless, they absorbed the Christian idea of the sinful nature of man and the guilt that went with it. For this reason, it was necessary to do penance for the shedding of blood after battle and make peace with God before it. However, there were ways in which the life of the warrior could conform to Christian ideals, through suffering as a form of penance. Eventually, mainly after our period, a mass of literature helped to create and reinforce the idea of warriorhood as asceticism and an embodiment of Christian values, chivalry. However, this concept truly began to penetrate Scandinavia only after the Viking Era, Denmark in the twelfth century and Norway and Sweden in the thirteenth.

War and religiosity

We are of course aware that many people are motivated to fight and often to die by their religious faith, and it is frequently repeated that wars are fought with more ferocity and hatred when the opposing sides have conflicting religious beliefs. However, there has been a tendency among historians of the modern period and military historians in general, insofar as they discuss them at all, to regard such beliefs as propaganda tools of political and military masters. This may be the case in modern conflicts, particularly in the West, where people live in a materialist society from which religiosity is largely absent, but this approach is much less appropriate to the Middle Ages. It is generally accepted that the idea of a division between religion and everyday life would have been beyond the comprehension of people in the pre-Christian era. For the pagan Vikings, the boundaries between this world and the otherworld(s) were not so pronounced and what we might define as the religious or spiritual was an integral part of daily life.

It follows that "religion" must have had an impact on the conduct of warfare by non-Christian and non-Moslem peoples. Moreover, those converted to the "religions of the book" also lived in a world in which God constantly intervened, and in which His purpose lay behind all events. There is no space to discuss fully the differences in conception that resulted from the conversion of Scandinavians to Christianity, a change that occurred slowly over several centuries, and not without a degree of syncretism. However, apart from the introduction of written rules and institutional management of spiritual affairs, it may be said that (in principle at least) a Christian hoping for the favor of God could ask, whereas his pagan predecessor could influence deities and spirits by magical means, and even oblige them to act in his or her favor. The use of ritual and magic before and during battle has already been discussed, but in this chapter the belief systems of the Viking Era as a motivator for war and the conduct of war concern us.

Much of the evidence we have for the beliefs of the majority of the non-Christian peoples of Europe in the Viking Era comes from material remains, especially those found with burials and cremations. Obviously burial and cremation represent methods utilized by the living to dispose of the dead, but the method of disposal and the objects that accompany the deceased inevitably reflect the values and ideals held by a society. The "warrior burial" tradition of the Viking Era has left us a lot of material, which in itself suggests a warrior ideology, but interpretation must be highly speculative without the support of written evidence. Quantity of material alone does not indicate the status of the deceased, nor can we assume that different metals or gemstones were valued in the same way that we value them. Accompanying weapons and equipment may have been intended for the use of the deceased in an afterlife, but they might also have been offerings to deities. Metals have an intrinsic value, but also a value in terms of the labor and technological skill required to produce the items, a value linked to method and difficulty of acquisition, and a value attached to the social status or office they or the items manufactured from them signified for their owner(s).

Our knowledge of ancient beliefs and psychology, derived from written sources, together with contemporary written evidence itself, has to be used to interpret material remains. Much of our knowledge comes from recorded mythology. Nowadays "myth" has a negative connotation as something without any truth in it, perhaps a product of some collective neurosis. However, myths contain elements of man's history in the context of religiosity, as tradition incorporating cult, ritual, and liturgy. Mythology may become transformed into sagas of the heroic past, but it still survives because it is relevant to those who memorize or record it, recite it, and listen to it. Even if myths outlive their usefulness as sacral support for the social structure, they may still maintain their appeal as some of the ideals embedded in them may still be relevant, while other mythological tradition could be reinterpreted to reinforce their reality. This is the case with the Norse material recorded in sagas and medieval "histories." Christian recorders of ancient myth were euhemerists, interpreting mythology as tradition or history distorted by the machinations of the devil, who had misled men into believing that other men were gods. We have to attempt to strip away their veneer to reveal a mythology that had the belief-world of the pre-Christian era embedded in it.

In the case of the Vikings, we have a distorted memory of their pagan beliefs in the writings of medieval Icelanders and Saxo Grammaticus. The warrior-band/*comitatus* structure of the Viking bands that penetrated the region that later became Russia probably aided them in achieving dominance over local tribes, the majority of whom were farmers and hunters. Like the warrior-bands of the earlier Germanic migration, they will have absorbed young men of the local tribes.[15] In all likelihood it was in this way that the Vikings provided the catalyst for the formation of the original elite of Kievan Rus. It is therefore extremely difficult to separate "Viking" and "Slavic" elements in Russian folklore. Moreover, although Slavic-speaking people undoubtedly migrated to the Balkans, the Middle Danube region and the lands east of the Elbe, the Slavic linguistic dominance of European Russia was only partially achieved by colonization, as there are clear indications that Baltic- and Finnic-speaking tribes were "slavicized," a process that continues to this day in the case of the latter. Their beliefs too must have been absorbed in the melting pot of Kievan Rus. We also know that there was Scandinavian settlement on the coasts of what is now Poland, Lithuania, and Latvia in the Vendel Period and later, so some Scandinavian input into West Slavic and Baltic culture is to be expected. Saxo even claimed that the Scandinavians taught the Kuronians to become sea raiders.

Shamanism and warfare

Shamanism is generally regarded as one of the earliest human belief-systems, because it has survived into modern times in hunter-gatherer societies thought to resemble the pre-farming societies of the Stone Age. Anthropologists have adopted more or less narrow definitions of shamanism: here the term is used to include all magical practices involving shape-shifting and communication with spirits or inhabitants of another world in order to gain benefit or foresee future events. In the view of Neil Price it encompasses the Viking practice of *seiðr*, which, as he says, has many features in common with the magic practiced by the Sami and other circumpolar peoples. He refers to a world-view which accepts communication between the human and animal worlds, shape-shifting, and possibly transformation into animal form.[16]

A modern tendency has been to see the actions of shamans as primarily "peaceful," part of a general view that hunter-gatherer communities were not warlike, a view proved false by the increasing evidence of pre-Neolithic mass killings. Shamans were no more or less peaceful than the people they lived amongst. They saw themselves as fighting a battle, and the clothes and protective amulets they wore as armor.[17] In all societies that have had recourse to shamanic magic and have been studied by anthropologists, the magic has been used for good or ill, in the sense that "good" is equated with the benefit of the community the shaman serves, "ill" the harm done to those perceived as disrupting or threatening that community. As in the case of the pagan Scandinavians, there is no evidence of any ethical dimension to their beliefs, in the sense of a moral code such as that of Christianity or Islam, sanctioned by a power external to human society. If shamanic magic was used to ward off disease, hunger and bad weather, often interpreted to be the work of evil spirits—why not also to ward off human enemies, bearing in mind that the spirit world and the tangible world were so closely linked? Prediction of success or failure in war, just as in the hunt, was one of the tasks of American Northwest Coast shamans.[18] Moreover, in various parts of the world shamans did not simply ward off threats, they created or summoned them: in Siberia and North America charms and ritual implements were used to attack enemies, while shamans of the Northwest Coast fought spiritual duels, that could result not only in their death but the deaths of others in their communities. They also accompanied war parties to fight their battles alongside the warriors who fought physically. North America in the early modern period is not Viking-Age Scandinavia, but these examples illustrate what might have been. It is safe to say that the Magyars had shamans when they arrived in the Carpathian Basin, and the Baltic Finns may have had them in the same period, while the Viking practitioners of *seiðr* inherited many of the shaman's methods.

It was possible to perceive of a hero as both shaman/magician and warrior, much as the peoples of the American Northwest Coast did. Some of the heroes of Baltic–Finnic heroic poetry, which remained as oral tradition until the eighteenth and nineteenth centuries, retain characteristics of both. When these characters acquired this form cannot be specified: the era of known and intense Scandinavian seafaring activity, the Vendel and Viking periods, appears most suitable as the era of epic poetry about warriors and travelers to distant lands, but its heroes might have belonged to any era from the Bronze Age to the period immediately before Christianization.[19] As regards tentative comparisons with Northwest Coast practices, one point of comparison is that, with the exception of Estonia, there is no evidence that the Baltic Finns had any political organization above village level.[20] If shamanism is characteristic of societies without complex political structures or social hierarchies, it may well have survived among them. Despite the probable small scale of the warfare north of the Gulf of Finland, we do know from the evidence of grave finds that there was a warrior culture among the Baltic–Finnic elite in the Vendel and Viking periods, while certain deities bear a resemblance to those of Viking Age Scandinavia: for instance, Ukko of the Finns and Taara (Tharapita) of the Estonian tribes have a Thor-like association with thunder.[21] The weapon finds of Estonia and central and western Finland were to all intents and purposes Germanic.

The Christian War

Despite the differences between pagan and Christian world-views touched on above, there was a similarity between the world of the monk and that of the shaman. Those who were dedicated to the service of God were also engaged in a war, in this case against the devil, and the imagery used in their texts and liturgy reflected this.[22] By Charlemagne's time the clergy saw themselves as soldiers of Christ (*milites Christi*), accepted concepts of just war and likened themselves to the Israelite warriors of the Old Testament. Just as the "historical" wars of the ancient Israelites were turned into allegories of Christ's spiritual conflicts, so those struggles were portrayed as combats, while Christ was also portrayed as a commander of celestial armies. The Church played its part in war by fighting the spiritual battle: prayers were believed to be powerful weapons and were therefore solicited by all army commanders.

But what of those who fought earthly battles, the majority of the male aristocracy in Viking Age Christian Europe? The Church's view of the continuing and ever-present war between forces of good and evil naturally penetrated their consciousness as well. Many of them were literate, but they are even less likely to have read biblical exegesis and theological tracts than they are to have read Vegetius. Their impression of the Bible and the demands of their religion was probably largely formed by sermons and the images of the scriptures painted on the interior walls of churches. Much of what they found in the Old Testament must have seemed familiar. The actions of the early Israelites provided an example of warlike behavior that must have found a willing audience among the warriors of northern and eastern Europe.

In the process of converting the pagan rulers of the polities that emerged from the former Western Roman Empire, Christianity became further adapted to the values of the warrior elite. Whether this made the Church more warlike is a moot point, as it already had a "warrior ethos," but Christianity appeared "warlike" in a way that the Germanic aristocracy could understand.[23] Throughout the Middle Ages the attitude of the Church to war was ambiguous. The justification for bloodshed was constantly under discussion, but the general view, following St. Augustine, was that warfare could be just in certain circumstances. However, those who truly wished to embrace Christ could not engage in warfare, although this attitude was modified in the Crusading Era. Since the fifth century, Church councils had repeatedly declared priests, monks, and canons (the lower clergy) exempt from military service. They were expected to refrain from warfare, even from hunting, and from the carrying of weapons. These bans were repeatedly reiterated throughout the period 750–1100, because many of the lower clergy were engaging in warfare: for instance, Frankish clergy regularly went on campaign and several took part in the Battle of Hastings.[24] Many warriors eventually retired to the cloister, although some took their armor and weapons with them.[25] As we have seen, the opposition of the Church to the shedding of blood by the clergy did not mean opposition to participation in war. Nevertheless, whatever cause was fought for, until the end of our period the general view remained that the warrior's calling "cannot be carried out without some doing of evil," as an anonymous penitentialist wrote.[26] This was reflected in the penances meted out to any who killed fellow-Christians in combat, even if, as in the case of William's expedition to England in 1066, such warfare had papal sanction.[27] Even the killing of pagans required a penance if it was done for the base motive of plunder.

During the eleventh century the idea of a Christian warrior whose actions were entirely just began to gain ground. In what appears to us a paradox, this was encouraged by the "Peace of God" movement: in opposing the destruction of church property and violence against women and children and merchants, a new warrior ideal was created—by the end of the eleventh century warriors had the opportunity to imitate Christ, just as the monks did, but by following their own profession. Even before this, however, it is likely that many knights believed themselves equal in status to monks as servants of God. Although our written evidence comes almost exclusively from the quills of clerics, one reason to suspect this is the presence of a considerable number of military saints and martyrs such as Maurice, supposedly a Roman soldier of the late third century. The lives of saints were examples to be followed, and there was no questioning their place among the highest servants of Christ. Moreover, most of those who were canonized in the Viking Era were men of noble stock from the Germanic warrior class, whereas many of the earlier saints had been brought up in a less warlike milieu.

Gods of war
Before embarking on a discussion of "war-deities" it should be pointed out that there were probably no pagan deities associated exclusively with warfare.

Neatly organized pantheons of related gods and goddesses for particular "peoples" or language groups, each deity with its own spheres of interest or jurisdiction, are a product of societies with a written culture, which enabled certain interpretations to become set in stone (or ink), and often a product of modern interpretations, which "bureaucratize" ancient otherworlds. In northern and central Europe during the Christian period compilers and scribes tried to make sense of confusing and often fragmentary information and naturally interpreted it in the light of what they were familiar with, as well as putting a Christian slant on it. The vast majority of them were certainly influenced by their knowledge of the Greco-Roman gods and the way in which they were organized. Before Christianization, even within regions occupied by recorded tribes or peoples, there must have been a huge variety of deities and spirits, just as there were a variety of customs for disposal of the dead. The spheres of interest of the higher deities will also have varied with time and place. Even with the knowledge that has been passed down to us by Christian or Moslem writers, it is clear that deities had overlapping interests, while the known beliefs about otherworlds and otherworldly beings often appear contradictory. They are contradictory to us, because we attempt to map them and fit them into a single universe, organized according to our rationality and our conception of space and geography.[28]

What we know of Slavic and Baltic religiosity does indeed suggest a bewildering collection of otherworldly beings. Some of these were mentioned in written sources of the early Middle Ages and occur in later folklore, and several had warlike attributes and associations with warriors. Svantevit is recorded by Helmold and Saxo as the god whose temple stood in Arkona on Rügen. The temple was the repository of booty gathered in war, stabled a white horse used for divination and was defended by a picked group of three hundred warriors. Clearly they owed some allegiance to the temple, but it is not clear who their military leader was or what status he had. If he was a chieftain of status, to all intents and purposes the band was a *comitatus*. The deity named Svantevit or the name as a component of place-names also occurs in Russia, Ukraine, Bulgaria, Serbia, Croatia, and Bosnia.

Another deity of Arkona was Rugiewit, also one of the three deities recorded by Saxo as worshipped in nearby Charenza (Venzer Burgwall).[29] Without much foundation, it has been suggested that Rugiewit was a Rani form of the god Perun, of which there are numerous but scattered records from Procopius to the *Primary Chronicle*.[30] According to the latter, he was made the chief deity of Kiev by Vladimir before his conversion to Christianity.[31] Among his many aspects was that of thunder god, a common attribute of numerous Indo-European gods also associated with war, who also used thunderbolts as weapons. That Perun had an ancient origin is also suggested by the remarkably similar characteristics (including the name) of the Baltic god Perkūnas. The reconstructed root is *perkwu*, which may have meant oak (another association) originally, but became linked to thunder-bolts and striking, as in Proto-Slavic *per*, "strike" or "kill." Place-names with components that probably derive from the name occur throughout the Slavic-speaking Balkans.[32] In some Slavic mythological tales Perun's wife is Zorya, although she is more often associated with the sun-god Dažbog, who appears in the *Primary Chronicle* and other medieval sources. Zorya appears as an armed warrior-maiden and protector of those she favored in battle. Unfortunately the medieval Slavs and Balts left us no corpus of skaldic verse, no sagas and no Poetic Edda. We can only surmise that their elite pagan warrior fraternities had links to specific deities associated with war because what little we know of their belief-world has close similarities to that of the Scandinavians.

In Norse mythology as it has come down to us through written sources of the High Middle Ages, Odin and Thor are the deities most frequently associated with war. In general Thor defends the ordered world (that is, the cosmos as habitable for humans and gods) against chaotic cosmic forces, whereas Odin engages in warfare amongst men, assisting those he has chosen to defeat others. Moreover, Odin has a strong motivation for his interference in earthly warfare. Both the poems *Hákonarmál*, and especially *Eiríksmál*, written in praise of dead kings, emphasize the gathering of a military retinue by Odin for the final battle at Ragnarǫk. Odin is assembling an army of the dead (*einherjar*) in Valhǫll, the hall of the *valr*, "those who die on the battlefield."[33]

Since *valr* usually appears as a word related to the slain on the field of battle, and never in skaldic verse to refer to Odin's companions in his hall, it may be of relatively late origin. The relationship of the *valr* with the *einherjar*, or how they became *einherjar*, is uncertain, but it is possible that they were thought of as valr until accepted among Odin's companions. The usual skaldic term for Odin's hall is Óðinns sal, but here the later *valhǫll*, undoubtedly the same place, is retained as the most familiar. Those who transport the fallen warriors to the hall, the valkyries, are often described as Odin's foster-daughters, just as the *einherjar* are foster-sons.[34] Among the names given to Freyja is Valfreyja, "Mistress of the Slain," the first of the valkyries, who serves ale at the feasts of the Aesir, just as the valkyries serve the *einherjar*.[35] It would be unsound simply to argue that Valhǫll was "devised" to provide an afterworld paradise as an incentive for bravery. In fact, it seems to be a development of an ancient myth involving the gathering of an otherworldly army to fight against evil (or chaotic) powers at the end of time, one which occurs in ancient Iranian and Indian sources of *c.* 1000 BC. Nor is there any indication that pagans had any conception of an afterlife as a paradise in the Christian or Moslem sense.

As an assistant in war, Odin is notoriously unreliable: he betrays those he has previously supported, such as Sigmundr in *Vǫlsunga saga*.[36] In *Eiriksmál* Odin himself explains this as necessary to prepare for Ragnarǫk, "the uncertainty of knowing when the grey wolf will attack the homes of the gods," when great kings will be needed to fight on their side. In *Hákonarsmál* the dead Håkon complains to the valkyries that he got no help from the gods in the battle in which he was slain, and then, when he arrives at the hall of the *valr*, that Odin seems most untrustworthy. This may be an addition by Christian writers who wished to denigrate pagan beliefs, but this need not be the case, as some mythological explanation was required for the fact that those who claimed a special relationship with Odin were all too often defeated and killed in the end.[37] In any case, although they may be forces for order as opposed to chaos, or fertility as opposed to barrenness, deities of pagan beliefs appear to have been more ambiguous in character than the God of the Judeo–Christian–Moslem tradition. Rather like nature itself, which in many ways they represented, they could turn against humans.

It is often repeated nowadays that Vikings believed only those who died in battle went to Valhǫll, a clear incentive for Vikings to fight ferociously and seek death in combat. However, there is no indication in any of our sources that Vikings fought more or less ferociously than their opponents, and certainly not that they hurled themselves at the enemy in an uncontrollable fury at every opportunity. Furthermore, since there was a good chance of famous warriors dying of a cause other than battle, all of these would be excluded from the army of the dead. The belief largely derives from a statement by Snorri Sturluson in *Gylfaginni*: "You say that all those men that have fallen in battle since the beginning of the world have now come to Odin in Valhǫll."[38] In Chapter 34 of *Gylfaginni* it is said that Hel 'has to administer board and lodging to those sent to her, and that is those who die of sickness or old age."[39] The first problem is that the source was written by a Christian three centuries after the conversion of Harald Bluetooth. In addition, the first quotation is clearly derived from some older sources, and in any case does not say that *only* those who have fallen in battle go to Valhǫll, while Snorri's contrast between Hel and Valhǫll may be influenced by the Christian Hell–Heaven model, although he does not imply that either Valhǫll or Hel were connected with reward or punishment. *Eiriksmál* and *Hákonarmál* tell of Odin welcoming dead kings into his hall, but not whether it was only the valr who resided there. Gisli *saga* appears to suggest that Hel was a general abode of the dead, when it says that there is a custom to tie Helshoes on those who walk to Valho ll.[40]

An unrelated source, *Voluspá*, does mention an unpleasant place of punishment for murderers, swearers of false oaths and seducers of other men's wives: "Corpsestrand."[41] Elsewhere there are indications that social class determined where someone ended up after death: for instance, *Hár-barðslióð* says Odin owned the jarls who fell in battle but Thor the slaves, a statement of exaggerated contrast that belongs to this type of literature.[42] In the Mälar region of Sweden many Thor's hammers have been found with urns containing ashes of the dead, many of them women. In *Grímnismál* Freyja is said to welcome half the fallen men in her hall at Fó lkvangr while Odin takes the other half.[43] In other Norse sources we hear of the dead living in the mounds in which they were buried, or going to the abode of the goddess Ran if they drowned. Furthermore, we know that one way in which pagan Viking, or for that matter, Slav or Magyar, religiosity was not the same as Christian belief was that there was no written word and no claim to universality or consistency. The localized nature of beliefs and cults is reflected in the variety of ideas about the afterlife and disposal of the dead, which included burial in mounds, cremation, ship-burial, possibly being cast out on the water in a burning ship, all of which were used for people of status. The famous description by the Arab traveler Ibn Falan of the funeral of a Rus chieftain on the Volga involved the sacrifice of a young slave woman, who was presumably supposed to accompany the dead chieftain in the afterlife. The women who were buried in ships at Oseberg (Norway) and Tuna (Sweden) clearly expected an afterlife, but we know nothing of its anticipated character.

It is difficult to connect any of the Scandinavian funeral rites known from archaeology with the Valhǫll myth. On the other hand, the Gotlandic picture stones may represent the transport of a fallen hero on horseback and his welcome by a valkyrie (the female figure with a drinking horn), as *Grímnismál* tells us that they served beer to the dead warriors. However, neither *Eiriksmál* nor *Hákonarmál* mention the method of transport to Valhǫll. There are other possible interpretations of the pictures; for instance, the rider may be Odin himself, given his eight-legged horse, and if he is not, the "woman" may be a death goddess, such as the one who appears to Balderus in Saxo's *Gesta Danorum*.[44] To compound the problem that our sources for pagan beliefs were passed down for over two centuries and filtered through Christian beliefs, it is improbable that there ever was a coherent view of the cosmos, the gods or the afterlife in pagan times.

Despite the difficulties, it does seem that there was a widespread acceptance of the existence of the *einherjar*, Odin's army of the dead. If it was not only those who died in battle who went to Valhǫll, who were they? It has been maintained that they were deified dead heroes or warriors. In his life of the missionary Ansgar, Rimbert mentioned Erik, a former king of the Svear, being worshipped as a god. As a Christian and non-Scandinavian source, this may be a misinterpretation, and even if some aristocracy of the highest status were thought of as such, it is improbable that all those who went to Valhǫll were. Alongside *Hárbarðslióð* mentioned above, other sources tell us that noble persons went to Valhǫll, for instance, *Eiriksmál* and *Hákonarmál* and Saxo's *Gesta Danorum*.[45] However, Jens Peter Schjødt has suggested that it was not only warriors who died in battle that joined them, but warriors who were ritually marked with a spear.[46] He cites a number of cases in which heroes are marked as about to die or are sacrificed to Odin with a spear, from *Ynglingasaga, Egils saga einhanda ok Ásmundar, Volsunga* saga and *Hávamál*. In *Ynglingasaga* 9 Odin himself is marked with a spear when he is about to die, "and he declared as his own all men who fell in battle." This suggests that the spear was used in ritual initiation (meaning death and rebirth). Elsewhere the spear also appears as a weapon of Odin, and throwing a spear at the enemy was also a way of dedicating the enemy to him.

It is probable that the myth of Odin welcoming his heroes to his hall formed some part of a warrior ideology in the pagan Viking period. Those who were expected to have this fate were elevated to an elite position in the minds of their followers in earthly life. Moreover, their power to choose their retinues, and therefore enable them to be chosen for Valhǫll as well, would have given them power over others. The members of those they selected for their retinue, or comitatus, would thus also acquire great honor. It is interesting that *Eiríksmál* and *Hákonarmál* were written for kings who were nominally Christian—Erik Bloodaxe and Håkon the Good.[47] Both seem to have tolerated the continuation of paganism in Norway and the praise poems are likely to reflect the beliefs of the poets as well as rulers. According to *Ágrip*, Håkon was buried in a mound, albeit in a stone coffin with only a sword and his clothes.[48] In Scandinavia the conversion to Christianity was a "top-down" process, in which rulers were converted first and then endeavored to convert their realms, so we may expect that the conversion of their peoples was a long process.

Reference has already been made to the spiritual war fought by churchmen against the devil, which was only a part of a much greater war fought by celestial armies. In a sense, Christ was seen as the supreme commander, with a host of subordinate leaders such as the Archangel Michael. The laity are unlikely to have shared allegorical interpretations of this struggle; if an aristocracy that inherited a warrior tradition from pre-Christian times needed a god of battles, they found him in the Old Testament. In Exodus, the Book of Joshua, Deuteronomy, Kings, Judges, and many other books the God of the Israelites had functioned as a tribal war god, protecting his people and smiting his enemies. For the laity who understood the Old Testament as an account of actual events, its laws, and the tales of actions based on them would have sanctioned practices inherited from the pagan past.

New ideals were incorporated into warriorhood as Christianity became entrenched, but the absorption of many old pagan concepts into Christianity during the mission period meant that God was seen in a rather different light by the kings and nobility of Germanic Europe than he was by the Church Fathers (the early Christian writers and teachers of the second to eighth centuries AD).[49] In 1098 Raymond of Aguilers, who was present at the prolonged and difficult siege of Antioch, declared explicitly (with the support of direct quotations from the Psalms) that the God of the Israelites had given victory to the crusaders.[50] Victory was a sign of God's favor, and He rewarded the victors just as He had rewarded the Hebrews of old. That in itself was not a new idea, but by 1098 the ideal of the holy warrior who could spill blood in defense of Christ, and in so doing achieve a status similar to that of a monk, had taken root.

Berserkers and their ilk

The popular conception of the Vikings, albeit somewhat eroded by a sustained effort to emphasize their contribution to art, navigation, and trade, probably owes more to the image of the berserker than to anything else. It is not surprising that warriors in an uncontrollable killing frenzy, biting shields, howling like animals and clad in their skins capture the imagination. Such warriors have come to symbolize the ferocity and pagan customs of the Vikings. The earliest description of them is probably Þórbjǫrn hornklofi's *Haraldskvæði* (*Hrafnsmál*), usually dated to *c.* 900. Its description of the Battle of Hafrsfjord (traditionally dated to 872) includes the following lines:

> They [the ships] were loaded with farmer chiefs and broad shields, with spears of Vestland and Frankish swords; berserkers yelled, the battle was on, *ulfheðnar* howled and shook their spears . . .
>   Of berserker fury I would ask, the drinkers of corpse-sea [blood], what are they like, those men who go happy into battle? . . .
>   *Ulfheðnar* they are called, they carry bloody shields in battle; they color their spears red when they join the fighting; there they are arranged for their task: there I know that the honorable prince places his faith in brave men who hack at shields.[51]

The etymology of the term *berserk* is uncertain. One possible meaning is "baresark" ("bare of shirt"), a possible reference to a habit of fighting unarmored or even without a shirt.[52] *Ynglingasaga* says that "they [Odin's warriors] went without coats of mail, and behaved madly like dogs and wolves. They bit their shields and were as strong as bears or boars and neither fire nor iron could hurt them. This is called going berserk."[53] The other proposed meaning is "bear-sark," referring to the habit of wearing a bear's skin, or perhaps that of another animal. This would correspond to the wearing of wolfskins by the *úlfheðnar*, clearly described in *Vatnsdæla Saga*: "With him [King Harald] were Rognvald of Møre and many other great chieftains and the berserker called *úlfheðnar*. They had wolfskins over their mail shirts and were at the prow of the king's ship, and the king himself defended the stern with the greatest courage and valor."[54]

Our problem is that all sources except *Haraldskvæði*, incorporated in the Saga of King Harald Fairhair, are from the twelfth to fourteenth centuries.[55] Did berserkers and wolf-coats really exist on the battlefields of the eighth, ninth and tenth centuries?

The berserkers of the Icelandic *Íslendingasögur* (Icelandic family sagas) are the sum of the negative aspects of male warrior fraternities described above: they exist outside the bounds of society, and they are cruel, violent, and threatening to women, but they have none of the "positive" traits such as heroism or procurers of wealth. In both *Íslendingasögur* and *Fornaldarsagor* (tales of past times) they function as foes for the heroes to cut down in droves, often coming from the periphery of the Norse world (from the West Norse point of view), for instance Sweden, and frequently appear as nothing more than stupid brutes. As Anatoly Liberman put it: "The berserks of the family sagas resembled the berserks of old only in name." There are nevertheless anomalies in their portrayal in some of these sagas. Liberman also declares that berserkers resembled or were identical with *úlfheðnar*, both of which roared and howled when they fought, and that they were elite troops, but that nothing supported Snorri's statement that berserkers were looked upon as Odin's associates.[56] The early source, *Haraldskvæði*, appears to differentiate berserkers from wolfskins, but this is not absolutely clear, while the writer/compiler of *Vatnsdæla saga* appears to think they were the same. As for the rejection of any relationship with Odin, the evidence for their presence in battle, let alone for their behavior if they did appear on the battlefield, is very limited, and there is as much "circumstantial evidence" to support a link with Odin.

The point has been made that if there really were groups of ferocious maniacs dressed in animal skins on the battlefield, this would surely have been mentioned by contemporary Christian sources, in which there is no sign of them.[57] These sources contain very few details of behavior on the battlefield, but in any case, absence of howlers and shield-biters does not rule out the existence of warrior fraternities called *berserkir* or *úlfheðnar* ("wolfcoats"), rather it suggests that if men known as such existed in the pagan Viking period, they were not quite as portrayed in later saga sources. In the *Battle of Maldon* Vikings are referred to as wolves, but this is more likely to be a general reference to their uncivilized and predatory character than to howling and the wearing of wolfskins. However, there is a description of wolf-like behavior in a Christian source, namely Leo the Deacon's account of the behavior of Sviatoslav's Rus army. In Book VIII he writes of the advancing Rus warriors before Preslav "roaring like beasts and uttering strange and weird howls," and later, in the first battle near Dorostolon, "charging with their habitual ferocity and passion ... bellowing as if possessed." In the third battle Sviatoslav (Sphendosthlavos) is described as "charging the Romans in a frenzied rage."[58] Whether Sviatoslav's army can be strictly described as a Viking army is debatable. There is no reason to doubt that he and many of his elite warriors were of Viking origin, while some may have been recent arrivals from Scandinavia, but the army must have included Slavs and possibly Finnic language troops as well. Nevertheless, this is an account of pagan warrior behavior that might have been described as "berserk" by Snorri and Saxo, by an eyewitness who was present at the battle in his capacity as secretary of the Byzantine emperor John Tzimiskes. The eleventh-century chronicler John Skylitzes also describes the piercing howls of the Rus mourning their dead, while Leo mentions the sacrifice of prisoners of both sexes that accompanied the night-time cremation of their dead on funeral pyres.[59]

Certain scholars have argued that there was a parallelism between the mythological world of the dead and the earthly world in Old Norse and Germanic society, the so-called *Männerbünde* existing in both. According to this theory, the berserker and *úlfheðnar* have a special relationship with Odin on earth, just as the army of the dead (*einherjar*) does in Valhǫll. Otto Höfler even maintained that the berserker/*úlfheðnar* had some kind of metaphorical relationship to the dead, and died and were reborn as *einherjar*. It is well known that humans often see the social structure of otherworldly beings in terms of their own, and that their own social structure is frequently maintained to be divinely sanctioned. In this sense Odin's *einherjar* could be the equivalent of the Viking chieftain's *comitatus*.

If we exclude their role as "sword-fodder" in the *Íslendingasögur*, there are certain features of the berserkers' role that consistently crop up in a number of sagas and may well derive from their actual function. One is that they appear as elite bodyguards or household troops of kings. An example is given above, referring to the Battle of Hafrsfjord. It was probably sources such as *Haraldskvæði* that Snorri used as a basis for his statement in *Heimskringla* that King Harald Fairhair's ship was manned by berserkers. Similarly, in *Hrólfs saga kraka*, although an even later source, the berserkers are the retinue of King Hrólfr. In *Asmundar saga kapabana (The Saga of Asmund the Champion-Killer*) berserkers appear as the elite followers of King Lazinus and Hildibrand Húnakappa (Hildibrand, Champion of the Huns). This is one role of berserkers in the *fornaldursagor*, but in others they simply appear as gangs of "wild men," or, more to the point, men who have begun to behave like predatory animals. Both images may represent echoes of the pagan period. The description of men who operated outside society as "wolves" occurs throughout history. This "anti-social" role of berserkers seems to accord all too well with the behavior of young male warrior fraternities studied by anthropologists. The reader may well wonder how different this berserk behavior was from that of medieval troops in general: the answer is probably that for them and their ilk it was a way of life, whereas others behaved in this way more rarely.

The berserkers of the kings' retinues appear in a rather less negative light than the wild men. In *Hrólfs saga kraka* there is even a hint that they were not so different from the *kappar*, the "champions" who are heroes of the saga, as they sit together at the feast table. Moreover, the leader of the *kappar*, Bǫðvarr Bjarki, apparently has the ability to transform himself into a bear, or at least the ability to create a projection of one, and was born of a father named Bjǫrn who had been turned into a bear by magic. Although such tales could be derived from common folktale motifs, it is quite possible that these are distorted memories of an association between bears and elite warriors called berserkers, who underwent some sort of ritual transformation into a bear. Similar warrior initiations are known to have occurred in other societies. In addition, there are a number of examples from the sagas in which a champion apparently has to prove that he can defeat a bear, or at least is prepared to fight one. In *Hrólfs saga kraka* the berserkers challenge all present in the hall as they enter it, asking if they think they are as strong as the berserkers themselves, perhaps a memory of such an initiation.[60]

The best known episode suggestive of an initiation is in *Volsunga saga*, in this case involving wolves. King Sigmundr and his son Sinfjǫtli put on wolf-coats which they cannot remove. They are transformed into wolves in the forest and proceed to fight several men at once and kill them. Sinfjǫtli is then bitten in the throat by Sigmundr after making some inadvisable remarks, before recovering with the aid of a leaf brought by a raven, after which they discard the wolfskins. As argued by the champions of the *Mannerbünde*, Lily Weiser and Otto Höfler, these incidents, together with several others in the saga, appear to be misunderstood initiation rituals involving death and rebirth, through which Sinfjǫtli becomes a warrior, and learns some "rules" in the process. The forest need not have been part of the earthly world in the ritual context, but an otherworld to which the hero travels.

Assuming that there were warrior-bands associated with bears or wolves in Scandinavia (which cannot be certain), were some associated with one and some the other, or were there bands associated with both? It is possible that our sources have confused different traditions and that there was only one animal associated with warriors, or more than two, since "shape-changing," the taking of animal form, was also connected with shamanic practices and belief in lycanthropy was otherwise widespread. In early medieval Rus there was even an epic tale of a werewolf prince, clearly based on the eleventh-century outcast Ruirikid prince of Polotsk, Vseslav.[61] Nor do we know, if warrior-bands connected with animals did exist, how long ago they existed. This brings us to the non-written evidence for animal warrior cults. The clearest image is on one of a set of bronze matrixes for making helmet plates, found at Torslunda on the Swedish island of Öland and dated to the seventh century, the Vendel Period. There is a one-eyed dancing warrior figure on the left, possibly Odin himself, and what seems to be a warrior armed with a spear and wearing a wolfskin with mask and tail on the right, in the process of drawing his sword. As noted above, the spear was associated with Odin and it is also the most common weapon of *úlfheðnar* in literary sources. Similar spear-armed figures and in one case a probable wolf-warrior are found on two earlier Migration Period mounts from Germany. Drawings also survive of anthropomorphic figures on fifth-century gilded silver drinking horns from Gallehus, Jutland (the horns themselves are now lost). Other animals are also represented in the Torslunda images, such as a chained monster led by a warrior and bears fighting with a warrior. Helmets have boar crests and the two horns with bird heads on the helmet of the "Odin figure" may represent ravens. This particular image was clearly familiar through the Iron-Age Germanic-speaking areas of Europe, as very similar ones appear on an amulet from Ekhammar and a pendant from Birka, both in Uppland, Sweden, and on the Finglesham buckle and a plate of the Sutton Hoo helmet from England. The Oseberg tapestry, pieced together from fragments found with the ninth-century boat burial of an aristocratic woman, also shows a man in an animal costume facing another

with a horned helmet and carrying crossed staves or spears. Women carrying shields and wearing animal (boar?) masks and skins form some sort of
ritual procession, perhaps representing the valkyries or their priestesses.[62]

Although there seems to be a remarkable continuity in the symbolism
of the artefacts mentioned above, whatever ritual practices they represent
may not have remained consistent in meaning over the centuries. There
are, nevertheless, two pieces of evidence for later warrior rituals of similar
type, the one a ceiling fresco in the Church of Hagia Sofia in Kiev, built by
Yaroslav the Wise in 1053, and the other a tenth-century account of a ritual
drama performed for the emperor in Constantinople. Emperor Constantine
VII's *Book of Ceremonies* (*c.* 953) names the performance "gothikon" and
lists "Gothic" as one of the languages, but he probably means Norse, as no
Goths can have served as late as the tenth century in the emperor's guard,
which consisted largely of Scandinavians or Rus.[63] The former "Goths" may
have come from Gotland or Götaland. In the dance some warriors were
skin-clad and some wore masks, and shields were struck with staves. Scenes
of entertainers at the Hippodrome of Constantinople adorn the walls of the
stairway in Hagia Sofia. On the ceiling above there is a fresco which shows
a spear-armed figure in a bird-like mask confronting a moustached figure
with a shield and an axe: this too may be a drama from the Hippodrome,
but it may also have links to warfare, as the *gothikon* apparently does.

Constantine's account is the only clear evidence we have that ritual
dramas related to warfare were performed in the Viking Era. Were these
initiation rituals, war dances, re-enactments of cosmic battles, or simply
games? There is a thin line between games and ritual. There are earlier
representations of warriors (or warrior gods) that may be dancing, such as
the single one on the Finglesham buckle and the pairs on the Torslunda,
Vendel, Valsgärde, and Sutton Hoo helmet plates. Earlier still, there are
references in Greek and Roman sources to chanting and dancing, in this
case just prior to or during the advance to combat. The *barritus*, referred
to by Ammianus in the fourth century as used both by Germanic troops
and Roman infantry, apparently involved rhythmic chanting or shouting,
swinging of shields in rhythm and keeping step to them. There are no references to such movements in battle in any source from the Viking Era,
but pagan warriors may well have employed war dances before battle, both
as a method of preparation, perhaps involving the honoring of deities or
summoning supernatural aid, and to work themselves into a frenzy. The

gothikon suggests that war dances and ritual dramas may still have been performed among Germanic troops in the Viking Era, although its age and origin cannot be certain. The accumulated evidence of images and written sources from the early Middle Ages indicates that a warrior ideology permeated at least a sector of society. However, we have no way of knowing whether warriors actually fought in wolfskins or bearskins in battle, or simply wore them for ritual occasions (which might include feasting), or only wore them in initiations, or even only in the otherworld. A bearskin would have been a severe hindrance in combat, and Leo the Deacon makes no mention of the Rus wearing animal skins.

How far did this "ritualized" or mythological war, perhaps involving animal-costume ceremonies and ritual combats or warrior dances, relate to reality? The argument might be made that like the battles of the shamans mentioned above, this "warfare" had more to do with the spirit realm or an otherworld than the "real world," but the multiple worlds of the Viking and Slav belief system impinged upon one another. What we do not know is whether the wearing of animal skins or costumes with magical or quasi-religious properties occurred on the field of battle, and, if it did, whether those who wore them were primarily warriors who engaged in physical combat or warriors who concentrated upon spiritual combat, as the shamans of the Northwest Coast seem to have done. To argue that all berserkers or "wolfskins" were actually spiritual warriors in the pre-Christian Era would be to assume a total confusion of their function by the time the sagas were written, and that Þórbjǫrn hornklofi was writing fantasy verse, which seems improbable. It is much more likely that the rituals prepared the warriors for war and in some way reiterated their special relationship with Odin and perhaps other deities.

It has been suggested that the role of berserkers may have been as elite household troops. If Schjødt is right, the berserkers, as warrior retinues of noble leaders, had a special relationship to Odin, something that should not come as a surprise, given that as we know him from High Medieval sources, he was the war-god who intervened most in human affairs. The benefits of belonging to such a retinue of a king in terms of wealth and social status have been mentioned, but they may have been greater still if kings or chieftains and their warrior followers were those selected by Odin as his companions after death, as they could offer a route to Valhǫll. This is one possible link between berserkers or *úlfheðnar* and Odin.

As to how they fought, we have no clue at all as to the role of *úlfheðnar*. Even if in a battle frenzy, there is no reason why berserkers or *úlfheðnar* should have lost all conception of duty to stand by their leader or standard and maintain the battle line. They may have fought in the forefront of their leader's troops, at the head of a wedge formation, or in the prows of the leading ships, but that does not mean they charged headlong and screaming at the enemy as soon as they saw them, the popular image of the fanatical warrior.[64] Leo the Deacon's account of Dorostolon may lack detail on many points, but he was particularly interested in bizarre behavior (to the Byzantine mind), and for all the howling and "madness" shown by the Rus in combat, he says nothing of suicide squads; and that is precisely what small bands of warriors would have been had they charged out well in front of the rest of their army against massed ranks of Byzantine spearmen and archers, or worse, against the *kataphraktoi*, unless the entire enemy host fled before them.

If berserkers were also members of the *comitatus*, they will have been inculcated with the rules that bound them to their leader as well as the rules of their fraternity. Berserkers and *úlfheðnar* may have made howling or roaring noises in battle, but the custom among almost all troops in this period was to make as much noise as possible and most regional contingents or retinues must have had their own war-cries. This may be what Snorri or his source meant by "they behaved like mad dogs and wolves." *Ynglingasaga* is also the only source which clearly says that berserkers went without armor. It is difficult to believe that troops of the *comitatus* would shun the use of armor, although this does not exclude the possibility that they sometimes threw it off in a battle frenzy, perhaps convinced that they were invulnerable. Body armor may have been relatively rare, but among the Vikings those closest to the chieftains would surely have been the first to have access to it. This should not rule out berserkers as elite troops of this type, nor should it exclude their use of armor; *Heimskringla* was written in the thirteenth century and it may have been colored by the later image of the berserker as completely wild, although it may also contain accurate information. Warrior fraternities that lived in the wild probably did go without armor; it is quite possible that this was the origin of such warriors, but that their customs were adopted into the *comitatus* as some of them were employed by chieftains, and thus became associated with Odin and his warrior rituals, but we can only speculate on this. No source says explicitly that *úlfheðnar* did not use armor; the translation of the quotation from *Vatnsdœla Saga* given above suggests that they did use it, but the Old Norse phrase, "Þeir höfðu vargstakka fyrir brynjur" could mean "They used wolf-skins *in place of armor*," rather than "over armor." This too, of course, was written centuries after the battle supposedly took place.[65]

As for their behavior, berserkers and *úlfheðnar* may also have fought in a crazed fashion within the battle line, but they will not have been alone in doing this. There are abundant accounts of battle-madness throughout history, even from modern times. Some of these involved peoples known to have performed pre-battle rituals involving dancing and chanting, such as the Zulus, but even modern western soldiers have described bizarre experiences and reckless behavior under the severe stress of combat.[66] Although such behavior was sometimes incited by intoxicants, it is quite clear that altered states of mind can be achieved without them. Since there is no account of berserkers taking them, any suggestion that they did so remains nothing more than speculation, albeit within the realms of possibility.[67]

The Jómsvikings

In a limited number of sources there are warrior fraternities of the Viking Era that are named or have named leaders. Of these, the Jómsvikings are the best known, but their existence is doubtful. They appear in *Fagrskinna*, *Heimskringla*, *Oláf Saga Tryggvasonar*, and, of course, the *Saga of the Jóms-vikings*. An important source for them was clearly skaldic verse, some of which they quoted, particularly oral tradition concerning the band's involvement in a tenth-century war between the Norwegian jarl of Lade, Håkon Sigurdsson, and the kings of Denmark. It is clear that the tale had been highly embellished with elements of "viking tradition" by the end of the twelfth century; on the other hand, it is rare that such a "historical" tale has absolutely no foundation in reality. The rules of membership, as described in the *Saga of the Jómsvikings*, are those common to warrior fraternities, including the *comitatus*: kinship was not to be taken into account in selection, no women were to be allowed in the fortress, all booty was to be placed at the standard for sharing, and each member was obliged to avenge any other as if he were a brother.[68] There was supposedly an internal hierarchy, the first leader being Palnatóki, who also passed judgement on those members who were found to have killed kin of other members before they had joined the fraternity. The *Saga* names their fortress as Jómsborg.

The site of Jómsborg has often been connected to Vineta, a mythical city of the south Baltic coast said to have been consumed by the waves, and Vetlaba, a large town alleged to be in the region and described by the envoy of the caliph of Córdoba, Ibrāhīm ibn Yaʿqūb: "They have a huge town on the Ocean, which has twelve gates. It has a haven for which they use tree trunks cut in half. They fight with Meszko and their military strength is huge. They do not have a king and do not allow one ruler to dominate them; they are governed by the elders."[69]

Alternative sites proposed, all in Pomerania, include one of the islands east of the island of Rügen and submerged in the fourteenth century, Barth on the north coast west of Rügen, Koserow on Usedom, and Wolin, nowadays in Poland but then situated in the territory of the Pomeranian Slavs. Adam of Bremen also refers to Jumne, "a most noble city," where Harald Bluetooth took refuge in 986.[70] Wolin is known to have been a trading emporium with a multi-ethnic population in the tenth century. Scandinavians appear to have been among them, although it was in the territory of the Pomeranian Slavs.[71] Possibly a warrior fraternity controlled it for a period, some of its members being Scandinavian, but the Slavs of the Baltic coast were no strangers to seafaring and used similar ships to the Vikings.

Despite the *Saga's* claim that no fear was to be shown by the Jómsvikings, and their subsequent reputation that has lasted to this day, the sagas suggest that they abandoned their allies or employers whenever the situation looked unfavorable. Sigvaldi did so at the Battle of Hjǫrungavágr (986, according to the sagas) and they betrayed Olaf Tryggvason before Svoldr (999 or 1000). If there is any truth in the reports that they went with Thorkell the Tall to England to assist Cnut in 1009, they did the same there, as Thorkell changed sides and fought for the English. Whatever oaths they swore and initiations they may have undergone, and however loyal they were to one another, in the service of others the Jómsvikings could not necessarily be relied upon. Any warrior-band that hired itself out to nearby rulers but owed no real allegiance to them would be all too likely to behave in such a fashion.

As it appears in the sagas, Jómsborg is a refuge for Scandinavians of standing who were expelled from their homelands. A multi-ethnic trading emporium such as Wolin would have been a suitable place for such people to go, even more so if it was the home of a warrior fraternity. One of them may have been Styrbjörn the Strong, who attempted to overthrow his uncle,

Erik the Victorious of Sweden, in 984 or 985. His attempt is said to have ended in disaster at the Battle of Fýrisvellir.[72] The Jómsvikings may also have been some of the Wendish allies of Sweyn Estridsen when he unsuccessfully tried to take Denmark from Magnus the Good, joint king of Norway and Denmark, in 1043. Although they are not named as such, Magnus is said to have destroyed the fortress of Jómsborg in the same year. The place-name Jómsborg is commonly considered a post-Viking Era invention. The town as well as the name may be a literary creation, on the assumption that the supposed warrior fraternity must have had (or ought to have had) such a home, or it may even be a conflation of several places in Pomerania. If there was a traditional base for bands of raiders or rebels, perhaps known as Jómsvikings, the idea that there was a single warrior fraternity that occupied the same site continuously for 150 years is likely to be an assumption made from the name used of successive bands by later skalds or saga writers, who then built the myth around it.

The *Saga of the Jómsvikings* claims that the band that later became the Jómsvikings was originally active around the Irish Sea: true or not, this makes the important point that many of the bands of raiders which set out for Britain, Ireland, Frankia, and other destinations may have adopted a similar ethos to the fraternities described above, although those with a looser organization and a lack of permanence are probably better characterized as simple raiding-parties. If one of these bands did settle in Wolin or nearby, they had no reason to exclude older warriors, possibly renegades from the emerging Scandinavian kingdoms. Nevertheless, it has long been argued that it was mainly the young men who went on long-distance expeditions. They might include those who were expected to leave the community for a while, as described above, who had yet to settle down as farmers or had not the possibility to do so. For a contemporary clerical view of the Scandinavians, we can look to Adam of Bremen, who mentions that their warriors paid tribute to the king of Denmark in return for the right to plunder the barbarians around the Baltic, but frequently plundered their own people, whom they did not hesitate to sell into slavery.

Wolves in sheep's clothing?

Having suggested that berserkers did exist in Scandinavian societies, even if the exact nature of their behavior and employment remains uncertain, were they as exceptional as often assumed? We know nothing of their behavior or customs, but Sviatoslav's warriors may have been associates of Perun or some other Slavic god rather than Odin (or of both). However, warrior fraternities that had close links to pagan deities were hardly likely to find favor with either the Roman or the Byzantine Churches after conversion. As we shall see, even when they were not overtly associated with paganism the mode of behavior of warrior fraternities became suspect in the eyes of clerical chroniclers and annalists. As in the case of the berserkers of the Icelandic sagas, there is some question as to whether these authors were referring to warriors of a mythical or fictional past or whether warriors with a similar ethos still existed in their day and in the Christianized parts of Europe. It is conceivable, even probable, that they had existed in pagan Ireland or England, but Christianity had been established for two centuries or more by the time the Vikings became a serious threat.

A case in point is the *Fenian* cycle, which was popular in Ireland from the tenth century onwards. It concerns the *fianna*, young men who lived in the wilderness and had supernatural or animal powers. One school of thought is that this is a record of the pagan past, drawing on oral tradition and maintained in the Christian period by those who wished to preserve their mythology. The opposing (and to my mind more convincing) view is that the monastic scribes who wrote down the tales were not consciously trying to preserve ancient tradition, but recording tales as they knew them, oral tradition that had continuously adapted to contemporary culture.[73] As suggested by Thomas Charles-Edwards, the early fianna may have been the *comitatus* of Irish chieftains or kings in the fifth century and conversion period, particularly those who raided Britannia. However, by the eighth century *fian* was not used to denote the retinues of established kings who had kindred or other close connections with monasteries, but to denote warbands that operated either as robber-bands or as followers of kings or chieftains who had no kindred within the Church, or who had been dispossessed. The term fian probably changed in character as result of the Church's opposition to some of its practices, such as the taking of "evil oaths" and general destruction of property and preying on settled communities.[74] Christian writers condemned the *fianna*, describing their bands as brigands and "consecrated to the devil." They were practicers of *diberg,* "brigandage," associated with destruction of churches, the murder of clerics, and the rape of any woman they could find. It was also associated with paganism. The *fianna* appear mainly in literature because the Irish annals are relatively terse and it seems that their activities had few political consequences. Nevertheless, they appear in an entry of the *Annals of Ulster* for 847, which also confirms the existence of such groups in the Viking Age: "Máel Sechnaill devastated the Island of Loch Muinremor, overcoming there a large warrior-band [*fian-lach*] of Luigni and Gailenga, who had been plundering the territories in the manner of the heathens."[75]

"In the manner of the heathens" draws an explicit comparison with the Vikings who were then plaguing Ireland. As if to emphasize the general characteristics of warrior-bands outlined above, the Irish law tract *Tecosca Cormaic* states, "every man is a fian member until [he obtains] landed property." Kim McCone concludes that the *fian* included both noble and royal sons undergoing their warrior education and outcasts from society, not necessarily of noble stock. Their life in the wilderness associated them with animals and mysterious or supernatural forces that were believed to flourish outside civilized society. We also find warriors who took wolf-form, like Laignech Fáeled in *Cóir Anmann*, and the *dord fiansa*, the war-chant of the fian, may even have involved howling. Initiation into the *fianna* involved an abrogation of social status and rights, and tests such as being hunted by existing *fianna* and dodging the spears of nine men.[76] In the High Middle Ages the *fianna* acquired an increasingly heroic image, divorced from the *diberg* with which they had once been associated.

Aside from the Scandinavian sources, the Irish provide the best evidence for warrior fraternities, but there is no question that they existed elsewhere in Europe. The Welsh *Mabinogian* provides literary examples of such bands, and "heroes" who operated with them, such as Culhwch. Evidence for Viking Era Wales is extremely poor, but the chronicle *Brut y Tywysogyon* describes violent war-bands of noble youths who plundered, raped, abducted and enslaved in the twelfth and thirteenth centuries.[77] These warriors are termed *ynfydyon*, "hotheads." Similarly, fraternities of lawless aristocratic young men who preyed upon citizens and peasants existed in later medieval France.[78] In both cases these bands acted on the fringes of the communities they came from and often provided services for local aristocracy, or paid them part of their proceeds in return for licence to continue their activities. We can guess that this is what Archbishop Hincmar of Reims was speaking of in the late ninth century when he complained that it was impossible to struggle against brigandage when the brigands were not only protected by the great but paid by them to act as assassins.

Few would argue with the statement that Anglo-Saxon England was a warrior society, certainly in origin. An analogue of Bǫðvarr Bjarki is Beowulf, who undergoes dangerous competitions and leaves his community with a warrior-band. His name may be a combination of words for bear and wolf and he has superhuman strength. Yet he is a protector of his community and loyal to his king, a Christian warrior worthy of God's protection and help. Whoever wrote or adapted the poem to the form we know, probably a cleric, adjusted the pagan warrior image to the Church's teaching. How far did the real aristocratic warriors of England follow suit? A succession of laws, from Ine's around the turn of the eighth century to Alfred's in the ninth and Æthelstan's in the early tenth, endeavored to curb the activities of marauders or lawless war-bands, the latter defined as over thirty-five men in Ine's Law. Both the later Laws imply that such brigands were receiving support from others within the community, nobles or commoners, just like the Welsh and French bands mentioned above. Most revealing is the *ASC*. It relates that in 1065 a band of Northumbrians took many people from the Midlands north with them as prisoners, so many that the effects were felt for many years.[79] In addition, the *ASC* gives numerous examples from both before and after the Norman Conquest of noblemen who, when outlawed or deprived of their lands, immediately organized their own band of warriors to launch raids on England. In the reign of Edward the Confessor they included Sweyn Godwineson in 1046, Osgod Clapa (who was actually Danish by birth) in 1049, Harold Godwineson, who raided in the Severn Estuary in 1052, and Earl Ælfgar of East Anglia, who returned to sack Hereford in concert with the Welsh in 1055. Their activities as exiles were no less violent than those of earlier Scandinavian raiders; for instance:

> Earl Harold came from Ireland with ships into the mouth of the Severn near the borders of Somerset and Devonshire, and raided there a lot: and the local people, both from Somerset and from Devonshire, gathered to oppose him, and he put them to flight and killed more than 30 good thegns besides other people . . . ."[80]

After the Conquest Harold's sons raided Devon from Ireland and Eadric "the Wild" and Hereward the Wake resisted in England. Nor were they alone in resisting, as bands of warrior-brigands operated from the wilds, called *silvatici* by the Normans. Eadric and Hereward may have been defenders of 'Englishness' in the face of Norman oppression, but perhaps not quite in the way that modern admirers would like to think. Post-conquest historians of the early twelfth century such as William of Malmesbury depict the English as reduced to slavery after the defeat of Hastings. Clearly this was not actually the case, but they mean disempowered by defeat, or, to employ a term used frequently of raped women, dishonored. It was not loss of freedom as we would understand it that they were most concerned about, but loss of status, most of all warrior status—a loss which equated the former warrior aristocracy with slaves. In the decade immediately following Hastings many men of thegn status or above were driven to rebellion by the seizure of their lands, which meant the denial of their ability to follow the path they were born for. The maintenance of honor (in the early medieval Germanic sense) demanded resistance: better to become a brigand, operating rather as the *fianlach* did in Ireland, than to accept shame. Eadric, Hereward and those like them were defending their rights and their form of Englishness, the way of the warrior elite, but they were not defenders of the English people as a whole, some of whom, as servants of the new landowning class, probably suffered from their activities alongside the Normans. We should bear in mind the pre-conquest behavior of the English warrior class, for whom plunder and rapine were proof of their prowess, a form of prowess the author of the early twelfth-century *Gesta Herewardi Saxonis* was keen to emphasize.[81]

Slavery and warriorhood

The raiders of the Viking Era did not seek only silver, but people. It is generally known that the Vikings and Arabs of this era were slave-traders. So were the Magyars, but perhaps more surprisingly to many, so were all the Christian peoples. On many occasions bands of warriors raided their own folk. As noted above, Adam of Bremen mentioned this as a practice of Scandinavian raiding bands. In the early eleventh century Archbishop Wulfstan (II) of York complained bitterly about the behavior of the English sexually abusing English women and selling them to heathens.[82] Some eighty years later his namesake, Bishop Wulfstan of Worcester, complained about the sale of English women to the Irish, albeit in an era when slavery in England was in decline under pressure from a new regime. Nevertheless, in the Viking Era slavery was endemic and an integral part of the early medieval European economy.

There are many contemporary accounts of attacks on communities in which the adult men were slaughtered and women and children taken as captives. This is a record of the year 844 from Ibn Hayyān's chronicle of al-Andalus: "Meanwhile the Norsemen—may God curse them!—had arrived, ship after ship, and occupied the city of Seville. They spent seven days there, killing the men and enslaving the women and children . . ."[83] Similar accounts of Viking-Rus activities were given by both Christian and Moslem annalists and chroniclers throughout the period 750–1100. In 955 the pagan Obodrites invaded Saxony and sacked Cocarescemier, killing the men of arms-bearing age and carrying off the women and children into slavery.[84] But Christians and Moslems behaved no differently. The twelfth-century Irish text *Cogadh Gaedhel re Gallaibh (The War of the Gaedhil with the Gaill)* tells us that after the Irish had captured Viking Limerick in 968, they "carried away their soft, youthful, bright, matchless girls; their blooming silk-clad young women; and their active, large, and well-formed boys." According to *ASC* (A), after the English had captured the Viking fort at Benfleet in 894, they "seized all that was inside it, both money and women and also children, and brought all into London." Some at least of these women are likely to have been Scandinavian, as they sometimes accompanied their husbands: the *ASC* mentions that in 896 the Vikings secured their women before leaving their fort on the Lea in East Anglia. Almost two hundred years later, after Gruffudd ab Cynan had won the Battle of Mynedd Carn in 1081:

> . . . after causing great havoc there and a lot of ravaging, Gruffudd marched towards Arwystli . . . and he destroyed and killed its people, he burned its houses, and took its women and maidens into captivity. Thus did he pay for like to Trahaearn.[85]

Accounts of Frankish or German activities normally refer simply to plundering, albeit often in exultant terms. However, particularly in the eastern Frankish realm, which became Germany, a large section of the peasantry who worked on the landed estates were slaves. In fact, it is to this that we owe the word "slave": from the end of the ninth century *sclavus* began to be used of slaves instead of the old Latin word *servus*, reflecting the Slavic origin of much of this labor.[86]

Furthermore, because it involved traffic in people and ultimately control of people, slavery had a significance beyond the simple making of profit.

There were sound practical reasons for the taking of women and children as slaves. They were easier to control and more dependent on their captors for sustenance then men, and therefore less likely to run away, while boys and girls who grew up as slaves became acculturated to their new society. However, the desire for women slaves also had other roots. Although many ended up in their captors' homelands, thousands of captives must have been sold quite soon after being captured, as it would have been quite impossible for either Vikings or Magyars to take all their captives with them on their long-distance journeys. Whatever the Church's teachings, it is certain that many Christian folk had no compunction about engaging in this trade. To take just one example, in the mid-tenth century the daughter of a Swabian count named Ernust was taken by the Magyars and bought from them by a townsman of Worms.[87]

Anyone taken as a slave could find themselves at the other end of Europe. This was not just a result of transport by sea to slave emporia in distant lands by Vikings, but movement of "goods," in this case people, across mainland Europe. As an example, large numbers of Slavs from the region east of the Elbe ended up in Moslem Spain, clearly not as a result of capture by the Moorish emirates or caliphates.[88] The greatest influx seems to have occurred in the mid-tenth century (the reign of Abd-al-Rahmán, Caliph of Cordoba), so it is likely to be connected with the campaigns of Henry the Fowler and Otto I on the eastern German frontier. However, there were slave markets in Slavic towns such as Prague as well, and the Slavic-speaking peoples also fought and enslaved one another. Reduction to slavery was one of the most unfortunate consequences of war for an individual. In England, the Frankish Empire and its successor kingdoms and Scandinavia male slaves had limited rights, for instance, to testify and to own certain possessions, but legal rights were severely restricted. In post-Viking Scandinavian sagas slaves were allotted the most demeaning tasks, such as dunging, digging and herding. Most significantly in the social system of the Viking Era, the slave had no kin and no personal autonomy—in other words, he had no honor. He could be sold or killed by his master and his wife could be taken from him whenever his master thought fit. The "light at the end of the tunnel" was that a slave could achieve freedom through hard work.

For all the destruction of the Norman conquest of England, it was the beginning of the end for slavery. The Normans, alongside their Frankish neighbors, had absorbed more of the Church's teaching on the evils of this institution than had the English nobility. The Church had always opposed the enslavement of Christians, but increasingly, from the late tenth century onwards, it opposed the institution altogether. This was largely because it encouraged immorality. The Church endorsed misogynist ideas about the innate promiscuity of women, which justified their control by men, but it did not encourage the possession of multiple "wives," whether the result of repudiation of one wife in favor of another, or the keeping of concubines, who were frequently wives in all but name. One reason was "God's Law," but a clear purpose was also the maintenance of order. Theft of women was a threat to this and so was female promiscuity or adultery, for which every law-code in Europe proscribed savage punishments, ranging from mutilation to death.[89] In Welsh Law the link between kin feud and such behavior is explicit, as it was an insult to the husband.[90] On a wider level the aristocratic practice of siring numerous sons by different women posed a threat to order and peace within Christian realms.

As the Viking Era progressed, the Church increasingly condemned violence between Christians and the activities of raiding bands which preyed on them, but the members of the aristocracies of the emerging Christian kingdoms were very slow in seeing anything wrong in their activities, except when they were the sufferers. Young aristocratic men continued to form warrior-bands that killed, robbed, and raped women long after 1100. At the same time ecclesiastical sources such as the Irish annals quoted above condemned them. They were seen as pirates and bandits, disapproved of by the Church, even when employed by legitimate rulers in time of war. Some of the nobility may have been indifferent to their activities, or even profited from them, but under the influence of those who employed the written word the members of such warrior-bands began their slow transformation from hero to criminal. In pre-Christian societies they may have been seen as disruptive in the sense that they could put the livelihood and social equilibrium of the community at risk, and it may often have been necessary to wreak vengeance on them, but their activites were not necessarily contemptible or inherently evil.

Women as victims

One aspect of the "anti-social" nature of young male warrior groups is that they were associated with abduction, rape, and the taking of female slaves. There is even a suggestion that Germanic ideas of marriage were founded on the forcible seizure of women by warriors: both the Old English word for marriage, *brydhlop*, and Old Norse *brúðhlaup* mean "bride-running." Internal conflicts were often characterized by abductions. Only towards the end of our period, in the eleventh century, did the Church begin to make an impression, at least in the west of Europe, in its campaign against bigamy and slavery. In the Icelandic sagas there are frequent cases of visits by unwanted suitors (often involving berserkers). The authors were Christians and portray these as resulting in feud and often the death of the visitor, but they were obviously concerned about such occurrences in the age when the sagas were written. In most cases abduction must have been a traumatic experience: noblewomen abducted for the purpose of marriage could expect to be raped, as "consummation" of the union. According to Dudo of Saint Quentin, Rollo (Hrólfr) of Normandy acquired Poppa, daughter of a count named Berenger, as a wife in a raid on Bayeux in 885 or 889. Similarly, Rogneda (Ragnhild), betrothed to Yaropolk Sviatoslavich, was seized and forced into marriage by his brother and rival Vladimir, whom Thietmar referred to as "fornicator maximus." He was said to have had at least four wives and eight hundred concubines.[91] Allowing for exaggeration, his behavior was typical of the pagan warrior elite and proof of his status. For most women taken by enemy in war abduction must have meant ruin, but a woman who remained free, and even sometimes a slave, who adapted to her new situation could become a valued concubine, a wife, and even a queen if she was from a suitable family and her captor was of sufficiently high status. However unpleasant her abduction, Rogneda did become a princess. In *Beowulf*, a tale from the other end of Europe, Hrothgar's queen is named *Wealhþeów*, "foreign slave," a clue that she or her prototype in an oral tale might have been the victim of an abduction in the past. Not all seizures of women were permanent: in 1046 Sweyn Godwineson "ordered [Eadgifu] the abbess of Leominster to be brought to him, and he kept her as long as it suited him, and then let her go home." Violent sexual domination, including rape and abduction, were an integral part of the warrior ethos all over Europe. The *Primary Chronicle* would have us believe that Vladimir's conversion to the True Faith wrought a dramatic change in his behavior; if so, he would have become an exception.

Possession of a woman provided more than sexual gratification—it subjected not only her, but her male relatives as well. For this reason the women of opponents were targeted for abduction or slavery. Women could be subjected through marriage, concubinage, fosterage, guardianship, service, or slavery. Although these differed in degree of subjection (even within each category), they all entailed possession and the women were frequently viewed as trophies, which signified a man's status and power. The higher a man's status, the greater the number of women he amassed, and his control over women contributed to his status in the hierarchy. Accumulation of females accompanied, or resulted from, the acquisition of military power and wealth. Purchase and the means to support slaves and concubines also enabled him to reward his followers, as women were redistributable wealth like any other valuable possessions. It seems that the value of female slaves was generally higher than that of male: in Ireland the word for female slave, *cumal*, also meant the highest value unit of land and was equivalent to eight or ten cows.[92] Enslavement was an essential aspect of the warrior's way of life, humiliating the foes whose women he had taken and increasing the esteem in which he was held. In addition, more women as sexual partners meant more offspring, including sons who would become warriors themselves, particularly if, as increasingly became the case, they were denied the inheritance a "legitimate" son might have. As a man's status increased he also acquired control of free women, as others entrusted him with the guardianship of their women.

Medieval chronicles tend to portray raped women as victims of excessive lust. The violence of the act is understated and little concern is shown for the women beyond the "dishonor" the act entails, with the implication that only women of a certain social status can suffer this. Rape is still employed as a means of terrorising opposing population groups, but as a weapon of war it was more than this. It was another method of subjecting women, and by extension humiliating their menfolk. Rape was one of the specified things for which the Norman conquerors of England were ordered to do penance by the papacy, while Orderic Vitalis lamented the dishonoring of noble women and girls, suggesting that the Normans had been no exception in using this method of humiliation (of both the women and their menfolk) and demonstration of their dominance. Nor had their Anglo-Saxon noble predecessors been strangers to the employment of it, as the example of Sweyn Godwineson demonstrates.

During their invasions of England the Vikings frequently occupied nunneries, perhaps in part a large-scale demonstration of English powerlessness as they failed to protect their womenfolk. An important aspect of this was that most nunneries of the early Anglo-Saxon kingdoms were royal foundations and frequently had abbesses of royal birth. In 804 the community of Lyminge in Kent had been forced to flee *en masse* to Canterbury, while occupied nunneries included Thanet (851, 853, 865), Sheppey (855), Repton (874) and Wareham (876).[93] The Viking Era saw a drastic decline in the number of nunneries in both England and Ireland, where nunneries also had close links to powerful families. Of course the Vikings targeted religious communities in general, both because they were wealthy and soft targets and because the buildings made useful defensible bases, but given the other evidence of their attitudes to their opponents' womenfolk it is difficult to avoid the suspicion that nunneries were especially tempting.

Between the period when they were lionized as progenitors of the British who created the empire and their rehabilitation as traders and makers of jewelry, the Vikings had a dreadful reputation for "rape and pillage," which ultimately derived from their bad press in the Christian writings of the Viking Period and High Middle Ages. However, in view of the evidence, as regards the assembling of numbers of women by powerful men, it is difficult to discern any clear distinction between the attitudes of Viking, Irish, English, Slav, Magyar or any other warriors. All raped, abducted, kept as slaves or concubines and bought and sold women. Alien as it is to us, these activities acted as proof of the warrior's virility.

Chapter 8

Concluding Words

There were dramatic changes in the period 750–1100: despite the problems with Viking, Magyar, and Saracen raids, the population of Europe grew, economic prosperity generally increased along with trade and the foundations of more stable states were laid. The dates are of course arbitrary, in this case chosen to encompass the period of Viking activity rather than any particular developments in European society or political history. In military terms, in many ways the practices of warfare remained the same as they had been before 750 and would be after 1100, with an emphasis on raids and devastation of enemy territory, often with limited objectives, and general avoidance of high-risk encounters such as battles in the open field. Insofar as battlefield tactics were concerned, there was a shift in most of Europe from the single line phalanx to a somewhat more flexible approach with separate "battles" often drawn up one behind the other, and increased used of massed archery. Cavalry became slowly but steadily more effective as its armor and the quality of mounts improved through breeding, but throughout the period it was most often employed in small groups that either launched "sting" attacks on enemy infantry lines or awaited their chance to exploit signs of disintegration or exhaustion in the enemy formation before leading the pursuit. Cavalry versus cavalry encounters probably consisted of "charging" into contact and a period of mêlée before each side broke apart and retired to reassemble if one side did not flee.

Without doubt the most significant development in European warfare during the Viking Era was the proliferation of fortifications, whether more or less planned like the burghal system of Wessex–Mercia or the frontier defenses of East Frankia–Germany, or private fortifications. The objectives of warfare increasingly became seizure of these strongpoints, while conquests were secured by their construction. This was accompanied by a slow increase in the sophistication of siege-craft in the former Frankish Empire, and by the end of the period in the West Slavic and Hungarian kingdoms

However, the era has been defined here by Viking activity, so we may ask what part the Vikings played in all this. In terms of the political map of Europe, Viking achievements were few. Their rule of parts of England was short-lived, and only a few towns in Ireland, the Western Isles and the Orkney and Shetland Islands remained of their conquests. In Rus they had made a significant contribution to the origin of the towns and principalities, but these had assumed a predominantly Slavic character. Lands had been granted to Vikings by the Franks on several occasions: in Frisia in 826, 850 (Rorik) and 882 (Godfred); in Brittany, including Nantes and territory around the Loire before 919 (Ragenold/Rögnvaldr); and around Rouen in 911 (Rollo/Hrolfr). Of these, only Normandy survived as a distinct entity, once again because it became "French." As in the case of their generally accepted contribution to trade and international contacts in Europe, their most significant military contribution was arguably unintended, in that their enemies had to innovate to counter their activities, by building fortifications and occasionally fleets. The one really significant Viking technical innovation was their ships, which gave them the mobility to operate over large distances and raid on a large scale.

There is no question that the mobility provided by their ships and their large-scale plundering and/or extraction of "protection money" posed a new and difficult problem for the victims of the Vikings. However, their record in battle was mixed. They suffered defeats in every region they attacked, including Wales and Ireland. Flodoard's accounts of Viking defeats in the tenth century may be exaggerated, particularly in terms of casualties, but it does seem that defeat in battle became more common on the continent after 900. By that time the Viking presence in Ireland was already limited to a few longphorts, and thereafter they could achieve little without Irish allies. In the use of the phalanx ("shield-wall") in battle the methods used by Viking armies did not differ significantly from those of their enemies in England, Francia and Germany, but the one-line phalanx remained its basis throughout the period. The Vikings did not attempt to develop the use of mounted troops in battle outside Scandinavia, despite facing them on many occasions. A desire to maintain the ability to move armies rapidly by longship may have been one contributory factor, but conservatism in military practice was probably another. Nevertheless, they may have used cavalry in Scandinavia, at least in Denmark and Sweden, as mounted warriors (possibly deities) are portrayed on the Gotland picture stones from the late Vendel or very early Viking Period and later we have the horseman burials in Denmark, but virtually nothing is known of land battles in these regions. New methods were eventually adopted in territories with ruling dynasties of Norse or partially Norse origin, in Normandy and Russia, but only after the Norse elements were absorbed by the native people and had adopted their customs.

Despite their adept use of fortifications in their campaigns, the Scandinavians seem to have generally regarded them as a short-term expedient. Only in a few trading site-ports in Denmark, Sweden, and Ireland were more permanent defenses built. Although they occupied parts of England, Scotland, and much of Brittany for some decades, there is no indication that any attempt was made to build anything more than isolated or temporary fortifications to retain those territories. In other words, the Vikings did not adopt the methods of defense in depth used in Wessex or on the East Frankish–German frontiers. Similarly, they did not show any particular inclination to conduct long sieges or adopt the methods of siege-craft used on the continent of Europe or Byzantium, except at Paris, an attempt which failed. Even when they were besieged they often preferred to come out and fight in the open, a practice that was probably partly "Viking custom," but may also have had a sound military basis in many cases, as most Viking forces trapped in defenses had little hope of the relief that English or Frankish forces may have had in their own lands.

To a large extent the Vikings retained a "raiding mentality" until Sweyn Forkbeard's campaigns in England were transformed into campaigns of conquest at the end of the tenth century. In their ninth-century conquests of the smaller Anglo-Saxon kingdoms, the Vikings had preferred to install puppet kings while their armies continued their rampages around Britain and Francia, the relatively small Kingdom of York being the only political product of their early conquests. Otherwise their territories were peripheral islands or isolated ports. The reasons for the Viking failure to conquer any substantial territory in Ireland, even though they were present in significant numbers in the ninth century, must have other explanations. Here it is suggested that the sheer number of kings and the complexity of the Irish political scene was a contributory factor. It is also uncertain that the Vikings made any real attempt to take over Irish kingdoms or the Pictish kingdom, although they inflicted a catastrophic defeat on the latter. Only in England were real attempts made to overrun all the Anglo-Saxon kingdoms and later the kingdom of England.

As far as their behavior was concerned, for all the rhetoric of our sources the Viking warrior ethos was not very different from that of their enemies.

After all, the elites who dominated the English and Frankish kingdoms had a similar Germanic cultural heritage. Nor, it appears, was this heritage very different from that of their Slavic and Baltic neighbors. Even the Viking destruction of churches and monasteries, which attracted especial horror, was exceptional only in its sheer scale. Conversion to Christianity slowly effected a dramatic change in Viking outlook on many things; for instance, it wholly changed their conception of time. Slowly but steadily, it probably also changed their priorities from earning honor in this life to earning an afterlife in paradise, but even in the later medieval sagas honor earned by warlike deeds remains a preoccupation, as it was still to an extent with their Christian enemies in the Viking Age. Christianity also incorporated a moral code that compelled warriors to justify their warlike actions, but the Germanic warrior culture was also absorbed into a Christian faith that already saw its purpose in terms of a cosmic war and adopted military imagery. Warfare was a natural, if unsatisfactory, state that would persist until the Second Coming, and moreover, it was sometimes necessary to spread the faith: in other words, warfare could be, and frequently was, justified.

The Vikings, like the Magyars, came from outside the established order of Christendom: not only was their ability to move great distances and attack unsuspecting communities terrifying, but their warfare, even if often conducted in a similar manner to their opponents, self-evidently had an evil purpose, as they were pagans. Once the Magyars converted to the True Faith, their long-range raiding ceased and they settled into a pattern of behavior similar to their neighbors, but the Vikings continued to raid even after they had converted, sometimes on an even bigger scale, and their long-established image as "heathens" was hard to shake off. Although the attitude of the Church to Viking or Magyar atrocities may appear inconsistent to us, the fact that they were not Christians was the decisive factor in this condemnation. Nor were churchmen blind to the violence of aristocratic warriors from Christianized realms, as they frequently condemned this also if its object was not to spread the faith or fight those who were threatening it: in other words, to repeat the words of the Irish annalist, if it was conducted "in the manner of the heathens."

It is often stated that "the Viking Age was over" after Stamford Bridge. This is a very Anglocentric view, and even then inaccurate, as Danish armies landed in England in 1069 and 1075, and Cnut (IV) planned an invasion in 1085. The Viking raiding mentality did not die overnight, as activity continued in the Irish Sea, the west and north of Scotland, and the Baltic, even into the twelfth century, but the development of more stable and centralized kingdoms in Scandinavia meant that increasingly raids in that area had to be made either by kings or with their blessing. On the continent of Europe, and in England after the Norman Conquest, military advances, especially the spread of fortifications, had already made raiding increasingly difficult. Nevertheless, by the mid-eleventh century most of Europe was free of a scourge that had lasted for almost three centuries, which those who recorded it had ensured would live on to this day as a byword for warlike behavior, terror, and destruction.

Notes

Abbreviations used in the bibliography and notes
Sources
AB—Annals of Saint-Bertain
AF—Annals of Fulda
ASC—*Anglo-Saxon Chronicle*
Hkr—Heimskringla (of Snorri Sturluson)
RFA—*Royal Frankish Annals*
Journals and book series
ANS—Anglo-Norman Studies
CG—Chateau-Gaillard
JMMH—Journal of Medieval Military History
MGH—Monumenta Germanica Historica
SRG—Scriptores Rerum Germanicarum in usum scholarum

Chapter 1: Viking-Age Warfare and History

1. Woolf, Rosemary, "The ideal of men dying with their lord in the Germania and in the *Battle of Maldon*," *Anglo-Saxon England* 5 (1976), 63–81.
2. The opposite extreme is represented by the *Song of Roland*, which supposedly relates the action at Roncesvalles in 778, but in which almost nothing bears any resemblance to what actually happened, only a couple of names being "historical."
3. Mia Münster-Swendsen, "Saxos skygge: Sven, Saxo og meningen med Lex castrensis," in Per Andersen and Thomas Heebøll-Holm, eds, *Saxo og hans samtid* (Århus: 2012), pp. 91–112. The text has a complicated history. It is sometimes called "Vederloven," but this name derives from the latest of three versions or paraphrases, Witherlax Ræt. Nowadays the reconstructed "version X" of the philologist Martin Clarentius Gertz (1915) is usually used, but this is not without some problems.
4. Birgit Sawyer, *The Viking-Age Rune-Stones*, esp. pp. 99–107, 116–22.
5. It is contrasted with eddic poetry, which is characterized as "timeless" and usually deals with mythological themes (a distinction that would not have been recognized by the Vikings themselves) and the Icelandic *rímur*. For a summary of skaldic poetry, its genres and sub-genres, see Bjarne Fidjestøl, "Skaldic Verse," in *Medieval Scandinavia*, ed. Phillip Pulsiano, Garland Encyclopedias of the Middle Ages, 1 (New York: 1993), pp. 592–4.
6. The most enthusiastic advocate of this approach is the Norwegian historian Rikke Malmros. See, for instance, the collection of her articles in *Vikingernes syn på militær og samfund: Belyst gennem skjaldenes fyrstedigtning* (Århus: 2010). Another who has made extensive studies of skaldic verse, Judith Jesch, is more cautious in her approach: see her *Ships and Men in the Late Viking Age: The Vocabulary of Runic Inscriptions and Skaldic Verse* (Woodbridge, Boydell: 2001).
7. Albert B. Lord, *The Singer of Tales* (Cambridge, MA: 1961). Also Alain Renoir, *A Key to Old Poems: The Oral-Formulaic Approach to the Interpretation of West Germanic Verse* (University Park, Penn.: 1987).

8. In the *Prose Edda*. See Snorri Sturluson, *Edda*, tr. A. Faulkes (London: 1987), "Skaldskaparmal" and "Hattatal," pp. 59–220. It should be noted that his authorship of *Heimskringla* is not certain, and that this attribution is based on the close stylistic similarities with his other known work.

9. Examples include *Vikinger i krig* by Kim Hjardar and Vegard Vike (Oslo: 2011) and Torgrim Titlestad's books *Slaget i Hafrsfjord* (Oslo: 2006) and *Harald Hårfagre* (Oslo: 2010). An English example is Charles Jones, *The Forgotten Battle of 1066: Fulford* (Stroud: 2006). All of these books are still worth reading, but the reader should bear in mind their uncritical attitude to the sagas. Ian Stephenson's attitude in his *Viking Warfare* (Stroud: 2012), that the sagas are worthless as history, goes to the other extreme. He in turn accepts virtually everything that is reported in Anglo-Saxon saints' legends!

10. Saxo, *Gesta Danorum*, 11:5.1. Valerius Maximus, *Facta et dicta memorabilia'* [Nine Books of] Memorable Deeds and Sayings' (3.2.23). This was Saxo's favorite source of classical Latin passages.

11. The Old Norse histories and sagas usually give figures in "tens," but these tens could be dozens, as they also used a duodecimal system of reckoning: in most cases we do not know which was intended in the original. Hence "four tens" could be forty, or forty-eight. The figures for these fleets could be 150 and 300, or 180 and 360.

12. For instance, Brian Murdoch, *The Germanic Hero: Politics and Pragmatism in Early Medieval Poetry* (Cambridge: 1996).

13. According to Ekkehard IV (d. 1060) *Waltharius* was written by the monk Ekkehard (I), presumably in the early tenth century, but he (IV) adjusted the Latin for the taste of Archbishop Aribo of Mainz, removing some of the germanisms.

14. Nithard, *De dissensionibus filiorum Ludovici pii (On the Dissensions of the Sons of Louis the Pious)*

15. Bishop of Auxerre, d. 448 in Ravenna.

16. See Chapter 7 for a discussion of this.

17. John Haldon, *The State and the Tributary Mode of Production* (London: 1993).

18. Ryan Lavelle, *Alfred's Wars: Sources and Interpretations of Anglo-Saxon Warfare in the Viking Age* (Woodbridge: 2010).

19. Josiah Cox Russell, "Population in Europe," in Carlo M. Cipolla, ed., *The Fontana Economic History of Europe*, vol. 1: The Middle Ages (Glasgow: 1972), pp. 25–71.

20. Guy Halsall, *Warfare and Society in the Barbarian West, 450–900* (London: 2003), pp. 165, 167. See the discussion of the Roman Republican soldier's method in the light of known equipment in Sam Koon, *Infantry Combat in Livy's Battle Narratives* (Oxford: 2010), pp. 8–14.

21. Joachim Henning, "Civilization versus Barbarians? Fortification Techniques and Politics in Carolingian and Ottonian Borderlands," in Florin Curta, ed., *Borders, Barriers and Ethnogenesis: Frontiers in Late Antiquity and the Middle Ages* (Turnhout: 2005), pp. 23–34 (p. 27).

Chapter 2: Equipment

1. See, for instance, the Franks Casket.

2. Richard Underwood, *Anglo-Saxon Weapons and Warfare* (Stroud: 2000), p. 44.

3. In this book, unless otherwise mentioned, the term "cavalry" refers to men mounted for combat: it does not imply that they were specialised mounted troops such as those of the modern period, who rarely if ever fought on foot. The problems related to mounted and foot combat in this era are discussed further in Chapter 5.

4. The best had the inscription "+vlfberh+t," but others had the second cross after the "t".

5. These results were obtained from tests done by Dr Alan Williams, an archaeometallurgist and consultant to the Wallace Collection in London, and Tony Fry, a senior researcher at the National Physical Laboratory in Teddington. Whereas the originals and their direct imitations

had the inscription +vlfberh+t, others were distinguished by an inscription with the second cross after the "t".

6. Peter Paulsen, *Axt und Kreutz in Nord-und Osteuropa* (Bonn: 1956), pp. 156–67; P. Hallinder, "Streit-und Arbeitsäxte," in Greta Arwidsson, ed., Birka II:2. *Systematische Analysen der Gräberfunde* (Stockholm: 1986), pp. 45–50 (p. 47).

7. For instance, the Utrecht Psalter, fols. 7, 14; Stuttgarter *Bilderpsalter* 1, fols. 48, 7 Iv, or an ivory book cover now in Zurich: J. Hubert, J. Porcher and W.F. Volbach, *L'empire carolingien* (Paris: 1968), fig. 228. These look like composite bows.

8. James Graham-Campbell, *Viking Artefacts: a Select Catalogue* (London: 1980), p. 74.

9. Abbo, *Abbonis Bella Parisiacae urbis* 1, line 275, 36; Miracula sancti *Martini Vertavenrir c. 5*: MGH SS rer Met 3.570–571.

10. Maurice, *Strategikon*, 1:2.

11. W.F. Paterson, "The Archers of Islam," *Journal of the Economic and Social History of the Orient*, 9:1/2 (1966), 69–87.

12. Charlotte Hedenstierna-Jonson, "The Birka Warrior: The Material Culture of a Martial Society," Doctoral Thesis in Archaeological Science (Stockholm: 2006), pp. 56–7.

13. St. Vigeans 1, Glenferness, Shandwick and Meigle.

14. Richer of Saint-Rémi, *Histories*, 2:92.

15. Bibliothèque Nationale de Paris, MS Lat. 12,302; David S. Bachrach, *Warfare in Tenth-Century Germany* (Woodbridge: 2012), p. 151.

16. The *Carmen* is attributed to Bishop Guy of Amiens and has often been claimed as a forgery, without good reason: see the edition of Frank Barlow, listed in the bibliography, in which he suggests that it was written as early as 1067.

17. Rabanus, *De procinctu Romanae miliciae*, 10; 1 Samuel 17:31–54.

18. D.S. Bachrach, *Warfare in Tenth-Century Germany*, p. 151.

19. Paul Martin, *Arms and Armor: From the 9th to the 17th Century* (Rutland, Vermont: 1968), pp. 8–9.

20. The Bible de Saint Pierre de Roda, Paris, Ms Lat 6, vol. III, fol. 144v°, Catalonia, and the Richelieu Manuscrits Latin 6 Bible, Catalonia, both in the Bibliothèque Nationale de France.

21. Adalbert of Magdeburg, *Continuatio*, 961.

22. For instance, in the battle scene on the eleventh-century MS Cotton Claudius B IV f24v manuscript in the British Library.

23. Nancy Edwards, *The Archaeology of Early Medieval Ireland* (London: 1996), p. 89.

24. C. Eggenberger, *Psalterium aureum sancti Galli: Mittelalterliche Psalterillustration im Kloster St. Gallen* (Sigmaringen: 1987), pics. 13–14.

25. Similar helmets can also be seen in the Utrecht Psalter 51 and the Bern *Psychomachia* 52 and on ivories such as a worn tablet now in the Louvre 53 and a diptych in Milan.

26. MS Cotton Claudius BIV f. 24v, British Library.

27. For example, Count Eccard of Macon included one brunia in his will and Eberhard of Friuli bequeathed no fewer than four: John Coupland, "Carolingian Arms and Armor in the Ninth Century," *Viator* 21 (1990), 29–50 (p. 35).

28. Ermold, *In honorem Hludovici imperatoris*, lines 574, 1710–1711.

29. Edictum Pistense c. 25: MGH Cap. 2.321.

30. Nicholas Brooks and H.E. Walker, 'The Authority and Interpretation of the Bayeux Tapestry', in Nicholas Brooks, *Communities and Warfare 700–1400* (London: 2000), pp. 197–8. See Chapter 5.

31. *Lex Ribuaria* 40.11; Notker, *De Carolo Magno* 2.17. Notker calls them greaves (*ocreae*), the classical term. His work is a collection of anecdotes about Charlemagne, some clearly outright inventions, some highly suspect, and some that have a basis in fact. Eberhard (c. 815–866) was

the Frankish Duke of Friuli from 846. He was an experienced soldier and many of his letters survive.

32. John Coupland, "Carolingian Arms and Armor in the Ninth Century," *Viator* 21 (1990), 29–50 (p. 7).

33. R.H.C. Davis, *Medieval Warhorse: Origin, Development and Redevelopment* (London: 1989), pp. 31–47. See especially the detail of the vicissitudes of the English horse-breeding industry from 1790 to 1950 on pp. 45–7.

34. The *Vita Corbiniani* of Bishop Arbeo of Freising. The saint lived c. 670–c. 730.

35. On the CV, see Davis, *Medieval Warhorse*, pp. 71–2. The importance of using the *CV* in conjunction with the *BE (Brevium Exempla ad describendas res ecclesiasticas et fiscales)* was shown by Carroll Gillmor, "The *Brevium Exempla* as a Source for Carolingian Warhorses," in *JMMH* 6 (2008), pp. 32–57. The two were bound together in the same manuscript, evidence that they were regarded as complementary by the Carolingian rulers themselves.

36. Lucius Junius Moderatus Columella, De Re Rustica; Rutilius Taurus Aemilianus Palladius, *Opus agriculturae*, also occasionally known as *De Re Rustica*. The titles of both works are usually translated "On Agriculture."

37. Carroll Gillmor, "The 791 Equine Epidemic and its Impact on Charlemagne's Army," in JMMH 3 (2003), pp. 23–45.

38. William of Apulia, *Gesta Roberti Wiscardi* ("The Deeds of Robert Guiscard"), composed between 1096 and 1099. There are three extant works about the Normans of southern Italy, all written in the same period and from the Norman point of view.

39. II Athelstan, trans. *English Historical Documents* 1, p. 420. See Chapter 3 on the interpretation of the "plough" regulation.

40. M. Mü ller-Wille, "Pferdegrab und Pferdeopfer im frü hen Mittelalter, mit einem Beitrag von H Vierck: Pferdegräber im angelsächsischen England," in *Berichten van de Rijksdienst voor het Ouheidkundig Bodemonderzoek, Jaargang* 20–21: 1970–1971 (1972), 119–248.

41. A. Hedman, *Gravar och bebyggelseutveckling i Arninge*. Riksantikvarieämbetet rapport 1996/108 (Stockholm: 1996). This was a cremation burial under a low mound. Those buried in the grave were a young woman, three men of different ages and a person of undetermined sex, seven horses, eleven dogs, two cats, three sheep, one goat, one pig, one lynx, and a number of birds including an eagle owl and a hawk. Undoubtedly many were sacrificed, probably including some of the humans.

42. Johan Engström, "The Vendel Chieftains: a study of military tactics," in Anne Nørgård Jørgensen and Birthe L. Clausen, eds, *Military aspects of Scandinavian Society in a European Perspective AD 1–1300* (Copenhagen: 1997), pp. 248–55.

43. Klaus Randsborg, *The Viking Age in Denmark: The Formation of a State* (London: 1980), pp. 126–7.

44. RFA, 804.

45. Saxo, *Gesta Danorum*, 13:2. In this campaign the Danish army, composed entirely of infantry, was harassed and worn down by Slav cavalrymen.

46. Saxo, *Gesta Danorum*, 10–11. These are more historical than the previous books, but contain limited information about actual events, even this tainted by suspect tradition and invention by the author.

47. A. Sundkvist, *Hästarnas land: aristokratisk hästhållning och ridkonst i Svealands yngre järnålder* (Uppsala: 2001), p. 194.

48. Wladyslaw Duczko, "Continuity and Transformation: the Tenth Century AD in Sweden," in Przemysław Urbánczyk, ed., *The Neighbors of Poland in the 10th Century* (Warsaw: 2000), pp. 7–36 (p. 22).

49. The Slavic or "Wendish" people that occupied the island of Rügen and adjacent areas across the Stralsund strait (Pomerania) from the ninth to the twelfth centuries.
50. Maurice, Strategikon, ed. Dennis, p. XVII.
51. For the first view, see Lynn White Jnr, *Medieval Technology and Social Change* (1962), pp. 1–38 and 135–53, and J.F. Verbruggen, "The Role of Cavalry in Medieval Warfare," JMMH 3 (2005), 46–71 (p. 62). For the counter-arguments, see R.H. Hilton and P.H. Sawyer, "Technological Determinism: the Stirrup and the Plough," *Past and Present*, 24 (1963), 90–100, and Bernard Bachrach, "Charles Martel, Mounted Shock Combat, the Stirrup, and Feudalism," in *Armies and Politics in the Early Medieval West* (Aldershot: 1993), pp. 49–75.
52. Initially it was claimed that the men had died in battle, defeated by the Estonians, but if this was the case, it seems odd that they were buried in such an orderly fashion unless the Estonians had taken to offering whole boatloads of men, equipment and animals as sacrifices, a previously unknown habit. On this burial, see Jü ri Peets, "Salme Ship Burials: Revealing a Grim Cargo of Elite Viking Warriors," *Current World Archaeology* 58, vol. 5:10 (2013), 18–24.
53. Tinna Damgård-Sørensen, Søren Nielsen and Erik Andersen, "Fuldblod på havet," in Niels Lund, ed., Beretning fra toogtyvende tværfaglige vikingesymposium (Højbjerg: 2004), pp. 4–50 (p. 44).
54. Rikke Malmros, *Vikingernes syn pÅmilitær og samfund* (Århus: 2010), pp. 69–79.
55. Harry Alopaeus, "Der Schiffsfun von Lapuri," in *Deutsches Schiffsarchiv 11:1988* (Hamburg: 1989), pp. 2134. The main difference between the Finnish boat and Scandinavian ones was the use of treenails as well as iron nails.
56. Denis Rixson, *The West Highland Galley* (Edinburgh: 1998).
57. Edwin and Joyce Gifford, "Alfred's New Longships," in Timothy Reuter, ed., *Alfred the Great: Papers from the Eleventh-Centenary Conferences* (Aldershot: 2003), pp. 281–9 (pp. 282–3).

Chapter 3: Military Organization and Training

1. Rosamond McKitterick, *The Frankish Kingdoms under the Carolingians 751–987* (London: 1983), pp. 146–9.
2. Despite this, they are often referred to in this book because, as they give more systematic accounts of tactics and formations, they are useful "control mechanisms" for what was possible in this period.
3. The author is unknown, but because it was formerly attributed to Hyginus Gromaticus he is now known as "Pseudo-Hyginus."
4. The ludicrous name ("Little key to the small cloth") almost certainly derives from a misreading of a lost Greek title. The earliest extant manuscript is eighth- or ninth-century, but it is a compilation of ancient and later material. See pp. 68–9.
5. Preface to Alfred's translation of Gregory the Great's *Pastoral Care*, in *Alfred the Great: Asser's Life of King Alfred and Other Contemporary Sources*, tr. and ed. Simon Keynes and Michael Lapidge (Harmondsworth: 1983), p. 126.
6. Richard P. Abels, *Alfed the Great: War, Kingship and Culture in Anglo-Saxon England* (London: 1998), pp. 219–57.
7. See *Alfred the Great*, ed. Keynes and Lapidge, pp. 124–5.
8. Wace, *Roman de Brut*, ed. Weiss, lines 13593–13604; GS 1.6:10 (Haddingus); Msk 12, pp. 139–40; FsK, 235, pp. 185–6; Hkr III, pp. 76–7 (all telling the tale of Harald Hardrade, alias Norðbrikt in Msk). On Olga's revenge, see Aleksandr Koptev, "Reconstructing the Funeral Ritual of the Kievan Prince Igor (*Primary Chronicle*, sub anno 945)," *Studia Mythologica Slavica* 13 (2010), 87 106 (pp. 87–100).
9. As David Bachrach has pointed out, in many works the term "warrior" has often been preferred to "soldier" because authors want to suggest that the armies of the early Middle Ages

were more or less disorganized hordes led by wealth-seeking warlords at the head of a feudal pyramid. See David S. Bachrach, *Warfare in Tenth-Century Germany* (Woodbridge: 2012), p. 13. The same work is invaluable for bringing to our attention the amount of militarily educative material that was available to officers of the ninth and tenth centuries.

10. Nithard, *Historiarum*, 3.6.

11. Liudprand of Cremona, *Antapodosis*, 2.31.

12. Regino of Prüm (*Chronicon*) appears to think that the wound was caused by the boar, but mentions that some thought one of Carloman's men had used his weapon carelessly and the king had kept this secret to prevent the execution of a man who had done this accidentally. The latter "conspiracy theory" is the explanation favored by the *Annals of St-Vaast (Annales Vedastini)* and the Annals of Fulda (*Annales Fuldenses*), and it is possible that a source at court or someone who was with the hunt "leaked" this information. A much later French king, Philip IV "the Fair," fell off his horse when charged by a boar and died from his injuries (1303).

13. There is no room to discuss this here, but the Iron Age concept of ownership may have been quite different from ours, as there were no written records or contracts and religious ideas may have included a different concept of land and its use. Nevertheless, from the advent of farming megalithic tombs may have marked an exclusive "right" of a certain kin-group to use certain areas of land, and by the Bronze Age there were boundary markers.

14. For instance, the families of St. Germanus of Auxerre and Gregory of Tours were descended from former senatorial Roman families.

15. See, for instance, Leszek Słupecki, "The temple in Rhetra-Riedegost: West-Slavic pagan ritual as described at the beginning of the eleventh century," in Anders Andrén, Kristina Jennbert and Catharina Raudvere, eds, *Old Norse religion in long-term perspectives: Origins, changes and interactions* (Lund: 2006), pp. 224–8 (pp. 224–5).

16. D.S. Bachrach, *Warfare in Tenth-Century Germany*, pp. 74–5.

17. Karl J. Leyser, *Medieval Germany and its Neighbors, 900–1250* (London: 1982), p. 62; Charles Bowlus, *The Battle of Lechfeld and its Aftermath, August 955* (Aldershot: 2006), p. 152.

18. Jean Durliat, "Le manse dans le polyptyque d'Irminon: nouvel essai d'histoire quantative," in Hartmut Atsma, ed., *La Neustrie: Les pays au nord de la Loire de 650 à 850: colloque historique international*, vol. 2 (Sigmaringen: 1989), pp. 467–504.

19. D.S. Bachrach, *Warfare in Tenth-Century Germany*, p. 89.

20. Carroll Gillmor, "The *Brevium Exempla* as a Source for Carolingian Warhorses," in *JMMH* 6 (2008), pp. 32–57 (p. 45).

21. Richard P. Abels, *Lordship and Military Obligation in Anglo-Saxon England* (London: 1988), pp. 43–57.

22. Nicholas Brooks, *Communities and Warfare 700–1400* (London: 2000), pp. 35–7.

23. Asser, Life of Alfred, 12; Janet L. Nelson, *Politics and Ritual in Early Medieval Europe* (Woodbridge: 1986), pp. 117–18.

24. *ASC* (E) 894 [893].

25. Both Keynes and Lapidge in their translation of Asser (p. 115 and p. 285, n. 4) and Michael Swanton in his translation of the *ASC* (p. 84 and p. 85, n. 14) draw a parallel with the division of the Amazon army into two in Orosius' *History*, but the former also point out that Asser mentions the division of Alfred's court and finances into three (n. 4), which would be a likely parallel to military organization, while Swanton (n. 14) suggests that Janet Bately (in her edition of the work) is correct in asserting that Alfred did not actually know Orosius' work, even though it was translated into Old English. However, see the criticism of Halsall's view in Brooks' review of his work: 2005, p. 425.

26.   26. Guy Halsall, *Warfare and Society in the Barbarian West, 450–900* (London: 2003), pp. 104–5. Building and maintenance of defenses were referred to as *waru* and *weal-stilling* in the Burghal Hidage.

27.   *ASC* (A, B, C, D).

28.   LawII Cnut 12, 14, 15, referring to his rights in Wessex, Mercia and the Danelaw, S 986. See F.E. Harmer, *Anglo-Saxon Writs* (Stamford: 1989), p. 73.

29.   Nicholas Hooper, "The Housecarls in England in the Eleventh Century," *ANS* 7 (1985), 161–76 (pp. 71–5).

30.   Ryan Lavelle, *Alfred's Wars: Sources and Interpretations of Anglo-Saxon Warfare in the Viking Age* (Woodbridge: 2010), p. 108.

31.   *ASC* (E), 1035; *ASC* (C, D), 1041.

32.   N.A.M. Rodger, *The Safeguard of the Sea: A Naval History of Britain 660–1649*, Naval History of Britain, vol. 1 (New York: 1999), p. 11.

33.   *ASC*, 934, and Flodoard, *Annales*, 939.

34.   Ann Williams, *Æthelred the Unready: The Ill-Counselled King* (London: 2003), p. 46.

35.   Edwin and Joyce Gifford, "Alfred's New Longships," in Timothy Reuter, ed., *Alfred the Great: Papers from the Eleventh-Centenary Conferences* (Aldershot: 2003), pp. 281–9 (p. 283).

36.   Lavelle, *Alfred's Wars*, p. 149.

37.   According to John of Worcester: 2:1040, in his mention of the abolition he explains that Æthelred had to feed and clothe Thorkell's men in return for their service.

38.   They are not named *butsecarls* in *ASC* (E), but it lists the ports from which Harold and God-wine took ships in 1052: Pevensey, Dungeness, Romney, Hythe, Folkestone and Sandwich. The men are referred to as *butsecarls* in the other manuscripts.

39.   Nicholas Hooper, "Some Observations on the Navy in Late Anglo-Saxon England," in Christopher Harper-Bill, Christopher Holdsworth and Janet L. Nelson, eds, *Studies in Medieval History presented to R. Allen Brown* (Woodbridge: 1989), pp. 203–13 (pp. 210–12).

40.   For instance, in Bishop Æthelric's will, made between 1001 and 1012. See *Anglo-Saxon Wills*, ed. and with a translation by Dorothy Whitelock (Cambridge: 1930), p. 141.

41.   Sean Davies, *Welsh Military Institutions 633–1283* (Cardiff: 2004), pp. 19–20.

42.   *Brut* (Pen. 20). The *Brut y Tywysogion* ("Chronicle of the Princes") is an annalistic chronicle. The most important versions are those in Peniarth MS. 20, which begins in 682 with the death of Cadwaladr and ends in 1332, and the *Red Book of Hergest*, which is less complete.

43.   *Historia Gruffudd vab kenan*, ed. D. Simon Jones (Cardiff: 1977), p. 68.

44.   David Crouch, *The Image of Aristocracy in Britain 1000–1300* (London: 1992), p. 165.

45.   S. Davies, *Welsh Military Institutions*, p. 31.

46.   The *Trioedd Ynys Prydein*, "Triads of the Island of Britain" are a group of related texts which include elements of Welsh historical tradition, mythology, and folklore. Objects are grouped together in threes, hence the name. Most are in the thirteenth-century manuscript *Peniarth 16*, but others are in the *Llyfr Gwyn Rhydderch* ("White Book of Rhydderch") and *Llyfr Coch Hergest* ("Red Book of Hergest") and other manuscripts.

47.   The collective name of the Middle Welsh histories, which claimed Brutus of Troy as the founder king. *Brut y Brenhinedd* ("Chronicle of the Kings") includes some sixty versions of the Welsh translation (with adaptations) of Geoffrey of Monmouth's Latin *Historia Regum Britanniae* ("History of the Kings of Britain").

48.   As suggested by Bernard Bachrach, "The Feigned Retreat at Hastings," *Mediaeval Studies* 33 (1971), 344–7.

49.   Patrick Galliou and Michael Jones, *The Bretons* (Oxford: 1991), pp. 152–5.

50.   Wendy Davies, *Small Worlds: The Village Community in Early Medieval Brittany* (London: 1988), pp. 138–9.

51. W. Davies, *Small Worlds*, p. 198.
52. W. Davies, *Small Worlds*, pp. 163–87 (p. 184).
53. K.H. Jackson, ed. and tr., *The Gaelic Notes in the Book of Deer* (Cambridge: 1972) (http:// www.ucc.ie/celt/published/G102007).
54. Dauvit Broun, "The Origin of Scottish Identity in its European Context," in Barbara Crawford, ed., *Scotland in Dark Age Europe* (St Andrews: 1994), pp. 21–31.
55. Gregory of Tours, *Historiae Franconum* 3:3, *Beowulf* 23, vv. 2354–66 (in which the name appears as Hygelac).
56. The modern Danish spelling. In the Middle Ages it appeared in various spellings, such as *lethang, leyding, lething.*
57. A fort of similar design at Borgeby, Scania, may also be one of Harald Bluetooth's.
58. Bjørn Myhre, "Boathouses and naval organization," in Anne Nørgård Jørgensen and Birthe L. Clausen, eds, *Military aspects of Scandinavian Society in a European Perspective AD 1–1300* (Copenhagen: 1997), pp. 169–83.
59. The ship was not accepted if it shipped more water than one man could bail out: *Gulatingslov* 295.
60. For instance, see Peter Heather, *Empires and Barbarians: Migration, Development and the Birth of Europe* (London: 2009), pp. 59–60, 174–7.
61. *Diplomatarium Danicum*, 1.2.21.
62. Niels Lund, *Lið, leding og landeværn* (Roskilde, Vikingeskibshallen: 1996), pp. 187–208.
63. Ger Atle Ersland and Terje H. Holm, *Norsk Forsvarshistorie, vol 1: Krigsmakt og Kongemakt 900–1814* (Bergen: 2000), p. 25.
64. Erik Kjersgaard, "Leding og landeværn," in Tage E. Christiansen, Svend Ellehøj and Erling Ladewig Petersen, eds, *Middelalderstudier tilegnede Aksel E. Christensen pÅtresårsdagen, 11 september 1966* (Copenhagen: 1966), pp. 113–40 (pp. 121–2).
65. *Gulatingslov* 20.
66. *Upplandslagen*, KgB 10:1.
67. *Västmannalagen*, KgB 7 and 8.
68. *Guta saga*, 2 and 4, pp. 6 and 12. Chapter 4 states that the Gotlanders agreed to send their ships against heathen countries, but not against Christian ones. Whether this levy had existed before the Gotlanders themselves were Christianized is not clear.
69. For instance, Mats G. Larsson, *Hamnor, Husbyar och ledung* (Lund: 1987), pp. 6–31.
70. See the collection of articles in Michael Olausson, ed., *En bok om Husbyar* (Stockholm: 2000).
71. Lund, *Lið, leding og landeværn*, pp. 155, 163.
72. ASMÆ, *Annales 1208–1288*, p. 260: this entry records the introduction of several taxes associated with the *ledung.*
73. *Sverris saga*, 87, 88, pp. 93–6.

Chapter 4: Campaigning

1. Hugh Kennedy, *The Armies of the Caliphs: Military and Society in the Early Islamic State* (London: 2001), pp. 97–9; John F. Haldon, *Warfare, State and Society in the Byzantine World* (London: 1999), pp. 96–106.
2. Vegetius, *Epitoma Re Militaris*, 1.9.19.
3. Donald W. Engels, *Alexander the Great and the Logistics of the Macedonian Army* (Berkeley: 1978), pp. 154–6; Martin van Creveld, Supplying War: *Logistics from Wallenstein to Patton* (Cambridge: 2004), pp. 28–9.
4. Modern horses are larger than those of the Viking Era, and need more than twice the amount of hard fodder. See Jonathan P. Roth, *The Logistics of the Roman Army at War (264 BC–AD235)*

(Leiden: 1999), p. 62; Ann Hyland, *Equus: The Horse in the Roman World* (London: 1990), p. 90.

5. Hyland, *Equus*, p. 96; Engels, *Alexander*, p. 127; Charles Gladitz, *Horse Breeding in the Medieval World* (Dublin: 1997), pp. 127–8.

6. Bernard S. Bachrach, "Animals and Warfare in Early Medieval Europe," in *Settimane di Studio de Centro Italiano Sull'alto Medievo* 31:1 (1985), pp. 707–64; John F. Haldon, ed., *General Issues in the Study of Medieval Logistics* (Leiden: 2006), p. 146.

7. Roth, *Logistics of the Roman Army*, pp. 21–5; Leo VI, Taktika, 6.29.

8. *Three Byzantine Military Treatises*, pp. 302–4.

9. Baudry of Bourgueil tells us that the ships and shipwrights came from many places. The number of ships is uncertain, but Wace's figure of 700 is generally regarded as too high. See Carroll Gillmor, "Naval Logistics of the Cross-Channel Operation, 1066," in Stephen Morillo, ed., *The Battle of Hastings* (Woodbridge: 1996), pp. 114–28 (pp. 119–Saxo24).

10. Saxo, *Gesta Danorum*, 14:1.6.

11. John Keegan, *The Face of Battle* (Harmondsworth: 1976), pp. 55–62.

12. *Capitularia Spuria*, p. 110.

13. David S. Bachrach, *Religion and the Conduct of War c. 300–c. 1215* (Woodbridge: 2003), p. 33.

14. Ralf Glaber, *Historiarum*, 4.23.

15. Nithard, *Historia*, 3:1.

16. Thietmar of Merseburg, *Chronicon*, 6.24 (1005).

17. Thietmar of Merseburg, *Chronicon*, 3.19.

18. *FRA*, 891.

19. *AF*, 896.

20. *AB*, 859.

21. Michael and Sean Davies, *The Last King of Wales: Gruffudd ap Llywelyn c. 1013–1063* (Stroud: 2012), pp. 106–7.

22. *ASC* (A, E), 971. It lists the locations of five, those in which the kings took part.

23. The travel accounts of Othere and Wulfstan were preserved in the Seven Books of Histories *Against the Pagans* by the fifth-century Spanish author Paulus Orosius (Alfred's version).

24. RFA, 791.

25. Charles R. Bowlus, *Franks, Moravians and Magyars: The Struggle for the Middle Danube, 788–907* (Philadelphia: 1995), pp. 5–18. The extent and location of Great Moravia is disputed; here Bowlus makes a case for a southern location of at least a substantial part of it.

26. Widukind, *Res gestae*, 3:8.

27. Alcuin, "Letter 16 to Ethelred of Northumbria," p. 42.

28. In *Ibn Fadlān and the Land of Darkness*, p. 145. The raid occurred in 912–13.

29. Ransom of valuable objects was probably the least common, but it did occur, particularly with objects that had religious significance, such as the ornate Gospel book from Canterbury, the *Codex Aureus*: see Leslie Webster and Janet Backhouse, *The Making of England: Anglo-Saxon art and culture, AD 600–900* (London: 1991), pp. 199–201.

30. On the early campaigns of William, see John Gillingham, "William the Bastard at War," in Stephen Morillo, ed., *The Battle of Hastings: Sources and Interpretations* (Woodbridge: 1996), pp. 95–112 (pp. 102–9).

31. *Annales Mettenses priores* (Earlier Annals of Metz), 805.

32. Hkr, *Ólafs saga helga*,9.

33. Flodoard, *Annales*,9.

34. Francis J. Byrne, *Irish Kings and High Kings* (Dublin: 2001 [1973]), p. 162.

35. *AB*, 868.

36. *ASC* (C, D, E), 1006.

37. Orderic Vitalis, *Ecclesiastical History*, vol. 2: Orderic was the son of a French priest and an English mother. His main source was William of Jumieges's *Gesta Guillelmi ducis Normannorum et regis Anglorum*, much of which has been lost.
38. William of Malmesbury, *Gesta regum anglorum*, 1: B.III, p. 283.
39. *AB*, 836; Rimbert, *Vita Anskarii*, 24. The emporia were centers of trade, especially in prestige goods: see Richard Hodges, *Dark Age Economics* (London: 1990), pp. 74–7, 122–5, and on the context of the Danish attacks on Frisia in general, Ian Wood, "Christians and pagans in ninth-century Scandinavia," in Birgit Sawyer, Peter Sawyer and Ian Wood, eds, *The Christianization of Scandinavia* (Alingsås: 1987), pp.36–67.
40. T.M. Charles-Edwards, *Early Christian Ireland* (Cambridge: 2000), p. 17.
41. On this, see especially Paul Gazzoli, *Anglo-Danish Relations in the Later Eleventh Century*, unpublished thesis, Cambridge University: 2010.
42. Ian Howard, *Swein Forkbeard's Invasions and Danish Conquest of England, 991–1017* (Woodbridge: 2003), pp. 114–17.

Chapter 5: Battle

1. Ryan Lavelle, *Alfred's Wars: Sources and Interpretations of Anglo-Saxon Warfare in the Viking Age* (Woodbridge: 2010), p. 264.
2. Despite a recent very poorly researched and badly argued attempt to argue that the battle was elsewhere (John Grehan and Martin Mace, *The Battle of Hastings: The Uncomfortable Truth* (Barnsley: 2013)), there is no question that this was the site of the battle.
3. *AF*, 876; *AB*, 876.
4. Neil S. Price, *The Viking Way: Religion and War in Late Iron Age Scandinavia* (Uppsala: 2002), p. 354.
5. All these practices come under the Norse term *seiðr*.
6. Widukind, *Res Gestae*, 1.36.
7. Guy Halsall, *Warfare and Society in the Barbarian West, 450–900* (London: 2003), pp. 180–1.
8. Regino of Prüm, *Chronicon*, 891.
9. Saxo, *Gesta Danorum*, 13:2.1.
10. Simon Franklin and Jonathan Shephard, *The Emergence of Rus 750–1200* (London: 1996), p. 149.
11. John Skylitzes, *Synopsis Historiarum*, 288:23–291.4.
12. Thomas S. Noonan, "The Scandinavians in European Russia," in Peter Sawyer, ed., *The Oxford Illustrated History of the Vikings* (Oxford: 1997), pp. 241–68 (p. 155).
13. Aleksandr Koptev, "The Story of 'Khazar Tribute': A Scandinavian Ritual Trick in the Russian *Primary Chronicle*," *Scando-Slavica* 56:2 (2010), 189–212.
14. *ASC* (A, B), line 21.
15. BL Harley MS 603, fol. 7v, an illustration of Psalm 13; BL MS Cotton Claudius B.IV, fol. 25v. Examples of other Old English manuscripts are Ælfric of Eynsham's "The Maccabees" and the Old English Orosius.
16. Regino of Prüm, *Chronicon*, 891.
17. See Bernard S. Bachrach, "The Angevin Strategy of Castle-Building in the reign of Fulk Nerra, 987–1040," *The American Historical Review*, 88/3 (1983), 533–60.
18. Charles Bowlus, *Battle of Lechfeld and its Aftermath, August 955: The End of the Age of Migrations in the Latin West* (Aldershot: 2006), p. 49.
19. Xenophon, *Hellenica* 6:4.9.
20. *ASC*, entry for 878 (not A).
21. Thietmar of Merseburg, *Chronicon*, 7.64. The goddess is unnamed.
22. Widukind, *Res Gestae*, 1.38.

23. Hkr, *Ólafs saga helga*, 221, pp. 508–9.

24. Franklin and Shepard, *Emergence of Rus*, p. 195. (PVL 1, p. 100.)

25. Nick Aitcheson, *The Picts and the Scots at War* (Stroud: 2003), pp. 84–5.

26. *Alfred the Great: Asser's Life of King Alfred and Other Contemporary Sources*, tr. and ed. Simon Keynes and Michael Lapidge (Harmondsworth: 1983), p. 79.

27. Hkr, *Ólafs saga helga*, 224–229, pp. 510–16.

28. Hkr, *Ólafs saga helga*, 226 (Hollander, p. 512)

29. Most emphasize the literal, e.g. V.D. Hanson, *The Western Way of War: Infantry Battle in Classical Greece* (New York: 1989), pp. 172–5, J.F. Lazenby, "The Killing Zone," in V.D. Hanson, ed., *Hoplites: The Classical Greek Battle Experience* (London: 1991), p. 97, but some think the term was more metaphorical, e.g. H. van Wees, "The Development of the Hoplite Phalanx: Iconography and Reality in the Seventh Century," in H. van Wees, ed., *War and Violence in Ancient Greece* (London: 2000), pp. 127–31.

30. M.J. Nicasie, *Twilight of Empire: The Roman Army from the Reign of Diocletian until the Battle of Adrianople* (Amsterdam: 1998), pp. 212–16, n. 109. He points out that Vegetius assumed the Roman file (*contubernium*) was of ten men, perhaps on the basis that its commander was a *decanus*, but there is no evidence of this officer in the imperial period.

31. Nikephoros Ouranos, *Taktika*, 1–15. See Eric McGeer, *Sowing the Dragon's Teeth: Byzantine Warfare in the Tenth Century* (Washington DC: 1995), pp. 89–97 and 275–7.

32. McGeer, *Sowing the Dragon's Teeth*, pp. 262–70, 276.

33. Vegetius, *Epitoma*, 2.23.

34. It should be noted here that, with the exception of the Spartans and other elite troops such as the Theban Sacred band, there is no evidence that Greek citizen hoplites were any better trained than medieval infantry. On the other hand, at least on occasion, the Greek *hoplon* had a rope round the inner rim which enabled each hoplite to grip his neighbor's shield, thus almost literally forming a "shield wall" and making movement of the line as a single unit easier.

35. Michael P. Speidel, *Ancient Germanic Warriors: Warrior Styles from Trajan's Column to Icelandic Sagas* (London: 2004), p. 107.

36. Maurice, *Strategikon*, 12:16.

37. Maurice, *Strategikon*, 12:7.

38. "Skirmishing," in *Three Byzantine Military Treatises*, ed. Dennis: 1985, pp. 145–237 (pp. 195, 219 etc.).

39. Gesta *principum polonorum*, pp. 221–4.

40. Alan Pittman, "'With your shield or on it': combat applications of the Greek hoplite spear and shield," in Barry Molloy, ed., *The Cutting Edge: Studies in Ancient and Medieval Combat* (Stroud: 2007), pp. 64–76 (p. 76). The study centers around the use of the spear and the *hoplon*, which was quite different from early medieval shields, but the observations on the integrity of the phalanx as a formation are applicable.

41. Saxo, *Gesta Danorum*, 7:10.6.

42. 42. Livy, *Ab Urbita Condita Libri*, 2.50.9; Caesar, *Bellum Gallicum*, 6.40; Ammianus, *Res Gestae*, 17.13.9, 24.2.14.

43. Vegetius, *Epitoma*, 3.19.

44. Saxo, *Gesta Danorum*, 8:4.8–9.

45. The *Praecepta militaria* of the Emperor Nikephoros Phokas, 3.1–3, in McGeer, *Sowing the Dragon's Teeth*, pp. 3–78 (p. 35).

46. *The History of Leo the Deacon*, 151.3–4. See McGeer, *Sowing the Dragon's Teeth*, pp. 315–16.

47. Richer of Saint-Rémi, *Histories*, 1:8.

48. Asser, "Life of King Alfred," 38.

49. This use of "boar" (Welsh *twrch*) was common in Welsh poetry, of which Asser must have had a good knowledge.

50. *Carmen de gestis Frederici* 2, lines 1171–90. See Claude Gaier, *Art et organization militaire dans la principauté de Liège et dans la comté de Looz au moyen âge* (Brussels: 1968), pp. 159–60.

51. Marjorie Chibnall, "Military Service in Normandy before 1066," in Stephen Morillo, ed. *The Battle of Hastings: Sources and Interpretations* (Woodbridge: 1996), pp. 79–92 (pp. 87–8).

52. See Chapter 4.

53. John France, "La guerre dans la France feodale àla fin du ix et au x siècle," *Revue Belge d'Histoire Militaire,* 23 (1979), 178–98 (pp. 194–8).

54. This is recorded in English sources as well as the kings' sagas.

55. John Skylitzes, Synopsis Historiarum, 357:54–60.

56. *Annals of Ulster to AD 1201,* http://www.ucc.ie/celt/published/T100001A/text487 (U918.4). This gives the most detailed account of any Viking-Age battle in the Irish Annals, one that occurred outside Ireland! The battle is also mentioned in the *Chronicle of the Kings of Alba and the Historia de Sancto Cuthberto* ("History of St. Cuthbert"). F.T. Wainwright argues that there were two battles, but I am in agreement with Clare Downham and Ian Walker that there was only one. See F.T. Wainwright, "The battles at Corbridge," in his *Scandinavian England* (Chichester: 1975), pp. 163–75, p. 168; Ian Walker, *Lords of Alba: The Making of Scotland* (Stroud: 2006), pp. 71–3.; Clare Downham, *The Dynasty of Ívarr to A.D. 1014* (Edinburgh: 2007), pp. 91–3.

57. *Annals of Ulster to AD 1201,* http://www.ucc.ie/celt/published/T100001A/text486 (U917.2).

58. Leo VI, *Taktika*, pp. 221–3.

59. Thietmar of Merseburg, *Chronicon*, pp. 143–4.

60. Leo VI, Taktika, pp. 456–7; Regino of Prüm, *Chronicon*, pp. 132–6.

61. See especially Bowlus, *Battle of Lechfeld*, on Magyar tactics and the aftermath of Lechfeld.

62. John France, *Victory in the East: A Military History of the First Crusade* (Cambridge: 1994), pp. 288–95.

63. Franklin and Shepard, *Emergence of Rus*, p. 274.

64. Regino of Prüm, *Chronicon*, 889.

65. *Gesta Sanctorum Rotonensium* and *Vita Conuuoionis* (Acts of the Saints of Redon, The Monks of Redon), ed. and trans. C. Brett (Woodbridge: 1989), 1.7; Regino of Prüm, *Chronicon*, 860.

66. *Gesta principum polonorum*, pp. 221–4.

67. Widukind, *Res gestae*, 3:69.

68. Hkr, *Magnú ss saga berfœtts*, 25, pp. 235–7; Fsk 84–85; Msk 59; *Annals of Ulster*, p. 541 (www.ucc.ie/ celt/published/T100). *Annals of the Four Masters*, p. 973 (www.ucc.ie/celt/published/ T100005B).

69. The *Chronicle of John of Worcester: Volume II* (1039).

70. See R. Allen Brown, "The Battle of Hastings," in *Proceedings of the Battle Conference in Anglo-Norman Studies 3*: 1980 (Woodbridge: 1981), pp. 1–21 (pp. 14–16), and Bernard S. Bachrach, "The Feigned Retreat at Hastings," *Mediaeval Studies* 33 (1971), 344–7. The *Carmen,* William of Poitiers and Orderic Vitalis all refer to pretended flight at Hastings, as do sources on the battles at Montbayou (1025), Messina, St Aubin-le-Cauf and Cassel (1071).

71. Nithard, *Histories*, 3:6. See also Bernard S. Bachrach, *Early Carolingian Warfare: Prelude to Empire* (Philadelphia: 2001), pp. 124–30.

72. Hkr, *Ólafs saga helga*, 223, p. 509.

73. Nithard, *Histories*, 3:6.

74. *RFA*, 782.

75. See Hanson, ed., *Hoplites*, and Hanson, *The Western Way of War*.

76. For instance, S.L.A. Marshall, *Men against Fire: The Problem of Battle Command* (Norman, OK: 2000 [1947]).
77. Halsall, *Warfare and Society*, p. 203.
78. *ASC* (A), entries for 851, 875, 882, 885.
79. John Haywood, *Dark Age Naval Power* (Frithgarth: 2006 [1999]), pp. 154–8.
80. See John H. Pryor and Elizabeth M. Jeffreys, *The Age of the DROMVN: The Byzantine Navy ca 500–1204* (Leiden: 2006), on the reason for the disappearance of the ram. It seems that it was effective only against ships of mortise and tenon plank construction, like those of the Mediterranean in the classical period.
81. *Morkinskinna*, 42, pp. 228–9. Hkr, *Haralds saga Sigurðarsonar*, 61–63, pp. 625–9.
82. Hkr, *Ólafs saga Tryggvasonar*, 106–7.
83. Hkr, *Haralds saga Hárfagra*, 18.
84. Hkr, *Ólafs saga helga*, 49; also Fagrskinna, p. 140.
85. Hkr, *Magnú ss saga Erlingssonar*, 7, pp. 381–3.
86. *Sverris saga*, 143.
87. F.P. Magoun, "King Alfred's Naval and Beach Battle with the Danes in 896," *Modern Language Review*, 37 (1942), pp. 409–14. The article is cited in full in Lavelle, *Alfred's Wars*, pp. 290–6.
88. The battle is described in *Heimskringla*, *Fagrskinna* and Saxo's *Gesta Danorum*, as well as in *Jómsvíkinga saga*. These are late literary accounts, although they probably have a limited basis in fact. The skaldic poetry includes verses by Þó rðr Kolbeinsson and Tindr Hallkelsson.
89. See Chapter 1 on skaldic verse.
90. *Fagrskinna*, 22; Hkr, *Ólafs saga helga*, 40–1.
91. McGeer, *Sowing the Dragon's Teeth*, p. 308.
92. *Egils saga*, 54.
93. Halsall, *Warfare and Society*, p. 202.
94. "AD 616: the Battle of Chester," *Current Archaeology*: 202 (3/4.2006), 517–24 (p. 518).
95. Pia Bennike, "Rebellion, Combat, and Massacre: A Medieval Mass Grave at Sandbjerg near Næstved in Denmark," in Ton Otto, Henrik Thrane, and Helle Vandkilde, eds, *Warfare and Society: Archaeological and Social Anthropological Perspectives* (Århus: 2006), pp. 305–18; Veronica Fiorato, Anthea Boylston and Christopher Knusel, eds, *Blood Red Roses: The Archaeology of a Mass Grave from the Battle of Towton, AD 1461* (Oxford: 2000). Recently over 1,000 skeletons of men who died violently were found in the Alken Enge wetlands near Lake Mossø in Jutland, Denmark. Typically, many have seized upon this as evidence of "sacrifice" as described by Tacitus in his account of the aftermath of the Teutoberg Forest débâcle in AD 9. The bodies were obviously dumped in the lake (now a bog), and as such could well be offerings to the gods, but all or many of them may have died on a battlefield in the slaughter that invariably followed the breaking of an ancient or medieval army. See http://sciencenordic.com/entire-army-sacrificed-bog (accessed 18.10.2012).
96. Richard P. Abels, "'Cowardice' and Duty in *Anglo-Saxon England*," *JMMH*, 4 (2006), 40.
97. Richard P. Abels, "English Tactics, Strategy and Military Organization in the Late Tenth Century," in Donald Scragg, ed., *The Battle of Maldon, 991 AD* (Oxford: 1991), p. 151; John of Worcester, 2, 1016, pp. 486–9. This particular anecdote is unlikely to be true, but reflects Eadric's reputation as a traitor.
98. The same betrayal theme is common to many non-English heroic battle poems, for instance, the *Song of Roland* version of the ambush of Charlemagne's rearguard in the Pyrenees and the Serbian poems of the Field of Blackbirds (Kosovo, 1389).
99. The same may be said of Moslem treatment of pagans. In this era Mahmud of Ghazni is supposed to have massacred hundreds of thousands of Indian idolators during his campaigns in northern India.

100. *ASC*, 870.
101. *Annals of Ulster*, www.ucc.ie/celt/published/T100001A/text414, *Book of Leinster*, Part 3, Do Flaithesaib Hérend Iar Creitim, www.ucc.ie/celt/online/G800011A Ms folio 25b, p. 97.
102. Widukind, *Res gestae*, 3.48, p. 128.
103. Karl Leyser, "The Battle on the Lech 955," *in Medieval Germany and its Neighbors 900–1250* (London: 1982), pp. 43–67 (p. 64).
104. William of Malmesbury, *De gestis regum*, 2, p. 303.
105. Lavelle, *Alfred's Wars*, p. 304.
106. Rodulfus Glaber, *Opera*, p. 61.
107. Bernard S. Bachrach, "The Combat Sculptures at Fulk Nerra's 'Battle Abbey,'" *Haskins Society Journal*, 3 (1991), 63–80.8.

Chapter 6: Fortifications and Siegecraft

1. Flodoard of Reims, *Annales*, 946.
2. *AB*, 864.
3. Jan van Doesburg, "Back to the Facts: New Evidence for and Thoughts on Early Medieval Earthworks in the Central Netherland," in CG 25 (Caen: 2012), 105–18 (pp. 108–14).
4. Joachim Henning, "Civilization versus Barbarians? Fortification Techniques and Politics in Carolingian and Ottonian Borderlands," in Florin Curta, ed., *Borders, Barriers and Ethnogenesis: Frontiers in Late Antiquity and the Middle Ages* (Turnhout: 2005), pp. 23–34 (p. 32).
5. Adam of Bremen, *History of the Archbishops of Hamburg-Bremen*, 2:68.
6. French *motte* (Lat. *mota*) initially meant turf, later bank, and by the end of our period the type of castle. North French *baille* meant "low/lower yard."
7. Stuart Prior, *A Few Well-Positioned Castles: The Norman Art of War* (Stroud: 2006), p. 75.
8. Bernard S. Bachrach, "The Angevin Strategy of Castle-Building in the reign of Fulk Nerra, 987–1040," *The American Historical Review*, 88/3 (1983), 533–60, pp. 541–2.
9. Prior, *A Few Well-Positioned Castles*, pp. 95–6.
10. Ian Ralston, *Celtic Fortifications* (Stroud: 2006), pp. 43–91.
11. This (slightly risky) statement is based on the opinions of modern researchers, but some Polish archaeologists still claim that certain strongholds now thought to be later originated in the sixth or seventh centuries: Andrzej Buko, *The Archaeology of Early Medieval Poland* (Leiden: 2008), pp. 86–7.
12. Buko, *Archaeology of Medieval Poland*, p. 94.
13. The name of the culture is derived from two groups of remains that have been studied in the vicinities of the city of Romny in Sumy Oblast and the village of Borshchevo in Voronezh Oblast.
14. *Primary Chronicle*, 61.
15. Długosz, *Annales*, 2:104–5.
16. Bruno of Querfurt, *Epistola*, 4:3.
17. Simon Franklin and Jonathan Shephard, *The Emergence of Rus 750–1200* (London: 1996), pp. 170–3.
18. See, for instance, Elsie Roesdahl, "The end of Viking-age fortifications in Denmark, and what followed," CG 12 (Caen: 1985), 39–47, pp. 39–42.
19. For example, Mats G. Larsson, *Götarnas riken: Upptäcksfärder till Sveriges enande* (Stockholm: 2002), pp. 49–50.
20. http://www.archeurope.com/index.php?page=sliasthorp (accessed 06.04.2013).
21. *RFA*, 808.
22. Helen Clarke and Björn Ambrosiani, *Towns in the Viking Age* (Leicester: 1995), p. 153.

23. Andres S. Dobat, "Danevirke revisited: An investigation into military and socio-political organization in South Scandinavia (c. AD 700–1100)," *Medieval Archaeology* 52 (2008), 27–67 (p. 49).

24. *Ibn Fadlān and the Land of Darkness*, p. 163.

25. The name in Latin, Birca, is probably derived from the word *birk*, meaning market place, and is not a historical Viking name for the site. At various times historians and archaeologists have claimed that Ansgar's Birka was Köpingsvik, Linköping, Saltvik on Åland and most recently near Kalmar (with the corollary that the *Sueones* are a different people from the *Svear*, contrary to the normal assumption). These arguments are beyond our scope—here the important factor is the site of Björkö.

26. James Graham-Campbell, *The Viking World* (London: 2001), p. 96.

27. A fort of similar design at Borgeby, Scania, may also be one of Harald Bluetooth's.

28. *Caithreim Cellachain Caisil*, sections 62–71. http://www.ucc.ie/celt/published/G100030/ index. html, accessed 30.11.2012. This source is from the 1400s and there is no clear evidence that it was copied in the same way as the annals, so there is no telling how reliable it is or what its sources were.

29. *AF*, 880.

30. *ASC* (A), 921.

31. Jean-Pierre Nicolardot and Philippe Guigon, "Une fortresse du Xe siècle: le Camp de Péran àPlédran (Côyes d'Armor)," *Revue archéologique de l'Ouest*, 8/8 (1991), pp. 123–57.

32. Flodoard of Reims, *Annales, 936; La Chronique de Nantes*, 89.

33. Flodoard of Reims, *Annales*, 925. Raoul (Rudolf) was Duke of Burgundy, but was elected king of the Franks in 923.

34. *ASC* (A, B, C, D), 914.

35. Richard Abels, *Alfred the Great: War, Kingship and Culture in Anglo-Saxon England* (London: 1998), pp. 91–3.

36. *ASC* (C, D, E) records the ravaging of Watchet, but this probably means the area. The *Vita Oswaldi*, p. 455, makes it clear that the place resisted. See also Eric John, "War and Society in the Tenth Century; The *Maldon* Campaign," *Transactions of the Royal Historical Society*, 5th ser., 27 (1977), 173–95, (pp. 184–5).

37. Ann Williams, "A Bell-house and a Burh-geat: Lordly Residences in England before the Norman Conquest," in Robert Liddiard, ed., *Anglo-Norman Castles* (Woodbridge: 2003), pp. 23–40 (p. 31).

38. Williams, "A Bell-house and a Burh-geat," pp. 35–6.

39. Sean Davies, *Welsh Military Institutions 633–1283* (Cardiff: 2004), pp. 195–6.

40. Tadhg O'Keeffe, Ireland's Round Towers (Stroud: 2004), p. 107.

41. *Fragmentary Annals*, Annal FA429, ?918: http://www.ucc.ie/celt/published/T100017/index. html. This text is probably eleventh-century, so it may not be reliable in its details.

42. Attributed to "Heron." See *Siegecraft: Two Tenth-Century Instructional Manuals by "Heron of Byzantium*," ed. and with a translation by Denis F. Sullivan (Washington DC: 2000), pp. 1–4.

43. *AB*, 973; Regino of Prüm, *Chronicon*, 873.

44. Flodoard of Reims, *Annales*, 949.

45. Thietmar of Merseburg, *Chronicon*, 6:15.

46. Richer of Saint-Rémi, *Histories*, 2.92 and 3.103.

47. This is the modern usage. In medieval Latin texts *ballistae* often denoted crossbows.

48. Donald R. Hill, "Trebuchets," *Viator* 4 (1973), 99–114 (pp. 100–4).

49. *Annales Quedlinburgenses*, 74.

50. Vegetius, *Epitoma*, 4:14. See also the translation of *Mappae clavicula: a little key to the world of medieval techniques*, ed. Cyril Stanley Smith and John G. Hawthorne (Philadelphia, PA: 1974), pp. 68–9.

51. Since the author draws heavily on Apollodorus here, it is not certain when "recently" was, but the Byzantine text and illustrations differ considerably from the German scholar Otto Lendle's 1975 reconstruction of Apollodorus of Damascus' (second-century) machine: Sullivan, pp. 172–3.

52. Vegetius, *Epitoma*, 2:25.

53. Richer of Saint-Rémi, *Histories*, 3:105.

54. Gerd Althoff, *Otto III* (University Park, PA: 2003 [1996]), pp. 118–20. The submission is recounted in Thangmar's *Vita Bernwardi*.

55. Flodoard, *Annales*, 933.

56. *Annals of Ulster*, 872.

57. Deuteronomy 20:16–18.

Chapter 7: The Way of the Warrior

1. Once again, this is a subject beyond the scope of this book, as it would fill several lengthy books on its own. See, for instance, T.M. Charles-Edwards, *Early Irish and Welsh Kinship* (Oxford: 1993), and Torben A. Vestergaard, "Marriage Exchange and Social Structure in Old Norse Mythology," in Ross Samson, ed., *Social Approaches to Viking Studies* (Glasgow: 1991), pp. 21–34.

2. In a cognatic system such as that of *Anglo-Saxon England*, the family line was derived from both males and females, in which case a marriage extended the kin, whereas in agnatic kinship societies the woman kept her own name and family identity. In the cognatic system she adopts the name of her new kin.

3. A term adopted in the late 'Middle Ages from the Gaelic *clann*. The clan "founder" may have been a real person in origin, but his deeds as related in clan circles were partly or wholly mythological.

4. ASC (C), 1049. *Niðing* was an abusive term of Scandinavian origin, which also appears in the later Norwegian law-codes. The *here* was the "armed host," those liable to military service—in effect, free men. It seems that Sweyn was exiled after his kidnap of Abbess Eadgifu in 1046, but the support of his father enabled him to go to Flanders, to Godwine's ally Count Baldwin. The incident is reported only in ASC (C). King Edward agreed to return his lands in 1049, but Harold and Bjorn opposed this. Sweyn then seized Bjorn and murdered him. There was also a tradition preserved at Worcester that he had claimed (perhaps an idle boast when drunk) to be a son of King Cnut after his return in 1050, a gross slur on his mother's reputation.

5. J.F. Verbruggen, *The Art of Warfare in Western Europe during the Middle Ages, from the eighth century to 1340* (Amsterdam: 1977), pp. 30–1; Marc Bloch, Feudal Society, vol. 1 (London: 1965 [1961]), pp. 125–30.

6. J.M. Wallace-Hadrill, *The Long-haired Kings and other Studies in Frankish History* (London: 1962), pp. 121–47 (p. 122).

7. Richard Fletcher, *Bloodfeud: Murder and Revenge in Anglo-Saxon England* (Oxford: 2003).

8. Stephen D. White, *Feuding and Peace-Making in Eleventh-Century France* (Aldershot: 2005), pp. 213–46.

9. Helle Vandkilde, "Warriors and Warrior Institutions in Copper Age Europe," in Ton Otto, Henrik Thrane, and Helle Vandkilde, eds, *Warfare and Society: Archaeological and Anthropological Perspectives* (Århus: 2006), pp. 393–422 (pp. 105–12).

10. As indicated in Tacitus's *Germania*, although this is a controversial source for Germanic society, as part of his purpose in writing it was to portray it as a contrast with supposed Roman decadence.

11. For discussion of the war-band/*comitatus* and its definition, see H. Kuhn, "Die Grenzen der germanischen Gefolgschaft," *Zeitschrift für Rechtsgeschichte (Germanistische Abteilung)* 73 (1956), 1–83 (p. 4); and A.K.G. Kristensen, "Tacitus's germanische Gefolgschaft," Det Kongelige Danske *Videnskabernes Selskab, Historisk-filosofiske meddelelser* 50:5 (1983), 71–86 (pp. 53–6).

12. It has been argued that a similar change in the character of the kings' military followings occurred even in Ireland. See T.M. Charles-Edwards, *Early Christian Ireland* (Cambridge: 2000), pp. 113, 464–8.

13. See the discussion of the Germanic terms for lord, *frô, truhtin* and *hêrro* in D.H. Green, *Language and History in the Early Germanic World* (Cambridge: 1998), pp. 102–20.

14. Saxo, *Gesta Danorum*, 2:7.13.

15. This is also a likely pattern for the success of "Anglo-Saxon" warrior-bands in forming the governing elite of post-Roman Britannia. In this case, they also achieved linguistic dominance, which did not happen in Rus: the relative number of incomers may have been lower in Rus (as in Normandy), but other possible reasons are that the Slavic component of the early Kievan princely *družina* was much more significant than the British component of the Germanic rulers' *comitatus* in eastern Britannia, and that the incomers to Rus included a very low proportion of women by comparison with Britain—it is the women who pass on the language.

16. Neil S. Price, *The Viking Way: Religion and War in Late Iron Age Scandinavia* (Uppsala: 2002). He thus chooses to see Viking belief in the supernatural primarily as a circumpolar phenomenon rather than Indo-European, Germanic, or Germano-Celtic. It could also be argued that this shamanic magic is a northern Eurasian phenomenon, as the Turkic (and Magyar) nomads who lived south of the forest-tundra zone still had shamans of similar type in the Viking Era.

17. See, for instance, Anna-Leena Siikala, *Suomalainen S`amanismi: mielikuvien historiaa* (Helsinki: 1994), pp. 294–6.

18. Price, *Viking Way*, p. 310.

19. Matti Kuusi, Keith Bosley and Michael Branch, eds, *Finnish Folk Poetry: Epic* (Helsinki: 1977), pp. 102–9, 525.

20. See Chapter 2.

21. There are arguments as to the origins of these names and whether the similar attributes were a consequence of Iron-Age Germanic influence on the Baltic Finns or much older influences or a common origin.

22. Katherine Allen Smith, *War and the Making of Monastic Culture* (Oxford: 2012), pp. 28–37, 112–55.

23. See James C. Russell, *The Germanization of Early Medieval Christianity: A Sociohistorical Approach to Religious Transformation* (New York: 1994). It is arguable that he overstates the impact of "Germanization" in making Christianity more militaristic, as it had adopted an aggressive warlike stance before the sixth century, but it is unquestionable that it further adopted a role as a religion of the warrior aristocracy.

24. On Carolingian clergy in war, see also David S. Bachrach, *Religion and the Conduct of War c. 300–c. 1215* (Woodbridge: 2003), pp. 45–7.

25. Smith, *War and the Making of Monastic Culture*, p. 96.

26. Quoted in Smith, War and the Making of Monastic Culture, p. 50.

27. See Karl Leyser, *Communications and Power in Medieval Europe: The Carolingian and Ottonian centuries* (London: 1994).

28. In passing, it may be noted that the ancient pagan pantheons as we know them are themselves rationalizations by compilers such as Hesiod or, in the case of the Near East and Egypt, priestly

bureaucracies. Near Eastern and Egyptian pantheons were periodically reorganized to reflect the interests of rulers from new cities or regions. Before the establishment of their written cultures Greek and Egyptian beliefs in the supernatural were probably as chaotic as those of the Slavic- and Germanic-speaking peoples of the northern and eastern European Iron Age.

29. Sven Wichert, "Beobachtungen zu Karentia auf Rügen im Mittelalter," in *Baltische Studien 2005—Pommersche Jahrbücher für Landesgeschichte*, Neue Folge Bd. 91 (2006), pp. 31–8.

30. Procopius, De bello Gothico, 7:14, 23–4. Perun is not named as such in this passage, but scholars agree that Procopius is describing this deity.

31. *Primary Chronicle*, yr 6488 (980).

32. Mike Dixon-Kennedy, *Encyclopedia of Russian and Slavic Myth and Legend* (Oxford: 1999), pp. 321–5.

33. Andreas Nordberg, *Krigarna i Odins sal: Dödsföreställningar och krigarkult i fornnordisk-religion* (Stockholm: 2004), pp. 56–60. Holl is probably derived from Old English heall, the equivalent of sal found in some skaldic verse, and may be of tenth-century origin. It is possible that *Eiríksmál* was composed in England, where Erik Bloodaxe (of York) was killed. *Óðinns sal* is the term used, for instance, in *Ragnarsdrapa* 12. In *Hákonardrápa* 5 it is called Sveigðis *[Óðinns] sal.*

34. See *Grimnismal* 36, *Gylfaginning* 36.

35. *Skaldskarpamal* 17.

36. *Vǫlsunga saga* 11.

37. Jens Peter Schjødt, "The Warrior in Old Norse Religion," in Gro Steinsland, Jó n Viðar Sigurðsson, Jan Erik Rekdal and Ian Beuermann, eds, *Ideology and Power in the Viking and Middle Ages: Scandinavia, Iceland, Ireland, Orkney and the Faeroes* (Leiden: 2011), pp. 269–96 (p. 277).

38. *Gylfaginning* 38.

39. *Gylfaginning* 34.

40. *Gísli saga* (short redaction) 14. See *Gisla saga Súrssonar*, ed. Finnur Jó nsson (Copenhagen: 1929); *The saga of Gisli*, tr. G. Johnston (London: 1963).

41. *Voluspá*, stanzas 38–9.

42. *Hárbarðslióð* 24.

43. *Grímnismál*, stanza 14.

44. Saxo, *Gesta Danorum*, 3:3.7.

45. Saxo, *Gesta Danorum*, 2:7.22.

46. Schjødt, "The Warrior . . .", pp. 284–5.

47. There are problems with the sources for Erik: if he was the same as the Erik who was king of York, he must have been a Christian for Æthelstan to tolerate his rule, and in the case of the Norwegian king, some of the sources are silent about his conversion. See Clare Downham, "Erik Bloodaxe—Axed? The Mystery of the Last Scandinavian King of York," *Medieval Scandinavia* 14 (2004), 51–77, on the possibility that the king of York and the king of Norway were not the same person.

48. *Ágrip 5:* see *Ágrip af Nóregs konungasǫgum*, ed. and tr. M.J. Discoll (London: 1995).

49. There were, of course, a huge variety of ideas expressed by these theologians, some of which were later condemned as heretical by the Roman or Byzantine Churches. However, none of them was preoccupied with the relationship of God or Christ to military and political leaders.

50. *Historia Franconum* 5. See Smith, *War and the Making of Monastic Culture*, pp. 10–15.

51. *Haraldskvæði* 8: 20, 21.

52. The recent tendency has been to reject this point of view, but see Kim McCone, "Hund, Wolf und Krieger bei den Indogermanen," in Wolfgang Meid, ed., *Studien zum indogermanishcen Wortschatzes* (Innsbruck: 1987), pp. 101–54 (p. 106), and the criticism of his view in Michael

Speidel, *Ancient Germanic Warriors: Warrior Styles from Trajan's Column to Icelandic Sagas* (London: 2004), p. 113.

53. Hkr, *Ynglingasaga*, p. 10.
54. *Vatnsdæla Saga* 9.
55. *Haralds saga Hárfagra*, 18; Hilda Ellis-Davidson, "Shape-Changing in the Old Norse Sagas," in J.R. Porter and W.M.S. Russell, eds, *Animals in Folklore* (Totowa, NJ: 1978), pp. 126–42.
56. Anatoly Liberman, "Berserks in History and Legend," *Russian History/Histoire Russe* 32: 3–4 (2005), 401–11 (p. 411).
57. I.P. Stephenson, *Viking Warfare* (Stroud: 2012), pp. 20–3.
58. *The History of Leo the Deacon*, tr. Alice-Mary Talbot and Denis F. Sullivan: 8, pp. 180, 185–6; 9, p. 196.
59. John Skylitzes, *Synopsis Historiarum*, p. 286; *History of Leo the Deacon*, 9, p. 193. Leo incorporates excerpts from Herodotus' description of the Skythians.
60. *Hrólfs saga kraka (The Saga of King Hrolf Kraki)*, 14.
61. See Roman Jakobson and Marc Szeftel, "The Vseslav Epos," in Roman Jakobson and Ernest J. Simmons, eds, *Russian Epic Studies* (Philadelphia: 1949), pp. 301–68.
62. See especially Terry Gunnell, *The Origins of Drama in Scandinavia* (Cambridge: 1995), pp. 60–76.
63. Constantine VII, *De ceremoniis aulae Byzantinae*, p. 231. See, for instance, Hilda Ellis-Davidson, *Pagan Scandinavia* (New York: 1967), p. 100.
64. See Chapter 6 on the possible use of the wedge (ON *svinfylkning*) in battle and the importance of maintaining formation.
65. In his translation in *The Sagas of Icelanders*, Andrew Wawn has translated "Þeir hö fðu vargstakka fyrir brynjur" as "They used wolf-skin cloaks for corslets . . . ." To me, this appears the less obvious translation, although he is a far superior translator of Old Norse! But it may be asked whether his translation has been influenced by the widespread view that neither berserkers nor *úlfheðnar* used armor. Michael Speidel, *Ancient Germanic Warriors*, insists that these troops did not use armor, although there is no clear evidence one way or the other.
66. On the Zulus, see Ian Knight, *The Anatomy of the Zulu Army: From Shaka to Cetshwayo* (London: 1995), especially his comments on their behavior at Isandhlwana (1879), pp. 221–2.
67. But see Howard D. Fabing, "On Going Berserk: A Neurochemical Inquiry," *The American Journal of Psychiatry* 113 (1956), 409–15, for a view that drugs or intoxicants might have been used, and J.G. Høyersten, "Berserkene—hva gikk det av dem?", *Tidskrift for den norske legeforening* 24 (2004), 124, 3247–50, for a further medical perspective on berserk behavior.
68. *Jómsvíkinga saga (The saga of the Jómsvikings)*, 6.
69. Quoted in Andrzej Buko, *The Archaeology of Early Medieval Poland* (Leiden: 2008), p. 247. See also the translation in *Ibn Fadlān and the Land of Darkness*, p. 166, which differs slightly, though not in any important respect. Ibrahim was a tenth-century traveler who journeyed from Tortosa (Spain) through central and eastern Europe. The probable main purpose of his journey was to head a delegation from the Umayyad caliph of Spain, Al-Hakam II (r. 961–976) to Emperor Otto I, and his original work was probably a report drafted for the caliph. Unfortunately, this has been lost and we have only excerpts in the works of later Arab geographers.
70. Adam of Bremen, *History of the Archbishops of Hamburg-Bremen*, 2:22.
71. Buko, *Archaeology of Medieval Poland*, pp. 246–50.
72. This event is probably that commemorated on three runestones: Högby, "the brave champion Asmund fell on the Fyrisvellir"; DR295, one of the Hällestad stones, "he did not flee at Uppsala"; and the Sjörup stone, "he did not flee at Uppsala, but slew as long as he had a weapon." Þórvaldr Hjaltason, the Icelandic skald who took part in the battle on Erik's side, also

commemorated it in poetic form. See *Poetry from the Kings' Sagas 1: From Mythical Times to c. 1035*, ed. Diana Whaley (Turnhout: 2012), p. 271.

73. As argued by Kim McCone in his *Pagan Past and Christian Present in Early Irish Literature* (Maynooth: 2000).

74. See Charles-Edwards, *Early Christian Ireland*, p. 113: The *Life of St Cainnech of Aghaboe* refers to some men "who took an evil oath, that is, they were *dibergich*."

75. CELT: Corpus of Electronic Texts: Annals of Ulster, U847.3 (http://143.239.128.67/celt/published/T100001A/index.html). I have substituted "warrior-band" as the translation for *fianlach*, in place of the translation given, "wicked men."

76. David Wyatt, *Slaves and Warriors in Medieval Britain and Ireland, 800–1200* (Leiden: 2009), p. 76.

77. A thirteenth-century version of an earlier Latin chronicle, generally regarded as a reliable source for the twelfth century onwards.

78. Georges Duby, *The Chivalrous Society* (Stanford: 1992), pp. 112–15.

79. *ASC* (E), 1065.

80. *ASC* (C), 1052 (also recorded in D and F).

81. Hugh M. Thomas, "The Gesta Herewardi," in *ANS* 11 (Woodbridge: 1999), pp. 214–32 (pp. 227–32).

82. Wulfstan II of York, *Sermo Lupi ad Anglos*, ed. Dorothy Whitelock (Exeter: 1976), pp. 57–8. This homily ("The Sermon of the Wolf to the English") was written in the context of English defeat by the Danes in 1014, and therefore assumed that they were being punished by God for their sins. Nevertheless, it is unlikely that he made up tales of Englishmen selling their countrywomen as slaves.

83. Quoted in *Ibn Fadlān and the Land of Darkness*, p.106. Ibn Hayyān lived from 987 to 1076, but he used earlier sources. Unlike the vast majority of medieval chroniclers, he named them, in this case Ahmad ibn Muhammad al-Rāzi (888–955) and his son 'Īsā.

84. Widukind, *Res Gestae Saxonicae* 3:52, p. 206.

85. *Historia Gruffudd vab kenan*, ed. D. Simon Jones (Cardiff: 1977), pp. 36–8.

86. Timothy Reuter, *Germany in the Early Middle Ages, 800–1056* (London: 1991), pp. 97–100; Eric J. Goldberg, *Struggle for Empire: Kingship and Conflict under Louis the German, 817–876* (Ithaca: 2006), p. 202.

87. Widukind, *Res Gestae Saxonicae*, 3:30, p. 184.

88. Petr Charvát, *The Emergence of the Bohemian State* (Leiden: 2010), pp. 154–8.

89. For instance, Laws of Cnut II, 53.

90. *Law of Hywel Dda*, tr. Dafydd Jenkins (Llandysul: 1986), p. 48.

91. *Primary Chronicle*, yr 6488 (980). This woman is said to have been a Greek nun earlier seized by Sviatoslav, the father of Yaropolk and Vladimir, during his Bulgarian campaign. If so, she had suffered the same fate at least once before.

92. Wyatt, *Slaves and Warriors*, p. 135.

93. All recorded in the *ASC*.

Bibliography

Primary Sources

Adam of Bremen, *Gesta Hammaburgensis ecclesiae pontificum*, ed. Bernard Schmeidler, MGH SRG 2 (Hanover: 1917).

Annales Suecici Medii Aevi: Svensk Medeltidsannalistik, ed. G. Paulsson (Lund: 1974).

Asser, *De rebus gestis Aelfredi*, ed. W.H. Stevenson (Oxford, Oxford University Press: 1959).

Annales Fuldenses sive annales regni Francorum orientalis, ed. Friedrich Kurze, MGH SRG 7 (Hanover: 1891).

Annales Mettenses priores, ed. Bernhard von Simson, MRG SRG Separate edition 10 (Hanover: 1905).

Annales Quedlinburgenses, ed. Martina Giese, MGH SRG Separate edition 72 (Hanover: 2004).

The Carmen de Hastingae Proelio of Guy, Bishop of Amiens, ed. and with a translation by Frank Barlow, 2nd edn (Oxford, Oxford University Press: 1999).

"Edictum Pistense," in Alfred Boretius and Victor Krause, eds, *Capitularia regum Francorum* 25, MGH Cap. 2.321 (Hanover: 1897).

The Chronicle of John of Worcester: Volume II: The Annals from 450 to 1066, ed. R.R. Darlington and P. McGurk, with a translation by P. McGurk and Jennifer Bray (Oxford, Oxford University Press: 1995).

Chronicon Æthelweardi: The Chronicle of Æthelweard, ed. and with a translation by Alistair Campbell (London, Nelson: 1962).

La chronique de Nantes, ed. Peter Merlet (Paris, A. Picard: 1896).

Constantine Porphyrogenitus, De Administrando Imperio, ed. Gyula Moravcsik, with a translation by R.J.H. Jenkins, *Corpus Fontium Historiae Byzantinae* 1, 2nd edn (Washington, DC, Dumbarton Oaks Center for Byzantine Studies: 1967).

Constantine VII Porphyrogenitus, De ceremoniis aulae Byzantinae, 2 vols, ed. Johan Jakob Reisky (Bonn, Impensis Ed. Weberi: 1829–30).

Diplomatarium Danicum, vol. 1:2, 1053–1169, ed. Lauritz Weibull, rev. Niels Skyum-Nielsen (Copenhagen: 1963).

The Ecclesiastical History of Orderic Vitalis, vol. 2 (Books 3 and 4), ed. and with a translation by Marjorie Chibnall (Oxford, Oxford University Press: 1991).

Egils saga Skalla-Grímssonar, ed. Sigurður Nordal, Íslenzk Fornrit 2 (Reykjavík, Hið íslenzka fornritfélag: 1933).

Encomium Emmae Reginae, ed. Alistair Campbell (Cambridge, Cambridge University Press: 1998).

Ermoldus Nigellus, *Carmina in honorum Hludovici imperatoris*, ed. E Dummier, MGH Scriptores (Hanover: 1826).

Gesta principum polonorum/Deeds of the Princes of the Poles, with an English translation by Paul W. Knoll and Frank Schauer, Central European Medieval Texts, 3 (Budapest, CEU: 2003).

Guta saga, ed. Christine Peel (London, Viking Society for Northern Research: 1999).

The History of Leo the Deacon, ed. and trans. Alice-Mary Talbot, Dumbarton Oaks Studies 41 (Harvard, Harvard University Press: 2005).

"Hrólfs saga kraka ok kappa hans," in *Fornaldarsögur Norðurlanda*, vol. 1, ed. Guðni Jónsson (Reykjavík, Íslendingasagnaútgáfan: 1954).

Íslendingabók, Landnámabók, ed. Jakob Benediktsson, Íslenzk fornrit I (Reykjavík, Hið íslenzka forn-ritfélag: 1968).

Johannes Skylitzes, *Synopsis Historiarum*, ed. Ioannes Thurn (Berlin, De Gruyter: 1973).

Jómsvíkinga saga (efter Cod. AM. 510, 4:to) *samt Jómsvíkinga drápa*, ed. Bjarni Kolbeinsson (Lund, Gleerup: 1879).

Lex Ribuaria Et Lex Francorum Chamavorum, ed. Rudolf Sohm, Monumentis Germaniae historicis recusae (Hanover: 1883).

Norges Gamle Love indtil 1387, vols 1-5, ed. R. Keyser and P.A. Munch (Christiania [Oslo]: 1845-1895).

Procopius, *History of the Wars, vol. IV, Books* 6.16-7.35, ed. and with an English translation by H.B. Dewing (Harvard: 1924).

"The *Praecepta militaria* of the Emperor Nikephoras II Phokas (963-969)," with a translation by Erik McGeer, in McGeer, 1995, pp. 12-59.

Rabanus Maurus, "*De procinctu Romanae miliciae*," ed. E. Dimmler, *Zeitschrift fur deutschen Altertum* 15 (1872), 443-51.

Rodulfus Glaber, *Opera*, ed. Neithard Bulst, and with a translation by John France and Paul Reynolds (Oxford, Oxford University Press: 1989).

Samling av Sveriges gamla lagar, vols 1-13, ed. H.S. Collin and C.J. Schlyter (Stockholm and Lund: 1827-1877); vol. 3: *Codex iuris Uplandici*, ed. C.J. Schlyter (1834); vol. 4: *Codex iuris Suderman-nici*, ed. C.J. Schlyter (1838); vol. 7: *Codex iuris Vestmannici*, ed. C.J. Schlyter (1841).

Saxo Grammaticus, *Gesta Danorum/Danmarkshistorien, 1: Bog 1-10*, ed. Karsten Friis-Jensen and with a Danish translation by Peter Zeeberg (Copenhagen, Det Danske Sprog-og Litteraturselskab & Gad: 2005).

Siegecraft: Two Tenth-Century Instructional Manuals by "Heron of Byzantium," ed. and with a trans-lation by Denis F. Sullivan, Dumbarton Oaks Studies 36 (Washington DC, Dumbarton Oaks Publications: 2000).

Sverris saga, etter Cod. AM 327 4°, ed. Gustav Indrebo (Kristiania [Oslo]: 1920).

The Taktika of Leo VI, with tr. and commentary by George T. Dennis, Dumbarton Oaks Texts 12 (Washington DC, Dumbarton Oaks: 2010).

"The *Taktika* of Nikephoras Ouranos, Chapters 56 through 65," with a translation by Erik McGeer, in McGeer, 1995, pp. 88-163.

Thietmari Merseburgensis episcopi Chronicon, ed. Frederick Kurze, MGH SRG (Hannover: 1889).

Three Byzantine Military Treatises, ed. and with a translation by George T. Dennis, Dumbarton Oaks Texts 9 (Harvard, Harvard University Press: 2009).

Vegetius Renatus, Flavius, *Epitome Rei Militaris*, ed. M.D. Reeve (Oxford, Oxford University Press: 2004).

Vǫlsunga saga, *Fornaldarsögur Norðurlanda*, vol. 1, ed. Guðni Jó nsson (Reykjavík, I slendingasa-gnaútgáfan: 1959).

Widukind von Corvey, *Res gestae Saxonicae/Die Sachsengeschichte*, ed. and with a German translation by Ekkehart Rotter and Bernd Schneidmü ller (Stuttgart, Philipp Reclam: 1981).

William of Malmesbury, *Gesta regum Anglorum*, 2 vols: vol. 1, ed. and with a translation by R.A.B. Mynors, R.M. Thomson and M. Winterbottom; vol. 2, General Introduction and Commentary, by M. Winterbottom and R.M. Thomson (Oxford, Oxford University Press: 1998-2002).

Sources in Translation

[Note: many of the above titles also have facing page translations.]

Adam of Bremen, *History of the Archbishops of Hamburg-Bremen*, tr. F.J. Tschan (New York: 2002).

Alfred the Great: Asser's Life of King Alfred *and Other Contemporary Sources*, tr. and ed. Simon Keynes and Michael Lapidge (Harmondsworth, Penguin: 1983).

The *Anglo-Saxon Chronicle*, tr. and ed. Michael Swanton (London, Dent: 1996).

The Annals of Fulda, tr. and annotated Timothy Reuter, Ninth-Century Histories, II (Manchester, Manchester University Press: 1992).

The Annals of Jan Dlugosz: A History of Eastern Europe from A.D. *965 to* A.D. *1480*, ed. and trans. Maurice Michael (Chichester: 1997).

The Annals of St-Bertin, tr. and annotated by Janet L. Nelson, Ninth-Century Histories 1 (Manchester, Manchester University Press: 1991).

Caithreim Cellachain Caisil: The Victorious Career of Cellachan of Cashel, or, the Wars Between the Irishmen and the Norsemen in the Middle of the 10th Century, ed. and tr. Alexander Bugge (Oslo: 2010 [1905]).

Carolingian Chronicles: Royal Frankish Annals and Nithard's Histories, ed. and with an introduction by Bernhard Walter Scholz and Barbara Rogers (University of Michigan Press: 1995 [1972]).

Carolingian Civilization: A Reader, tr. Paul Dutton (Peterborough, Ont., Broadview Press: 1993).

Egil's saga, tr. Christine Fell (London, Dent: 1975).

Fagrskinna: a Catalogue of the Kings of Norway, tr. and with an introduction by Alison Finlay (Leiden, Brill: 2004).

Grettirs *Saga*, trans. by Denton Fox and Hermann Palsson (Toronto, University of Toronto Press: 1961).

History and Politics in Late Carolingian and Ottonian Europe: The Chronicle of Regino of Prüm and Adalbert of Magdeburg, tr. and annotated by Simon MacLean (Manchester, Manchester University Press: 2009).

The History of Leo the Deacon: Byzantine Military Expansion in the Tenth Century, tr. Alice-Mary Talbot and Denis F. Sullivan (Washington DC, Dumbarton Oaks: 2005).

Ibn Fadlan and the Land of Darkness: Arab Travellers in the Far North, tr. Caroline Stone and Paul Lunde (Harmondsworth, Penguin: 2011).

John Skylitzes, *A Synopsis of Byzantine History 811–1057*, tr. John Wortley (Cambridge, Cambridge University Press: 2010).

The Book of Settlements: Landnamabok, ed. Hermann Palsson and Paul Edwards (Winnipeg, University of Manitoba Press: 2007).

"*Mappae clavicula*: a little key to the world of medieval techniques," ed. Cyril Stanley Smith and John G. Hawthorne, *Transactions of the American Philosophical Society*, 64 (Philadelphia, PA, American Philosophical Society: 1974).

Morkinskinna: The Earliest Icelandic Chronicle of the Norwegian Kings (1030–1157), ed. and with an introduction by Theodore M. Andersson and Kari Ellen Gade, Islandica 51 (Ithaca, NY, Cornell University Press: 2000).

Ottonian Germany: The Chronicle of Thietmar of Merseburg, tr. and annotated by David A. Warner (Manchester, Manchester University Press: 2001).

Richer of Saint-Remi, Histories, Vol. I, Books. 1–2, ed. and tr. Justin Lake (Harvard, Harvard University Press: 2011).

The Russian Primary Chronicle: Laurentian Text, tr. and ed. Samuel Hazzard Cross and Olgerd P. Sherbowitz-Wetzor (Cambridge, MA, Mediaeval Academy of America: 1953).

The Saga of King Sverrir of Norway, tr. J. Sephton, facsimile reprint (London, David Nutt: 1994 [1899]).

The Saga of the Volsungs, tr. Jesse Byock (Berkeley, LA, University of California Press: 1990).

The Saga of the Jomsvikings, tr. Lee M. Hollander (Austin, TX, University of Texas Press: 1955).

Saxo Grammaticus, *The History of the Danes, Books I–IX*, tr. Peter Fisher, ed. and commentary Hilda Ellis Davidson (Cambridge, D.S. Brewer: 1996).

Snorri Sturluson, *Heimskringla: History of the Kings of Norway*, ed. and with an introduction by Lee M. Hollander (Austin, TX, American–Scandinavian Foundation: 1964).

——— , *Edda*, tr. A. Faulkes (London, Everyman: 1987).

Secondary Sources

Listed here are a few of the most important works and some that give a historical background; there are many others listed in the Notes which are omitted here because of lack of space. Edited collections are listed when almost all the articles in them are of interest.

Abels, Richard P., *Lordship and Military Obligation in Anglo-Saxon England* (London: 1988).

Bachrach, Bernard S., "Logistics in Pre-Crusade Europe," in John A. Lynn, ed., *Feeding Mars: Logistics in Western Warfare from the Middle Ages to the Present* (Boulder, CO, Westview Press: 1993), pp. 57–78.

Bachrach, David S., *Religion and the Conduct of War c.300–c.1215* (Woodbridge, Boydell: 2003).

——, *Warfare in Tenth-Century Germany* (Woodbridge, Boydell: 2012).

Brooks, Nicholas, *Communities and Warfare 700–1400* (London, Hambledon Press: 2000).

Charles-Edwards, T.M., "Irish warfare before 1100," in Thomas Bartlett and Keith Jeffery, eds, *A Military History of Ireland* (Cambridge, Cambridge University Press: 1996), pp. 26–51.

Chibnall, Marjorie, "Military Service in Normandy before 1066," in Stephen Morillo, ed., *The Battle of Hastings: Sources and Interpretations* (Woodbridge, Boydell: 1996), pp. 79–92.

Clarkson, Tim, *The Men of the North: The Britons of Southern Scotland* (Edinburgh, John Donald: 2010).

Cooper, Janet, ed., *The Battle of Maldon: Fiction and Fact* (Hambledon Press: 1993).

Crumlin-Pedersen, Ole, ed., *Aspects of Maritime Scandinavia* A.D. 200–1200: *Proceedings of the Nordic Seminar on Maritime Aspects of Archaeology, Roskilde, 13th–15th March 1989* (Roskilde, Vikingeskibshallen: 1991).

Davies, Sean, *Welsh Military Institutions 633–1283*, Studies in Welsh History, 21 (Cardiff, University of Wales: 2004).

Ellis-Davidson, Hilda R., *The Battle God of the Vikings* (York, University of York Center for Medieval Studies: 1972).

Ersland, Ger Atle, and Terje H. Holm, *Norsk Forsvarshistorie, vol. 1: Krigsmakt og Kongemakt 900–1814* (Bergen, Eide: 2000).

Fitzpatrick, Elizabeth, "Raiding and warring in monastic Ireland," *History Ireland* 1:3 (1993), 13–18.

France, John, "La guerre dans la France feodale àlafinduixet auxsiècle," *Revue Belge d'Histoire Militaire* 23 (1979), 178–98.

Franklin, Simon, and Shephard, Jonathan, *The Emergence of Rus 750–1200* (London, Longman: 1996).

Glover, Richard, 'English Warfare in 1066', *English Historical Review* 67 (1952), 1–18.

Goldberg, Eric J., *Struggle for Empire: Kingship and Conflict under Louis the German, 817–876* (Ithaca, Cornell University Press: 2006).

Halsall, Guy, *Warfare and Society in the Barbarian West, 450–900* (London, Routledge: 2003).

——, ed., Violence and Society in the Early Medieval West (Woodbridge, Boydell: 2002).

Hawkes, S.C., ed., *Weapons and Warfare in Anglo-Saxon England* (Oxford, Oxford University Committee for Archaeology: 1989).

Herrmann, Joachim, ed., Die *Slawen in Deutschland. Geschichte und Kultur der slawischen Stämme westlich von Oder und Neiße vom 6. bis 12. Jahrhundert* (Berlin, Akademie-Verlag: 1985).

Hill, David H., and Alexander R. Rumble, eds, *The Defense of Wessex: The Burghal Hideage and Anglo-Saxon Fortifications* (Manchester, Manchester University Press: 1996).

Hooper, Nicholas, "The Housecarls in England in the Eleventh Century," 7 (1985), 161–76.

——, "Some Observations on the Navy in Late *Anglo-Saxon England*," in Christopher Harper-Bill, Christopher Holdsworth and Janet L. Nelson, eds, *Studies in Medieval History presented to R. Allen Brown* (Woodbridge, Boydell: 1989), pp. 203–13.

Howard, Ian, *Swein Forkbeard's Invasions and Danish Conquest of England, 991–1017* (Woodbridge, Boydell: 2003).

Hudson, Benjamin, *Viking Pirates and Christian Princes: Dynasty, Religion and Empire in the North Atlantic* (Oxford, Oxford University Press: 2005).

Hultgård, Anders, "Óðinn, Valhǫll and the Einherjar. Eschatological Myth and Ideology in the Late Viking Period," in Gro Steinsland, Jó n Viðar Sigurðsson, Jan Erik Rekdal and Ian Beuermann, eds, *Ideology and Power in the Viking and Middle Ages: Scandinavia, Iceland, Ireland, Orkney and the Faeroes* (Leiden, Brill: 2011), pp. 297–328.

Jørgensen, Anne Nørgård and Birthe L. Clausen, eds, *Military aspects of Scandinavian Society in a European Perspective AD 1–1300* (Copenhagen, National Museum of Denmark: 1997).

Jørgensen, Anne Nørgård, John Pind, Lars Jørgensen, and Birthe Clausen, eds, *Maritime Warfare in Northern Europe: Technology, organization, logistics, and administration 500 BC–1500 AD*, Publications from the National Museum Studies in Archaeology and History 6 (Copenhagen: National Museum: 2002).

Kershaw, Priscilla K., *The One-eyed God: Odin and the (Indo-)Germanic Männerbünde* (Washington DC, Journal of Indo-European Studies: 2000).

Lavelle, Ryan, *Aethelred II: King of the English 978–1016 (Stroud, Tempus: 2002).*

——— , *Alfred's Wars: Sources and Interpretations of Anglo-Saxon Warfare in the Viking Age* (Woodbridge, Boydell: 2010).

Liberman, Anatoly, 'Berserks in History and Legend', *Russian History/Histoire Russe* 32: 3–4 (2005), 401–11.

Livingstone, Michael, ed., *The Battle of Brunanburh: A Casebook* (Exeter, University of Exeter Press: 2011).

Lund, Niels, *Lið, leding og landeværn* (Roskilde, Vikingeskibshallen: 1996).

McGeer, Eric, *Sowing the Dragon's Teeth: Byzantine Warfare in the Tenth Century*, Dumbarton Oaks Studies, 33 (Washington DC, Dumbarton Oaks: 1995).

McGrath, S.F.-P. "The Battles of Dorostolon (971): Rhetoric and Reality," in Thomas S. Miller and John Nesbitt, eds, *Peace and war in Byzantium: Essays in Honor of George T. Dennis, S.J.* (Washington DC, Catholic University of America: 1995), pp. 152–64.

MacLean, Simon, *Kingship and Politics in the Late Ninth Century: Charles the Fat and the End of the Carolingian Empire* (Cambridge, Cambridge University Press: 2003).

Morillo, Stephen, ed., "The 'Age of Cavalry' Revisited," in Donald J. Kagay and L.J. Andrew Villalon, *The Circle of War in the Middle Ages: Essays on Medieval Military and Naval History* (Woodbridge, Boydell: 1999).

Nelson, Janet L., *Charles the Bald* (London, Longman: 1992).

Nordberg, Andreas, *Krigarna i Odins sal: Dödsföreställningar och krigarkult i fornnordisk-religion* (Stockholm, Stockholms universitet: 2004).

O Cróinín, Dáibhí, ed., *A New History of Ireland, Volume I: Prehistoric and Early Ireland* (Oxford, Oxford University Press: 2008).

Price, Neil S., *The Viking Way: Religion and War in Late Iron Age Scandinavia* (Uppsala, Uppsala University: 2002).

Pryor, John H., ed., *Warfare and Military Organization in Pre-Crusade Europe* (Aldershot, Ashgate: 2002).

Pullen-Appleby, John, *English Sea Power c.871 to 1100* (Hockwold-cum-Wilton, Anglo-Saxon Books: 2005).

Purton, Peter, *A History of the Early Medieval Siege, c.450–1200* (Woodbridge, Boydell: 2009).

Randsborg, Klaus, *The Viking Age in Denmark: The Formation of a State* (London, Duckworth: 1980).

Reuter, Timothy, "The End of Carolingian Military Expansion," in Peter Godman and Roger Collins, eds, *Charlemagne's Heir: New Perspectives on the Reign of Louis the Pious* (Oxford, Oxford University Press: 1990), pp. 391–405.

————— , "Carolingian and Ottonian Warfare," in Maurice Keen, ed., *Medieval Warfare: A History* (Oxford, Oxford University Press: 1999), pp. 13–35.

Rodger, N.A.M., *The Safeguard of the Sea: A Naval History of Britain 660–1649, Naval History of Britain, vol. 1* (New York, Norton: 1999).

Roesdahl, Elsie, "The Danish geometrical fortresses and their context," in R. Allen Brown, ed., *Anglo-Norman Studies IX* (Woodbridge, Boydell: 1987), pp. 108–26.

Schoenfeld, Edward J., "Anglo-Saxon 'Burhs' and Continental 'Burgen': Early Medieval Fortifications in Constitutional Perspective," *The Haskins Society Journal*, 6 (1994), 49–66.

Schjødt, Jens Peter, "Óðinnn, Warriors, and Death," in Judy Quinn, Kate Heslop and Tarin Wills, eds, *Learning and Understanding in the Old Norse World: Essays in Honor of Margaret Clunies Ross* (Odense, University Press of Southern Denmark: 2007), pp. 137–51.

Scragg, Donald, ed., *The Battle of Maldon, 991 AD* (Oxford, Oxford University Press: 1991).

Szameit, Erik, "Frankische Reiter des 10. Jahrhunderts," in Matthias Puhle, ed., *Otto der Große. Magdeburg und Europa. Katalog zur Austellung 2* (Mainz, Philipp von Zabern: 2001), pp. 254–61.

Underwood, Richard, *Anglo-Saxon Weapons and Warfare* (Stroud, The History Press: 2000).

Váňa, Zdeněk, *The World of the Ancient Slavs* (London, Orbis: 1983).

Werner, Karl Ferdinand, "Heersorganization und Kriegsfü hrung im deutschen Kö nigreich des 10. und 11. Jahrhunderts," *Settimane di Studio de Centro Italiano Sull'alto Medievo 15* (1968), 791–843.

Williams, Ann, *Æthelred the Unready: The Ill-Counselled King* (London, Hambledon Continuum: 2003).

Woolf, Alex, *From Pictland to Alba: Scotland, 789 to 1070* (Edinburgh, Edinburgh University Press: 2007).

Index

Names of written works are given in the form most likely to be encountered by an English-speaking reader, with translations below. Where authors are known or attributed, written works are listed under the author.

Abbreviations of titles: k.—king, e.—earl, el.—ealdorman, j.—jarl, d.—duke, c.—count, p.—prince, cs.—countess, mg.—margrave, q.—queen, cal.—caliph, emp.—emperor, hk.—high king, b.—bishop, ab.—archbishop. Period of office or reign is given in parentheses after the title.

Notes to Index

1. Deeds of the Bishops of the Hamburg Church; **2.** Synoptic History of the Norwegian Kings; **3.** Propositions to sharpen the Young; **4.** "Things done" ("The deeds" . . ., i.e. of the Romans after Tacitus' history ended); **5.** *Annales Fuldenses*; **6.** *Annales Bertiniani*; **7.** *Annales Vedastini*; **8.** *Annales Xantenses*; **9.** The Saga of Asmund the Champion-slayer; **10.** *Vita Ælfredi regis Angul Saxonum*; **11.** Chronicle of the Princes; **12.** On the Management of Royal Estates; **13.** Song of the Battle of Hastings; **14.** The Victorious Career of Cellachan of Cashel; **15.** Chronicle of the Irish ("Scots"); **16.** The War of the Irish with the Foreigners; **17.** The Fitness of Names; **18.** Book of Ceremonies of the Byzantine Palace ("Three Treatises on Military Expeditions" is an appendix); **19.** On the Fortifications of Military Camps; **20.** *De moribus et actis primorum Normanniæ ducum*; **21.** *Annales Mettenses priores*; **22.** Egil's Saga; **23.** The Saga of Egil the One-handed and Asmund Berserk-slayer; **24.** The Life of Charlemagne; **25.** The *Encomium of Queen Emma*; **26.** In honor of Emperor Louis; **27.** Eymunds Saga; **28.** "Fair parchment"; **29.** "Tales of former times"; **30.** The Law of Frostating (Trøndelag); **31.** The Deeds of the princes of the Poles; **32.** *Psalterium aureum*; **33.** "Grey Goose" (collection of Icelandic laws); **34.** The Lay/Sayings of Grímnir; **35.** The Law of Gulating (Hordaland, Sogn and Fjordane); **36.** The Lay of Håkon; **37.** The Saga of King Håkon Håkonsson; **38.** The Deeds of Harald Fairhair (The Raven's song); **39.** The Saga of Harald Fairhair; **40.** The Lay/Song of Hárbard; **41.** The Sayings of the High One (Odin); **42.** The Saga of King Hrolf Kraki; **43.** Icelandic family sagas; **44.** A Synopsis of History; **45.** Saga of the Jomsvikings; **46.** The Law of Jutland; **47.** King Valdemar's Land Register; **48.** The Law of the Ripuarian Franks; **49.** The Law of the Saxons; **50.** Retribution; **51.** The Lay of Ludwig (Louis); **52.** "The Little Key to the Small Cloth"; **53.** "Mouldy parchment"; **54.** *PM* is a title given by its first modern editor, Kulakovsky (1908): the Greek title translates as "Presentation and Composition on Warfare of the Emperor Nikephoros"; **55.** The Histories or On the Dissensions of the Sons of Louis the Pious; **56.** "Concerning Charlemagne" (collection of anecdotes); **57.** Instructions on Siege Warfare; **58.** *Historia Longobardum*; **59.** Histories in Four Books; **60.** Life of Ansgar; **61.** History in five books from 900 *AD* to 1044 *AD* (*Historiarum libri quinque ab anno incarnationis DCCCC usque ad annum MXLIV*); **62.** *Royal Frankish Annals*; **63.** The Deeds of the Danes; **64.** The Law of Scania; **65.** The Saga of the Ynglings (*Heimskringla*, ch. 1); **66.** The Tricking of Gylfi (first part of the Prose Edda); **67.** The Law of the Retainers; **68.** The Saga of King Sverre; **69.** The Instructions of Cormac (law tract); **70.** The Law of Uppland; **71.** The Law of Västmanland; **72.** The saga of the people of Vatnsdal; **73.** The Epitome of Military Science; **74.** On Architecture; **75.** The Saga of the Volsungs; **76.** The Prophecy of the Seeress; **77.** The Deeds of the Saxons; **78.** The Deeds of Robert Guiscard; **79.** The Deeds of the Kings of the English; **80.** On Greek affairs.